T0210720

Lecture Notes in Computer Science 9138

Commenced Publication in 1973
Founding and Former Series Editors:
Gerhard Goos, Juris Hartmanis, and Jan van Leeuwen

Jean Krivine · Jean-Bernard Stefani (Eds.)

Reversible Computation

7th International Conference, RC 2015
Grenoble, France, July 16–17, 2015
Proceedings

 Springer

Editors
Jean Krivine
CNRS/Université Paris Diderot
Paris
France

Jean-Bernard Stefani
Inria
St. Ismier Cedex
France

ISSN 0302-9743   ISSN 1611-3349   (electronic)
Lecture Notes in Computer Science
ISBN 978-3-319-20859-6   ISBN 978-3-319-20860-2   (eBook)
DOI 10.1007/978-3-319-20860-2

Library of Congress Control Number: 2015942240

LNCS Sublibrary: SL2 – Programming and Software Engineering

Springer Cham Heidelberg New York Dordrecht London

Printed on acid-free paper

Springer International Publishing AG Switzerland is part of Springer Science+Business Media
(www.springer.com)

Preface

This volume contains the proceedings of RC 2015, the 7th International Conference on Reversible Computation. RC 2015 took place during July 16–17, 2015, in Grenoble, France, and was hosted by Inria, the French National Research Institute on Computer Science and Control, at its Grenoble research center.

RC 2015 was the seventh event in a series of annual meetings designed to gather researchers from different scientific disciplines for the discussion and dissemination of recent developments in all aspects of reversible computation. Reversible computation refers to computing models where computational processes are in some sense reversible, whether in a physical sense (e.g., as in isentropic processes) or logical (e.g., as in undoable or invertible programs). Reversible computation ideas have appeared in a broad range of areas, including, for instance, low-power circuit design, quantum computing, coding/decoding, program debugging, scientific computation, discrete event simulation, database systems, robotics, and the modeling of biochemical systems. Previous RC events took place in York, UK (2009), Bremen, Germany (2010), Ghent, Belgium (2011), Copenhagen, Denmark (2012), Victoria, Canada (2013), and Kyoto, Japan (2014).

The RC 2015 conference included two invited talks by Vincent Danos and Elham Kashefi, and six technical sessions. RC 2015 attracted 30 submissions. All papers were reviewed by three members of the Program Committee or their designated sub-reviewers. From these, the Program Committee selected 15 full papers and four short papers for inclusion in these proceedings and for presentation at the conference.

We would like to thank all who contributed to making RC 2015 a successful event: the authors for submitting the results of their research to RC 2015; our two invited speakers for their inspiring talks and their time; the Program Committee of RC 2015 and their sub-reviewers for their hard work under tight time constraints, and their dedication to the quality of the conference; the Steering Committee of the Reversible Computation series, with special mention of Irek Ulidowski and Robert Wille, for their guidance and wisdom; the attendees of the events for their interest in the presentations and the constructive discussions; the people at the University of Bremen for running the conference website and dealing with the publicity aspects, with special thanks to Lisa Jungmann and Robert Wille; the people at Inria Grenoble for taking care of the organization of the event and the myriad details that go into it, with special thanks to Sophie Azzaro, Martine Consigney, Alain Kersaudy, Clara Peuget, and Vanessa Peregrin.

We benefited greatly from the EasyChair conference management system, which simplified greatly the handling of the submission, review, discussion, and proceedings preparation processes. Finally we would like to express our appreciation to Inria for supporting RC 2015.

July 2015

Jean Krivine
Jean-Bernard Stefani

Organization

Program Committee Chairs

Jean Krivine   CNRS, France
Jean-Bernard Stefani Inria, France

Program Committee

Holger Axelsen   DIKU, Denmark
Bob Coecke   University of Oxford, UK
Vincent Danos   CNRS, France
Alexis De Vos   Universiteit Gent, Belgium
Gerhard Dueck   University of New Brunswick, Canada
Simon Gay   University of Glasgow, UK
Markus Grassl   Max Planck Institute for the Science of Light, Germany
Matthew Hennessy   Trinity College Dublin, Ireland
Niraj Jha   Princeton University, USA
Ivan Lanese   University of Bologna/Inria, Italy
Cosimo Laneve   University of Bologna, Italy
Michael Miller   University of Victoria, Canada
Iain Phillips   Imperial College London, UK
Ilia Polian   University of Freiburg, Germany
Indranil Sengupta   Indian Institute of Technology, Kharagpur, India
Michael Kirkedal   University of Bremen, Germany
  Thomsen
Irek Ulidowski   University of Leicester, UK
Daniele Varacca   LACL - Université Paris Est Créteil, France
Paul Vitanyi   CWI, Amsterdam, The Netherlands
Janis Voigtländer   University of Bonn, Germany
Robert Wille   University of Bremen, Germany
Shigeru Yamashita   Ritsumeikan University, Japan
Tetsuo Yokoyama   Nanzan University, Japan

Additional Reviewers

Giachino, Elena   Mogensen, Torben
Kaarsgaard, Robin   Morrison, Daniel
Kole, Abhoy   Piccolo, Mauro
Koutavas, Vasileios   Sacerdoti Coen, Claudio
Mezzina, Claudio   Soeken, Mathias

Contents

Design of Reversible Circuits

Circuit Synthesis

Short Papers

Invited Paper

Moment Semantics for Reversible Rule-Based Systems

Vincent Danos[1]([⊠]), Tobias Heindel[2], Ricardo Honorato-Zimmer[2], and Sandro Stucki[3]

[1] Département d'Informatique, École Normale Supérieure, Paris, France
vincent.danos@gmail.com
[2] School of Informatics, University of Edinburgh, Edinburgh, UK
[3] Programming Methods Laboratory, EPFL, Lausanne, Switzerland

Abstract. We develop a notion of stochastic rewriting over marked graphs – i.e. directed multigraphs with degree constraints. The approach is based on double-pushout (DPO) graph rewriting. Marked graphs are expressive enough to internalize the 'no-dangling-edge' condition inherent in DPO rewriting. Our main result is that the linear span of marked graph occurrence-counting functions – or *motif functions* – form an algebra which is closed under the infinitesimal generator of (the Markov chain associated with) any such rewriting system. This gives a general procedure to derive the moment semantics of any such rewriting system, as a countable (and recursively enumerable) system of differential equations indexed by motif functions. The differential system describes the time evolution of moments (of any order) of these motif functions under the rewriting system. We illustrate the semantics using the example of preferential attachment networks; a well-studied complex system, which meshes well with our notion of marked graph rewriting. We show how in this case our procedure obtains a finite description of all moments of degree counts for a fixed degree.

Keywords: Stochastic processes · Moment semantics · Reversible Computing · Graph rewriting · Rule-based systems

1 Introduction

To explain the purpose of this paper, we start with a simple case of stochastic Petri net (PN) using the following pair of reactions:

$$A \xrightarrow{k_0} 2A \qquad\qquad (\rho_0)$$

$$A \xrightarrow{k_1} \varnothing \qquad\qquad (\rho_1)$$

This work was sponsored by the European Research Council (ERC) under the grants DOPPLER (587327) and RULE (320823).

J. Krivine and J.-B. Stefani (Eds.): RC 2015, LNCS 9138, pp. 3–26, 2015.
DOI: 10.1007/978-3-319-20860-2_1

The PN has a single species (or place) A and two reactions (or transitions) modelling the birth and death of cells. Given a mother cell, reaction ρ_0 will produce one daughter cell. Reaction ρ_1 models the death of cells. The firing rate of the reactions is given by the law of *mass action* and depends on the number N of cells present in the system as well as the rate constants k_0, k_1 of the reactions:

$$\theta_0 = k_0 N, \qquad\qquad \theta_1 = k_1 N.$$

The physical interpretation of the law of mass action states roughly that the propensity of a reaction is proportional to the concentration of the reactants, that is, the occupants of the left-hand side (LHS) of the reaction. We get a more computational interpretation by treating reactions such as ρ_0 and ρ_1 as *rewrite rules* over the state space of the PN. In order to apply a rule, we first need to *pattern-match* its LHS against the current state of the PN. The PN itself can then be seen as a labelled transition system, where transitions are rule applications, that is, they are identified by a rule together with an associated match of the LHS in the current state. If we assign the same constant transition rate to all applications of a given rule, the overall firing rate of that rule is exactly the product of said rate constant and the number of matches of the LHS in the current state. Returning to our birth and death model, the activity of the rule ρ_0 is k_0 times the number of ways one can match a single cell in a population of N, which is just $k_0 N$. These transitions and associated rates define a *continuous-time Markov chain* (CTMC), which provides the stochastic semantics of the PN. The CTMC is often expressed as a so-called *master equation* (ME), a system of differential equations describing the time evolution of the probability of finding the PN in a particular state [27].

As far as PNs go, the birth and death model is simple. Yet, because ρ_0 creates cells, its state space is countably infinite, and so is the number of equations in the ME. Nonetheless, the average evolution of the number of cells can be compactly described by the single rate equation (RE)

$$\tfrac{d}{dt}\mathbf{E}(N) = k_0\,\mathbf{E}(N) - k_1\,\mathbf{E}(N).$$

Indeed, the average occurrence count of any species in a given PN can always be approximated by a finite set of REs, providing us with a differential semantics for PNs [17,27].

1.1   Our Goal

In this paper, we wish to investigate similar REs but for models of dynamic networks that are more richly structured than PNs. We are looking for the following two ingredients:

1. a simple formal language that is flexible enough to capture a broad class of network dynamics
2. a method to generate REs for motif functions for any model of the above class

Regarding point 1, we propose a notion of *stochastic marked graph rewriting* which follows the general guidelines of the theory of graph transformation systems (GTS) [6,7,15,16,25,29]. Stochastic processes are modelled as rewrite rules over directed multigraphs with *marks* allowing for pre- and post-conditions on node degrees. Marked graphs double as a simple query language for identifying subgraphs subject to degree constraints. This provides a formal modeling framework in which we develop the method of point 2. We show how to generate (in general) countable systems of ordinary differential equations (ODEs) describing the mean evolution of marked graph motifs counts, or any higher-order statistics thereof. In fact, these ODEs completely describe the dynamics of the moments of marked graph observables. We therefore refer to them as the *moment semantics* of the rewrite system.

1.2   Preferential Attachment

We can elaborate on our basic birth and death model to illustrate these ideas. In the following, unless stipulated otherwise, graph is short for directed multigraph.

We start by endowing the model with a network structure. While the PN model allows us to track the evolution of a population over time, it does not capture mother-daughter relationships among cells. We now extend the PN model to a simple GTS that will do exactly that. The state of the PN is replaced by a directed multigraph with cells as nodes and edges pointing from daughters to mothers; the reactions of the PN are replaced by graph rewrite rules. This extension allows us to track "genealogical patterns" such as the number of sibling relationships. The updated rules of the birth and death model are

$$A \xrightarrow{\ k_0\ } A \leftarrow A' \qquad\qquad (\alpha_0)$$

$$A \xrightarrow{\ k_1\ } \varnothing \qquad\qquad (\alpha_1)$$

The birth rule α_0 introduces a new node A' (the daughter indicated by a prime) and a new edge $A \leftarrow A'$ representing the mother-daughter relationship; the death rule α_1 is identical to its counterpart ρ_1 from the PN model.

We can express sibling relationships through the motif

$$A' \twoheadrightarrow A \leftarrow A''$$

Tracking the number of such motifs amounts to counting the number of subgraphs in the state of our system that are isomorphic to the sibling graph.

So far, the sole purpose of edges in our model is to track relationships. This does not do justice to the expressive power of our rewrite formalism. In particular, there is no reason edges should not also influence the dynamics of the model. Let us add a third rule to illustrate this principle.

$$A' \twoheadrightarrow A \xrightarrow{\ k_2\ } A' \twoheadrightarrow A \leftarrow A'' \qquad\qquad (\alpha_2)$$

On their own, the rules α_0, α_1 model the evolution of a culture of rather uniform cells: any cell can divide or die at any time. Rule α_2, on the other hand, reflects the fact that some cells may be more prolific than others: if a cell already has a daughter, it is likely to divide again. This positive feedback, known as *preferential attachment* (PA) or the *Matthew effect*, appears in many real-world complex systems and has been extensively studied [3,4,11,12].

At a first glance, the preferential attachment rule α_2 looks rather innocuous. It seems to be just a special case of the birth rule α_0. However, having a closer look at the right-hand side (RHS) of α_2, we realise that this rule directly creates siblings. Hence, we should expect a high k_2/k_0 ratio to increase the occurrence of siblings dramatically.

Just as for the simpler PN system, we can employ an RE to describe the evolution of the average number of sibling relationships over time. The RE consists in the following system of ordinary differential equations (ODE), with S, N and E counting siblings, cells (single nodes) and mother-daughter relationships (single edges), respectively:

$$\frac{d}{dt}\mathbf{E}(S) = 2(k_0 + k_2)\mathbf{E}(E) + 2k_2\mathbf{E}(S) - 3k_1\mathbf{E}(S)$$

$$\frac{d}{dt}\mathbf{E}(N) = k_0\mathbf{E}(N) + k_2\mathbf{E}(E) - \ k_1\mathbf{E}(N)$$

$$\frac{d}{dt}\mathbf{E}(E) = k_0\mathbf{E}(N) + k_2\mathbf{E}(E) - 2k_1\mathbf{E}(E)$$

It is easy enough to convince ourselves that (in the absence of parallel edges) this system of ODEs does indeed describe the evolution of the preferential attachment process: the equations for N and E follow the law of mass action (modulo symmetry factors); the equation for S essentially says that one needs to create daughters in order to create siblings. Note also the positive feedback of E on itself: thanks to the positive dependency of S on E, a high k_2/k_0 ratio will indeed lead to an explosion in siblings. With these intuitions in mind, a clever modeller could certainly have come up with these equations. Yet, this manual process is error-prone and does not scale well. The combinatorics involved are non-trivial: as we will see later, more complex models can involve hundreds or thousands of equations. This prompts the need for tools to automate the derivation of REs from GTS similar to those available for PNs.

Consider now a more complex motif (which can be expressed directly using marked graphs). Define $N_i(G)$ as the number of nodes in the graph G that have in-degree *exactly* i (i.e. mothers with exactly i daughters). Note that N_i does indeed more than counting subgraphs: contrary to what one might think, N_i does *not* count the number of subgraphs in G that consist of a central node with i incident edges (i.e. i-stars) as that would also cover all the nodes in G with in-degree larger than i. In particular, N_2 is *not* the sibling pattern. Instead, we think of N_i as counting the number of matches of the single-node graph A in G, subject to the condition that the matching node have exactly i incident edges. For reasons that will become clear later, we call such pairs of graphs and associated degree conditions *marked graphs*. Perhaps surprisingly, we can write REs even for marked graph observables. The RE system for N_i, $i \in \mathbb{N}$ (which is derived explicitly in the next Section) is given by the following system of ODEs:

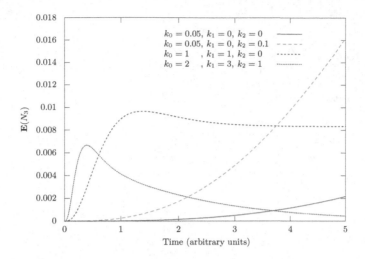

Fig. 1. Mean number of vertices with in-degree 3 (N_3) for various k_0, k_1, k_2

$$\tfrac{d}{dt}\mathbf{E}(N_i) = (k_0 + k_2(i-1))\,\mathbf{E}(N_{i-1}) - (k_0 + k_1(i+1) + k_2 i)\,\mathbf{E}(N_i) \quad \text{for } i \geq 1$$
$$\tfrac{d}{dt}\mathbf{E}(N_0) = k_0\,\mathbf{E}(N) + k_2\,\mathbf{E}(E) - (k_0 + k_1)\,\mathbf{E}(N_0)$$

Combined with the equations above for E and N, we have a set of equations which allows for a complete determination of the mean number of nodes of a given degree (with the size of the system being linear in the degree).

Fig. 1 shows the solutions of the RE for the case of $i = 3$ and various combinations of rates k_0, k_1, k_2. Note that the mean number of degree-three nodes is unbounded for low death rates, decays for high death rates, but reaches an equilibrium if the rates are suitably balanced. Yet it is unclear from these results alone *(i)* if N_3 converges in variance, and *(ii)* if its distribution around the mean is skewed. To answer *(i)* and *(ii)* we need to look at the *higher-order moments* of N_i. Luckily, we can derive ODEs not just for the mean but for arbitrary higher-order moments of marked graph observables. Due to the combinatorics involved, the resulting system of ODEs consists of 2097 equations! We therefore confine ourselves to presenting a plot (Fig. 2) summarising its solutions for the choice $k_0 = 1$, $k_1 = 2$ and $k_2 = 2$ of rates,[1] which shows that, despite the mean reaching an equilibrium, the skew and variance of N_i diverge over time. Clearly, the manual derivation of such an RE is beyond hope. We therefore developed a small, proof-of-concept tool for generating the REs in this example. The source code of our tool is freely available [1], and demonstrates that our construction can indeed be automated.

---

[1] It took approx. half a minute to generate the 2097 equations and another 33 minutes to solve them using GNU/Octave on a Intel Core i7 CPU.

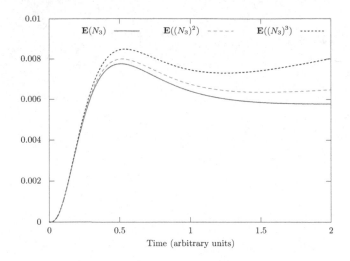

Fig. 2. The first three moments for the number of vertices with in-degree 3 (N_3) when $k_0 = 1, k_1 = 2, k_2 = 2$. The mean $\mathbf{E}(N_3)$ converges while the other moments may not.

1.3   A Sketch of the Solution

Let us briefly sketch our solution of the problem. Given a *marked graph observable* $[\tilde{G}](X)$, meaning a function counting the occurrences of the marked graph $\tilde{G}$ in the state X, we generate an ODE which describes the rate at which the mean occurrence count $\mathbf{E}([\tilde{G}](X(t)))$ changes over time. Careful inspection reveals that terms in the ODE are derived from the set of *minimal gluings* (MG) of the pattern $\tilde{G}$ with the LHS and RHS of the extant rules describing $X(t)$. (Note that the construction can thus be made incremental in the set of rules considered.) In particular, each term in $[\tilde{G}]$'s ODE depends on the current state *only* via expressions of the form $\mathbf{E}([\tilde{H}])$ for $\tilde{H}$ a pattern defining a new observable. This key property is referred to in the main part as *jump-closure* of graph observables. Each fresh observable $[\tilde{H}]$ can then be submitted to the same treatment.

To obtain higher-order moments, we exploit the commutative algebra structure of the linear space of pattern observables. We can compute $\mathbf{E}([\tilde{G}][\tilde{H}])$, i.e. covariances, etc. by expressing the product $[\tilde{G}][\tilde{H}]$ as a linear combination of motifs corresponding to the (minimal) gluings of $\tilde{G}$ and $\tilde{H}$. Though finite, the number of terms in the resulting expression is subject to the potentially high combinatorics of repeated pattern gluing.

As the generation of moment semantics is a symbolic procedure we can pursue it in principle to any order. This means that the order of the approximation is no longer limited to the humanly computable, and can be pushed further to acquire more accurate dynamics.

1.4   Related Work

Rate equations, and more generally mean field theories (MFT), are ubiquitous in the study of complex dynamics. Examples include, walkers on biopolymers [18,35]; models of epidemic spreading [21]; and of the evolution of social networks [13]. These examples witness both the power and universality of MFTs, and the fact that they are pursued in a seemingly ad hoc, and case-by-case fashion.

Conversely, various tools have been developed to automate the generation and solution of the ME and REs for the case of PNs [19,30,36]. But they suffer the limited expressivity of PNs as discussed above.

This paper follows ideas on applying the methods of abstract interpretation to the differential semantics of *site graph* rewriting [9,20,22]. From the GTS side, the theory of site graph rewriting had long been thought to be a lucky anomaly until a recent series of work showed that most of its ingredients could be made sense of, and given a much larger basis of applications, through the use of algebraic graph-rewriting techniques [2,23,24]. These latter investigations motivated us to try to address these questions at a higher level of generality [8]. Another more remote influence is Lynch's finite-model theoretic approach to rate equations [32].

1.5   Outline

The paper is organised as follows: §2 introduces the algebraic blueprint to build moment semantics and the notion of *jump-closure* of an algebra of observables; preferential attachment networks are used as an illustration; §3 introduces *marked graphs* and develops a formal stochastic graph transformation (GTS) framework based on *double-pushout* (DPO) rewriting of marked graphs; marks on graphs serve as simple *application conditions* and give rise to an algebra of *marked graph observables*, which are shown to be jump-closed with respect to the Markov chains generated by marked rewrite rules in §4; this is sufficient to derive the associated moment semantics.

2   The Blueprint of Moment Semantics

In this section we establish sufficient conditions for the existence of moment semantics for observables of suitable stochastic processes. These conditions provide the foundation on which we develop the moment semantics of concrete class of graphical rule-based systems in §3. We start with the necessary probabilistic preliminaries.

2.1   Markov Chains, Master Equation

Let S be an at most countable set, and write $\mathbb{R}^S$ for the vector space of real sequences indexed by S. We think of S as the state space of some process and of elements of $\mathbb{R}^S$ as real-valued *observables* on that process. Let X_t, $t \geq 0$ be a continuous-time Markov chain (CTMC) with state-space S and *row-finite* rate matrix Q; we say an $S \times S$ matrix is row-finite if it has only finitely many non-zero coefficients per row. Write $p_x(t)$, or simply p_x, for the probability of X_t being at x, and let $p(t)$, or simply p, be the vector in $\mathbb{R}^S$ with coordinates p_x. Note that Q is a linear operator on $\mathbb{R}^S$. The evolution of p can be described by the *forward equation*, also known as the *master equation* (ME), which is the following linear ordinary differential equation (ODE) with values in $\mathbb{R}^S$ [27,33]:

$$\tfrac{d}{dt}p^T = p^T Q \tag{1}$$

In explicit coordinate form:

$$\tfrac{d}{dt}p_x = \sum_y p_y q_{yx} - p_x \sum_y q_{xy}.$$

The ME has unique (minimal non-negative) solutions at all times and for all initial conditions [33]. One caveat is that for *explosive* X_t, which have non-zero probability to complete countably many jumps in finite time, the resulting p is a sub-probability.

Example 1 (CTMC of the PA example). For the case of preferential attachment, we take the state space S to be a countable set of finite directed graphs G with finite node and edge sets V_G, E_G. We associate rate matrices Q_i, $i = 0, 1, 2$ to each of the rules α_i, where the rate q_{GH}^i of transitioning from a graph G to a graph H via the rule α_i, is given by the number of ways in which the LHS of α_i occurs as an isomorphic subgraph in G in such a way that replacing said subgraph with the RHS of α_i in G produces H:

$$q_{GH}^0 = |\{n \in V_G \mid H = G^+(n)\}|$$
$$q_{GH}^1 = |\{n \in V_G \mid H = G^-(n)\}|$$
$$q_{GH}^2 = |\{e \in E_G \mid H = G^+(t(e))\}|$$

where $t(e)$ denotes the target node of the edge e, and $G^+(n)$, $G^-(n)$ are the graphs obtained, respectively, by adding a new node to G and connecting it to n, and by removing the node n and its edges from G. The overall rate matrix Q is given by $Q = \sum_i k_i Q_i$.

2.2   ODEs of Means

The rate matrix Q defines a linear transformation on $\mathbb{R}^S$ as follows:

$$(Qf)(x) = \sum_y q_{xy}(f(y) - f(x)). \tag{2}$$

Since the sum above is finite, Qf is indeed a well-defined element of $\mathbb{R}^S$. We call Qf the *jump* of f relative to Q. Intuitively, Qf is the expected rate of change in f given that the process sits at x. This interpretation of Q as a linear operator on observables (rather than probabilities) is similar to predicate transformer semantics [5].

Given an observable f, we write $\mathbf{E}_p(f) := p^T f$ for the expected value of f according to p. From the (1) we can derive formally the following:

$$\tfrac{d}{dt}\mathbf{E}_p(f) \;=\; \tfrac{d}{dt}p^T f \;=\; p^T Q f \;=\; \mathbf{E}_p(Qf), \tag{3}$$

giving us an equation for the rate of change of the mean of $f(X_t)$. As such this equation is not very useful, $\mathbb{R}^S$ being an even larger index set than S. Indeed, unless S is finite, $\mathbb{R}^S$ does not even have a countable basis. But, suppose we are given a linear subspace $\mathscr{A}$ of $\mathbb{R}^S$ which (i) has a countable basis $\mathscr{B}$, and (ii) is jump-closed in the sense that $Q\mathscr{B} \subseteq \mathscr{A}$. Jump-closure means that for g in $\mathscr{B}$, one can write its jump Qg as:

$$Qg = \textstyle\sum_{h \in \mathscr{B}} a_{g,h} h,$$

with finitely many non-zero coefficients $a_{g,h}$. By substituting this expression in (3), we get a linear ODE indexed by $\mathscr{B}$:

$$\tfrac{d}{dt}\mathbf{E}_p(g) = \textstyle\sum_{h \in \mathscr{B}} a_{g,h}\,\mathbf{E}_p(h). \tag{4}$$

Note that the dependence in the probability distribution $p(t)$ of X_t has vanished! Thanks to jump-closure, (4) completely bypasses the probabilistic behaviour of the model, and predicts directly the mean evolution of the processes g_t for g in $\mathscr{B}$. The mean of any other observable f in $\mathscr{A}$ can then be expressed as a linear combination of the solutions of (4).

The vector space $\mathbb{R}^S$ can be equipped with the product topology. A linear map on $\mathbb{R}^S$ is continuous for that choice of topology iff it is row-finite. By a result of Shkarin [34, Theorem 2.3], any row-finite linear system of differential equations over $\mathbb{R}^S$ has solutions defined at all times and for all initial conditions. As $\mathscr{B}$ is countable, Shkarin's Theorem guarantees all-time (but, in general, non-unique) solutions for (4).

Example 2 (REs for Preferential Attachment). We will illustrate this idea by deriving the REs for the fixed-degree node-counting observable N_i from §1. We start by computing the jump of N_i with respect to Q_0 as given in Example 1. Expanding the definition of Q_0 in (2) and simplifying a bit, we get

$$(Q_0 N_i)(G) = \sum_{n \in V_G} (N_i(G^+(n)) - N_i(G)).$$

It is easy to verify that, for all $i \geq 1$, the difference under the sum is equal to -1 if n has in-degree i, to 1 if n has in-degree $(i-1)$, and to 0 otherwise. Hence the above simplifies to

$$Q_0 N_i = N_{i-1} - N_i, \qquad\qquad \text{for } i \geq 1.$$

Proceeding similarly for $Q_1 N_i$ and $Q_2 N_i$, one obtains

$$QN_i = (k_0 + k_2(i-1))N_{i-1} - (k_0 + k_1(i+1) + k_2 i)N_i$$

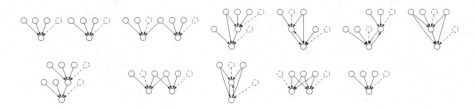

Fig. 3. The eleven graph patterns $(S_3 + S_3)$, $G_1, \ldots, G_9$ and S_3 corresponding to base observables of the vector space containing $([S_3])^2$. Dotted nodes and edges represent negative existence conditions, i.e. ths absence of an additional edge; later to be represented by marks (see next Section).

for $i \geq 1$, suggesting $\{N_i\}_{i \in \mathbb{N}}$ as a candidate for the basis $\mathscr{B}$. However, the jump of N_0 depends on two additional observables, namely $N(G) = |V_G|$ and $E(G) = |E_G|$, counting the number of nodes and edges, respectively, in G:

$$QN_0 = k_0 N + k_2 E - (k_0 + k_1)N_0.$$

Expressing N as the infinite sum $N = \sum_{i=0}^{\infty} N_i$ does not solve the problem as a linear combination may only involve a finite number of vectors. Similarly, it is not clear how one would express the observable E in terms of N_i. Fortunately, the jumps of N and E do not involve any additional observables:

$$QN = k_0 N + k_2 E - k_1 N$$
$$QE = k_0 N + k_2 E - 2k_1 E$$

and we conclude that $\mathscr{B} = \cup_i \mathscr{B}_i$ with $\mathscr{B}_i = \{N, E\} \cup \{N_k\}_{k=0}^i$ form a jump-closed basis which indexes the RE for the N_i motifs. In this favourable case, each finite $\mathscr{B}_i$ spans a finite-dimensional subspace which is already jump-closed. Hence, solutions of the RE exist and are unique for all times and initial conditions.

2.3   Higher-Order Moments

So far, we have only considered the mean evolution of observables f in $\mathscr{A}$. One might also be interested in higher-order statistics of f, such as its standard deviation or skewness. Suppose then that $\mathscr{A} = \text{lin}(\mathscr{B})$ is a subspace of $\mathbb{R}^S$ as above, and additionally, that $\mathscr{A}$ is closed under (pointwise) product. One can write the powers of any f in $\mathscr{A}$, as a linear combination

$$f^n = \sum_{h \in \mathscr{B}} b_{f,h,n} h, \qquad\qquad n \geq 1,$$

where only finitely many of the coefficients $b_{f,h,k}$ are non-zero. Thus, solutions of (4) already describe *arbitrary* moments of observables. (Considerations on the existence and uniqueness of solutions remain the same.)

Example 3 (Higher moments of N_i). Suppose we want to compute the variance of N_i with respect to p, that is,

$$\mathbf{V}_p(N_i) = \mathbf{E}_p\big((N_i - \mathbf{E}_p(N_i))^2\big) = \mathbf{E}_p\big((N_i)^2\big) - \mathbf{E}_p(N_i)^2.$$

We already have an RE describing the mean of N_i, and we need one for the second moment of N_i, $\mathbf{E}_p((N_i)^2)$. To apply the above idea, it is enough to find a sub-algebra $\mathscr{A}$ which contains $\mathscr{B}$ and has a countable basis; the linear span of $\mathscr{B}$ alone does not work as we cannot even express the square N^2 of its "simplest" observable N as a linear combination in $\mathscr{B}_i$.

At this point it is worth making the following observation: all of the observables we have considered so far count the occurrences of degree-constrained graph patterns, that is, given a graph G, they count the number of subgraphs in G that are isomorphic to a fixed graph, subject to conditions fixing the degrees of some nodes. For example, the observable $N_i(G)$ counts the number of occurrences of the single-node graph in G that have in-degree i, while the observable $E(G)$ counts the number of single-edge graphs with no additional conditions. Later, we call such graph-counting functions *marked graph observables* and prove that they span a sub-algebra of $\mathbb{R}^S$. (A proof of this fact along with a more detailed account of marked graph observables is given in §3.3.)

To illustrate this point, consider first the simple node-counting observable N. Writing A for the single-node pattern (with no extra conditions), $A + A$ for its disjoint union, the two-node pattern, and $[P]$ for the observable counting the pattern P, we can express the second moment of N as the sum

$$\mathbf{E}_p(N^2) = \mathbf{E}_p\big(([A])^2\big) = \mathbf{E}_p([A + A] + [A])$$
$$= \mathbf{E}_p([A + A]) + \mathbf{E}_p([A]) = \mathbf{E}_p([A + A]) + \mathbf{E}_p(N).$$

Intuitively, we can write the product of any two pattern observables $[P_1]$, $[P_2]$ as a sum over all possible overlaps of P_1 and P_2 (including the trivial one). In the case of the pattern A, there are just two such overlaps, namely the trivial one, $A + A$, and the complete overlap A. We make this intuition precise in §3.3 by introducing the notion of *minimal gluings*.

A more complex example is the pattern S_k, which we define to be the k-*star*, that is, the graph consisting in a *hub* node n with k neighbours $m_1, \ldots, m_k$, each connected to the hub through a *spoke* (m_i, n). Furthermore, we impose the condition on S_k that the in-degree of its hub be exactly k. The motifs N_k and $[S_k]$ are related through the equation $[S_k] = k!N_k$, where the factor $k!$ is due to the internal symmetries of S_k. Hence it is enough to express $\mathbf{E}_p(([S_k])^2)$, to complete the example.

To find this expression, we proceed as in the simple case above and compute all overlaps of S_3 with itself (Fig. 3). The square $[S_k]^2$ can then be expressed as

$$[S_3]^2 = [S_3 + S_3] + 9[G_1] + 36[G_2] + 9[G_4] + 36[G_5]$$
$$+ 6[G_6] + 18[G_7] + 6[G_9] + 36[G_3] + 18[G_8] + 6[S_3].$$

where the patterns $(S_3 + S_3)$, $G_1, \ldots, G_9$ and S_3 are those shown in Fig. 3 (in that order). The combinatorial integer coefficients are the multiplicities of non-isomorphic overlaps resulting in the same graph; e.g. we can obtain G_1 in $9 = 3 \times 3$ different ways, as each copy of S_3 must decide independently which of its three peripheral nodes to share with the other copy.

For more complex patterns, such as S_k, the manual enumeration of overlaps becomes difficult due to the combinatorics involved. They are therefore best automated. To this end, we developed a small, proof-of-concept tool [1] for generating ODEs of higher-order moments of S_k. In fact, the equation and diagrams in this example and those of the previous section have been automatically generated.

We can summarise the above discussion.

Suppose given a triple $(S, Q, \mathscr{A})$, with S an at most countable set, Q a row-finite $S \times S$ rate matrix, and $\mathscr{A}$ a linear sub-space of $\mathbb{R}^S$ with a countable basis $\mathscr{B}$ such that $Q\mathscr{B} \subseteq \mathscr{A}$ (jump-closure). We can define a linear ODE system indexed by $\mathscr{B}$:

$$\tfrac{d}{dt}\mathbf{E}_p(g) = \sum_{h \in \mathscr{B}} a_{g,h}\,\mathbf{E}_p(h),$$

with finitely many non-zero coefficients $a_{g,h}$. The ODE can be described more concisely as $\frac{d}{dt}X = Q_{\mathscr{B}}^T X$ with $Q_{\mathscr{B}}$ the restriction of Q to $\mathscr{B}$ (which exists by jump closure), and $X(t) \in \mathbb{R}^{\mathscr{B}}$. One sees this to be just the master equation (1) restricted to $\mathscr{B}$.

If in addition $\mathscr{A}$ is a sub-algebra of $\mathbb{R}^S$, by linear combinations, we can derive from the above equations for any moment formed over $\mathscr{B}$.

It remains now to build an interesting example of this situation. In the next section we develop our concrete graphical framework of stochastic rule-based systems and associated observables, for which moment semantics can be built.

3   Reversible Stochastic Graph Rewriting

We turn now to the GTS framework for which we will derive moment semantics as outlined in §2. We build on a well-known approach from algebraic graph rewriting, namely the *double pushout* (DPO) approach [7,28]. The reasons for this choice are twofold: first, we profit from a solid body of preexisting work, and second, it allows for an "axiomatic" presentation abstracting over the details of the graph-like structures that are being rewritten. Indeed, while we only treat the case of directed multigraphs (graphs with an arbitrary number of directed edges between any two nodes), the theory generalizes to DPO rewriting in other adhesive categories [29] with negative application conditions [14,26].

We start with preliminaries on directed multigraphs, followed by a brief summary of the DPO approach and its stochastic semantics [25]. Next, we introduce *marked graphs* as a means to add simple application conditions to graph rewrite rules. We establish two key properties of marks: firstly, we show that marks are sufficient to internalize the reversibility conditions inherent in DPO rewriting into rewrite rules; secondly, marked graphs give rise naturally to a class of observables over graphs with the algebraic structure outlined in §2. As we will see in §4, such observables are jump-closed with respect to CTMCs defined by any finite set of marked rewrite rules.

3.1 Graph-Theoretic Preliminaries and DPO Rewriting

A *finite directed multigraph* (henceforth simply *graph*) G consists of a finite set of *nodes* V_G, a finite set of *edges* E_G, and *source* and *target* maps $s_G, t_G \colon E_G \to V_G$. A *morphism* $f \colon G \to H$ between graphs G and H is a pair of maps $f_V \colon V_G \to V_H$, $f_E \colon E_G \to E_H$ on edges and nodes, such that for every edge e in E_G,

$$s_H(f_E(e)) = f_V(s_G(e)) \qquad \text{and} \qquad t_H(f_E(e)) = f_V(t_G(e)).$$

The graphs G and H are called the *domain* and *codomain* of f, respectively. Given a pair $f \colon F \to G$, $g \colon G \to H$ of morphisms, their *composition* $(g \circ f) \colon F \to H$ is defined as $(g \circ f) = (g_V \circ f_V, g_E \circ f_E)$. A graph morphism $f \colon G \to H$ is a *monomorphism*, or simply a *mono*, if f_V and f_E are injective; it is a *graph inclusion* if both f_V and f_E are inclusion maps, in which case G is a *subgraph* of H and we write $G \subseteq H$. Every morphism $f \colon G \to H$ defines a subgraph $f(G) \subseteq H$ called the *direct image* (or just the *image*) of f in H, such that $V_{f(G)} = f_V(V_G)$ and $E_{f(G)} = f_E(E_G)$. Finally, a graph morphism $f \colon G \to H$ is an *isomorphism*, or simply an *iso*, if f_V and f_E are bijections. Given an iso $f \colon G \to H$, we say that G is *isomorphic* to H and write $G \simeq H$.

Graph morphisms provide us with a notion of *pattern matching* on graphs. We restrict pattern matching to monos: a *match* of G in H is a mono $f \colon G \to H$. This restriction ensures that $f(G) \simeq G$ if f is a match, that is, matches of G in H identify subgraphs in H that are isomorphic to G. It is easy to verify that the composition of two matches is again a match. We write $[G; H]$ for the set of matches of G in H.

The main ingredient for graph rewriting are rewrite rules. A *rule* $\alpha \colon L \rightharpoonup R$ with *left-hand side* (LHS) L and *right-hand side* (RHS) R is a pair $\alpha_1 \colon K \to L$, $\alpha_2 \colon K \to R$ where both α_1 and α_2 are monos. Given a rule $\alpha \colon L \rightharpoonup R$, we define its *inverse* $\alpha^\dagger \colon R \rightharpoonup L$ as $(\alpha_1, \alpha_2)^\dagger = (\alpha_2, \alpha_1)$.

By combining matches and rules, we obtain *derivations*, the basic rewrite steps of a GTS. We first describe them informally. Fig. 4 shows a derivation with a match $f \colon L \to G$ on the left and a rule $\alpha \colon L \rightharpoonup R$ on top. The match f identifies the subgraph in G that is to be modified, while the rule α describes how to carry out the modification. In order to obtain the *comatch* $g \colon R \to H$ on the right, one starts by removing nodes and edges from $f(L)$ which do not have a preimage under $f \circ \alpha_1$ (colored red in the figure). This operation is allowed only if it leaves no edges dangling in G, that is, a node may be removed only if all its incident edges are also removed. To complete the derivation, one extends the resulting match $h \colon K \to D$ by adjoining to D the nodes and edges in R that do not have a preimage under α_2 (colored green in the figure). The two monos β_1 and β_2 witness, respectively, the deletions from G and additions to D, and form the *corule* of the derivation.

Derivations constructed in this way have the defining property of being *double pushouts* (DPO): they consist of a pair of *pushout squares* (PO) of graph morphisms [7,28].

There are certain points worth noting. Firstly, not every pair $f \colon L \to G$, $\alpha \colon L \rightharpoonup R$ of compatible matches and rules gives rise to a derivation. The reason

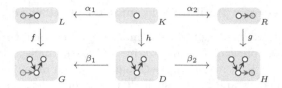

Fig. 4. A simple derivation or rewrite step: one starts with a match f for the left-hand side L of the rule in G; then, one constructs D by deleting nodes in G which correspond to nodes in L with no preimage in K; finally, one adds nodes and edges found in R but not in K

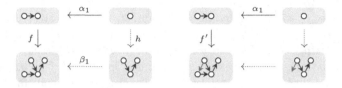

Fig. 5. The pair f, α_1 of monos has a POC, while the pair f', α_1 does not

is that the required left-hand PO does not exist for every pair $f\colon L \to G$, $\alpha_1\colon L \to K$ of monos. A suitable pair $h\colon K \to D$, $\beta_1\colon D \to G$ of monos, called *pushout complement* (POC) of f and α_1, exists iff the removal of nodes from G does not result in dangling edges. Fig. 5 illustrates this point. If a POC h, β_1 exists for f, α_1, then it is unique up to (unique) iso on D. Secondly, given a pair $h\colon K \to D$, $\alpha_2\colon K \to R$ of monos, the right-hand PO always exists, and the corresponding pair $g\colon R \to H$, $\beta_2\colon D \to H$ of monos is unique up to (unique) iso on H. Thirdly, if there is a derivation of g from f by α, then by symmetry, there is also a derivation of f from g via $\alpha^\dagger$.

Importantly, derivations *compose* and *split* (Fig. 6). Given a derivation of g_1 from f_1 by α with corule γ (the top DPO) and a derivation of g_2 from f_2 by γ with corule β (the bottom DPO), one obtains a composite derivation of $g = g_2 \circ g_1$ from $f = f_2 \circ f_1$ via α with corule β, by pasting together the two DPO diagrams. Conversely, derivations split along factorizations of matches: given the outer and top derivations of g from f and g_1 from f_1 via α, with corules β and γ, respectively, there is, for every f_2 such that $f = f_2 \circ f_1$, a unique bottom derivation with rule γ, comatch g_2 and corule β, such that $g = g_2 \circ g_1$.

Whenever there is a derivation with match f, comatch g and rule α, we say g is α-*derivable* from f and write $f \Rightarrow_\alpha g$. A pair of matches $f\colon G \to H$, $f'\colon G \to H'$ of a graph G is said to be isomorphic if there is an iso $u\colon H \to H'$ such that $f' = u \circ f$. It follows directly from the above discussion that the binary relation $\Rightarrow_\alpha$ is *(i)* partial, in that not every match of the LHS of α extends to a derivation, *(ii)* functional up to iso, that is, if $f \Rightarrow_\alpha g$ and $f \Rightarrow_\alpha g'$ then $g \simeq g'$, and *(iii)* injective up to iso, that is, if $f \Rightarrow_\alpha g$ and $f' \Rightarrow_\alpha g$ then $f \simeq f'$.

The fact that derivations are only defined up to iso is convenient as it allows us to invert them without paying attention to the concrete naming of nodes and

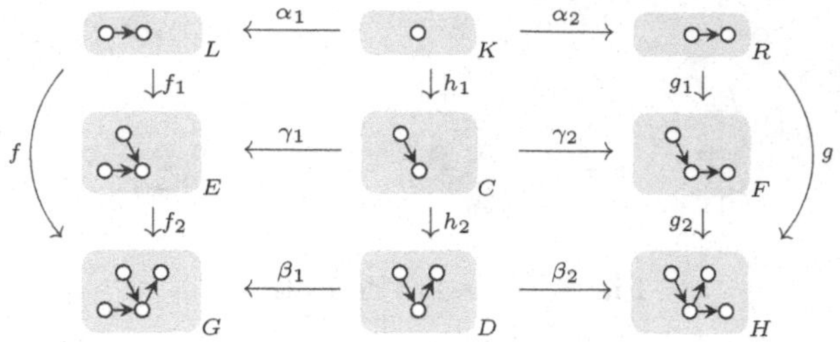

Fig. 6. A vertical composition of derivations

edges. Indeed, the inverse of $\Rightarrow_\alpha$ is just $(\Rightarrow_\alpha)^{-1} = (\Rightarrow_{\alpha^\dagger})$. On the other hand, when defining the stochastic semantics of rule-based systems, it is more convenient to restrict $\Rightarrow_\alpha$ to a properly functional relation. To this end, we fix once and for all a (countable) set $\mathscr{G}$ of *representatives* from every isomorphism class of graphs, and denote by $\alpha(f)$ and $f(\alpha)$, for any given rule $\alpha \colon L \rightharpoonup R$ and match $f \in \mathrm{dom}(\Rightarrow_\alpha)$, the unique comatch $\alpha(f) \colon R \to H$ and corule $f(\alpha)_1 \colon D \to G$, $f(\alpha)_2 \colon D \to H$ of the unique derivation for which both D and H are in $\mathscr{G}$. Note that the partial maps $\alpha(-)$ and $\alpha^\dagger(-)$ need not be inverses. Indeed, if α involves node deletions, one cannot choose $\alpha(-)$ and $\alpha^\dagger(-)$ such that $\alpha^\dagger(\alpha(f)) = f$ for all $f \in \mathrm{dom}(\Rightarrow_\alpha)$ because the node and edge sets of the respective codomains differ in general.

Given a rule $\alpha \colon L \rightharpoonup R$, define the rate matrix Q_α over $\mathscr{G}$ as

$$q^\alpha_{GH} = |\{f \in [L; G] \mid f \in \mathrm{dom}(\Rightarrow_\alpha) \text{ and } \alpha(f) \in [R; H]\}| \qquad \text{for } G \neq H,$$

$$q^\alpha_{GG} = \sum_{H \neq G} -q^\alpha_{GH} \qquad\qquad\qquad . \qquad\qquad\qquad \text{otherwise.}$$

Given a finite set of rules $\mathscr{R}$ and a *rate map* $k \colon \mathscr{R} \to \mathbb{R}^+$, let

$$Q(\mathscr{R}, k) = \sum_{\alpha \in \mathscr{R}} k(\alpha) Q_\alpha.$$

This defines a CTMC over $\mathscr{G}$. As $\mathscr{R}$ is finite, the rate matrix $Q(\mathscr{R}, k)$ is row-finite.

3.2   Marked Graphs

So far, our notion of pattern matching is rather limited. While monos identify (isomorphic) images of a "pattern" (i.e. their domain) in other graphs, they provide no way of imposing additional conditions on the image of the pattern. We have seen examples in §1 and §2 where such conditions were used to count the number of nodes with a particular in-degree. But conditions are also useful for rewriting: by equipping the LHS and RHS of rules with conditions, one obtains more expressive rewrite formalisms. A particular case which has been studied in the DPO setting is that of *negative application conditions* (NAC), where the

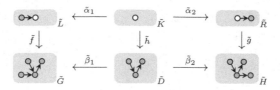

Fig. 7. A marked derivation

set of derivations under a rule α is restricted to instances where the match and comatch respect conditions associated with the LHS and RHS of α [14,26]. In this section, we extend graphs with simple degree conditions which we call *marks*. Marks can be seen as a very simple type of NAC. Yet, they are expressive enough to cover the example patterns[2] form §1 and §2, and to internalize the dangling-edge conditions seen in the previous section into the LHS of rules.

A *marked graph* $\tilde{G}$ is a graph G together with a *marking* predicate $M_G \subseteq V_G$ over nodes. We say a node $x \in V_G$ is *marked* if $x \in M_G$ and *unmarked* otherwise. We write $\overline{M}_G$ for the complement $V_G \setminus M_G$ of the marking M_G. We say a marked graph $\tilde{G}$ is *complete* if all its nodes are marked, that is, $M_G = V_G$.

A *marked morphism* $\tilde{f} \colon \tilde{G} \to \tilde{H}$ is a graph morphism $f \colon G \to H$ that *preserves* marks, that is, $f_V(M_G) \subseteq M_H$. Marked morphisms compose as their underlying graph morphisms. The definitions of subgraphs, inclusions and monos generalize straightforwardly to marked graphs and morphisms. It is easy to see that isos *reflect* marks, that is, a marked morphism $\tilde{f} \colon \tilde{G} \to \tilde{H}$ is a marked iso if its underlying graph morphism f is an iso and $f_V(M_G) = M_H$. We define the marking of the direct image $\tilde{f}(\tilde{G})$ of a marked morphism $\tilde{f} \colon \tilde{G} \to \tilde{H}$ by $M_{\tilde{f}(\tilde{G})} = f_V(M_G)$, that is, marks on nodes in $f(H)$ that are provided only by $\tilde{H}$ are not considered part of the marking of $\tilde{f}(\tilde{G})$. Fig. 7 shows a marked version of Fig. 4 where marked nodes are colored in dark gray, unmarked nodes in white. The graphs in the bottom row of Fig. 7 are complete while those in the top row are not. All morphisms in the figure are marked monos.

We interpret marks as conditions on node degrees: a *marked match* of $\tilde{G}$ in $\tilde{H}$ is a marked mono $\tilde{f} \colon \tilde{G} \to \tilde{H}$ that preserves and reflects the degrees of marked nodes, that is, for all $x \in M_G$, $\mathrm{indeg}_H(f_V(x)) = \mathrm{indeg}_G(x)$ and $\mathrm{outdeg}_H(f_V(x)) = \mathrm{outdeg}_G(x)$. Given a marked graph $\tilde{G}$, and an unmarked match $f \colon G \to H$, we say f *extends* to a marked match $\tilde{f} \colon \tilde{G} \to \tilde{H}$ if there is at least one marking on H for which $\tilde{f}$ is a marked match. Such an extension will exist iff nodes marked in $\tilde{G}$ are mapped by f to nodes of same degree in H. The composition of marked matches is again a marked match. We write $[\tilde{G}; \tilde{H}]$

---

[2] Strictly speaking, the example patterns in §1–2 require a slightly more expressive type of NACs than the one described in this section. In particular, they require separate conditions on in and out-degrees of nodes, where as we only consider conditions on the overall node degree here. However, the theory extends straight-forwardly to the case where in and out-degrees are represented by separate markings. We have implemented the more general case in [1].

for the set of marked matches of $\tilde{G}$ in $\tilde{H}$. All the morphisms in Fig. 7 except $\tilde{\beta}_1$ and $\tilde{\beta}_2$ are marked matches.

By allowing rules to be marked, we obtain a simple form of NACs. Marks in the LHS act as *preconditions* on a rule, marks in the RHS as *postconditions*. We further restrict the type of morphisms that may appear in rules to *rigid monos*: we say a marked mono $\tilde{f} \colon \tilde{G} \to \tilde{H}$ is rigid if every node in $\tilde{H}$ is marked unless it is the image of an unmarked node in $\tilde{G}$, that is, $\overline{M}_H = f_V(\overline{M}_G)$. A *marked rule* $\tilde{\alpha} \colon \tilde{L} \rightharpoonup \tilde{R}$ is a pair $\tilde{\alpha}_1 \colon \tilde{K} \to \tilde{L}$, $\tilde{\alpha}_2 \colon \tilde{K} \to \tilde{R}$ of rigid marked monos. We say $\tilde{\alpha}$ is *minimally marked* if $M_K = \varnothing$. We write $\tilde{\alpha}^\dagger$ for the inverse $(\tilde{\alpha}_2, \tilde{\alpha}_1)$ of a marked rule $\tilde{\alpha}$. The rules $\tilde{\alpha}$ and $\tilde{\beta}$ in Fig. 7 are marked but only $\tilde{\alpha}$ is minimally marked. (Minimally marked rules are used later to embed normal DPO rewriting into our marked graph rewriting.)

The rigidity condition on rules ensures that rules are well-behaved in the following way: given a marked rule $\tilde{\alpha} \colon \tilde{L} \rightharpoonup \tilde{R}$ with underlying (unmarked) rule α and an unmarked match $f \colon L \to G$ of its LHS,

1. there is a g such that $f \Rightarrow_\alpha g$ if f extends to a marked match, and
2. g extends to a marked match if f does.

The first point internalizes the no-dangling-edge condition into rules and roughly corresponds to a notion of type safety: if both the rule α and its "argument" f are "well-marked", then α can be applied safely to f. The second point is reminiscent of a predicate transformer semantics: the marking on $\tilde{R}$ is the "strongest postcondition" given the marking on the LHS $\tilde{L}$. Conversely, the marking on $\tilde{L}$ is the "weakest precondition" given $\tilde{R}$. Note that, by symmetry, the same holds for $\tilde{\alpha}^\dagger$ so that the pre and postcondition uniquely determine each other.

A PO of a pair $\tilde{f} \colon \tilde{G} \to \tilde{H}$, $\tilde{f}' \colon \tilde{G} \to \tilde{H}'$ of marked morphisms, is a commuting square of marked morphisms (see (5) below), where the underlying graph morphisms form a PO (6), and $M_F = g_V(M_H) \cup g'_V(M_{H'})$.

$$
\begin{array}{ccc}
\tilde{G} & \xrightarrow{\tilde{f}'} & \tilde{H}' \\
{\scriptstyle \tilde{f}}\downarrow & & \downarrow{\scriptstyle \tilde{g}'} \quad (5) \\
\tilde{H} & \xrightarrow{\tilde{g}} & \tilde{F}
\end{array}
\qquad\qquad
\begin{array}{ccc}
G & \xrightarrow{f'} & H' \\
{\scriptstyle f}\downarrow & & \downarrow{\scriptstyle g'} \quad (6) \\
H & \xrightarrow{g} & F
\end{array}
$$

A *marked derivation* is a DPO of marked monos such as in Fig. 7, with $\tilde{f}$, $\tilde{g}$, $\tilde{h}$ marked matches and $\tilde{\alpha}$, $\tilde{\beta}$ marked rules. We call $\tilde{g}$ the *marked comatch* and $\tilde{\beta}$ the *marked corule* of the derivation.

POs of marked monos have interesting properties when one mono is rigid.

Lemma 1. *A pair of marked monos $\tilde{f} \colon \tilde{G} \to \tilde{H}$, $\tilde{g} \colon \tilde{H} \to \tilde{F}$ where $\tilde{f}$ is rigid, has a POC if $\tilde{g}$ is a marked match. (If in addition, $\tilde{G}$ is markless, then $\tilde{g}$ must be a marked match for a POC to exist.)*

Lemma 2. *Let* (5) *be a PO of marked monos, with $\tilde{f}'$ rigid. Then*

1. $\tilde{g}$ *is rigid,*
2. $\tilde{f}$ *is a marked match iff $\tilde{g}'$ is,*
3. *the pair $\tilde{f}, \tilde{g}$ is the unique (up to unique iso) POC of $\tilde{f}', \tilde{g}'$ and*

$$M_H = g_V^{-1}(M_F \setminus g_V'(M_{H'})) \cup f_V(M_G).$$

The two lemmas above are sufficient to establish the properties of marked rules outlined before; besides they also allow one to prove that marked derivations compose and split along marked matches (which is key to the proof in the next section).

Write $\tilde{f} \Rightarrow_{\tilde{\alpha}} \tilde{g}$ if $\tilde{g}$ is $\tilde{\alpha}$-derivable from $\tilde{f}$. Just as its unmarked counterpart, the binary relation $\Rightarrow_{\tilde{\alpha}}$ is functional and injective up to iso. However, *contrary to* $\Rightarrow_{\alpha}$, the relation $\Rightarrow_{\tilde{\alpha}}$ is also total (by Lemma 1). We fix again a (countable) set $\tilde{\mathscr{G}}$ of representatives from every isomorphism class of marked graphs. Given any marked rule $\tilde{\alpha}\colon \tilde{L} \rightharpoonup \tilde{R}$ and match $\tilde{f}\colon \tilde{L} \to \tilde{G}$, the definitions of the maps $\tilde{\alpha}(-)$ and $\tilde{f}(-)$, as well as the $\tilde{\mathscr{G}} \times \tilde{\mathscr{G}}$ rate matrix $Q_{\tilde{\alpha}}$ associated with $\tilde{\alpha}$, are completely analogous to those for the unmarked case.

At this point, the reader might be wondering whether the restrictions imposed on marked rules cause any loss of expressivity with respect to unmarked DPO rewriting. They do not. Indeed, one can build an embedding of unmarked DPO rewriting in the marked variant. We start by noticing that for every (unmarked) graph G there is a unique complete marked graph $\tilde{G}_K$, and for every (unmarked) rule $\alpha\colon L \rightharpoonup R$ there is a unique minimally marked rule $\tilde{\alpha}_{\min}\colon \tilde{L}_{\min} \rightharpoonup \tilde{R}_{\min}$. To every match $f\colon L \to G$ of an LHS L in some G corresponds a unique marked mono $\tilde{f}\colon \tilde{L}_{\min} \to \tilde{G}_K$. By Lemma 1, there is a derivation $f \Rightarrow_{\alpha} g$ for some $g\colon R \to H$ iff $\tilde{f}$ is a marked match and by Lemma 2 this uniquely determines an extension $\tilde{g}\colon \tilde{R}_{\min} \to \tilde{H}_K$ of g to a marked match. Note that due to the rigidity of $\tilde{\alpha}_{\min}$, the codomain $\tilde{H}_K$ of $\tilde{g}$ must be complete.

Although we have only presented the case of directed multigraphs, marked stochastic DPO rewriting also straight-forwardly extends to other graph-like structures, such as typed graphs or hypergraphs. Another example is that of PNs, when seen as rewriting discrete typed graphs (graphs with no edges). Since nodes in a discrete graph have degree zero, any match trivially extends to a marked match.

3.3 Minimal Gluings and the Algebra of Marked Graph Observables

Given a marked graph $\tilde{G}$ in $\tilde{\mathscr{G}}$, define the *marked graph observable* $[\tilde{G}]\colon \tilde{\mathscr{G}} \to \mathbb{N}$ to be the integer-valued function $[\tilde{G}](\tilde{H}) = |[\tilde{G}; \tilde{H}]|$ counting the number of occurrences (i.e. marked matches) of $\tilde{G}$ in any given graph $\tilde{H}$ in $\tilde{\mathscr{G}}$. Marked graph observables turn out to be the natural choice of observable functions over which to construct moment semantics for marked DPO rewriting. In this section, we present their algebraic structure, establishing the connection to the framework developed in §2. To do so, we first need to introduce a key ingredient: *minimal gluings* (MG).

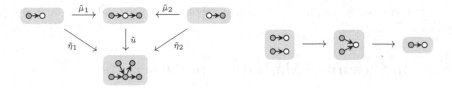

Fig. 8. Left: a gluing $\tilde{\eta}$ of the marked graphs $\tilde{L}$ and $\tilde{R}$ from Fig. 7 and the corresponding MG $\tilde{\mu}$. Right: the codomains of the MGs in $\tilde{L} * \tilde{L}$ ordered by (non mono) marked graph morphisms among them

Given a pair of subgraphs $G_1 \subseteq H$, $G_2 \subseteq H$ of a graph H, the *union* of G_1 and G_2 in H is the unique subgraph $G_1 \cup G_2$ of H, such that $V_{(G_1 \cup G_2)} = V_{G_1} \cup V_{G_2}$ and $E_{(G_1 \cup G_2)} = E_{G_1} \cup E_{G_2}$. The union $\tilde{G}_1 \cup \tilde{G}_2 \subseteq \tilde{H}$ of a pair of marked subgraphs $\tilde{G}_1 \subseteq \tilde{H}$, $\tilde{G}_2 \subseteq \tilde{H}$ has $G_1 \cup G_2$ as its underlying graph and $M_{G_1} \cup M_{G_2}$ as its marking. A *gluing* $\tilde{\eta}$ of a pair $\tilde{G}_1$, $\tilde{G}_2$ of marked graphs is a pair of marked matches $\tilde{\eta}_1 \colon \tilde{G}_1 \to \tilde{U}$, $\tilde{\eta}_2 \colon \tilde{G}_2 \to \tilde{U}$ with common codomain $\mathrm{cod}(\tilde{\eta}) = \tilde{U}$. We say $\tilde{\eta}$ is *minimal* if $\mathrm{cod}(\tilde{\eta}) = \tilde{\eta}_1(\tilde{G}_1) \cup \tilde{\eta}_2(\tilde{G}_2)$. Two gluings $\tilde{\eta}$ and $\tilde{\mu}$ are *isomorphic* if there is a marked iso $\tilde{u} \colon \mathrm{cod}(\tilde{\eta}) \to \mathrm{cod}(\tilde{\mu})$, such that $\tilde{\mu}_1 = \tilde{u} \circ \tilde{\eta}_1$ and $\tilde{\mu}_2 = \tilde{u} \circ \tilde{\eta}_2$. Write $\tilde{G}_1 *_{\simeq} \tilde{G}_2$ for the set of isomorphism classes of minimal gluings of $\tilde{G}_1$ and $\tilde{G}_2$, and $\tilde{G}_1 * \tilde{G}_2$ for a choice of representatives from each class in $\tilde{G}_1 *_{\simeq} \tilde{G}_2$ such that $\mathrm{cod}(\tilde{\mu}) \in \mathcal{G}$ for all $\tilde{\mu}$ in $\tilde{G}_1 * \tilde{G}_2$. It is easy to verify the following:

Lemma 3. *Let $\tilde{G}_1$, $\tilde{G}_2$ be marked graphs, then (i) $\tilde{G}_1 * \tilde{G}_2$ has $O(2^{N+M})$ elements, with $N = |V_{G_1}| + |V_{G_2}|$, $M = |E_{G_1}| + |E_{G_2}|$, and (ii) for every gluing $\tilde{\eta}$ of $\tilde{G}_1$ and $\tilde{G}_2$, there is a unique MG $\tilde{\mu}$ in $G_1 * G_2$ and marked match $\tilde{u} \colon \mathrm{cod}(\tilde{\eta}) \to \mathrm{cod}(\tilde{\mu})$ such that $\tilde{\eta}_1 = \tilde{u} \circ \tilde{\mu}_1$ and $\tilde{\eta}_2 = \tilde{u} \circ \tilde{\mu}_2$.*

Fig. 8 shows a gluing $\tilde{\eta}$ and its corresponding MG $\tilde{\mu}$ on the left, and the codomains of a set of minimal self-gluings on the right.

Thanks to MGs, marked graph observables form an algebra.

Theorem 1. *Let $\mathscr{B}$ be the set of marked graph observables. The linear space $\mathscr{A} = \mathrm{lin}(\mathscr{B})$ spanned by $\mathscr{B}$ is a sub-algebra of $\mathbb{R}^{\mathcal{G}}$, that is, $\mathrm{poly}(\mathscr{A}) = \mathscr{A}$.*

Proof. As $\mathscr{A}$ is a linear subspace of $\mathbb{R}^{\mathcal{G}}$, it suffices to show that $\mathscr{B}$ is closed under product. First, note that the product of any two marked graph observables $[\tilde{G}_1]$ and $[\tilde{G}_2]$ in $\mathscr{B}$ counts exactly the number of gluings $\tilde{G}_1 \to \tilde{H} \leftarrow \tilde{G}_2$ of marked matches in some common $\tilde{H} \in \mathcal{G}$. By Lemma 3, we can express such products as a (finite) linear combination of observables $[\mathrm{cod}(\tilde{\mu})]$ corresponding to the (codomains of) the MGs under $\tilde{G}_1$ and $\tilde{G}_2$:

$$[\tilde{G}_1](\tilde{H})[\tilde{G}_2](\tilde{H}) = |[\tilde{G}_1; \tilde{H}]| \cdot |[\tilde{G}_2; \tilde{H}]| = |\{\tilde{G}_1 \xrightarrow{\tilde{\eta}_1} \tilde{H} \xleftarrow{\tilde{\eta}_2} \tilde{G}_2 \mid \tilde{\eta} \text{ a gluing}\}|$$

$$= \sum_{\tilde{\mu} \in \tilde{G}_1 * \tilde{G}_2} [\mathrm{cod}(\tilde{\mu})](\tilde{H}).$$

Since $\mathrm{cod}(\tilde{\mu}) \in \mathcal{G}$ for all $\tilde{\mu}$ in $\tilde{G}_1 * \tilde{G}_2$, the result is again in $\mathscr{A}$. $\qquad\square$

Note that the set $\tilde{\mathscr{G}}$ contains the empty graph $\varnothing$, which makes $\mathscr{A}$ a *unitary* algebra with unit $[\varnothing]$.

4   Jump-Closure of Marked Graph Observables

We now have all the ingredients in place to derive moment semantics for (DPO-based) marked graph rewriting. The set $\tilde{\mathscr{G}}$ forms a countable state space over which we generate CTMCs from finite sets of marked rules and associated rate maps. The space $\mathscr{A}$ spanned by marked graph observables provides us with a candidate sub-algebra of $\mathbb{R}^{\tilde{\mathscr{G}}}$. It remains to show that $\mathscr{A}$ is jump-closed with respect to the CTMCs generated by marked rules.

Theorem 2. *Let $\mathscr{R}$ be a finite set of marked rules with associated rate map $k\colon \mathscr{R} \to \mathbb{R}^+$, and $\mathscr{B}$ the set of marked graph observables. The linear subspace $\mathscr{A}$ of $\mathbb{R}^{\tilde{\mathscr{G}}}$ spanned by $\mathscr{B}$ is closed under the action of the infinitesimal generator $Q(\mathscr{R}, k)$. In particular, for each marked rule $\tilde{\alpha}\colon \tilde{L} \rightharpoonup \tilde{R}$ in $\mathscr{R}$ and marked graph $\tilde{G}$ in $\tilde{\mathscr{G}}$, we have*

$$Q_{\tilde{\alpha}}[\tilde{G}] = \sum_{\tilde{\mu} \in \tilde{R} * \tilde{G}} [\mathrm{cod}(\tilde{\alpha}^\dagger(\tilde{\mu}_1))] - \sum_{\tilde{\mu} \in \tilde{L} * \tilde{G}} [\mathrm{cod}(\tilde{\mu})].$$

Proof. Let $\tilde{F}$ be some marked graph in $\tilde{\mathscr{G}}$ and $\tilde{\alpha}\colon \tilde{L} \rightharpoonup \tilde{R}$ a rule in $\mathscr{R}$. By (2) and the definition of $Q_{\tilde{\alpha}}$, we have

$$(Q_{\tilde{\alpha}}[\tilde{F}])(\tilde{G}) = \sum_{\tilde{H} \in \tilde{\mathscr{G}}} q^{\tilde{\alpha}}_{\tilde{G}\tilde{H}}([\tilde{F}](\tilde{H}) - [\tilde{F}](\tilde{G}))$$

$$= \sum_{\tilde{f} \in [\tilde{L};\tilde{G}]} |[\tilde{F}; \mathrm{cod}(\tilde{\alpha}(\tilde{f}))]| - \sum_{\tilde{f} \in [\tilde{L};\tilde{G}]} |[\tilde{F};\tilde{G}]|.$$

Recall that $\tilde{\alpha}(\tilde{f})$ denotes the representative comatch derived from $\tilde{f}$ by $\tilde{\alpha}$, and hence $\mathrm{cod}(\tilde{\alpha}(\tilde{f}))$ is just the marked graph derived from $\tilde{G}$ via $\tilde{\alpha}$ and $\tilde{f}$. The action of $Q_{\tilde{\alpha}}$ at $\tilde{G}$ thus naturally decomposes into two terms $Q^+_{\tilde{\alpha}}$ and $Q^-_{\tilde{\alpha}}$ describing, respectively, the production and consumption of instances of $\tilde{F}$. By Lemma 3, the consumption term $Q^-_{\tilde{\alpha}}$ is equal to

$$Q^-_{\tilde{\alpha}}[\tilde{F}](\tilde{G}) = |[\tilde{L};\tilde{G}]| \cdot |[\tilde{F};\tilde{G}]| = \sum_{\tilde{\mu} \in \tilde{L} * \tilde{F}} |[\mathrm{cod}(\tilde{\mu}); \tilde{G}]|$$

which is a linear combination of a finite number of elements in $\mathscr{B}$.

Applying the same decomposition Lemma 3 to the production term $Q^+_{\tilde{\alpha}}$, we obtain a more complicated expression:

$$Q^+_{\tilde{\alpha}}[\tilde{F}](\tilde{G}) = \sum_{\tilde{\mu} \in \tilde{R} * \tilde{F}} \sum_{\tilde{f} \in [\tilde{L};\tilde{G}]} |\{\tilde{u} \in [\mathrm{cod}(\tilde{\mu}); \mathrm{cod}(\tilde{\alpha}(\tilde{f}))] \mid \tilde{u} \circ \tilde{\mu}_1 = \tilde{\alpha}(\tilde{f})\}|.$$

To simplify this expression, we use properties of marked derivations seen in §3.2. First, recall that the relation $\Rightarrow_{\tilde{\alpha}}$ between marked matches under $\tilde{L}$ and $\tilde{R}$ has $\Rightarrow_{\tilde{\alpha}^\dagger}$ as its inverse. The first match $\tilde{\mu}_1$ of any MG $\tilde{\mu}$ in $\tilde{R} * \tilde{F}$ thus has a preimage $\tilde{\alpha}^\dagger(\tilde{\mu}_1)$ under $\Rightarrow_{\tilde{\alpha}}$, as well as an associated corule $\tilde{\mu}_1(\tilde{\alpha}^\dagger)$. Write $\tilde{\mu}_1^\dagger$ for $\tilde{\alpha}^\dagger(\tilde{\mu}_1)$, $\tilde{\alpha}_\mu^\dagger$ for $\tilde{\mu}_1(\tilde{\alpha}^\dagger)$, and $\tilde{U}$, $\tilde{U}^\dagger$ for the codomains of $\tilde{\mu}_1$, $\tilde{\mu}_1^\dagger$. Recall that $\tilde{\alpha}_\mu^\dagger \colon \tilde{U} \rightharpoonup \tilde{U}^\dagger$ is again a marked rule, and hence there is an associated map $\tilde{\alpha}_\mu^\dagger(-)$ between matches under $\tilde{U}$ and $\tilde{U}^\dagger$. As $\tilde{\alpha}(\tilde{f}) \Rightarrow_{\tilde{\alpha}^\dagger} \tilde{f}$, the fact that derivations split along factorizations of matches means that $\tilde{\alpha}_\mu^\dagger(-)$ restricts to a bijection

$$\{\tilde{u} \in [\tilde{U}; \mathrm{cod}(\tilde{\alpha}(\tilde{f}))] \mid \tilde{u} \circ \tilde{\mu}_1 = \tilde{\alpha}(\tilde{f})\} \quad \simeq \quad \{\tilde{v} \in [\tilde{U}^\dagger; \tilde{G}] \mid \tilde{v} \circ \tilde{\mu}_1^\dagger = \tilde{f}\}$$

which allows us to simplify our previous expression for $Q_{\tilde{\alpha}}^+[\tilde{F}]$ to

$$Q_{\tilde{\alpha}}^+[\tilde{F}](\tilde{G}) = \sum_{\tilde{\mu} \in \tilde{R} * \tilde{F}} \sum_{\tilde{f} \in [\tilde{L}; \tilde{G}]} |\{\tilde{u} \in [\tilde{U}; \mathrm{cod}(\tilde{\alpha}(\tilde{f}))] \mid \tilde{u} \circ \tilde{\mu}_1 = \tilde{\alpha}(\tilde{f})\}|$$

$$= \sum_{\tilde{\mu} \in \tilde{R} * \tilde{F}} \sum_{\tilde{f} \in [\tilde{L}; \tilde{G}]} |\{\tilde{v} \in [\tilde{U}^\dagger; \tilde{G}] \mid \tilde{v} \circ \mu_1^\dagger = \tilde{f}\}| = \sum_{\tilde{\mu} \in \tilde{R} * \tilde{F}} |[\tilde{U}^\dagger; \tilde{G}]|.$$

This is again a linear combination of a finite number of elements in $\mathscr{B}$, concluding the proof of Theorem 2. □

Before we move on, a few remarks about the above theorem and its proof are in order. Firstly, the theorem is a statement about marked graph observables rather than individual derivations. Although the observables in question depend on the LHS and RHS of rules, the explicit dependency of (2) on the rate matrix $Q_{\tilde{\alpha}}$ has vanished along with the corresponding dependencies on derivations in the definition of $Q_{\tilde{\alpha}}$. This is made possible by two key insights from §3.2 and §3.3, namely *(i)* that rules internalize application conditions and hence every marked match of an LHS extends to a derivation, and *(ii)* that application conditions in rules can be combined algebraically, by means of minimal gluings, with those in marked graph observables.

Secondly, the proof makes use of reversibility of derivations in several places. Nevertheless, Theorem 2 also holds for CTMCs generated by a significant class of irreversible graph transformation systems. In particular, our approach extends to single pushout (SPO) and sesqui-pushout (SqPO) rewriting, both of which deal with irreversible derivations [6,15,31]. In both cases the rigidity constraints on (marked) rules need to be relaxed as they would otherwise force rules to be reversible. For Theorem 2 to hold, it is sufficient to restrict rules to spans of monos and impose a strongest postcondition on their RHS (note that the latter does not restrict the expressivity of rules). Although $\Rightarrow_{\tilde{\alpha}^\dagger}$ is no longer the inverse of $\Rightarrow_{\tilde{\alpha}}$ in this setting, it can still be used to split derivations "backwards" along factorizations of comatches, leading to a bijection argument akin to that in the above proof.

Combining Theorems 1 and 2, we obtain the moment semantics for any finite rule set $\mathscr{R}$ and associated rate map k. In particular, the expected value of a marked graph observable $\tilde{G}$ will satisfy the following differential equation:

$$\frac{d}{dt}\mathbf{E}_p([\tilde{G}]) = \sum_{\tilde{\alpha}\in\mathscr{R}} k(\tilde{\alpha}) \sum_{\tilde{\mu}\in\tilde{R}(\tilde{\alpha})*\tilde{G}} \mathbf{E}_p([\mathrm{cod}(\tilde{\alpha}^{\dagger}(\tilde{\mu}_1))]) - \sum_{\tilde{\alpha}\in\mathscr{R}} k(\tilde{\alpha}) \sum_{\tilde{\mu}\in\tilde{L}(\tilde{\alpha})*\tilde{G}} \mathbf{E}_p([\mathrm{cod}(\tilde{\mu})])$$

(7)

where $\tilde{L}(\tilde{\alpha})$ and $\tilde{R}(\tilde{\alpha})$ denote, respectively, the LHS and RHS of the marked rule $\tilde{\alpha}$. Since, $\mathrm{poly}(\mathscr{A}) = \mathscr{A}$, ODEs for the higher moments can be generated by the exact same procedure.

The number of terms in (7) depends on the size of the relevant sets of left and right-hand MGs, which is worst-case exponential in the size of the graphs involved (Lemma 3). In practice, one often finds many pairs of *irrelevant* MGs, the terms of which cancel out exactly. This reduces the effective size of the equations but not the overall complexity of generating them.

Second, as said in §1.3, the repeated application of (7) will lead to an infinite expansion in general. In practice, the system of ODEs needs to be truncated. For concrete models, static analysis might help finding invariants in the underlying rewrite system and find a finite closure even for models where the set of reachable states is demonstrably infinite [10]. We have seen a simple example in §1.

5 Conclusion

Consider again the example of preferential attachment presented in the first two sections. In this case, we can automatically derive systems of ODEs that are finite; however, we have to cope with the combinatorial blow-up. This bring us to the most exciting direction for future work: mean field approximations of moment semantics. In the literature, one often finds graphical approximation techniques based on conditional independence assumptions to control the size of patterns used in observables, such as so-called pair approximation [13, 21]. It is known that these methods can be more accurate than naive truncation of ODEs. In a natural next step, we would like to understand if and how these can be brought inside our formal approach.

References

1. The Preferential Attachment ODE Generator (2015). https://github.com/sstucki/pa-ode-gen/
2. Bapodra, M., Heckel, R.: From graph transformations to differential equations. ECEASST **30** (2010)
3. Barabási, A.L., Albert, R.: Emergence of scaling in random networks. Science **286**(5439), 509–512 (1999)
4. Barabási, A.L., Albert, R., Jeong, H.: Mean-field theory for scale-free random networks. Physica A: Statistical Mechanics and its Applications **272**(1), 173–187 (1999)
5. Chaput, P., Danos, V., Panangaden, P., Plotkin, G.D.: Approximating Markov processes by averaging. Journal of the ACM **61**(1), 5 (2014)

6. Corradini, A., Heindel, T., Hermann, F., König, B.: Sesqui-pushout rewriting. In: Corradini, A., Ehrig, H., Montanari, U., Ribeiro, L., Rozenberg, G. (eds.) ICGT 2006. LNCS, vol. 4178, pp. 30–45. Springer, Heidelberg (2006)

7. Corradini, A., Montanari, U., Rossi, F., Ehrig, H., Heckel, R., Löwe, M.: Algebraic approaches to graph transformation. Part I: basic concepts and double pushout approach. In: Handbook of Graph Grammars and Computing by Graph Transformation, pp. 163–245 (1997)

8. Danos, V., Heindel, T., Honorato-Zimmer, R., Stucki, S.: Approximations for stochastic graph rewriting. In: Merz, S., Pang, J. (eds.) ICFEM 2014. LNCS, vol. 8829, pp. 1–10. Springer, Heidelberg (2014)

9. Danos, V., Honorato-Zimmer, R., Jaramillo-Riveri, S., Stucki, S.: Deriving rate equations for site graph rewriting systems. In: SASB (2013)

10. Danos, V., Honorato-Zimmer, R., Jaramillo-Riveri, S., Stucki, S.: Coarse-graining the dynamics of ideal branched polymers. In: Electronic Notes in Theoretical Computer Science, Workshop on Static Analysis and Systems Biology, SASB 2012, Deauville, pp. 47–64, April 2015

11. Dorogovtsev, S.N., Mendes, J.F.F.: Evolution of networks with aging of sites. Phys. Rev. E **62**, 1842–1845 (2000)

12. Dorogovtsev, S.N., Mendes, J.F.F., Samukhin, A.N.: Structure of growing networks with preferential linking. Phys. Rev. Lett. **85**, 4633–4636 (2000)

13. Durrett, R., Gleeson, J.P., Lloyd, A.L., Mucha, P.J., Shi, F., Sivakoff, D., Socolar, J.E., Varghese, C.: Graph fission in an evolving voter model. Proceedings of the National Academy of Sciences **109**(10), 3682–3687 (2012)

14. Ehrig, H., Ehrig, K., Habel, A., Pennemann, K.H.: Theory of constraints and application conditions: From graphs to high-level structures. Fundamenta Informaticae **74**(1), 135–166 (2006)

15. Ehrig, H., Heckel, R., Korff, M., Löwe, M., Ribeiro, L., Wagner, A., Corradini, A.: Algebraic approaches to graph transformation. Part II: Single pushout approach and comparison with double pushout approach. In: Rozenberg, G. (ed.) Handbook of Graph Grammars and Computing by Graph Transformation, pp. 247–312. World Scientific, River Edge (1997)

16. Ehrig, H., Pfender, M., Schneider, H.J.: Graph-grammars: an algebraic approach. In: 14th Annual IEEE Symposium on Switching and Automata Theory, pp. 167–180 (1973)

17. Ethier, S.N., Kurtz, T.G.: Markov Processes: Characterization and Convergence. Wiley (1986)

18. Evans, M.R., Ferrari, P.A., Mallick, K.: Matrix representation of the stationary measure for the multispecies TASEP. Journal of Statistical Physics **135**(2), 217–239 (2009)

19. Fages, F., Soliman, S.: Formal cell biology in Biocham. In: Bernardo, M., Degano, P., Zavattaro, G. (eds.) SFM 2008. LNCS, vol. 5016, pp. 54–80. Springer, Heidelberg (2008)

20. Feret, J., Danos, V., Harmer, R., Krivine, J., Fontana, W.: Internal coarse-graining of molecular systems. PNAS **106**(16), 6453–6458 (2009)

21. Gleeson, J.P.: High-accuracy approximation of binary-state dynamics on networks. Physical Review Letters **107**(6), 068701 (2011)

22. Harmer, R., Danos, V., Feret, J., Krivine, J., Fontana, W.: Intrinsic information carriers in combinatorial dynamical systems. Chaos **20**(3) (2010)

23. Hayman, J., Heindel, T.: Pattern graphs and rule-based models: the semantics of Kappa. In: Pfenning, F. (ed.) FOSSACS 2013 (ETAPS 2013). LNCS, vol. 7794, pp. 1–16. Springer, Heidelberg (2013)

24. Heckel, R.: DPO transformation with open maps. In: Ehrig, H., Engels, G., Kreowski, H.-J., Rozenberg, G. (eds.) ICGT 2012. LNCS, vol. 7562, pp. 203–217. Springer, Heidelberg (2012)
25. Heckel, R., Lajios, G., Menge, S.: Stochastic graph transformation systems. Fundam. Inform. **74**(1), 63–84 (2006)
26. Heckel, R., Wagner, A.: Ensuring consistency of conditional graph grammars - a constructive approach. Electronic Notes in Theoretical Computer Science **2**(0), 118–126 (1995)
27. van Kampen, N.: Stochastic processes in physics and chemistry, 3rd edition, North-Holland (2007)
28. Lack, S., Sobociński, P.: Adhesive categories. In: Walukiewicz, I. (ed.) FOSSACS 2004. LNCS, vol. 2987, pp. 273–288. Springer, Heidelberg (2004)
29. Lack, S., Sobocinski, P.: Adhesive and quasiadhesive categories. Theoretical Informatics and Applications **39**(2), 522–546 (2005)
30. Lopez, C.F., Muhlich, J.L., Bachman, J.A., Sorger, P.K.: Programming biological models in Python using PySB. Molecular Systems Biology **9**(1) (2013)
31. Löwe, M.: Algebraic Approach to Single-Pushout Graph Transformation. Theoretical Computer Science **109**(1&2), 181–224 (1993)
32. Lynch, J.F.: A logical characterization of individual-based models. In: 23rd Annual IEEE Symposium on Logic in Computer Science, LICS 2008, pp. 379–390. IEEE (2008)
33. Norris, J.R.: Markov chains. Cambridge series in statistical and probabilistic mathematics. Cambridge University Press (1998)
34. Shkarin, S.A.: Some results on solvability of ordinary linear differential equations in locally convex spaces. Mathematics of the USSR-Sbornik **71**(1), 29 (1992)
35. Stukalin, E.B., Phillips III, H., Kolomeisky, A.B.: Coupling of two motor proteins: a new motor can move faster. Physical Review Letters **94**(23), 238101 (2005)
36. Thomas, P., Matuschek, H., Grima, R.: Intrinsic noise analyzer: a software package for the exploration of stochastic biochemical kinetics using the system size expansion. PloS ONE **7**(6), e38518 (2012)

Reversible Machines

A Hierarchy of Fast Reversible Turing Machines

Holger Bock Axelsen[1], Sebastian Jakobi[2], Martin Kutrib[2(✉)],
and Andreas Malcher[2]

[1] Department of Computer Science, University of Copenhagen,
Universitetsparken 5, Copenhagen, Denmark
funkstar@di.ku.dk
[2] Institut für Informatik, Universität Giessen, Arndtstr. 2,
35392 Giessen, Germany
{jakobi,kutrib,malcher}@informatik.uni-giessen.de

Abstract. Reversible Turing machines with a working tape and a one-way or two-way read-only input tape are considered. We investigate the classes of languages acceptable by such devices with small time bounds in the range between real time and linear time, *i.e.*, time bounds of the form $n+r(n)$ where $r \in o(n)$ is a sublinear function. It is shown that there exist infinite time hierarchies of separated complexity classes in that range. We then turn to the question of whether reversible Turing machines in the range of interest are weaker than general ones or not. This is answered in the affirmative by proving that there are languages accepted by irreversible one-way Turing machines in real time that cannot be accepted by any reversible one-way machine in less than linear time.

Keywords: Reversible Turing machines · Structural computational complexity · Time hierarchies · Fast computations · Real time vs. linear time

1 Introduction

One of the great early results of computational complexity is that for single-tape Turing machines, the real-time and linear-time complexity classes are equal [5]. Although a wonderful result, for deterministic machines this is quite sensitive to variations in static resources, in particular the number and character of the input and work tapes. There are languages that can be accepted in real-time by deterministic Turing machines equipped with a one-way read-only input tape and a separate work tape, but which cannot be accepted in real-time by one-tape deterministic Turing machines.[1] Also, for multi-tape models, linear time is strictly more powerful than real time, in the strong sense that there are languages that can be accepted in linear time with a one-way read-only input tape and a single work tape, but which are not real-time for any number of tapes [12]. Furthermore, for such machines there are infinite hierarchies between real-time

---

[1] Consider the mirror language of marked palindromes, $w\$w^R$.

© Springer International Publishing Switzerland 2015
J. Krivine and J.-B. Stefani (Eds.): RC 2015, LNCS 9138, pp. 29–44, 2015.
DOI: 10.1007/978-3-319-20860-2_2

and linear-time computations, among the languages accepted under time bounds of form $n + r(n)$ with $r \in o(n)$ [7], where n is the input length.

In contrast, the structural complexity theory of fast *reversible* computations is not well-understood. Although techniques exist that can yield inclusion results between deterministic and reversible complexity classes, these techniques usually rely on reversible simulation of irreversible machines, *cf.* [2,8,14]. In [6] reversible one-tape Turing machines are studied from the viewpoint of invertible functions. The invertible partial functions are exactly those that can be computed without surplus information by such Turing machines. Moreover, the question is raised whether the invertible functions that can be computed in polynomial time can also be computed in reversible polynomial time. Reversible simulation introduces static resource or complexity overheads, *e.g.* extra tapes and larger alphabets, or increased time or space complexities, which are then inherited by the machine performing the simulation. For instance, using a *history* to simulate irreversible Turing machines requires the addition of an extra work tape. This can take us out of the model under consideration if the number of work tapes is an issue, but removing the tape from the simulation apparently requires (reversible) tape reduction such as in [1], incurring a time penalty which may also take us out of the range of interest. This limits the usefulness of reversible simulation techniques in discerning reversible structural complexity, in particular in the lower end of the spectrum, such as the fast (irreversible) computations mentioned above.

Here, we investigate the range between real time and linear time for reversible Turing machines with a one-way or two-way read-only input tape and a single work tape. It is evident that reversible simulation is too costly for the reversible machines to inherit the deterministic hierarchies, so we shall here show directly that there exists such infinite reversible hierarchies. To this end we develop a notion of time constructibility for reversible Turing machines. We then give languages L_r such that if r is the *inverse* of a reversibly time-constructible function, then L_r can be accepted by a one-way reversible Turing machine in time $n + r(n)$, but not by any two-way RTM in less time. Since the languages that witness the separations in the reversible case are different from the ones that witness separation in the irreversible case [7], we cannot derive the relationship between the reversible and deterministic classes from this result alone. By carefully combining incompressibility and crossing sequence arguments, we find that the reversible and deterministic machines in this range have different computational capacities: we show that there are languages accepted by one-way deterministic Turing machines in real-time that cannot be accepted in less than linear time by any one-way reversible Turing machine. Although fine-grained, to the best of our knowledge this is the first such unconditional separation of reversible and deterministic classes for Turing machines.

2   Preliminaries

We denote the non-negative integers $\{0, 1, 2, \dots\}$ by $\mathbb{N}$. The *empty word* is denoted by λ and the *reversal* of a word w by w^R. For the *length* of w we

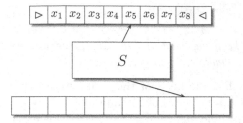

Fig. 1. Turing machine with a working tape and an input tape

write $|w|$. We use $\subseteq$ for *inclusions* and $\subset$ for *strict inclusions*. For a function $f : \mathbb{N} \to \mathbb{N}$ we denote its *i*-fold composition by $f^{[i]}$, $i \geq 1$. A function f is said to be *increasing* if $m < n$ implies $f(m) \leq f(n)$. The *inverse* of an increasing function $f : \mathbb{N} \to \mathbb{N}$ is defined as $f^{-1}(n) = \min\{\, m \in \mathbb{N} \mid f(m) \geq n \,\}$. The identity function $n \mapsto n$ is denoted by id. As usual we define the set of functions that grow strictly slower than f by

$$o(f) = \{\, g : \mathbb{N} \to \mathbb{N} \mid \lim_{n \to \infty} \frac{g(n)}{f(n)} = 0 \,\}.$$

In terms of orders of magnitude, f is an upper bound of the set

$$O(f) = \{\, g : \mathbb{N} \to \mathbb{N} \mid \exists\, n_0, c \in \mathbb{N} : \forall\, n \geq n_0 : g(n) \leq c \cdot f(n) \,\}.$$

Conversely, f is a lower bound of the set $\Omega(f) = \{\, g : \mathbb{N} \to \mathbb{N} \mid f \in O(g) \,\}$, and $\Theta(f)$ is defined to be $O(f) \cap \Omega(f)$.

A deterministic Turing machine consists of an initially blank read-write working tape, a read-only input tape whose inscription is the input word in between two endmarkers, and a finite-state control. At the outset of a computation the Turing machine is in the designated initial state, and the head of the input tape scans the left endmarker. Dependent on the current state and the currently scanned symbols on the tapes, the Turing machine changes its state, rewrites the current symbol on the working tape, and moves the heads independently one cell to the left, one cell to the right, or not at all. The machines have no separate output tape and the states are partitioned into accepting and rejecting states; this is a model for language acceptance. Fig. 1 shows the conceptual layout of a Turning machine in this model.

Definition 1. *A deterministic two-way Turing machine (abbreviated as 2DTM) is a system $M = \langle S, \Gamma, \Sigma, \rhd, \lhd, \delta, s_0, F \rangle$, where*

1. *S is the finite set of internal states,*
2. *Γ is the finite set of tape symbols, containing the blank symbol $\sqcup$,*
3. *Σ is the finite set of input symbols,*
4. *$\rhd \notin \Gamma \cup \Sigma$ is the left and $\lhd \notin \Gamma \cup \Sigma$ is the right endmarker,*
5. *$s_0 \in S$ is the initial state,*
6. *$F \subseteq S$ is the set of accepting states, and*

7. $\delta : S \times (\Sigma \cup \{\triangleright, \triangleleft\}) \times \Gamma \to S \times \{-1,0,1\} \times \Gamma \times \{-1,0,1\}$ *is the partial transition function, where* -1 *means to move the head one square to the left,* 0 *means to keep the head on the current square, and* 1 *means to move one square to the right.*

It is understood that the head of the input tape never moves beyond the endmarkers. Moreover, if the head of the input tape may never move to the left, we call the Turing machine *one-way* and abbreviate it as 1DTM.

A *configuration* of a Turing machine $M = \langle S, \Gamma, \Sigma, \triangleright, \triangleleft, \delta, s_0, F \rangle$ is a quintuple (s, w, h_0, β, h_1), where $s \in S$ is the current state, $w \in \Sigma^*$ is the input, $h_0 \in \{0, 1, \ldots, |w| + 1\}$ is the current head position on the input tape, $\beta : \mathbb{Z} \to \Gamma$ is a function that maps the tape cells of the working tape to their current contents, and $h_1 \in \mathbb{Z}$ is the current position of the working tape head. The *initial configuration* for input w is set to $(s_0, w, 0, \beta_{\sqcup}, 0)$, where $\beta_{\sqcup}$ maps all cells to the blank symbol. During the course of its computation, M runs through a sequence of configurations. One step from a configuration to its successor configuration is denoted by relation $\vdash$, defined by

$$(s, w, h_0, \beta[h_1 \mapsto a], h_1) \vdash (t, w, h_0 + d_0, \beta[h_1 \mapsto b], h_1 + d_1),$$

if $\delta(s, w_{h_0}, a) = (t, d_0, b, d_1)$, with $w_0 = \triangleright$, $w_{n+1} = \triangleleft$ for input $w = w_1 w_2 \cdots w_n$.

A Turing machine *halts* if the transition function is undefined for the current configuration. An input word w is *accepted* if the machine halts at some time in an accepting state, otherwise it is *rejected*. The *language accepted* by M is $L(M) = \{ w \in \Sigma^* \mid w$ is accepted by $M \}$.

Let $t : \mathbb{N} \to \mathbb{N}$, $t(n) \geq n + 1$, be a function. A Turing machine is said to be *t-time-bounded* or of *time complexity* t if and only if it halts on every input of length n after at most $t(n)$ time steps.

The family of all languages which can be accepted by 1DTM (resp. 2DTM) with time complexity t is denoted by $\mathsf{1DTIME}(t)$ (resp. $\mathsf{2DTIME}(t)$.) If t is the function $\mathrm{id} + 1$ then acceptance is said to be in *real-time*.

Now we turn to *reversible* (one-way) Turing machines. Basically, reversibility is meant with respect to the possibility of stepping the computation back and forth. So, the machines have also to be backward deterministic. In particular for the read-only input tape, the machines reread the input symbol which they read in a preceding forward computation step. So, for reverse computation steps of *one-way* machines the head of the input tape is either moved to the *left* or stays stationary.

A 1DTM (or 2DTM) is said to be *reversible*, abbreviated as 1RTM (respectively 2RTM), if for any two *distinct* transitions

$$\delta(p, x_0, x_1) = (q, d_0, y_1, d_1) \quad \text{and}$$
$$\delta(p', x'_0, x'_1) = (q', d'_0, y'_1, d'_1),$$

if $q = q'$, then $(d_0, d_1) = (d'_0, d'_1)$ and $(x_0, y_1) \neq (x'_0, y'_1)$.

The first condition means that transitions yielding the same state all have to move the heads the same way. The second condition says that for any configuration the predecessor state and the predecessor work tape symbol are uniquely determined by the state (which then implies the head movements), the input tape symbol read, and the work tape symbol written.

As above, the families of all languages accepted by 1RTM and 2RTM in time t is denoted by $\mathsf{1RTIME}(t)$ respectively $\mathsf{2RTIME}(t)$, with id $+1$ being real-time.

In order to prove tight time hierarchies in almost all cases constructible time bounding functions are required. Usually the notion "constructible" is concretized in terms of computations with respect to the device in question.

Definition 2. *A function* $f : \mathbb{N} \to \mathbb{N}$ *is said to be* 1RTM-time-constructible *iff there exists a* 1RTM *that (i) reads its unary input w in $|w| + 1$ time steps, (ii) halts after exactly $f(|w|)$ time steps, and (iii) halts with its work tape head on the rightmost (or leftmost) square of a distinguishable block of length $|w|$.*

The third condition of this definition means that there are $|w|$ consecutive tape squares with inscriptions from some known set of symbols, and that these squares are bordered by symbols not belonging to that set. This condition has been added to the definition with an eye towards later applications.

In order to clarify this notion we continue with an example of a 1RTM that time-constructs a fast-growing function.

Example 3. There is an increasing function of order $\Theta(2^{2^n})$ which is 1RTM-time-constructible. We construct a 1RTM $M = \langle S, \Gamma, \Sigma, \rhd, \lhd, \delta, p_0, F \rangle$ as follows. Set

$$S = \{p_0, p_1, p_2, p_f, q_a, q_e, q_l, q_r, q_Y, q_Z, r_a, r_e, r_r, r_X\},$$
$$\Gamma = \{\sqcup, 0, 1, !, \bar{0}, \bar{1}, \bar{!}, \$, X, Y, Z\},$$
$$\Sigma = \{a\} \text{ and } F = \emptyset.$$

In a first phase, M reads the input a^m and writes the string $X^{m-1}!\$$ to its working tape:

1. $\delta(p_0, \rhd, \sqcup) = (p_0, 1, \sqcup, 0)$
2. $\delta(p_0, a, \sqcup) = (p_1, 1, \sqcup, 1)$
3. $\delta(p_1, a, \sqcup) = (p_1, 1, X, 1)$
4. $\delta(p_1, \lhd, \sqcup) = (p_2, 0, !, 1)$
5. $\delta(p_2, \lhd, \sqcup) = (q_Z, 0, \$, 1)$

In a second phase, M successively increases a binary counter with the symbols from $\{0, 1, !\}$, where ! denotes the leading 1. The counter is realized in the X-block of the working tape, starting on the right of the block with the most significant bit on the left. Separated by the $\$$, on the right of the counter a string of the form Y^*Z is established, where one symbol is added for each incrementation of the counter. State q_a is used to increment the counter, where state q_e is entered when the length of the counter has to be increased. After the incrementation, state q_r is used to move back to the $\$$ symbol. The phase ends when the extension of the counter would exceed the X-block:

6. $\delta(q_Z, \lhd, \sqcup) = (q_l, 0, Z, -1)$
7. $\delta(q_l, \lhd, \$) = (q_a, 0, \$, -1)$
8. $\delta(q_l, \lhd, Y) = (q_l, 0, Y, -1)$
9. $\delta(q_a, \lhd, 0) = (q_r, 0, 1, 1)$
10. $\delta(q_a, \lhd, 1) = (q_a, 0, 0, -1)$

11. $\delta(q_a, \lhd, !) = (q_e, 0, 0, -1)$
12. $\delta(q_r, \lhd, 0) = (q_r, 0, 0, 1)$
13. $\delta(q_r, \lhd, \$) = (q_Y, 0, \$, 1)$
14. $\delta(q_e, \lhd, X) = (q_r, 0, !, 1)$
15. $\delta(q_e, \lhd, \sqcup) = (r_X, 0, \sqcup, 1)$

After having reached the $\$$ in state q_r, M uses the states q_Y, q_Z, and q_l to add a new symbol to the string of the form Y^*Z and to return to the beginning of the counter. Subsequently, the counter is increased again:

16. $\delta(q_Y, \lhd, Y) = (q_Y, 0, Y, 1)$ 17. $\delta(q_Y, \lhd, Z) = (q_Z, 0, Y, 1)$

The third phase is preceded by a sweep from the left end of the counter to its right end in state r_X, whereby the digits (only 0 may appear) are overwritten by X again (this will be the distinguishable block required by Definition 2). After the sweep, a second binary counter with symbols from $\{\bar{0}, \bar{1}, \bar{!}\}$ is successively increased. The counter is realized in the Y-block of the working tape, starting on the left of the block with the most significant bit on the right. Similar as in the second phase, state r_a is used to increment the counter, where state r_e is entered when the length of the counter has to be increased. After the incrementation, state r_r is used to move back to the $\$$ symbol. The phase ends in state p_f which is entered when the extension of the counter would exceed the Y-block, that is, when the Z appears. State p_f is finally used to move the head of the working tape to the left until the rightmost of the m consecutive symbols X appears. The block of m consecutive symbols X is bordered by $\sqcup$ and $\$$.

18. $\delta(r_X, \lhd, 0) = (r_X, 0, X, 1)$
19. $\delta(r_X, \lhd, \$) = (r_e, 0, \$, 1)$
20. $\delta(r_e, \lhd, Y) = (r_r, 0, !, -1)$
21. $\delta(r_e, \lhd, Z) = (p_f, 0, Z, -1)$
22. $\delta(r_r, \lhd, \$) = (r_a, 0, \$, 1)$
23. $\delta(r_r, \lhd, \bar{0}) = (r_r, 0, \bar{0}, -1)$

24. $\delta(r_a, \lhd, \bar{0}) = (r_r, 0, \bar{1}, -1)$
25. $\delta(r_a, \lhd, \bar{1}) = (r_a, 0, \bar{0}, 1)$
26. $\delta(r_a, \lhd, \bar{!}) = (r_e, 0, \bar{0}, 1)$
27. $\delta(p_f, \lhd, \bar{0}) = (p_f, 0, \bar{0}, -1)$
28. $\delta(p_f, \lhd, \$) = (p_f, 0, \$, -1)$

The reversibility of M is straightforwardly verified by inspecting the transition function and checking the two conditions from above. So, the running time of M remains to be considered.

The first phase takes $m + 3$ time steps. For calculating the number of steps of the second and third phase, we apply the known result that a Turing machine needs no more than $O(f(n))$ steps for successively increasing the binary counter from 1 to $f(n)$. (For example, note that during every second incrementation only the least significant bit has to be changed. See e.g. [10] for further details.) Clearly, the task takes also at least $f(n)$ steps. In addition, for every incrementation the string Y^*Z is extended by one symbol. Since the counter is increased up to 2^m, altogether the extension of the string takes $\Theta(2^{2m})$ steps. Therefore, the second phase is performed by M in $\Theta(2^{2m})$ steps. During the third phase, the second counter is incremented up to 2^{2^m} and the head is finally moved to the leftmost X. This together takes $\Theta(2^{2^m})$ steps. So, we conclude that M obeys a time bound of $\Theta(2^{2^m})$. ∎

The following definition summarizes the properties of reversibly constructible functions and names them.

Definition 4. *The set of all increasing, unbounded* 1RTM-*time-constructible functions f with the property $O(f(n)) \leq f(O(n))$ is denoted by $T(1\mathrm{RTM})$. The set of their inverses is $T^{-1}(1\mathrm{RTM}) = \{\, f^{-1} \mid f \in T(1\mathrm{RTM}) \,\}$.*

The properties increasing and unbounded are straightforward. The property $O(f(n)) \leq f(O(n))$ means that

$$\forall c \geq 1 : \exists n_0, c' \geq 1 : \forall n \geq n_0 : c \cdot f(n) \leq f(c' \cdot n).$$

That is, f grows fast enough that any post-application constant factor can be overcome by a pre-application constant factor. At first glance this seems to be restrictive, but it is not: it is easily verified that almost all of the commonly considered time complexities have this property. We shall use this property for the hierarchy separation result. Currently, there is no well-developed theory of time-constructible functions for reversible Turing machines. However, it is evident that Example 3 can be modified to show that there are functions of order $\Theta(2^n)$ as well as $\Theta(2^n \circ 2^n \circ \cdots \circ 2^n)$ belonging to $T(1\mathrm{RTM})$, where $\cdot \circ \cdot$ denotes function composition.

3   The Hierarchy Between Real-Time and Linear-Time

This section develops the strict and tight hierarchy between real time and linear time. To this end, we use witness languages as follows. Let r be a function from $T^{-1}(1\mathrm{RTM})$, *i.e.*, that there exists a function $f \in T(1\mathrm{RTM})$ so that $r = f^{-1}$. We set

$$L_r = \{\, a^m b^{f(m)-m} \# v_1 \$ v_2 \$ \cdots \$ v_k \mathord{\text{¢}} \$^{k-i} u \mid k, m \geq 1, i \in \{1, 2, \ldots, k\},$$
$$|\# v_1 \$ v_2 \$ \cdots \$ v_k| = m, v_i = u^R, |u| \geq 1, v_j \in \{a, b\}^*, 1 \leq j \leq k \,\}.$$

That is, L_r consists of words of the form of m occurrences of a, followed by exactly $f(m) - m$ occurrences of b, followed by a delimited sequence of \$-separated words over $\{a, b\}^*$ with total length m. One of these subwords, indexed by a subsequent number of \$'s, is then repeated in reverse at the end of the word.

Any non-constant time-constructible function grows faster than id, but since here we are interested in sublinear functions r, the inverses of constructible functions are used. Next we show that the languages L_r are on a certain level of the hierarchy.

Lemma 5. *For all functions $r \in T^{-1}(1\mathrm{RTM})$, the language L_r belongs to the class* 1RTIME($id + r$).

Proof. Let $C = \langle S_c, \Gamma_c, \Sigma_c, \triangleright, \triangleleft, \delta_c, s_{0,c}, \emptyset \rangle$ be a 1RTM that time-constructs f. In order to show the assertion, a 1RTM $M = \langle S \cup S_c, \Gamma \cup \Gamma_c, \Sigma, \triangleright, \triangleleft, \delta, s_{0,c}, F \rangle$ is constructed, with

$$S = \{s_0, s_m, s_d, s_a, s_b, s_f, s_{acc}\},$$
$$\Gamma = \{\sqcup, a, b, \#, \$\},$$
$$\Sigma = \{a, b, \#, \$, \mathcol{c}\} \text{ and } F = \{s_{acc}\},$$

where the unions are disjoint, and which works as follows.

In a first phase, M basically simulates C on the input prefix $a^m b^q \#$. By definition, C reads its unary input (here a^m) without stationary moves on the input tape. Then, C continues its computation with the input head scanning the right endmarker. Here C is modified so that it reads one input symbol b in each step, instead of stationarily scanning the endmarker. The phase succeeds if the simulation would halt at that time step the input head has moved out of the b's, that is, the head is moved onto the new symbol $\#$. In this situation $q = f(m) - m$ has been verified, and the working tape head is located on the, say, rightmost square of a distinguishable block of length m. For simplicity we may safely assume that this block has the form X^m. Let M be in state p_f at this time. Next, M performs the transition:

1. $\delta(p_f, \#, X) = (s_0, 1, \#, -1)$

The reversibility of C (and, thus, of M) is not affected by the modifications. Phase 1 requires $f(m) + 2$ time steps.

In the second phase, the condition $|\#v_1\$v_2\$ \cdots \$v_k| = m$ is verified. To this end, M continues to read its input and stores its reversal onto the distinguished block (now of the form $X^{m-1}\#$.) The condition is satisfied if and only if the $\mathcal{c}$ is read from the input exactly at the time at which the first symbol outside the distinguished block is read from the working tape (here we use the blank symbol $\sqcup$ for simplicity[2]):

2. $\delta(s_0, a, X) = (s_0, 1, a, -1)$ 4. $\delta(s_0, \$, X) = (s_0, 1, \$, -1)$
3. $\delta(s_0, b, X) = (s_0, 1, b, -1)$ 5. $\delta(s_0, \mathcal{c}, \sqcup) = (s_m, 1, \sqcup, 0)$

Phase 2 requires m time steps.

In the third phase, the head of the working tape is moved onto the last symbol of the subword v_i whose reverse has to be matched with u. State s_m is used to move the working tape head one subword ahead for each $\$$ read in the input (using state s_d to move across the subword.) Once no more $\$$'s are read, matching of the current subword and u can begin, using s_a or s_b to store the initial symbol of u.

---

[2] To see that these simplifying assumptions about the distinguished block are sound, consider the use of two distinct tracks on the work tape: one for the simulation of C and one for the copy of the $\$$-separated sequence.

6. $\delta(s_m, \$, \sqcup) = (s_d, 0, \sqcup, 1)$
7. $\delta(s_m, a, \sqcup) = (s_a, 1, \sqcup, 1)$
8. $\delta(s_m, b, \sqcup) = (s_b, 1, \sqcup, 1)$
9. $\delta(s_m, \$, \$) = (s_d, 0, \$, 1)$
10. $\delta(s_m, a, \$) = (s_a, 1, \$, 1)$

11. $\delta(s_m, b, \$) = (s_b, 1, \$, 1)$
12. $\delta(s_d, \$, a) = (s_d, 0, a, 1)$
13. $\delta(s_d, \$, b) = (s_d, 0, b, 1)$
14. $\delta(s_d, \$, \$) = (s_m, 1, \$, 0)$

Finally, in a fourth phase, M uses the states s_a and s_b to verify $v_i = u^R$. Comparison between the input and the work tape is performed one step out of sequence, and the lengths of these two subwords are identical if and only if after the comparison the input head reads the right endmarker (for the first time) and the working tape head scans the separating symbol $\$$ or #. This is checked by the state s_f, and the sole accepting state is s_{acc}:

15. $\delta(s_a, a, a) = (s_a, 1, a, 1)$
16. $\delta(s_a, b, a) = (s_b, 1, a, 1)$
17. $\delta(s_a, \lhd, a) = (s_f, 0, a, 1)$
18. $\delta(s_b, a, b) = (s_a, 1, b, 1)$

19. $\delta(s_b, b, b) = (s_b, 1, b, 1)$
20. $\delta(s_b, \lhd, b) = (s_f, 0, b, 1)$
21. $\delta(s_f, \lhd, \$) = (s_{acc}, 0, \$, 0)$
22. $\delta(s_f, \lhd, \#) = (s_{acc}, 0, \#, 0)$

During the third and fourth phase, the working tape head is moved in every step across the tape inscription $(\#v_1\$v_2\$ \cdots \$v_k)^R$, except for the very last step and steps where a $\$$ is read. So, both phases together require at most $m + (k - i)$ time steps.

We conclude that the total running time of M is at most

$$f(m) + 2 + m + m + (k - i) = f(m) + 2m + 2 + (k - i).$$

The length n of the whole input is $f(m) + m + 1 + (k - i) + |u|$. Therefore, M takes $m + 1 - |u|$ time steps beyond id. Since $|u| \geq 1$ this is at most m. On the other hand, since f belongs to $T(\text{1RTM})$ it is increasing and therefore $r = f^{-1}$ is increasing as well. So, we obtain

$$r(n) = r(f(m) + m + 1 + (k - i) + |u|) \geq r(f(m)) = f^{-1}(f(m)) = m$$

and, thus, the time complexity id $+ r$ is obeyed by M. □

Now we move on to show that the witness languages L_r cannot be accepted with time complexities whose part beyond id grows strictly slower than r, even for two-way reversible Turing machines. Due to the small time bounds the machines are too weak for diagonalization, so counting arguments are applied in order to separate the complexity classes. The method has, at least implicitly, been used several times in connection with real-time computations – for example in [4, 7, 12] for Turing machines and in [3] for iterative arrays.

Lemma 6. *Let $r : \mathbb{N} \to \mathbb{N}$ and $r' : \mathbb{N} \to \mathbb{N}$ be two functions. If $r \in T^{-1}(\text{1RTM})$ and $r' \in o(r)$ then language L_r does not belong to the class $\text{2RTIME}(id + r')$.*

Proof. For the purpose of contradiction, assume that language L_r is accepted by some 2RTM $M = \langle S, \Gamma, \Sigma, \rhd, \lhd, \delta, s_0, F \rangle$ with time complexity id $+r'$.

Recall that r is the inverse of a time-constructible function f. We now consider words of the form $a^m b^{f(m)-m} \#v_1 \$ v_2 \$ \cdots \$ v_k$ where $v_i \in \{a,b\}^k$ for all $1 \le i \le k$, $v_i \ne v_j$ for $i \ne j$, and $|\#v_1 \$ v_2 \$ \cdots \$ v_k| = m$. So, we have $m = k(k+1) = k^2 + k$. The number of distinct such words is trivially bounded below by the number of different k-element sets $\{v_1, v_2, \ldots, v_k\}$, $v_i \in \{a,b\}^k$. Given that $|\{a,b\}^k| = 2^k$, this is

$$\binom{2^k}{k} \ge \left(\frac{2^k}{k}\right)^k = \left(2^{k-\log k}\right)^k \ge 2^{\frac{k^2}{2}} = 2^{\Omega(k^2)}$$

for all sufficiently large k, with the inequalities provided by $\binom{n}{k} \ge \left(\frac{n}{k}\right)^k$ and $\frac{k}{2} \ge \log k$.

Next we provide these words as input prefixes to M and consider the possible situations M could be in immediately after processing the prefix in an accepting computation. The length of the remaining input is at most $2k$ for accepting computations. The remaining computation depends only on the current internal state and the contents of the at most $2(2k + r'(n)) + 1$ reachable squares on each tape: there are at most $2k + r'(n)$ steps left of the time bound id $+r'$, and the factor of 2 is due to M being two-way. Let $\ell = \max\{|\Sigma|, |\Gamma|, |S|\}$. For the $2(2k + r'(n)) + 1$ squares of both tapes there are at most $\ell^{4(2k+r'(n))+2}$ different inscriptions. Including the current state we obtain at most $\ell^{4(2k+r'(n))+3}$ different situations.

In general, r' is not necessarily increasing. Therefore, let $r''(1) = r'(1)$ and $r''(n) = \max\{r'(n), r''(n-1)\}$, for $n \ge 2$. Clearly, $r' \le r''$ and we obtain

$$\ell^{4(2k+r'(n))+3} \le \ell^{4(2k+r''(n))+3}.$$

For accepted words with the given prefix, the word length is

$$n \le f(m) + m + 2k \le f(m) + m + 2m \le 4 \cdot f(m) = 4 \cdot f(k^2 + k),$$

since $f \ge$ id, as f is increasing and unbounded by belonging to $T(\mathrm{1RTM})$. Because r'' is increasing by construction, this gives us

$$\ell^{4(2k+r''(n))+3} \le \ell^{4(2k+r''(4 \cdot f(k^2+k)))+3}$$
$$\le \ell^{4(2k+1)+4 \cdot r''(4 \cdot f(k^2+k))}.$$

From $r = f^{-1}$ it follows that r is increasing. By $r' \in o(r)$ and the construction of r'' we conclude $r'' \in o(r)$. Furthermore, we know $O(f(n)) \le f(O(n))$, so we obtain for sufficiently large k:

$$\ell^{4(2k+1)+4 \cdot r''(4 \cdot f(k^2+k))} \le \ell^{4(2k+1)+4 \cdot r''(f(c_1(k^2+k)))}, \text{ for some } c_1 \ge 1$$
$$= \ell^{4(2k+1)+4 \cdot o(r(f(c_1(k^2+k))))}$$
$$= \ell^{4(2k+1)+4 \cdot o(c_1(k^2+k))}$$
$$= \ell^{4(2k+1)+o(k^2)}$$
$$= \ell^{o(k^2)}$$
$$= 2^{o(k^2)}.$$

So, there are more words than situations. This means that there are two different words $w = a^m b^{f(m)-m} \# v_1 \$ v_2 \$ \cdots \$ v_k$ and $w' = a^m b^{f(m)-m} \# v'_1 \$ v'_2 \$ \cdots \$ v'_k$ of the form above for which the situation for the remaining computation is identical if the remaining input has the same length. Since w and w' are different, there exists an $i \in \{1, 2, \ldots, k\}$ with $v_i \neq v'_i$. Moreover, since $w \notin \$^{k-i} v_i^R$ belongs to L_r and, thus, is accepted by M, $w' \notin \$^{k-i} v_i^R$ is accepted by M as well. However $w' \notin \$^{k-i} v_i^R$ does not belong to L_r, contradicting that M accepts L_r.   □

Now the tight and infinite hierarchies in between real-time and linear-time follow immediately from Lemmas 6 and 5.

Theorem 7. *Let $r : \mathbb{N} \to \mathbb{N}$ and $r' : \mathbb{N} \to \mathbb{N}$ be two functions. If $r \in T^{-1}(1RTM)$ and $r' \in o(r)$ then*

$$\mathsf{1RTIME}(id + r') \subset \mathsf{1RTIME}(id + r) \text{ and } \mathsf{2RTIME}(id + r') \subset \mathsf{2RTIME}(id + r).$$

A taste of the hierarchies is given in the following example.

Example 8. As mentioned above, Example 3 can be generalized in a straightforward way to show that there are functions in $\Theta((2^n)^{[i]})$, for all $i \geq 1$, that belong to $T(1RTM)$. So, the functions $\log^{[i]}$, $i \geq 1$, belong to $T^{-1}(1RTM)$. Therefore, an application of the hierarchy theorem yields

$$\mathsf{1RTIME}(id + 1) \subset \cdots \subset \mathsf{1RTIME}(id + \log^{[i+1]})$$
$$\subset \mathsf{1RTIME}(id + \log^{[i]}) \subset \cdots \subset \mathsf{1RTIME}(id + id).$$

and

$$\mathsf{2RTIME}(id + 1) \subset \cdots \subset \mathsf{2RTIME}(id + \log^{[i+1]})$$
$$\subset \mathsf{2RTIME}(id + \log^{[i]}) \subset \cdots \subset \mathsf{2RTIME}(id + id).$$

∎

Here we have considered reversible Turing machines with a read-only input tape and a read-write working tape. Further natural variants for consideration would be one-tape machines and multitape machines.

For the one-tape variant, where there is only one read-write tape on which the input is provided, there is no hierarchy between real-time and linear-time, as mentioned above. By the results in [5,13] the real-time and linear-time classes for such not necessarily reversible machines coincide, and characterize the regular languages. Since every regular language can be accepted already by a *reversible* one-tape Turing machine, also the reversible classes coincide.[3]

In the proof of Lemma 6 it has been argued that the number of distinguishable situations for processing the last at most $2k$ input symbols depends on the

---

[3] Even though these classes characterize the regular languages, reversible finite automata are strictly less powerful than irreversible finite automata in general [11], so the capabilities of the Turing machine model are required to force this collapse.

current internal state and the contents of the at most $2(2k + r'(n)) + 1$ reachable squares on each tape. In the calculation of the number of different situations, the number of tapes therefore manifests itself only as a constant factor in the exponent. So, the order of magnitude $2^{o(k^2)}$ is not affected by the number of tapes. Therefore, the hierarchy results hold for m-tape machines as well (cf. [7] for similar results for not necessarily reversible Turing machines).

4 Reversibility Versus Irreversibility

We now turn to the question whether reversible Turing machines in the range of interest are weaker than general ones or not; it turns out that they are. In fact, there are languages accepted by irreversible one-way Turing machines in real time that cannot be accepted by any reversible one-way machine in less than linear time. The basic idea of the proof is to use the mirror language with a particular regular language in the center, utilizing that not all regular languages can be recognized by reversible finite automata. Irreversible Turing machines can check the infix from the regular language without moving the working tape head. However, if the regular language cannot be accepted by any reversible deterministic finite automaton, a reversible one-way Turing machine *has* to use its working tape to check the infix. This is exploited to force the working tape head away from any information stored to verify the mirror language part of the input.

We first develop the regular language and consider reversible Turing machines that accept it. To this end, we will use Kolmogorov complexity and incompressibility arguments. General information on this technique can be found, for example, in the canonical textbook [9, Ch. 7]. Let $w \in \{0,1\}^*$ be an arbitrary binary string. The Kolmogorov complexity $C(w)$ of w is defined to be the minimal size of a program (Turing machine) describing w. The following key component for using the incompressibility method is well known: there are binary strings w of *any* length so that $|w| \leq C(w)$.

We encode words $w \in \{0,1\}^*$ as follows. From left to right the digits are represented alternating by a's and b's so that a 0 is represented by a single letter and a 1 by a double letter. For example, the word 010110 is encoded as *abbabbaab*. Let $t(w)$ denote the code of w. Clearly, the set of code words for all $w \in \{0,1\}^*$ form the regular language $L_{bin} = ((aa + a)(bb + b))^*(aa + a + \lambda)$.

Lemma 9. *Any 1RTM accepting L_{bin} uses $\Omega(|w|)$ working space for infinitely many inputs w.*

Proof. Assume for the purpose of contradiction that L_{bin} is accepted by some 1RTM $M = \langle S, \Gamma, \Sigma, \triangleright, \triangleleft, \delta, s_0, F \rangle$ that uses $o(|w|)$ working space for all inputs w. We now choose a (long enough) word $w \in \{0,1\}^*$ with $C(w) \geq |w|$, consider an accepting computation on $t(w)$, and show that w can be compressed.

Ignoring the second (input) component w, every configuration (s, w, h_0, β, h_1) of M can be encoded with

$$O(\log(|S|) + \log(|w|) + \log(|\Gamma|^{o(|w|)}) + \log(o(|w|)))$$
$$= O(\log(|w|) + o(|w|)) = O(o(|w|)) = o(|w|)$$

bits. If we know the Turing machine M, the length of w, and the *accepting* configuration without the input w, we can reconstruct w as follows. For each candidate string x of length $|w|$, simulate M on x. If the simulation accepts in the (known) accepting configuration of M on w, we have $x = w$ and, thus, reconstructed w.

In order to show the correctness of the reconstruction, *i.e.*, that only w is accepted in the given configuration, assume on the contrary that there is a string $x \neq w$ such that x accepted by M in the accepting configuration of w. Let $w = w_1 w_2 \cdots w_n$ and $x = x_1 x_2 \cdots x_n$. From the accepting configuration, run M *backwards* (using the reversibility of M) for as long as the suffixes of w and x are identical. This eventually reaches configurations (s, w, h_0, β, h_1) and (s, x, h_0, β, h_1), differing only in their inputs, such that $w_i = x_i$ for $h_0 \leq i \leq n$, and $w_{h_0-1} \neq x_{h_0-1}$. Because M is one-way, this implies that M behaves identically in the two configurations on *all* input symbols from this point on, not just the particular suffix shared by x and w. Now, w_{h_0} is either a or b, say b. That is, $w_{h_0} = x_{h_0} = b$ and $w_{h_0-1} \neq x_{h_0-1}$. This implies that precisely one of w_{h_0-1} and x_{h_0-1} is b, say, $w_{h_0-1} = b$ and $x_{h_0-1} = a$. Since the string $x_1 x_2 \cdots x_{h_0} b$ belongs to L_{bin} it is accepted by M, and because M is one-way, the computation must reach configuration $(s, x_1 x_2 \cdots x_{h_0} b, h_0, \beta, h_1)$. Since M, when run on input $w_1 w_2 \cdots w_{h_0} b$, must reach configuration $(s, w_1 w_2 \cdots w_{h_0} b, h_0, \beta, h_1)$, $w_1 w_2 \cdots w_{h_0} b$ must also be accepted by M. However, the input $w_1 w_2 \cdots w_{h_0} b$ ends with three b's and, thus, does not belong to L_{bin}. Thus only w is accepted in the given accepting configuration.

However, we then have $C(w) \leq C(M) + \log(|w|) + o(|w|) + |p| = o(|w|)$, where $|p|$ is the constant size of the above program reconstructing w. We conclude $C(w) < |w|$, for w long enough, contradicting that $C(w) \geq |w|$. Therefore, M cannot accept L_{bin} in $o(|w|)$ space. $\qquad\square$

Lemma 10. *There is a language accepted by a 1DTM in real time that cannot be accepted by any 1RTM in less than linear time.*

Proof. The witness language for the assertion is

$$L = \{\, w u w^R \mid w \in \{0,1\}^*, u \in L_{bin}, |u| \geq 1 \,\}.$$

Language L is accepted by a 1DTM in real time as follows. First, the leading $w \in \{0,1\}^*$ is copied to the working tape. When the first symbol from $\{a, b\}$ appears in the input, the infix u starts. Now, the working tape head is kept at its current position, and the internal states of the machine are used to verify that u belongs to the regular language L_{bin}. If yes, upon reading the first symbol from $\{0, 1\}$, the machine starts to compare the trailing w^R with the tape inscription, whereby the working tape head is moved from the end of the inscribed w to its beginning, accepting if these are equal.

It remains to be shown that L is not accepted by any 1RTM in less than linear time. Assume on the contrary that there is a 1RTM $M = \langle S, \Gamma, \Sigma, \rhd, \lhd, \delta, s_0, F \rangle$ which accepts L in time id $+o(\text{id})$.

By Lemma 9, we know that there are words u of arbitrary lengths so that M has to use $\Omega(|u'|)$ working tape space for any prefix u' of u. More precisely, there is a constant $c_0 \geq 1$ so that M extends the length of the non-blank working tape inscription by i symbols for each block of at most $c_0 \cdot i$ input symbols.

Now we consider input prefixes wu and take a closer look at three particular configurations. The first configuration is reached at the first time step at which the word w has been read and the working tape head is located at an end of the non-blank part of the working tape. At this point w and possibly some symbols from u have been read. Let v be the inscription of the working tape and u_1 be the prefix of u that has been read at this time. From above we derive that the length of u_1 is at most $c_0 \cdot |w|$. Denote this configuration $C_{w,1} = (p, wu_1, |wu_1|, v, |v|)$.

The second configuration is reached when M has extended its working tape inscription by another $|w|$ symbols and the working tape head is located at the (same) end of the non-blank part of the working tape. Let $v'v_1$ be the inscription of the working tape at that time, where $|v'| = |v|$ and $|v_1| = |w|$, and let u_2 be the next part of the input that has been read to reach this configuration. Again, from above we derive $|u_2| \leq c_0 \cdot |w|$. Denote this configuration $C_{w,2} = (q, wu_1u_2, |wu_1u_2|, v'v_1, |v'v_1|)$.

The third configuration is reached when M has extended its working tape inscription by another $2|w|$ symbols, so that the working tape head is located at the (same) end of the non-blank part of the working tape. Similar to before, let $v''v_1'v_2$ be the inscription of the working tape at that time, where $|v''| = |v|$, $|v_1'| = |v_1| = |w|$, and $|v_2| = 2|w|$, and let u_3 be the next part of the input that has been read to reach this configuration. We know $|u_3| \leq 2c_0|w|$ from above. Denote this configuration $C_{w,3} = (s, wu_1u_2u_3, |wu_1u_2u_3|, v''v_1'v_2, |v''v_1'v_2|)$.

In the next step of the proof, extended crossing sequences are used. The notion of crossing sequences was introduced in [5] for one-tape machines. In that setting, the *crossing sequence* at location i was defined to be the sequence of states a Turing machine is in when its head crosses the boundary between tape square i and $i + 1$. Since here we are dealing with an additional input tape, the notion is extended as follows. Crossing sequences are now defined for the squares of the working tape, such that for each state in the sequence, the current input head position is also listed. Such crossing sequences are denoted $CS_i(x)$, for a Turing machine run on input x.

Next we consider a word $\hat{w} \in \{0,1\}^*$ such that $|w| = |\hat{w}|$ and $w \neq \hat{w}$, and determine the configurations

$$C_{\hat{w},1} = (\hat{p}, \hat{w}\hat{u}_1, |\hat{w}\hat{u}_1|, \hat{v}, |\hat{v}|),$$
$$C_{\hat{w},2} = (\hat{q}, \hat{w}\hat{u}_1\hat{u}_2, |\hat{w}\hat{u}_1\hat{u}_2|, \hat{v}'\hat{v}_1, |\hat{v}'\hat{v}_1|), \text{ and}$$
$$C_{\hat{w},3} = (\hat{s}, \hat{w}\hat{u}_1\hat{u}_2\hat{u}_3, |\hat{w}\hat{u}_1\hat{u}_2\hat{u}_3|, \hat{v}''\hat{v}_1'\hat{v}_2, |\hat{v}''\hat{v}_1'\hat{v}_2|)$$

as for w with the same u. That is, $\hat{u}_1\hat{u}_2\hat{u}_3$ is again a prefix of u. Let $u_1u_2u_3$ be longer than $\hat{u}_1\hat{u}_2\hat{u}_3$ (if not, interchange the roles played by w and $\hat{w}$ in the following.)

Now we consider the complete inputs $wu_1u_2u_3w^R$ and $\hat{w}u_1u_2u_3\hat{w}^R$, both belonging to L. Assume that one of the crossing sequences appearing on the working tape somewhere in the inscription v_1', that is, $CS_i(wu_1u_2u_3w^R)$, for some $|v''| \leq i \leq |v''v_1'|$, is the same as one of the crossing sequences appearing on the working tape somewhere in the inscription $\hat{v}_1'$, that is, $CS_j(\hat{w}u_1u_2u_3\hat{w}^R)$, for some $|\hat{v}''| \leq j \leq |\hat{v}''\hat{v}_1'|$. Since input positions and, thus, the input symbol associated with the states in the crossing sequence are the same, the behavior of M to the right of i is identical to the behavior to the right of j.

The total lengths of both inputs are at most $|w| + 4c_0|w| + |w| \in O(|w|)$. Since $|v_2| = 2|w|$ there is not enough time to move the working tape head back across v_2 while processing the suffix w^R, as doing this would imply a time complexity of at least linear time. So, the working tape head remains to the right of location i. This would imply that $\hat{w}u_1u_2u_3w^R$ is accepted by M as well, but $\hat{w}u_1u_2u_3w^R \notin L$. In turn, this means that all the crossing sequences $CS_i(wu_1u_2u_3w^R)$, for $|v''| \leq i \leq |v''v_1'|$, must be different from all the crossing sequences $CS_j(\hat{w}u_1u_2u_3\hat{w}^R)$, for $|\hat{v}''| \leq j \leq |\hat{v}''\hat{v}_1'|$.

We now consider the length of these crossing sequences. There are $2^{|w|}$ different input prefixes of length $|w|$ for which all the crossing sequences in the locations under question have to be different. Further, for M to use only $\mathrm{id} + o(\mathrm{id})$ time, most of these crossing sequences have to be short. Now, with only $|S|$ different states and at most $3c_0|w|$ input positions between $|wu_1|$ and $|wu_1u_2u_3|$ there are at most $\sum_{i=0}^{3c_0}(|S| \cdot 3c_0|w|)^i < (|S| \cdot 3c_0|w|)^{3c_0+1}$ possible crossing sequences of length $3c_0$ or less available. Since this is only polynomial in $|w|$, there is an input prefix of length $|w|$ for which all the $|w|$ crossing sequences in the locations under question are at least of length $3c_0 + 1$ (these do not have to be all different.) This implies that M spends at least $3c_0|w| + |w|$ time steps for performing these crossing sequences, while processing at most $|u_2u_3| \leq 3c_0|w|$ of the input, and so M spends at least $\mathrm{id} + |w|$ steps in total on this particular input. Because the total length of the input was of order $O(|w|)$, this means that M uses strictly more than $\mathrm{id} + o(\mathrm{id})$ time steps on some words in L.   □

As an immediate corollary to Lemma 10 we get the proper inclusions of the following theorem.

Theorem 11. *Let* $r : \mathbb{N} \to \mathbb{N}$ *be a function so that* $r \in o(\mathrm{id})$. *Then*

$$\mathrm{1RTIME}(\mathrm{id} + r) \subset \mathrm{1DTIME}(\mathrm{id} + r).$$

5   Conclusion

In this paper, Turing machines equipped with one working tape and a one-way or two-way read-only input tape have been investigated toward their ability to perform fast reversible computations. A main result is that there exist infinite hierarchies in between real time and linear time for such reversible Turing machines.

Furthermore, this result holds for multitape Turing machines as well. One essential step for proving these hierarchies was to translate the notion of time constructibility from arbitrary Turing machines to reversible Turing machines.

A primary motivation was the question of whether reversible Turing machines are less powerful than irreversible Turing machines under the above conditions. Here, the result is that Turing machines with one working tape and one-way input tape working in any given time complexity in between real time and linear time become less powerful when their computations have to be reversible. It is currently not clear, and an interesting topic for further research, whether the latter result can be generalized to Turing machines with a two-way input tape, or to Turing machines with more than one working tape.

Acknowledgments. H.B. Axelsen was supported by the Danish Council for Independent Research | Natural Sciences under the *Foundations of Reversible Computing* project. Thanks are due to Robin Kaarsgaard for comments on a draft of this paper.

References

1. Axelsen, H.B.: Time complexity of tape reduction for reversible turing machines. In: De Vos, A., Wille, R. (eds.) RC 2011. LNCS, vol. 7165, pp. 1–13. Springer, Heidelberg (2012)
2. Bennett, C.H.: Time/space trade-offs for reversible computation. SIAM J. Comput. **18**, 766–776 (1989)
3. Cole, S.N.: Real-time computation by n-dimensional iterative arrays of finite-state machines. IEEE Trans. Comput. **18**, 349–365 (1969)
4. Hartmanis, J., Stearns, R.E.: On the computational complexity of algorithms. Trans. Amer. Math. Soc. **117**, 285–306 (1965)
5. Hennie, F.C.: One-tape, off-line Turing machine computations. Inform. Control **8**, 553–578 (1965)
6. Jacopini, G., Mentrasti, P., Sontacchi, G.: Reversible Turing machines and polynomial time reversibly computable functions. SIAM J. Disc. Math. **3**, 241–254 (1990)
7. Klein, A., Kutrib, M.: Deterministic Turing machines in the range between real-time and linear-time. Theoret. Comput. Sci. **289**, 253–275 (2002)
8. Lange, K.J., McKenzie, P., Tapp, A.: Reversible space equals deterministic space. J. Comput. System Sci. **60**, 354–367 (2000)
9. Li, M., Vitányi, P.M.B.: An Introduction to Kolmogorov Complexity and Its Applications. Springer (1993)
10. Paul, W.J.: Komplexitätstheorie. Teubner (1978)
11. Pin, J.: On the language accepted by finite reversible automata. In: Ottmann, T. (ed.) Automata, Languages and Programming. LNCS, vol. 267, pp. 237–249. Springer, Heidelberg (1987)
12. Rosenberg, A.L.: Real-time definable languages. J. ACM **14**, 645–662 (1967)
13. Trakhtenbrot, B.A.: Turing machine computations with logarithmic delay. Algebra i Logika **3**, 33–48 (1964)
14. Vitányi, P.M.B.: Time, space, and energy in reversible computing. In: Bagherzadeh, N., Valero, M., Ramírez, A. (eds.) Computing Frontiers (CF 2005), pp. 435–444. ACM (2005)

Real-Time Methods in Reversible Computation

Tommi Pesu and Iain Phillips[✉]

Imperial College London, London, UK
{tommi.pesu13,i.phillips}@imperial.ac.uk

Abstract. Bennett has shown how to simulate arbitrary forwards-only computations by fully reversible computation. In particular he has given a space-efficient linear time simulation. After describing a different linear-time reversible simulation with improved space efficiency, we initiate the study of real-time simulations. In addition to being linear-time, these must offer continuous progress, meaning that the delay between successive forward events must be bounded by a constant.

1 Introduction

Intel's co-founder Gordon E. Moore famously predicted in 1965 that the computational performance of modern computers would double every 18 months (Moore's Law). At the moment his law is being obeyed, due to continuous development in the area of minimising elements which make up the computer. As pointed out in [3], a linear increase in clock frequency is associated with a quadratic increase of elementary gates per unit area, leading to a cubic increase in heat dissipation if the energy expended per event remains constant. Thus the increase under Moore's Law has only been possible due to a vast increase in energy efficiency of elementary logical gates.

However there exists a physical limit of $kT \ln 2$ which is about 3×10^{-21} Joule at room temperature. This is the minimum amount of energy that a computer must waste to perform a calculation. With current advances following Moore's Law, this limit will be reached in about ten years [9]. Therefore in the near future something drastic will need to be done for computation power to be able to increase at the pace defined by Moore's Law.

A possible solution to this problem was suggested by Landauer [4], who argued that the thermodynamic limit of $kT \ln 2$ only applies to calculation performed in a irreversible way. Therefore if the calculation is performed in a reversible way then the cost of a calculation operation can be below the limit $kT \ln 2$ given by thermal noise.

Lecerf and Bennett continued this line of thought, proving independently that an irreversible Turing Machine can be simulated by a reversible Turing machine [1,6].

The next development in reversible computation was more space efficient reversible simulation. Bennett [2] showed how to obtain a more space optimised version of reversible computation. Li and Vitányi [8] also looked at trade-offs between space and time, and trade-offs between space and irreversible erasure.

© Springer International Publishing Switzerland 2015
J. Krivine and J.-B. Stefani (Eds.): RC 2015, LNCS 9138, pp. 45–59, 2015.
DOI: 10.1007/978-3-319-20860-2_3

Lange, McKenzie and Tapp [5] gave a method to perform reversible simulation in linear space; however it comes at the cost of exponential time. Williams [10] generalised the results of [2,5]. Buhrman, Tromp and Vitányi proved an upper bound on the trade-off between time and space, and showed that one can simultaneously achieve sub-exponential time and sub-quadratic space [3].

In this paper we are interested in real-time reversible simulations. Such simulations must in particular be linear-time, but we identify a further stronger property they should satisfy, which we call *continuous progress*. This means that the simulation of each forward step should not be indefinitely delayed. More precisely, there is a fixed finite bound p, independent of the time taken by the original forwards-only computation, such that when p steps of the simulation are performed, at least one step of advancement is made with respect to the original forwards-only computation. As far as we are aware, real-time reversible simulations have not been studied previously.

If interactive systems or systems that need to stream out data at constant intervals are ever implemented in practice with reversible computation, then it is critical that the algorithm that performs the simulation satisfies the definition of continuous progress. For example users of said computer would quite quickly get frustrated if the execution of their program occasionally stalled for an undefined amount of time.

An example of a program that needs to stream out data at a constant rate is an mp3 decoder/player. If the program stalls and fails to send frequency information to the physical speakers at a constant rate the listening experience will be poor. Therefore it is a necessary condition that all reversible computation simulations for playing music and displaying video use an algorithm that satisfies continuous progress.

Plenty of examples can also be found in computation systems in finance. For example in algorithmic trading the trading systems emit information about the market and if the sending of the information is delayed it might be too late to trade based on this information.

Given that details on how exactly reversible computation will work with programs where information is non-deterministically streamed in computation have not yet been fully studied, it is hard to say how exactly continuous progress will fit in. However, it can be said with high confidence that continuous progress is a crucial requirement once a physical reversible computer can be built and actual real world programs are run on these computers.

As far as linear-time simulations are concerned, the most efficient presently known is due to Bennett [2]. We offer an improvement on his linear-time algorithm, which we call the k-ratic algorithm. This operates at essentially the same rate as Bennett's algorithm, but uses roughly half as much space.

Neither algorithm satisfies the continuous progress property, since an unbounded amount of time is taken up in periodic releasing of memory. We show how to modify each algorithm to ensure continuous progress, using multiple threads.

The paper is organised as follows. In Section 2 we look at the relevant previous work. Then in Section 3 we introduce the k-ratic algorithm. In Section 4 we describe changes to Bennett's linear-time algorithm and to the k-ratic algorithm to allow them to make continuous progress. We finish with some conclusions.

2 Previous Work on Linear-Time Simulations

This section will review existing research related to linear-time reversible simulations of forwards-only computation. The section starts off with Bennett's original 1973 algorithm. We then discuss the pebble game, a tool commonly used in the study of reversible computation. Finally we look at Bennett's 1989 algorithm, which has improved space efficiency compared to the original 1973 version.

2.1 Bennett's 1973 Simulation

The basic idea of Bennett's simulation is to construct reversible versions of all the elementary operations of a Turing machine. Doing this for a universal Turing machine will mean that all possible computer programs can be reversibly simulated.

We simulate a 1-tape Turing machine with a 3-tape Turing machine. The three tapes of the simulating machine are the work tape, the history tape and the output tape. At the beginning, the work tape contains the input of the machine and the other two tapes are empty. In the first stage the original computation is performed and at the same time the history tape is filled with padding from each single computational step to make the computation reversible. In the second stage the output is copied from the work tape onto the output tape. Finally in the third stage the work tape is converted back to the initial input with the help of the history tape. We are left with the input on the work tape and the output on the output tape, with the history tape empty.

Let the original computation take space S and time T, and let the reversible version of this computation take space S' and time T'. The work tape will take up space S. The history tape will at worst take up space $O(T)$. Finally the output will in the worst case take as much space as the work tape. Therefore space usage will be in the worst case $S' = 2S + T = O(S + T)$. Performing the first stage will take time $O(T)$. In the worst case the output will be as big as the amount of computation done, and so the second stage takes at most $O(T)$. Finally the third stage also takes $O(T)$. This sums up to $T' = O(T)$.

Bennett's simulation is very memory hungry. Note that T can be as much as $O(2^S)$, so that $S' = O(2^S)$ in terms of S alone. Considering that most modern computers can perform more computations per second than they have bytes of RAM, the simulation is infeasible in practice. Therefore a better implementation for reversible simulation that uses less space is needed.

2.2 The Pebble Game

The pebble game was briefly introduced by Bennett in [2], and later taken up by other researchers [8]. The pebble game has a board with an unbounded number of squares labelled with natural numbers from 1 upwards, and the player is given m pebbles. Each pebble represents δ steps of computation. The kth square on the board represents computation from the $(k-1)\delta$th step to the $k\delta$th step in the original forwards-only computation. If a pebble is placed on the kth square it means that enough information is stored so that the kth segment of δ steps can be performed reversibly using Bennett's 1973 method.

The pebble game has the following rules.

- Initially all the squares of the board are not pebbled.
- The player can place a pebble on the board either at square 1, or at square k if the $(k-1)$th square has been pebbled.
- The player can remove a pebble either at square 1 or at a square k if the $(k-1)$th square has been pebbled.
- The objective of the game is to place a pebble as far as possible in the list of squares and then clear the board to a situation where only the furthest pebble (the one with the greatest advancement) remains on the board.[1]
- The player can have a maximum of m pebbles on the board at the same time.

The number of pebbles allowed represents the space usage of the reversible simulation. Bennett's 1973 algorithm can be interpreted in the pebble game as follows. To advance n squares with n pebbles, first lay down n pebbles in order from square 1 to square n. Then remove the pebbles in reverse order by starting from $n-1$ and going down back to 1.

2.3   Bennett's 1989 Simulation

In 1989 Bennett presented an algorithm to reversibly simulate a machine running in time T and space S. Given a constant k, he shows how to place pebbles on up to k^n squares using $n(k-1)+1$ pebbles, with $(2k-1)^n$ moves in the pebble game.

Bennett proved that the simulation operates in time $T' = O(T^{1+\epsilon})$ (so non-linear) and space $O(S \log T)$. His analysis was later refined by Levine and Sherman [7], who demonstrated that there is a big constant factor in the memory bound that grows exponentially in terms of ϵ^{-1}. They state the time and space bounds as $T' = \Theta(T^{1+\epsilon}/S^\epsilon)$ and $S' = \Theta(S(1 + \ln(T/S)))$ with a constant factor in the space bound of approximately $\epsilon 2^{1/\epsilon}$.

In Bennett's algorithm, k is constant while n varies. Bennett remarks briefly that a linear-time variant can be obtained by holding n fixed and varying k. We next look at this in more detail. Note that we swap over n and k to reflect their new statuses.

Let us denote Bennett's algorithm for parameters n and k by $B(n,k)$. It works as follows. Let the original forwards-only computation use space S. Each

---

[1] In the game as described in [8] all pebbles are removed from the board, but the present formulation, matching Bennett's original description, is more convenient for the algorithms considered here.

square in the pebble game represents $m \approx S$ steps in the original computation. Using the 1973 algorithm these m steps can be performed in time $O(S)$ and space $O(S)$.

In order to advance by n^k squares in the pebble game, we pebble n blocks of n^{k-1} by calling $B(n, k-1)$ successively on blocks 1 to n. This gives us single pebbles at the end of each of the n blocks. We refer to the computation so far as the *advancement phase*. We then use $B(n, k-1)$ in reverse on blocks $n-1$ down to 1. We are left with a single pebble at square n^k. We refer to this latter part of the computation as the *clearing phase*. For the base case $k = 0$ a single pebble is placed on the first square.

Remark 2.1. The case for $k = 1$ is effectively Bennett's original 1973 algorithm.

The recurrence relation for the number of steps of $B(n, k)$ is

$$R(n, 0) = 1$$
$$R(n, k+1) = (2n - 1)R(n, k) \qquad (k \geq 0)$$

with solution $R(n, k) = (2n - 1)^k$.

Remark 2.2. Note that we count the number of steps in the pebble game, even though in fact each pebble placed represents $m \approx S$ steps.

The number of pebbles used by $B(n, k)$ is given by

$$P(n, 0) = 1$$
$$P(n, k+1) = P(n, k) + n - 1 \qquad (k \geq 0)$$

with solution $P(n, k) = k(n - 1) + 1$.

The time T taken by the original computation is mn^k. The time T' taken by $B(n, k)$ satisfies $T' = O(T)$, since

$$\frac{R(n, k)}{n^k} = \left(\frac{2n - 1}{n}\right)^k \leq 2^k. \tag{1}$$

So the algorithm runs in linear time. The space usage is $S' = (k(n-1)+1)O(S) = O(ST^{1/k})$.

3 The *k*-ratic Algorithm

We present a new linear-time reversible simulation algorithm, which we call the *k-ratic* algorithm. Like Bennett's algorithm, it splits the computation into blocks. However they are no longer of equal size; each successive block is smaller than its predecessor. In a sense the algorithm is greedier in using pebbles; Bennett's algorithm leaves more pebbles unused when executing the earlier blocks.

Let the *k*-ratic algorithm with parameters n and k be denoted by $K(n, k)$. It will use n pebbles, and works as follows. We first call $K(n-1, k-1)$ on block 1. This will leave a single pebble at the end of the block. We then successively call $K(n-2, k-1), \ldots, K(1, k-1)$ on blocks $2, \ldots, n-1$, respectively. We are now left with pebbles at the end of $n-1$ blocks. We place the final pebble after block $n-1$. As with Bennett's algorithm, we refer to the computation so far as the *advancement phase*. If we stop at this point we refer to this as the *advancement-only k-ratic* algorithm.

For the *full k-ratic* algorithm we must remove the first $n-1$ pebbles representing intermediate checkpoints. We do this by successively calling each of $K(1, k-1), \ldots, K(n-1, k-1)$ in reverse. We are left with a single pebble immediately after the end of the last block. As before, we refer to this latter part of the algorithm as the *clearing phase*.

In the base case for $k = 0$ we simply place a pebble on the first square and terminate.

Remark 3.1. In the case for $k = 1$, note that $K(n, 1)$ is the same as $B(n, 1)$, and is effectively Bennett's original algorithm of [1]. Just place n pebbles on successive squares, and then remove pebbles $n-1, \ldots, 1$ to leave only the last pebble.

A graphical demonstration of the method for $k = 2$ can be seen in Figure 1.

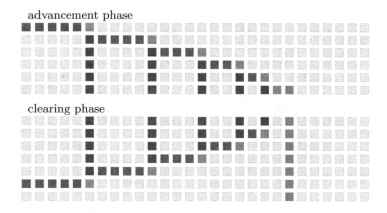

Fig. 1. Performing the k-ratic algorithm with $n = 7$ and $k = 2$

Let us call the number of the square with the last pebble the *advancement* of $K(n, k)$; we denote it by $A(n, k)$. We get the following recurrence relation:

$$A(n, 0) = 1$$
$$A(n, k+1) = 1 + \sum_{i=1}^{n-1} A(i, k) \qquad (k \geq 0)$$

Thus $A(n, 1) = n$ and

$$A(n, 2) = 1 + \sum_{i=1}^{n-1} A(i, 1) = 1 + \sum_{i=1}^{n-1} i = \frac{n(n-1)}{2} + 1.$$

The recurrence relation for the number of steps of $K(n, k)$ is

$$S(n, 0) = 1$$
$$S(n, k+1) = 1 + 2\sum_{i=1}^{n-1} S(i, k) \qquad (k \geq 0)$$

Thus $S(n, 1) = 2n - 1$ and

$$S(n, 2) = 1 + 2\sum_{i=1}^{n-1} S(i, 1) = 1 + 2\sum_{i=1}^{n-1}(2i - 1) = 2(n-1)^2 + 1.$$

Let us denote the running time of the advancement-only k-ratic algorithm by $S_A(n, k)$. Then

$$S_A(n, k) = \frac{S(n, k) + 1}{2}.$$

We now calculate an estimate of the advancement $A(n, k)$, using the following standard result.

Lemma 3.2. Let $f : \mathbb{R} \to \mathbb{R}$ be continuous and non-decreasing on the range $[0, n]$. Then

$$\int_0^{n-1} f(x)\,dx \leq \sum_{i=1}^{n-1} f(i) \leq \int_1^n f(x)\,dx.$$

Proposition 3.3. For any $n \geq 1$, $k \geq 1$ we have $A(n, k) = (n^k/k!) + O(n^{k-1})$.

Proof. We first show $A(n, k) \leq (n^k/k!) + O(n^{k-1})$ by induction on k. Clearly $A(n, 1) \leq n^1 + O(1)$. Suppose that $A(n, k) \leq (n^k/k!) + O(n^{k-1})$. Then using Lemma 3.2

$$
\begin{aligned}
A(n, k+1) &= 1 + \sum_{i=1}^{n-1} A(i, k) \\
&\leq 1 + \sum_{i=1}^{n-1}(i^k/k!) + \sum_{i=1}^{n-1} O(i^{k-1}) \\
&\leq 1 + \int_1^n x^k/k!\,dx + \sum_{i=1}^{n-1} O(i^{k-1}) \\
&= 1 + (n^{k+1} - 1)/(k+1)! + (n-1)O(n^{k-1}) \\
&= (n^{k+1}/(k+1)!) + O(n^k)
\end{aligned}
$$

We now show $A(n, k) \geq (n^k/k!) + O(n^{k-1})$. Clearly $A(n, 1) \geq n^1 + O(1)$. Suppose that $A(n, k) \geq (n^k/k!) + O(n^{k-1})$. Then using Lemma 3.2

$$
\begin{aligned}
A(n, k+1) &= 1 + \sum_{i=1}^{n-1} A(i, k) \\
&\geq 1 + \sum_{i=1}^{n-1}(i^k/k!) + \sum_{i=1}^{n-1} O(i^{k-1}) \\
&\geq 1 + \int_0^{n-1} x^k/k!\,dx + \sum_{i=1}^{n-1} O(i^{k-1}) \\
&= 1 + (n-1)^{k+1}/(k+1)! + (n-1)O(n^{k-1}) \\
&= (n^{k+1}/(k+1)!) + O(n^k)
\end{aligned}
$$

We deduce that $A(n, k) = (n^k/k!) + O(n^{k-1})$ as required. $\qquad \square$

The running time of $K(n, k)$ is no more than 2^k times the advancement:

Proposition 3.4. *For any $n \geq 1$, $k \geq 0$ we have $S(n, k) \leq 2^k A(n, k)$.*

Proof. By induction on k. It clearly holds for $k = 0$. Suppose $S(n, k) \leq 2^k A(n, k)$. Then

$$
\begin{aligned}
S(n, k + 1) &= 1 + 2\sum_{i=1}^{n-1} S(i, k) \\
&\leq 1 + 2\sum_{i=1}^{n-1} 2^k A(i, k) \\
&= 2^{k+1}(1 + \sum_{i=1}^{n-1} A(i, k)) - (2^{k+1} - 1) \\
&= 2^{k+1} A(n, k + 1) - (2^{k+1} - 1) \\
&\leq 2^{k+1} A(n, k + 1)
\end{aligned}
$$

$\square$

The k-ratic algorithm $K(n, k)$ achieves advancement of $A(n, k)$ squares in $S(n, k)$ steps. As before, each square in the pebble game corresponds to $m \approx S$ steps in the original computation. So we simulate $T = O(A(n, k))$ steps of the original computation in time $T' = O(S(n, k))$. It is clear from Proposition 3.4 that the k-ratic algorithm runs in linear time since $T' = O(T)$, just as for Bennett's algorithm. Indeed the ratio of 2^k of the number of steps of the simulating algorithm to the advancement achieved is the same in both cases, comparing Proposition 3.4 and Equation (1). The space usage is $S' = nO(S) = O(ST^{1/k})$ as in Bennett's algorithm.

However if we look in more detail at space, the k-ratic algorithm improves on Bennett's. Let us fix values for T/S, and for k. Bennett's algorithm uses $p_1 = k(n - 1) + 1$ pebbles with $n^k = T/S$. Thus $p_1 \approx (k^k T/S)^{1/k}$. The k-ratic algorithm uses $p_2 = n$ pebbles with $n^k/k! \approx T/S$. Thus $p_2 \approx (k!T/S)^{1/k}$. This gives us a ratio of $p_1/p_2 = (k^k/k!)^{1/k}$.

Proposition 3.5.

$$
\lim_{k \to \infty} (k^k/k!)^{1/k} = e
$$

Proof. This is a consequence of Stirling's formula $n! \sim \sqrt{2\pi n}(n/e)^n$. $\square$

By Proposition 3.5, p_1/p_2 tends to e as k increases; in fact it has a value ≥ 2 for $k \geq 6$. Thus the k-ratic algorithm uses roughly half as much space, a modest improvement.

The improvement is larger if we consider how much advancement can be made for a given amount of space (number of pebbles). Suppose we are given $k(n - 1) + 1$ pebbles as in Bennett's algorithm. Then $B(n, k)$ advances by n^k squares. The k-ratic algorithm can advance by

$$
A(k(n - 1) + 1, k) = ((k(n - 1) + 1)^k/k!) + O(n^{k-1}) = (k^k/k!)n^k + O(n^{k-1})
$$

The ratio $k^k/k!$ is of course simply a constant, but it is quite large for even small values of k:

Proposition 3.6. *For $k \geq 1$, $k^k/k! \geq 2^{k-1}$.*

Proof. By induction. It clearly holds for $k = 1$. We have

$$\frac{(k+1)^{k+1}}{(k+1)!} = \frac{(k+1)^k}{k!} \geq \frac{k^k + k.k^{k-1}}{k!} = 2\frac{k^k}{k!}$$

Hence result.   □

In fact $10^{10}/10! = 2755.7$. Thus even for modest values of k we get an improvement on advancement for the same amount of space usage.

We now turn to the issue of how to choose a suitable value of the parameter k. Even though the reversible simulation of T steps is linear with respect to T, the constant factor 2^k grows exponentially. This makes it in practice necessary to choose a small value of k. This is further supported by the diminishing returns of lower memory usage as k increases.

$$T' = \Theta(2^k T) \tag{2}$$

$$S' = \Theta(S \sqrt[k]{(T/S)k!}) \tag{3}$$

In the formal definition of big-O notation the $k!$ and 2^k should not exist in the notations as they are constant. However in this case they are quite large and might in practice have a significant impact on the computation time and space usage.

We now consider what value of k we should choose for optimal results, given a particular value of T/S. By Proposition 3.5 we have $\sqrt[k]{k!} = \Theta(k)$, which using Equation (3) gives us

$$S' = \Theta(kS \sqrt[k]{(T/S)}) .$$

To find the value of k for which S' reaches a minimum, we differentiate the function $y = x(T/S)^{1/x}$:

$$dy/dx = (T/S)^{1/x}(x - \ln(T/S))/x$$

meaning that $k \approx \ln(T/S)$ is the minimum.

As an example, if $T/S = 10^{20}$, space S' would improve up to roughly $\ln 10^{20} = 46.05$. However such a value of k would be far too large as far as time is concerned, given the 2^k slowdown in Equation (2). As far as space is concerned, after about $k = 7$ diminishing returns set in on the improvement in memory compared to the extra time.

Clearly there is a trade-off between space and time when choosing the value of k. How to resolve this will depend on the particular application. However we can estimate a suitable value of k based on the following heuristic. For a given value of T/S we decide on a value of k by finding the greatest k such that increasing from $k - 1$ to k doubles the space usage. Increasing k further would mean that we were doubling the time taken but not halving the space. Call this value $k_M(T/S)$. See Figure 2 for a plot of k_M for values up to 10^{100}, yielding e.g. a value of 17 for $T/S = 10^{100}$. Note that the horizontal axis is log-scale.

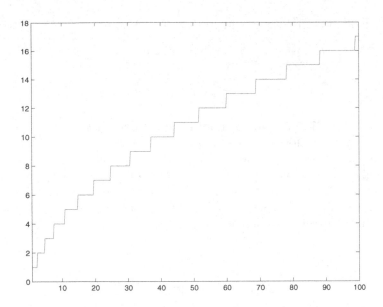

Fig. 2. Plot of $k_M(T/S)$ against $\log_{10}(T/S)$

4   Continuous Progress

We are interested in real-time reversible simulations of forwards-only computations. As stated in the Introduction, we identify *continuous progress* as a requirement for a simulation to be real-time. It will be convenient to allow multiple threads in the simulating program. A single step of the simulation means that each of its threads makes a step (or idles). Simulating programs can take a variable parameter n which allows for the capacity to simulate an indefinitely increasing number of steps depending on n (with a corresponding increase in memory usage).

Definition 4.1. *A (multi-threaded) simulation program* $\mathsf{Sim}(n)$ *makes continuous progress if and only if there is some constant* $p \in \mathbb{N}$ *(not depending on* n*) such that for every* n*, the program that is being simulated advances at least one computational step for every* p *steps of computation performed by the simulating program* $\mathsf{Sim}(n)$*. If such a* p *exists, we call it the* progression factor *of the simulation.*

Remark 4.2. If the simulation is reversible, it may have to perform further computation after reaching maximum advancement, i.e. after the forward computation has been fully simulated. We will still allow such a simulation to satisfy the condition for continuous progress.

A progression factor greater than one does not prevent a simulation in real time, as long as the simulating computation is run on a faster processor than the original computation.

From Definition 4.1 it follows that the simulation operates in linear time compared to the program being simulated. If the latter makes T steps, then the former makes $\leq pT = O(T)$ steps. However continuous progress is a stricter requirement than just linear time simulation, as it could be the case that on average the simulation advances linearly, but occasionally progress hangs for arbitrarily long time.

Example 4.3. Consider a simulation that takes the following amount of steps per progression of the program being simulated; it is linear time but not continuously progressing:

$$F(n) = \begin{cases} n & \text{if } n \text{ is a power of 2} \\ 1 & \text{otherwise} \end{cases}$$

Letting $k = \lfloor \log n \rfloor$ we have

$$\sum_{i=0}^{n} F(i) = (n+1) - (k+1) + \sum_{j=0}^{k} 2^j = (2^{k+1} - 1) + n - k \leq 3n \,.$$

Therefore on average to progress n steps in the original computation approximately $3n$ steps need to be performed by the simulation. Hence the simulation is linear time. However it is not continuously progressing due to the increasing stalls in progress that happen at powers of two. Such stalls also occur in Bennett's algorithm $B(n,k)$ described in Section 2.3, and in the k-ratic method $K(n,k)$ described in Section 3; in both cases the interval between successive advancement steps can be as much as $O(n^{k-1})$ steps of simulation.

Lemma 4.4. *If a q-threaded algorithm has a progression factor of p then there is a corresponding single-threaded algorithm with progression factor qp.*

Proof. Simply schedule the q threads onto a single thread in a round-robin fashion. ☐

In particular cases where different threads carry out different amounts of work, we may be able to improve on the bound given by Lemma 4.4, of course.

Both Bennett's 1989 linear-time algorithm (Section 2.3) and the k-ratic algorithm (Section 3) fail to exhibit continuous progress, due to the interruptions to forward progress for the clearing phases. We now look at how to reprogram them onto multiple concurrent threads to ensure continuous progress. Multiple threads are not essential by Lemma 4.4, of course.

A natural point to utilise multi-threading in algorithms such as we have considered is at the point when the advancement phase for a block finishes. At this point there is a need to backtrack and erase previously laid pebbles before proceeding to the next block. It is possible to multi-thread this part by having one thread continue forward while another thread frees the pebbles laid down in the past.

We start by allowing a comparatively large number of threads, namely $O(2^k)$, where k is the constant parameter in the algorithms described earlier. In the case of Bennett's algorithm by using 2^{k-1} threads we can get a progression factor of one.

Theorem 4.5. *For $k \geq 1$, we can program $B(n,k)$ onto 2^{k-1} threads with a progression factor of* 1.

Proof. By induction. The base case $k = 1$ with a single thread is clear. To perform $B(n, k+1)$ on n blocks, we divide the 2^k threads into 2^{k-1} used for advancement, and an equal number used for clearing. We start by using the advancement threads to perform the advancement phase of $B(n,k)$ on block 1. We know by induction that the progression factor is 1. Then for $i = 1, \ldots, n-1$, we simultaneously perform the clearing phase of $B(n,k)$ on block i and the advancement phase of $B(n,k)$ on block $i+1$. Again the progression factor is 1. Hence result.   ◻

By using 2^{k-1} threads we have improved the parallel time for the advancement phase to be equal to the advancement n^k. This is a 2^{k-1} speed-up compared to the sequential version. The total number of pebbles used is given by

$$P'(n,1) = n$$
$$P'(n,k+1) = 2P'(n,k) + n - 2 \qquad (k \geq 1)$$

with solution $P'(n,k) = (2^k-1)(n-1)+1$. This may be compared with $P(n,k) = k(n-1)+1$ for the original algorithm.

Suppose now that we have fewer than 2^{k-1} threads available. Let the number of threads be 2^j where $0 \leq j < k$. Then we can run the algorithm of Theorem 4.5 on 2^j threads by time-sharing as in Lemma 4.4. We still get continuous progress, with a progression factor of 2^{k-1-j}. The pebble usage will still be $P'(n,k)$.

In particular, if we take the 2^{k-1}-thread version and schedule it onto a single processor, we get a progression factor of 2^{k-1}. The pebble usage is of course greater than the $P(n,k)$ of the original algorithm, though only by a constant factor.

If we wish to economise on memory, as an alternative to Theorem 4.5 we can use k threads instead of 2^{k-1}.

Theorem 4.6. *For $k \geq 2$, we can program $B(n,k)$ onto k threads with a progression factor of 2^{k-2}.*

Proof. By induction on k. For $k = 1$ we have one thread and we have a progression factor of $1 = 2^{k-1}$.

Suppose true for $k \geq 1$. The threaded algorithm for $k+1$ uses $k+1$ threads. The algorithm divides the work into n blocks $1, 2, \ldots, n$, each of size n^k. We perform each successive advancement of block i using threads 1 to k, but slowed down by a factor of 2 compared to the threaded algorithm for k, except if $k = 1$, when we proceed at the usual rate. Once block i is finished we clear it up using thread $k+1$ operating at the normal rate, while threads 1 to k are advancing through the next block $i+1$. The time taken by thread $k+1$ is $R(i,k)/2 \leq 2^{k-1}n^k$ using Equation (1). The time taken by threads 1 to k on block $i+1$ is

$2.2^{k-2}n^k = 2^{k-1}n^k$ if $k \geq 2$, and $1.2^{k-1}n^k = 2^{k-1}n^k$ if $k = 1$. Hence thread $k+1$ will finish no later than threads 1 to k. The progression factor is 2^{k-1}. Hence result. □

When scheduling onto a single processor we get a progression factor of $k2^{k-2}$, which is not quite as good as the 2^{k-1} offered by Theorem 4.5. However the space usage improves. The method of Theorem 4.6 uses $P''(n,k)$ pebbles where

$$P''(n,1) = P(n,1)$$
$$P''(n,k+1) = P''(n,k) + P(n,k) + n - 2 \qquad (k \geq 1)$$

with solution $P''(n,k) = k(k+1)(n-1)/2 + 1$.

We can obtain a result similar to Theorem 4.6 for the k-ratic algorithm, but the progression factor increases by a multiple of two, due to the blocks being of different sizes, rather than all the same size. We first state a lemma concerning the advancement $A(n,k)$ of the k-ratic algorithm $K(n,k)$.

Lemma 4.7. *For $n \geq 2$ and $k \geq 0$ we have $A(n,k) \leq 2A(n-1,k)$.*

Proof. By induction on k. We easily check the case for $k = 0$. Suppose $A(n,k) \leq 2A(n-1,k)$ for all $n \geq 2$.

$$
\begin{aligned}
A(n,k+1) &= 1 + \sum_{i=1}^{n-1} A(i,k) \\
&= 1 + A(1,k) + \sum_{i=2}^{n-1} A(i,k) \\
&\leq 1 + A(1,k) + \sum_{i=2}^{n-1} 2A(i-1,k) \\
&= 1 + A(1,k) + 2\sum_{i=1}^{n-2} A(i,k) \\
&= 1 + 1 + 2(A(n-1,k+1) - 1) \\
&= 2A(n-1,k+1)
\end{aligned}
$$

□

The ratio of 2 in Lemma 4.7 is the best possible in general, since e.g. $A(1,2) = 1$ and $A(2,2) = 2$.

Remark 4.8. In fact for any $k \geq 0$, $\lim_{n\to\infty} A(n,k)/A(n-1,k) = 1$. To see this note that it is easy to show that $A(n,k) = A(n-1,k) + A(n-1,k-1)$ for any $k \geq 1$, $n \geq 2$. Also by Proposition 3.3 we have $\lim_{n\to\infty} A(n,k-1)/A(n,k) = 0$.

Theorem 4.9. *The k-ratic algorithm $K(n,k)$ can be programmed with k threads with a progression factor of 2^{k-1}.*

Proof. By induction on k. For $k = 1$ we have one thread. The progression factor is clearly $1 = 2^{k-1}$.

Suppose true for k. The threaded algorithm for $k+1$ uses $k+1$ threads. The algorithm divides the work into $n-1$ blocks $1, 2, \ldots, n-1$, where block i has size $A(n-i,k)$. We perform each successive advancement of block i using threads 1 to k, but slowed down by a factor of two compared to the threaded algorithm for k. Once block i is finished we clear it up using thread $k+1$ operating at the normal rate, while threads 1 to k are advancing through the next block $i+1$.

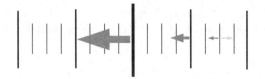

Fig. 3. Multi-threading with $k = 4$

We illustrate this in Figure 3, which shows the way in which different erasure threads (in red) have to operate at increasing rates in order to keep up with forward progression (in green).

The time taken by thread $k + 1$ is $S(i, k)/2 \leq 2^k A(i, k)/2 \leq 2^k A(i - 1, k)$ using Proposition 3.4 and Lemma 4.7. The time taken by threads 1 to k on block $i + 1$ is $2.2^{k-1} A(i - 1, k) = 2^k A(i - 1, k)$. Hence thread $k + 1$ will finish no later than threads 1 to k. The progression factor is $2.2^{k-1} = 2^k$. Hence result.   □

The number of pebbles used by the method of Theorem 4.9 is $k(n - 1) - 1$, compared to n for the original algorithm $K(n, k)$.

5   Conclusions

We have studied real-time reversible simulations of forwards-only computations. As far as we are aware, such simulations have not been studied previously.

The first part of this paper presented a new algorithm for reversible computation called the k-ratic method. The k-ratic method is a technique to reversibly simulate a forward-only computation. Letting T and S be the time and space used by the forwards-only computation, the k-ratic method uses $O(2^k T)$ time and $O(kS \sqrt[k]{T/S})$ space, where k is a constant. It also uses up to a factor of e less space than Bennett's linear-time algorithm. We considered how to pick a suitable value for k, taking into account the trade-off between time and space.

The latter part of the paper introduced the notion of continuous progress. For a program to satisfy the condition of continuous progress it is necessary that a upper bound must exist on the number of steps the simulating program can advance without the advancement of the program being simulated. The paper then explored how Bennett's technique and the k-ratic method can be modified with the help of multi-threading to satisfy the definition of continuous progress.

Two different ways to achieve continuous progress are discussed. The first method uses $O(2^k)$ threads and increases memory usage by a factor of $O(2^k)$. However it is able to achieve an upper bound of one for continuous progress. The second method increases memory usage by a factor of $O(k)$. However it is only able to provide a continuous progress upper bound of $O(2^k)$.

References

1. Bennett, C.: Logical reversibility of computation. IBM Journal of Research and Development **17**, 525–532 (1973)

 2. Bennett, C.: Time/space trade-offs for reversible computation. SIAM Journal on Computing **18**(4), 766–776 (1989)
 3. Buhrman, H., Tromp, J., Vitányi, P.: Time and space bounds for reversible simulation. In: Orejas, F., Spirakis, P.G., van Leeuwen, J. (eds.) ICALP 2001. LNCS, vol. 2076, pp. 1017–1027. Springer, Heidelberg (2001)
 4. Landauer, R.: Irreversibility and heat generation in the computing process. IBM Journal of Research and Development **5**, 183–191 (1961)
 5. Lange, K., McKenzie, P., Tapp, A.: Reversible space equals deterministic space. Journal of Computer and System Sciences **60**(2), 354–367 (2000)
 6. Lecerf, Y.: Machines de Turing réversibles. Récursive insolubilité en $n \in N$ de l'équation $u = \theta^n u$, où θ est un "isomorphisme de codes". Comptes Rendus **257**, 2597–2600 (1963)
 7. Levine, R., Sherman, A.: A note on Bennett's time-space tradeoff for reversible computation. SIAM Journal on Computing **19**(4), 673–677 (1990)
 8. Li, M., Vitányi, P.: Reversibility and adiabatic computation: trading time and space for energy. Proc. Royal Society of London, Series A **452**, 769–789 (1996)
 9. Vitányi, P.: Time, space, and energy in reversible computing. In: Proceedings of the Second Conference on Computing Frontiers, 2005, Ischia, Italy, May 4–6, 2005, pp. 435–444. ACM (2005)
10. Williams, R.: Space-efficient reversible simulations (2000). http://www.stanford.edu/rrwill/spacesim9_22.pdf

Reversible Ordered Restarting Automata

Friedrich Otto[1]([✉]), Matthias Wendlandt[2], and Kent Kwee[1]

[1] Fachbereich Elektrotechnik/Informatik, Universität Kassel,
34109 Kassel, Germany
{otto,kwee}@theory.informatik.uni-kassel.de
[2] Institut für Informatik, Universität Giessen,
Arndtstr. 2, 35392, Giessen, Germany
matthias.wendlandt@informatik.uni-giessen.de

Abstract. Stateless deterministic ordered restarting automata characterize the class of regular languages. Here we introduce a notion of *reversibility* for these automata and show that each regular language is accepted by such a reversible stateless deterministic ordered restarting automaton. We study the descriptional complexity of these automata, showing that they are exponentially more succinct than nondeterministic finite-state acceptors. We also look at the case of unary input alphabets.

Keywords: Restarting automaton · Reversibility · Descriptional complexity

1 Introduction

Reversibility is a property that has been investigated for various types of automata. It means that every configuration has a unique successor configuration and a unique predecessor configuration, that is, the automaton considered is forward and backward deterministic. The main motivation for studying this notion is the observation that information is lost in computations that are not reversible. Each Turing machine can be simulated by a reversible Turing machine [1], which shows that reversible Turing machines are just as expressive as general Turing machines. On the other hand, reversible deterministic finite-state acceptors (DFAs) are strictly less expressive than DFAs [13]. The notion of reversibility has also been studied for other types of automata, e.g., for pushdown automata [5] and for queue automata [6].

Here we introduce a notion of *reversibility* for a rather restricted class of restarting automata, the *stateless deterministic ordered restarting automata*. The restarting automaton was introduced in [4] as a formal device to model the linguistic technique of *analysis by reduction*. Since then many variants and extensions of the basic model have been introduced and studied (for an overview, see, e.g., [11]), and several classical families of formal languages, like the regular languages, the deterministic context-free languages, and the context-free languages, have been characterized by certain types of restarting automata.

© Springer International Publishing Switzerland 2015
J. Krivine and J.-B. Stefani (Eds.): RC 2015, LNCS 9138, pp. 60–75, 2015.
DOI: 10.1007/978-3-319-20860-2_4

The *deterministic ordered restarting automaton* (or *det-ORWW-automaton*) was introduced in [10] in the setting of picture languages. A det-ORWW-automaton has a finite-state control, a tape with end markers that initially contains the input, and a window of size three. Based on its state and the content of its window, the automaton can perform one of three types of operations: it may perform a *move-right step*, it may perform a combined *rewrite/restart step*, or it may perform an *accept step* (see Section 2 for details). The nondeterministic variant of the ordered restarting automaton accepts some languages that are not even context-free, but the deterministic variant accepts exactly the regular languages [10]. In fact, each det-ORWW-automaton can be simulated by a det-ORWW-automaton with only a single state [12]. As for the latter, states are essentially useless, they are called *stateless* det-ORWW-automata, or stl-det-ORWW-automata for short. In [12] the descriptional complexity of stl-det-ORWW-automata is investigated, using the size of the working alphabet as a complexity measure. It is shown that there is a double exponential trade-off when changing from a stl-det-ORWW-automaton to an equivalent DFA. Accordingly, we think that the stl-det-ORWW-automaton is a very interesting type of automaton, as it is a simple deterministic device that, nevertheless, yields succinct representations for the regular languages.

Here we introduce a notion of *reversibiliy* for stl-det-ORWW-automata, and we show that each regular language is accepted by a stl-det-ORWW-automaton that is reversible by presenting a transformation that turns a given stl-det-ORWW-automaton into an equivalent stl-det-ORWW-automaton that is reversible. This construction yields an exponential upper bound for the size increase of this transformation, but unfortunately we do not yet have a matching lower bound. Then we investigate the descriptional complexity of a reversible stl-det-ORWW-automaton in relation to the size of an equivalent DFA or NFA. We recall a simulation of stl-det-ORWW-automata by NFAs from [7], which also applies to stl-det-ORWW-automata that are reversible, and by considering a specific class of example languages we show that the resulting trade-off is indeed exponential. For DFAs, the corresponding trade-off is even double exponential. Finally, we consider the problem of turning a unary NFA into an equivalent stl-det-ORWW-automaton that is reversible. Here we obtain a quadratic size increase, but it remains open whether there is a matching lower bound. The paper closes with a short summary and a list of open problems.

2   Stateless Deterministic Ordered Restarting Automata

A *stl-det-ORWW-automaton* is a one-tape machine that is described by a 6-tuple $M = (\Sigma, \Gamma, \rhd, \lhd, \delta, >)$, where Σ is a finite input alphabet, Γ is a finite tape alphabet such that $\Sigma \subseteq \Gamma$, the symbols $\rhd, \lhd \notin \Gamma$ serve as markers for the left and right border of the work space, respectively,

$$\delta : (((\Gamma \cup \{\rhd\}) \cdot \Gamma \cdot (\Gamma \cup \{\lhd\})) \cup \{\rhd\lhd\}) \dashrightarrow \{\mathsf{MVR}\} \cup \Gamma \cup \{\mathsf{Accept}\}$$

is the (partial) *transition function*, and $>$ is a *partial ordering* on Γ. The transition function describes three different types of transition steps:

(1) A *move-right step* has the form $\delta(a_1a_2a_3) = \mathsf{MVR}$, where $a_1 \in \Gamma \cup \{\rhd\}$ and $a_2, a_3 \in \Gamma$. It causes M to shift the window one position to the right.

(2) A *rewrite/restart step* has the form $\delta(a_1a_2a_3) = b$, where $a_1 \in \Gamma \cup \{\rhd\}$, $a_2, b \in \Gamma$, and $a_3 \in \Gamma \cup \{\lhd\}$ such that $a_2 > b$ holds. It causes M to replace the symbol a_2 in the middle of its window by the symbol b and to restart, that is, the window is repositioned on the left end of the tape.

(3) An *accept step* has the form $\delta(a_1a_2a_3) = \mathsf{Accept}$, where $a_1 \in \Gamma \cup \{\rhd\}$, $a_2 \in \Gamma$, and $a_3 \in \Gamma \cup \{\lhd\}$. It causes M to halt and accept. In addition, we allow an accept step of the form $\delta(\rhd\lhd) = \mathsf{Accept}$.

If $\delta(u)$ is undefined for some u, then M necessarily halts, when it sees u in its window, and we say that M *rejects* in this situation. Further, the letters in $\Gamma \smallsetminus \Sigma$ are called *auxiliary symbols*.

A *configuration* of a stl-det-ORWW-automaton M is a pair of words (α, β), where $|\beta| \geq 3$, and either $\alpha = \lambda$ (the empty word) and $\beta \in \{\rhd\} \cdot \Gamma^+ \cdot \{\lhd\}$ or $\alpha \in \{\rhd\} \cdot \Gamma^*$ and $\beta \in \Gamma \cdot \Gamma^+ \cdot \{\lhd\}$; here $\alpha\beta$ is the current content of the tape, and it is understood that the window contains the first three symbols of β. In addition, we admit the configuration $(\lambda, \rhd\lhd)$. A *restarting configuration* has the form $(\lambda, \rhd w \lhd)$ (usually simply written as $\rhd w \lhd$); if $w \in \Sigma^*$, then $(\lambda, \rhd w \lhd)$ is also called an *initial configuration*. Further, we use Accept to denote an *accepting configuration*, which is a configuration that M reaches by an accept step.

A computation of a stl-det-ORWW-automaton M consists of certain phases. A phase, called a *cycle*, starts in a restarting configuration, the head is moved along the tape by MVR steps until a rewrite/restart step is performed and thus, a new restarting configuration is reached. If no further rewrite operation is performed, any computation necessarily finishes in a halting configuration – such a phase is called a *tail*. By $\vdash_M^c$ we denote the execution of a complete cycle, and $\vdash_M^{c*}$ is the reflexive transitive closure of this relation.

An input $w \in \Sigma^*$ is accepted by M, if the computation of M which starts with the initial configuration $\rhd w \lhd$ ends with an accept step. The language consisting of all words that are accepted by M is denoted by $L(M)$.

Theorem 1. [10,12] $\mathsf{REG} = \mathcal{L}(\mathsf{det\text{-}ORWW}) = \mathcal{L}(\mathsf{stl\text{-}det\text{-}ORWW})$.

3   Reversibility for stl-det-ORWW-Automata

Let $M = (\Sigma, \Gamma, \rhd, \lhd, \delta, >)$ be a stl-det-ORWW-automaton. A combined rewrite/restart step of the form $\delta(abc) = b'$ takes M from a configuration of the form $(\rhd u, abcv\lhd)$ to the restarting configuration $\rhd uab'cv\lhd$. Now it is not at all clear how a *reverse transition function* could be designed that would transform the latter configuration back to the former configuration. Therefore, we consider a different notion of reversibility for our automata, a notion that is more in the spirit of restarting automata.

Definition 2. *A stl-det-ORWW-automaton* $M = (\Sigma, \Gamma, \rhd, \lhd, \delta, >)$ *is called* reversible, *if there exists a* reverse transition function

$$\delta^R : ((\Gamma \cup \{\rhd\}) \cdot \Gamma \cdot (\Gamma \cup \{\lhd\})) \dashrightarrow \{\mathsf{MVR}\} \cup \Gamma$$

such that, for all restarting configurations $\triangleright w \triangleleft$ *and* $\triangleright w' \triangleleft$ *that can occur within computations of* M, $\triangleright w \triangleleft \vdash^c_M \triangleright w' \triangleleft$ *iff* $\triangleright w' \triangleleft \vdash^R_M \triangleright w \triangleleft$. *Here* $\vdash^R_M$ *denotes a cycle that is realized by using the reverse transition function* δ^R. *We describe the above reversible stl-det-ORWW-automaton as* $M = (\Sigma, \Gamma, \triangleright, \triangleleft, \delta, \delta^R, >)$, *and we use the prefix rev- to denote reversible automata.*

Observe that in the definition above, we require that a cycle must be reversible by δ^R only for the case that the corresponding restarting configurations occur in a valid computation of M, that is, there exists an input $x \in \Sigma^*$ such that $\triangleright w \triangleleft$ is reached from the initial configuration $\triangleright x \triangleleft$ of M. This corresponds to the way reversibility is defined for queue automata in [6].

Obviously, rev-stl-det-ORWW-automata can only accept certain regular languages. However, in contrast to the situation for DFAs, they actually accept all regular languages, as we have the following result.

Theorem 3. *For each stl-det-ORWW-automaton* M *working on an alphabet with* n *letters, there exists a rev-stl-det-ORWW-automaton* R *with* $2^{O(n)}$ *letters such that* $L(R) = L(M)$ *holds.*

For deriving this result we need the following normal form result for stl-det-ORWW-automata. Here the *right distance* of a cycle $C : \triangleright uabcv \triangleleft \vdash^c_M \triangleright uab'cv \triangleleft$ of a stl-det-ORWW-automaton M is defined as $D_r(C) = |v|+1$, where $|v|$ denotes the length of the word v. Thus, $D_r(C)$ is the distance from the window to the right end of the tape at the time of rewriting in cycle C.

Definition 4. *A stl-det-ORWW-automaton* $M = (\Sigma, \Gamma, \triangleright, \triangleleft, \delta, >)$ *is said to be in* normal form *if it satisfies the following two conditions:*

1. *In any computation* $(C_0, C_1, C_2, \ldots, C_m)$ *of* M, $|D_r(C_i) - D_r(C_{i-1})| \leq 1$ *holds for all* $i = 1, \ldots, m$.
2. M *only accepts with the right delimiter* $\triangleleft$ *in its window.*

Lemma 5. *For each stl-det-ORWW-automaton* M *working on an alphabet with* n *letters, there exists an equivalent stl-det-ORWW-automaton* $\hat{M}$ *with an alphabet of size at most* $2(n+1)$ *that is in normal form.*

Proof. From M we obtain an equivalent stl-det-ORWW-automaton $M' = (\Sigma, \Gamma, \triangleright, \triangleleft, \delta', >')$ that only accepts with the right delimiter in its window by using one extra symbol, that is, $|\Gamma| = n + 1$ [7]. From M' we construct the stl-det-ORWW-automaton $\hat{M} = (\Sigma, \Delta, \triangleright, \triangleleft, \delta, >)$ as follows:

- $\Delta = \Gamma \cup \{\underline{a} \mid a \in \Gamma\}$, which implies that $|\Delta| = 2 \cdot |\Gamma| = 2(n+1)$;
- $a > \underline{a}$ for all $a \in \Gamma$, and $\underline{a} > b$ for $a, b \in \Gamma$, if $a >' b$ holds;
- the transition function δ is defined as follows, where $a, b, c, d \in \Gamma$:

$$\delta(\triangleright a \triangleleft) = \delta'(\triangleright a \triangleleft) \text{ for } a \in \Gamma \cup \{\lambda\}, \quad \delta(ab\triangleleft) = \delta'(ab\triangleleft),$$

$$\delta(\triangleright ab) = \begin{cases} c, & \text{if } \delta'(\triangleright ab) = c, \\ \underline{a}, & \text{if } \delta'(\triangleright ab) = \text{MVR}, \end{cases} \quad \delta(\underline{a}bc) = \begin{cases} d, & \text{if } \delta'(abc) = d, \\ \underline{b}, & \text{if } \delta'(abc) = \text{MVR}, \end{cases}$$

$$\delta(\triangleright \underline{a}b) = \begin{cases} c, & \text{if } \delta'(\triangleright ab) = c, \\ \text{MVR}, & \text{if } \delta'(\triangleright ab) = \text{MVR}, \end{cases} \quad \delta(\underline{a}\,\underline{b}c) = \begin{cases} d, & \text{if } \delta'(abc) = d, \\ \text{MVR}, & \text{if } \delta'(abc) = \text{MVR}, \end{cases}$$

$$\delta(\triangleright \underline{a}\,\underline{b}) = \text{MVR} \qquad\qquad\qquad\qquad \delta(\underline{a}\,\underline{b}\,\underline{c}) = \text{MVR}.$$

The automaton $\hat{M}$ simulates a computation of M' by proceeding as follows. Assume that on input $x = x_1 \ldots x_m$, M' will perform the cycle

$$(\lambda, \triangleright x \triangleleft) = (\lambda, \triangleright x_1 \ldots x_{i-1} x_i x_{i+1} \ldots x_m \triangleleft) \vdash_M^c (\lambda, \triangleright x_1 \ldots x_{i-1} a x_{i+1} \ldots x_m \triangleleft).$$

Then $\hat{M}$ will first rewrite x_j, $j = 1, \ldots, i-1$, into $\underline{x}_j$, and then it will rewrite x_i into a, producing the restarting configuration $(\lambda, \triangleright \underline{x}_1 \ldots \underline{x}_{i-1} a x_{i+1} \ldots x_m \triangleleft)$. For the next cycle of M', there are three possibilities:

1. M' may rewrite x_{i-1} into a symbol b. Then $\hat{M}$ will rewrite $\underline{x}_{i-1}$ into b.
2. M' may rewrite a into a symbol b. Then so will $\hat{M}$.
3. Finally, M' may rewrite a symbol x_j for some $j \geq i+1$ into a symbol b. Then $\hat{M}$ will replace the symbols $a, x_{i+1}, \ldots, x_{j-1}$ from left to right by the symbols $\underline{a}, \underline{x}_{i+1}, \ldots, \underline{x}_{j-1}$, and then it will rewrite x_j into b.

Thus, in each cycle $\hat{M}$ either rewrites the first symbol from Γ from the left, or it rewrites the last symbol from $\Delta \smallsetminus \Gamma$ from the left. It now follows easily that $\hat{M}$ is in normal form, and that $L(\hat{M}) = L(M') = L(M)$ holds.   □

Now we can give the proof of Theorem 3.

Proof. Let $M = (\Sigma, \Gamma, \triangleright, \triangleleft, \delta_M, >)$ be a stl-det-ORWW-automaton with $n = |\Gamma|$. Without loss of generality we can assume that M only accepts with the right marker $\triangleleft$ in its window. By Lemma 5 we can construct a stl-det-ORWW-automaton $\hat{M} = (\Sigma, \overline{\Gamma}, \triangleright, \triangleleft, \hat{\delta}, >)$ that is equivalent to M and in normal form. Here $\overline{\Gamma} = \Gamma \cup \underline{\Gamma}$, where $\underline{\Gamma} = \{ \underline{a} \mid a \in \Gamma \}$, and hence, $\hat{M}$ has $2n$ letters.

From $\hat{M}$ we construct a rev-stl-det-ORWW-automaton $R = (\Sigma, \Delta, \triangleright, \triangleleft, \delta, \delta^R, >)$ such that $L(R) = L(\hat{M}) = L(M)$ as follows:

- The tape alphabet Δ contains the input alphabet Σ and all triples of the form (L, W, R), where

  - W is a sequence of letters $W = (w_1, \ldots, w_k)$ from $\overline{\Gamma}$ of length $1 \leq k \leq 2n$ such that $w_1 > w_2 > \cdots > w_k$,
  - L is a sequence of positive integers $L = (l_1, \ldots, l_{k-1})$ of length $k-1$ such that $l_1 \leq l_2 \leq \cdots \leq l_{k-1} \leq 2n$, and
  - R is a sequence of positive integers $R = (r_1, \ldots, r_{k-1})$ of length $k-1$ such that $r_1 \leq r_2 \leq \cdots \leq r_{k-1} \leq 2n$.

  As in [7] the idea is that W encodes the sequence of letters that are produced by $\hat{M}$ in an accepting computation for a particular field, and L and R encode the information on the neighbouring letters to the left and to the right that are used to perform the corresponding rewrite operations. For example, the triple $(l_1, w_1, r_1) \in (L, W, R)$ means that w_1 is rewritten into w_2, while the left neighbouring field contains the l_1-th letter of its sequence W', and the right neighbouring field contains the r_1-th letter of its sequence W''. To simplify the discussion below, we simply interpret a symbol $a \in \Sigma \cup \{\triangleright, \triangleleft\}$ as the triple $(L, W, R) = (\emptyset, (a), \emptyset)$.

Further, in order to ensure that triples in neighbouring fields are consistent with each other, the following notion has been introduced in [7]. For two finite non-decreasing sequences of integers $R' = (r'_1, \ldots, r'_k)$ and $L = (\ell_1, \ldots, \ell_s)$, where $k, s \geq 0$, we define a multiset order(R', L) as follows:

$$\text{order}(R', L) = \{\, r'_i + i - 1 \mid i = 1, \ldots, k \,\} \cup \{\, \ell_j + j - 1 \mid j = 1, \ldots, s \,\}.$$

Now a pair of triples $((L', W', R'), (L, W, R))$ is called *consistent*, if order$(R', L) = \{1, 2, \ldots, k+s\}$, that is, it is the integer interval $[1, k+s]$. This notion of consistency will be of importance in the definition of the transition functions below.

– The ordering $>$ on Δ is defined by taking $(L, W, R) > (L', W', R')$, if there exist $b \in \overline{\Gamma}$ and $l, r \in \mathbb{N}$ such that $L' = (L, l)$, $W' = (W, b)$, and $R' = (R, r)$.

– For a triple $(L, W, R) = ((l_1, \ldots, l_{k-1}), (w_1, \ldots, w_k), (r_1, \ldots, r_{k-1}))$, we take $\pi((L, W, R)) = w_k$ and $\|(L, W, R)\| = k$. The transition function δ is defined as follows, where $A, B, C \in \Delta \cup \{\triangleright, \triangleleft\}$ satisfy the condition that the pair (A, B) and the pair (B, C) are both consistent (see above):

$$\delta(ABC) = \begin{cases} \text{MVR}, & \text{if } \hat{\delta}(\pi(A)\pi(B)\pi(C)) = \text{MVR}, \\ \text{Accept}, & \text{if } \hat{\delta}(\pi(A)\pi(B)\pi(C)) = \text{Accept}, \\ ((L, \|A\|), (W, b), (R, \|C\|)), & \text{if } B = (L, W, R) \text{ and} \\ & \quad \hat{\delta}(\pi(A)\pi(B)\pi(C)) = b. \end{cases}$$

Thus, instead of replacing the symbol $\pi(B)$ by the symbol b, as $\hat{M}$ does, the automaton R appends the symbol b to the sequence of symbols W at the corresponding position. In addition, it appends the integers $\|A\|$ and $\|C\|$ to the lists L and R at this position, as these numbers point to the symbols (within the corresponding lists) that are at this moment contained in the neighbouring positions. Observe that $\delta(ABC)$ is undefined, if any of the pairs (A, B) or (B, C) is not consistent.

– Finally, the reverse transition function δ^R is defined as follows, where it is again required that the pairs (A, B) and (B, C) are consistent:

$$\delta^R(ABC) = \begin{cases} (L, W, R), & \text{if } B = ((L, l), (W, b), (R, r)), \ l = \|A\|, \ r = \|C\|, \\ & \quad \text{and } \hat{\delta}(\pi(A)\pi((L, W, R))\pi(C)) = b, \\ \text{MVR}, & \text{if } C \neq \triangleleft \text{ and the above conditions are not met}, \\ \text{undefined}, & \text{if } C = \triangleleft \text{ and the above conditions are not met}. \end{cases}$$

It remains to verify that R accepts the same language as M, and that R is indeed reversible.

Claim 1. $L(R) = L(M)$.

Proof. Let $w \in \Sigma^*$ such that $w \in L(M) = L(\hat{M})$ holds. Assume that $|w| = m \geq 1$. As $w \in L(\hat{M})$, the computation of $\hat{M}$ on input w is accepting, that is, it consists of a sequence of $s \geq 0$ cycles and an accepting tail. If $s = 0$, then $\hat{M}$ simply scans w from left to right, and it accepts on reaching the symbol $\triangleleft$. From the definition of δ it follows that R does exactly the same on input w, that is, $w \in L(R)$ holds in this case. If $s \geq 1$, then the accepting computation of $\hat{M}$ on input w looks as follows:

$$(\lambda, \triangleright w \triangleleft) \vdash^c_{\hat{M}} (\lambda, \triangleright w_1 \triangleleft) \vdash^c_{\hat{M}} \cdots \vdash^c_{\hat{M}} (\lambda, \triangleright w_s \triangleleft) \vdash^*_{\hat{M}} (\triangleright w'_s, bc \triangleleft) \vdash_{\hat{M}} \text{Accept},$$

where $w_1, \ldots, w_s \in \overline{\Gamma}^m$ and $w_s = w'_s bc$ for some letters $b, c \in \overline{\Gamma}$.

Let us look at the first cycle $(\lambda, \triangleright w \triangleleft) \vdash^c_{\hat{M}} (\lambda, \triangleright w_1 \triangleleft)$. It consists of $t_1 \geq 0$ move-right steps and a rewrite/restart step that replaces the symbol at position $t_1 + 1$ of w by a smaller symbol from $\overline{\Gamma}$, that is, $w = w'aw''$ for some $w' \in \Sigma^{t_1}$, $a \in \Sigma$, and $w'' \in \Sigma^{m-t_1-1}$, and $w_1 = w'bw''$ for some $b \in \overline{\Gamma}$ such that $a > b$ holds. From the definition of δ we see that, starting from the configuration $(\lambda, \triangleright w \triangleleft)$, the automaton R will execute the following cycle:

$$(\lambda, \triangleright w \triangleleft) = (\lambda, \triangleright w'aw'' \triangleleft) \vdash^c_R (\lambda, \triangleright w'Bw'' \triangleleft),$$

where $B = ((1), (a, b), (1))$. Thus, after simulating the first cycle the tape of R contains all the information on the tape content of $\hat{M}$ plus the information on the rewrite step that was executed during the first cycle. Observe that for all factors AB occurring on the tape of R during this computation, the corresponding pair (A, B) is trivially consistent.

Inductively it can be shown that R simulates the above computation of $\hat{M}$ cycle by cycle, in each rewrite/restart step not only simulating the corresponding rewrite/restart step of $\hat{M}$, but also encoding information on this very step. Hence, R accepts on input w, too, which shows that $L(M)$ is contained in $L(R)$.

Now assume conversely that $w \in \Sigma^*$ is accepted by R. As $w \in L(R)$, the computation of R on input w is accepting, that is, it consists of a sequence of $s \geq 0$ cycles and an accepting tail. If $s = 0$, then it follows from the definition of δ that R simply scans w from left to right and accepts on reaching the right delimiter $\triangleleft$. However, this means that on input w, $\hat{M}$ does exactly the same, that is, $w \in L(M)$ also holds in this case. Finally, if $s \geq 1$, then the computation of R on input w looks as follows:

$$(\lambda, \triangleright w \triangleleft) \vdash^c_R (\lambda, \triangleright W_1 \triangleleft) \vdash^c_R \cdots \vdash^c_R (\lambda, \triangleright W_s \triangleleft) \vdash^*_R (\triangleright W'_s, BC \triangleleft) \vdash_R \text{Accept},$$

where $W_1, \ldots, W_s \in \Delta^m$ and $W_s = W'_s BC$ for some letters $B, C \in \Delta$. Interpreting π as a morphism from Δ^* to $\overline{\Gamma}^*$, it follows that the computation of $\hat{M}$ on input w looks as follows:

$$(\lambda, \triangleright w \triangleleft) \vdash^c_{\hat{M}} (\lambda, \triangleright \pi(W_1) \triangleleft) \vdash^c_{\hat{M}} \cdots$$
$$\vdash^c_{\hat{M}} (\lambda, \triangleright \pi(W_s) \triangleleft) \vdash^*_{\hat{M}} (\triangleright \pi(W'_s), \pi(B)\pi(C) \triangleleft) \vdash_{\hat{M}} \text{Accept},$$

which means that $w \in L(M)$. Here the consistency of each pair (A, B) that corresponds to a factor AB of the tape contents of R implies that the corresponding steps of $\hat{M}$ are indeed possible. It follows that $L(R) = L(M)$ holds. $\square$

We now complete the proof of Theorem 3 by establishing the following claim.

Claim 2. The stl-det-ORWW-automaton R is reversible.

Proof. Let $w, z \in \Delta^m$ such that $(\lambda, \triangleright w \triangleleft) \vdash^c_R (\lambda, \triangleright z \triangleleft)$ holds. Then $w = uAv$ and $z = uBv$ for some $u \in \Delta^r$, $A, B \in \Delta$, and $v \in \Delta^{m-r-1}$, that is, $u = U_1 \ldots U_r$, $V = V_1 \ldots V_{m-r-1}$ for some $U_1, \ldots, U_r, V_1, \ldots, V_{m-r-1} \in \Delta$, and

$$(\lambda, \triangleright w \triangleleft) \vdash^r_R (\triangleright U_1 \ldots U_{r-1}, U_r A V_1 \ldots V_{m-r-1} \triangleleft)$$
$$\vdash_R (\lambda, \triangleright U_1 \ldots U_r B V_1 \ldots V_{m-r-1} \triangleleft).$$

From the definition of δ we can conclude the following properties:

1. The pairs $(\triangleright, U_1), (U_1, U_2), \ldots, (U_{r-1}, U_r), (U_r, A), (A, V_1)$ are all consistent, as the factors $\triangleright U_1$, $U_1 U_2, \ldots, U_{r-1} U_r, U_r A$, and $A V_1$ are all scanned by R during this cycle.
2. $\delta(\triangleright U_1 U_2) = \delta(U_1 U_2 U_3) = \cdots = \delta(U_{r-1} U_r A) = \mathsf{MVR}$, and so $\mathsf{MVR} = \hat{\delta}(\triangleright \pi(U_1) \pi(U_2)) = \hat{\delta}(\pi(U_1) \pi(U_2) \pi(U_3)) = \cdots = \hat{\delta}(\pi(U_{r-1}) \pi(U_r) \pi(A))$.
3. $\delta(U_r A V_1) = B$, and so $\hat{\delta}(\pi(U_r) \pi(A) \pi(V_1)) = \pi(B)$, where $A = (L, W, R)$ and $B = ((L, \|U_r\|), (W, b), (R, \|V_1\|))$.

It follows immediately that also the pairs (U_r, B) and (B, V_1) are consistent. Now we apply the reverse transition function δ^R starting with the configuration $(\lambda, \triangleright z \triangleleft) = (\lambda, \triangleright U_1 \ldots U_r B V_1 \ldots V_{m-r-1} \triangleleft)$. It looks for the first position from the left where a rewrite can be 'undone.' Obviously, if the factor $U_r B V_1$ is reached, then $B = ((L, \|U_r\|), (W, b), (R, \|V_1\|))$ is rewritten into $A = (L, W, R)$, which yields the cycle

$$(\lambda, \triangleright z \triangleleft) \vdash^{c^R}_R (\triangleright U_1 \ldots U_{r-1}, U_r A V_1 \ldots V_{m-r-1} \triangleleft) = (\lambda, \triangleright w \triangleleft).$$

So we must argue that there is no factor $U_{i-1} U_i U_{i+1}$, $1 \leq i \leq r$, such that δ^R would rewrite the letter U_i. Assume to the contrary that such an index exists, that is, $U_i = ((L', l'), (W', b'), (R', r'))$ such that $\|U_{i-1}\| = l'$, $\|U_{i+1}\| = r'$, and $\hat{\delta}(\pi(U_{i-1}) \pi((L', W', R')) \pi(U_{i+1})) = b'$ for some $i \leq r$. Hence, starting from the configuration $(\lambda, \triangleright \pi(U_1) \ldots \pi(U_{i-1}) \pi((L', W', R')) \pi(U_{i+1}) \ldots \pi(V_{m-r-1}) \triangleleft)$, $\hat{M}$ would rewrite the letter $\pi((L', W', R'))$ into the letter b'. As $\hat{M}$ is in normal form, its next rewrite would occur at position $i - 1$, i, or $i + 1$, which means that R, which simulates $\hat{M}$ step by step, would also perform a rewrite at one of these positions when starting from the configuration $(\lambda, \triangleright w \triangleleft)$. Thus, it follows that $i = r$, that is, we have $U_r = (((L', l'), (W', b'), (R', r')), \|U_{r-1}\| = l'$, and $\|B\| = r'$. However, as the right sequence (R', r') of U_r ends with $r' = \|B\|$, while the left sequence $(L, \|U_r\|)$ of B ends with the number $\|U_r\|$, we see that the pair $((R', r'), (L, \|U_r\|))$ is not consistent, which contradicts our observation above. Thus, when using the reverse transition function δ^R, the above cycle is indeed inverted. $\square$

This completes the proof of Theorem 3. $\square$

Hence, we obtain the following characterization.

Corollary 6. $\mathsf{REG} = \mathcal{L}(\text{rev-stl-det-ORWW})$.

4   Descriptional Complexity

We are interested in the descriptional complexity of rev-stl-det-ORWW-auto-mata and its relation to that of DFAs and NFAs, where we use the number of states as a measure for the size of a DFA or NFA, and we use the number of symbols in its tape alphabet as the complexity measure for a stl-det-ORWW-automaton.

Theorem 7. *For each DFA $A = (Q, \Sigma, q_0, F, \varphi)$, there exists a rev-stl-det-ORWW-automaton $M = (\Sigma, \Gamma, \rhd, \lhd, \delta, \delta^R, >)$ such that $L(M) = L(A)$ and $|\Gamma| = |Q| \cdot (|\Sigma| + 1)$.*

Proof. Let $A = (Q, \Sigma, q_0, F, \varphi)$ be a DFA that accepts a language $L \subseteq \Sigma^*$. We take $\Gamma = \Sigma \cup (Q \times \Sigma)$, define $a > (q, a)$ for all $a \in \Sigma$ and all $q \in Q$, and define the transition functions δ and δ^R as follows, where $a, b, c \in \Sigma$ and $p, q, q' \in Q$:

$$
\begin{array}{llll}
\delta(\rhd\lhd) & = \mathsf{Accept}, \text{ if } \lambda \in L(A), & \delta(\rhd(q,a)b) & = \mathsf{MVR}, \\
\delta(\rhd a \lhd) & = \mathsf{Accept}, \text{ if } a \in L(A), & \delta(\rhd(q,a)(p,b)) & = \mathsf{MVR}, \\
\delta(\rhd ab) & = (q,a), \text{ if } \varphi(q_0,a) = q, & \delta((p,a)(q,b)(q',c)) & = \mathsf{MVR}, \\
\delta((q,a)bc) & = (p,b), \text{ if } \varphi(q,b) = p, & \delta((p,a)(q,b)c) & = \mathsf{MVR}, \\
\delta((q,a)b\lhd) & = (p,b), \text{ if } \varphi(q,b) = p, & \delta((q,a)(p,b)\lhd) & = \mathsf{Accept}, \text{ if } p \in F, \\[2mm]
\delta^R(\rhd(q,a)b) & = a, \quad \text{ if } \varphi(q_0,a) = q, & \delta^R(\rhd(p,a)(q,b)) & = \mathsf{MVR}, \\
\delta^R((p,a)(q,b)c) & = b, \quad \text{ if } \varphi(p,b) = q, & \delta^R((p,a)(q,b)(q',c)) & = \mathsf{MVR}. \\
\delta^R((p,a)(q,b)\lhd) & = b, \quad \text{ if } \varphi(p,b) = q, &&
\end{array}
$$

Thus, given $w = a_1 \ldots a_n$ as input, where $n \geq 2$ and $a_1, \ldots, a_n \in \Sigma$, M rewrites w from left to right into the word $(q_1, a_1) \ldots (q_{n-1}, a_{n-1})(q_n, a_n)$, where $q_i = \varphi(q_0, a_1 \ldots a_i)$, $1 \leq i \leq n$, and this word is then accepted in a tail computation if $q_n \in F$, that is, M accepts on input w iff $\varphi(q_0, a_1 \ldots a_n) = \varphi(\varphi(q_0, a_1 \ldots a_{n-1}), a_n) = \varphi(q_{n-1}, a_n) = q_n \in F$, that is, iff A accepts on input w. Hence, we see that $L(M) = L$ holds.

From the definition of δ^R it follows immediately that by δ^R, a restarting configuration of the form $\rhd(q_1, a_1) \ldots (q_{i-1}, a_{i-1})(q_i, a_i)a_{i+1} \ldots a_n \lhd$ is transformed back into the restarting configuration $\rhd(q_1, a_1) \ldots (q_{i-1}, a_{i-1})a_i a_{i+1} \ldots a_n \lhd$. Thus, M is indeed reversible in the sense of the above definition. $\square$

Hence, each DFA can be simulated by a rev-stl-det-ORWW-automaton of about the same size and, correspondingly, each NFA of size n can therefore be simulated by a rev-stl-det-ORWW-automaton of size $O(2^n)$. Unfortunately, we do not yet have a corresponding lower bound.

Next we turn to the converse transformation. In [7] the following result is shown, which, of course, also holds for stl-det-ORWW-automata that are reversible.

Theorem 8. [7] *For each stl-det-ORWW-automaton M with n letters, there exists an NFA A with $2^{O(n)}$ states such that $L(A) = L(M)$ holds.*

In particular, it follows that, for each (reversible) stl-det-ORWW-automaton M with n letters, there exists an equivalent DFA B with $2^{2^{O(n)}}$ states. We will now prove that these upper size bounds for turning a rev-stl-det-ORWW-automaton into an equivalent NFA (DFA) are sharp (up to the O-notation). For this, we consider a collection of example language B_n $(n \geq 3)$ that are slight variations of languages considered in [14].

Let $\Sigma = \{0, 1, \#, \$\}$. For $n \geq 3$, let B_n be the following regular language:

$$B_n = \{\, v_1 \# v_2 \# \ldots \# v_m \$ u \mid m \geq 1,\, v_1, \ldots, v_m, u \in \{0,1\}^n,\, \exists i : v_i = u \,\}.$$

Using standard techniques the following results can be shown on B_n.

Lemma 9. (a) *Every NFA for B_n has at least 2^n states.*
(b) *Every DFA for B_n has at least 2^{2^n} states.*

Now the following technical result yields the intended lower bounds.

Proposition 10. *The language B_n is accepted by a rev-stl-det-ORWW-automaton that has a tape alphabet of size $O(n)$.*

Proof. It has already been observed in [12] that the language B_n is accepted by a stl-det-ORWW-automaton that only uses $O(n)$ letters, but here we have to show that this also holds for a stl-det-ORWW-automaton that is reversible.

The rev-stl-det-ORWW-automaton $M = (\Sigma, \Gamma, \triangleright, \triangleleft, \delta, >)$ for B_n will work in n phases. Let $w = v_1 \# \ldots \# v_m \$ u$ be given as input, where $m \geq 1$ and $v_1, \ldots, v_m, u \in \{0,1\}^n$, and let $v_j = v_{j,1} \ldots v_{j,n}$, $1 \leq j \leq m$, and let $u = u_1 \ldots u_n$. In phase i, M will shift the information about the letter u_i to the left until this information reaches the letter $v_{1,i}$. While doing so, it compares this letter to the letter $v_{j,i}$ for all $j = 2, \ldots, m$, storing the results of these comparisons by replacing the symbol $v_{j,i}$ by some appropriate auxiliary symbol. Finally, after phase n has been completed, M moves across the current tape content and checks whether there is a syllable v_j all of its letters have been matched successfully. Now we describe the automaton M in some detail.

First we define the tape alphabet Γ as

$$\Gamma = \Sigma \cup \{\, [*, s, a, i, b] \mid 1 \leq i \leq n, a \in \Sigma, b \in \{0,1\}, s \in \{+, -\} \,\} \cup$$
$$\{\, [b, i], [a, i, b], [s, a, i, b] \mid 1 \leq i \leq n, a \in \Sigma, b \in \{0,1\}, s \in \{+, -\} \,\} \cup$$
$$\{\, \underline{[b, i]}, \underline{[a, i, b]}, \underline{[s, a, i, b]} \mid 1 \leq i \leq n-1, a \in \Sigma, b \in \{0,1\}, s \in \{+, -\} \,\},$$

that is, Γ contains $68n - 22 \in O(n)$ letters. Next we define the partial order on Γ as follows, where $a, b_1, b_2, b_3 \in \{0,1\}$ and $s \in \{+, -\}$:

$$a > [a, i] > [a, i, b_1] > [s, a, i, b_2] > [*, s, a, i, b_3] \text{ for all } 1 \leq i \leq n,$$
$$[\$, i, b_1] > \underline{[\$, i, b_1]} > [\$, i+1, b_2] \text{ for all } 1 \leq i \leq n-1,$$
$$[\#, i, b_1] > \underline{[\#, i, b_1]} > [\#, i+1, b_2] \text{ for all } 1 \leq i \leq n-1,$$
$$[s, a, i, b_1] > [a, i] > [a, i, b_1] > [s, a, i, b_2] > [a, i+1, b_3] \text{ for all } 1 \leq i \leq n-1.$$

Finally, we define the transition functions δ and δ^R, dividing this description into n phases as mentioned above.

1. M moves its read/write window to the letter u_1, rewrites u_1 into $[u_1, 1]$, and moves the information on u_1 to the left. Here the following transitions are used, where $a_1, a_2, a_3, b \in \{0, 1\}$ and $s \in \{+, -\}$:

$$\delta(\triangleright a_1 a_2) = \mathsf{MVR}, \qquad \delta(a_1 a_2[\$, 1, b]) = [a_2, 1, b],$$
$$\delta(a_1 a_2 a_3) = \mathsf{MVR}, \qquad \delta(a_1 a_2[a_3, 1, b]) = [a_2, 1, b],$$
$$\delta(a_1 a_2 \#) = \mathsf{MVR}, \qquad \delta(\# a_1[a_2, 1, b]) = [+, a_1, 1, b], \quad \text{if } a_1 = b,$$
$$\delta(a_1 \# a_2) = \mathsf{MVR}, \qquad \delta(\# a_1[a_2, 1, b]) = [-, a_1, 1, b], \quad \text{if } a_1 \neq b,$$
$$\delta(\# a_1 a_2) = \mathsf{MVR}, \quad \delta(a_1 \#[s, a_2, 1, b]) = [\#, 1, b],$$
$$\delta(a_1 a_2 \$) = \mathsf{MVR}, \qquad \delta(a_1 a_2[\#, 1, b]) = [a_2, 1, b],$$
$$\delta(a_1 \$ a_2) = \mathsf{MVR}, \qquad \delta(\triangleright a_1[a_2, 1, b]) = [*, +, a_1, 1, b], \text{ if } a_1 = b,$$
$$\delta(\$ b a_2) = [b, 1], \qquad \delta(\triangleright a_1[a_2, 1, b]) = [*, -, a_1, 1, b], \text{ if } a_1 \neq b.$$
$$\delta(a_1 \$[b, 1]) = [\$, 1, b],$$

It is easily seen that these steps can be reversed by defining the reverse transition function δ^R accordingly.

2. In the following $n-1$ phases M does the same with the remaining letters of u. In each of these phases M first marks all letters previously rewritten by an underline until it reaches the next symbol of u. Here we skip the transitions for these rewrite steps, continuing with those transitions that are used when u_i is encountered. Here $a_1, a_2, a_3, b, b_1 \in \{0, 1\}$ and $s_1, s_2 \in \{+, -\}$:

$$\delta([\underline{a_1, i-1}]ba_2) = [b, i] \qquad\qquad \text{for } 2 \leq i \leq n-1,$$
$$\delta([\underline{a_1, n-1}]b\triangleleft) = [b, n],$$
$$\delta([\$, 1, \underline{b_1}][\underline{b_1, 1}][\overline{b}, 2]) = [b_1, 2, b],$$
$$\delta([\underline{a_1, i-1, b_1}][\underline{b_1, i-1}][\overline{b}, i]) = [b_1, i, b] \qquad \text{for } 3 \leq i \leq n,$$
$$\delta([\underline{a_1, i-1, b_1}][\$, i-1, b_1][a_2, i, b]) = [\$, i, b] \qquad \text{for } 2 \leq i \leq n,$$
$$\delta([\$, i-1, b_1][\underline{a_1, i-1, b_1}][a_2, i, b]) = [a_1, i, b] \qquad \text{for } 3 \leq i \leq n,$$
$$\delta([\underline{a_1, i-1, b_1}][a_2, i-1, b_1][a_3, i, b]) = [a_2, i, b] \qquad \text{for } 2 \leq i \leq n,$$
$$\delta([\underline{a_1, i-1, b_1}][a_2, i-1, b_1][\$, i, b]) = [a_2, i, b] \qquad \text{for } 2 \leq i \leq n,$$
$$\delta([+, a_1, i-1, b_1][b, i-1, b_1][a_3, i, b]) = [+, b, i, b] \qquad \text{for } 2 \leq i \leq n,$$
$$\delta([+, a_1, i-1, b_1][a_2, i-1, b_1][a_3, i, b]) = [-, a_2, i, b] \qquad \text{for } 2 \leq i \leq n$$
$$\qquad\qquad\qquad\qquad\qquad\qquad\qquad\qquad\qquad\qquad \text{and } a_2 \neq b,$$
$$\delta([-, a_1, i-1, b_1][a_2, i-1, b_1][a_3, i, b]) = [-, a_2, i, b] \qquad \text{for } 2 \leq i \leq n,$$
$$\delta([\#, i-1, b_1][s_1, a_2, i-1, b_1][s_2, a_3, i, b]) = [s_1, a_2, i, b] \quad \text{for } 2 \leq i \leq n,$$
$$\delta([\underline{a_1, i-1, b_1}][\#, i-1, b_1][s_1, a_2, i, b]) = [\#, i, b] \qquad \text{for } 2 \leq i \leq n,$$
$$\delta([\underline{a_1, i-1, b_1}][a_2, i-1, b_1][\#, i, b]) = [a_2, i, b] \qquad \text{for } 2 \leq i \leq n-1,$$
$$\delta([+, a_1, n-1, b_1][b, n-1, b_1][\#, n, b]) = [+, b, n, b],$$
$$\delta([+, a_1, n-1, b_1][a_2, n-1, b_1][\#, n, b]) = [-, a_2, n, b] \quad \text{for } a_2 \neq b,$$
$$\delta([-, a_1, n-1, b_1][a_2, n-1, b_1][\#, n, b]) = [-, a_2, n, b],$$
$$\delta([s_1, a_1, i-1, b_1][s_2, a_2, i-1, b_1][s_3, a_3, i, b]) = [s_2, a_2, i, b] \quad \text{for } 3 \leq i \leq n,$$
$$\delta([*, +, a_1, n-1, b_1][b, n-1, b_1][\#, n, b]) = [*, +, b, n, b],$$
$$\delta([*, +, a_1, n-1, b_1][a_2, n-1, b_1][\#, n, b]) = [*, -, a_2, n, b] \text{ for } a_2 \neq b,$$
$$\delta([*, -, a_1, n-1, b_1][a_2, n-1, b_1][\#, n, b]) = [*, -, a_2, n, b],$$
$$\delta([*, +, a_1, i-1, b_1][b, i-1, b_1][a_2, i, b]) = [*, +, b, i, b] \quad \text{for } 2 \leq i \leq n-1,$$
$$\delta([*, +, a_1, i-1, b_1][a_2, i-1, b_1][a_2, i, b]) = [*, -, a_2, i, b] \quad \text{for } 2 \leq i \leq n-1$$
$$\qquad\qquad\qquad\qquad\qquad\qquad\qquad\qquad\qquad\qquad \text{and } a_2 \neq b,$$
$$\delta([*, -, a_1, i-1, b_1][a_2, i-1, b_1][a_2, i, b]) = [*, -, a_2, i, b] \quad \text{for } 2 \leq i \leq n-1.$$

From the information stored within the letters that are used to replace the letters $v_{1,1}$ to $v_{1,n}$ it is easily seen that also these transitions can be reversed by defining δ^R accordingly.

3. Finally M checks whether the final tape contents contains a factor of the form $[*, +, a_1, n, b][*, +, a_2, n, b][\#, n, b]$, $[+, a_1, n, b][+, a_2, n, b][\#, n, b]$, $[*, +, a_1, n, b][*, +, a_2, n, b][\$, n, b]$, or $[+, a_1, n, b][+, a_2, n, b][\$, n, b]$, and it accepts in the affirmative.

It remains to argue that $L(M) = B_n$ holds. From the construction it is rather straightforward to see that M accepts all words from the language B_n. Hence, it remains to show that M does not accept any other words.

So let $w \in \Sigma^*$ be a given input word that M accepts. We must show that w meets all of the following properties:

(a) $w = v_1 \# v_2 \# \ldots \# v_m \$ u$, where $m \geq 1$ and $v_1, \ldots, v_m, u \in \{0, 1\}^*$.
(b) $|u| = n$.
(c) $|v_1| = \ldots = |v_m| = n$.
(d) There exists an index $i \in \{1, \ldots, m\}$ such that $v_i = u$ holds.

In each phase i, the rewriting process is initialised by rewriting the letter u_i into the symbol $[u_i, i]$. The symbol $[u_1, 1]$ can only be rewritten if it is immediately to the right of the symbol $\$$, and, for $2 \leq i \leq n$, the symbol $[u_i, i]$ is produced only immediately to the right to a symbol $[u_{i-1}, i - 1]$. Finally, $[u_n, n]$ can only be written immediately to the left of the symbol $\lhd$. This ensures property (b). In addition, the MVR steps of the initial phase make sure that (a) holds. The rules for the comparison mark exactly one letter of v_i in each phase, which ensures property (c), and the final scan only accepts if there is a syllable v_i that coincides with u, which proves (d). Thus, $L(M) = B_n$ follows.   □

Together with Theorem 8 these results show the following.

Corollary 11. (a) *There is an exponential trade-off for turning a rev-stl-det-ORWW-automaton into an equivalent NFA.*
(b) *There is a double exponential trade-off for turning a rev-stl-det-ORWW-automaton into an equivalent DFA.*

5   Unary Languages

From Theorem 7 we know that a DFA with n states and an input alphabet of size m can be converted into an equivalent rev-stl-det-ORWW-automaton that has an alphabet of size $n \cdot (m + 1)$. For an NFA with n states, we thus obtain an equivalent rev-stl-det-ORWW-automaton with an alphabet of size $2^n \cdot (m + 1)$. Here we prove that in the unary case, that is, if $m = 1$, we can do better.

Theorem 12. *From an NFA A with n states that accepts a unary language $L(A)$, an equivalent rev-stl-det-ORWW-automaton M with an alphabet of size $O(n^2)$ can be constructed.*

Proof. In [2] it is shown that each NFA with n states can be converted into an equivalent NFA with $O(n^2)$ states that is in *Chrobak normalform*, which means that the latter NFA consists of a chain of states of length at most n^2 which leads to a finite number of disjoint loops that have altogether at most n states.

So from A we first construct an NFA $B = (S, \{a\}, s_0, F, \delta_B)$ in Chrobak normalform, where $S = C \cup P$. Here $C = \{s_0, c_1, \ldots, c_k\}$ is a chain of length $k \leq n^2$ and $P = \bigcup_{i=1}^{l} P_i$, where, for $i = 1, \ldots, l$, $P_i = \{(0, p_i), (1, p_i), \ldots, (p_i - 1, p_i)\}$ is a loop of length p_i such that $\sum_{i=1}^{l} p_i \leq n$.

The tape alphabet of the rev-stl-det-ORWW-automaton $M = (\{a\}, \Gamma, \triangleright, \triangleleft, \delta, \delta^R, >)$ is

$$\Gamma = \{a\} \cup C \cup (P \times \{<, >\}) \cup (P \times \{0, 1, \ldots, l - 1\}),$$

where the components $\{<, >\}$ are used to locate the cell where the last rewrite operation has been performed. We see that Γ contains $O(n^2)$ letters.

M works as follows. As long as B is still within the chain C, M processes the input letter by letter from left to right by replacing each letter a by the state which B reaches by reading the current input symbol:

$$\delta(\triangleright aa) = c_1 \text{ and } \delta(c_i aa) = c_{i+1} \text{ for } 1 \leq i \leq k - 1.$$

After each restart M has to find the next a. In addition, M must accept if it reaches the right end in a final state:

$$\begin{aligned}
\delta(\triangleright c_1 a) &= \mathsf{MVR}, \\
\delta(\triangleright c_1 c_2) &= \mathsf{MVR}, \\
\delta(c_i c_{i+1} c_{i+2}) &= \mathsf{MVR} \quad \text{for } 1 \leq i \leq k - 2, \\
\delta(c_i c_{i+1} a) &= \mathsf{MVR} \quad \text{for } 1 \leq i \leq k - 1, \\
\delta(c_i c_{i+1} \triangleleft) &= \mathsf{Accept}, \text{ if } c_{i+1} \in F.
\end{aligned}$$

Clearly this part is reversible.

If the length of the input a^m exceeds the length k of the chain C, M simulates the computations of B for all loops P_i, $1 \leq i \leq l$, simultaneously. For that l subsequent symbols $(i_l, p_l, z_l), (i_{l-1}, p_{l-1}, z_{l-1}), \ldots, (i_1, p_1, z_1)$, where $z_l, \ldots, z_1 \in \{<, >\}$, are used to represent the states within the different loops that B could be in. So for an input a^{k+l+r}, M will reach the tape content

$$\triangleright c_1 \cdots c_k (i_l, p_l, z_l)(i_{l-1}, p_{l-1}, z_{l-1}) \cdots (i_1, p_1, z_1) a^r \triangleleft$$

after $k + l$ cycles. This is interpreted as follows: B is in the state (i_1, p_1) after reading a^{k+l} and using the first loop P_1, it is in state (i_{l-1}, p_{l-1}) after reading a^{k+2} and using the loop P_{l-1}, and it is in state (i_l, p_l) after reading a^{k+1} and using the loop P_l. So the different possible ways B can use are tried sequentially by M. The computation continues by shifting the information on the various loops to the right step by step, beginning with the state of loop P_1. Here the third components $z_j \in \{<, >\}$ are used to indicate the position at which the next rewrite must be performed. After processing another factor a^j, the tape contains the prefix $\triangleright c_1 \cdots c_k$, which is followed by the factor

$$(i_{l,0}, p_l, z_{l,0})(i_{l,1}, p_l, z_{l,1}) \cdots (i_{l,j}, p_l, z_{l,j})(i_{l-1,j}, p_{l-1}, z_{l-1,j}) \cdots (i_{1,j}, p_1, z_{1,j}),$$

which is followed by the suffix $a \cdots a \triangleleft$. The corresponding transitions are defined as follows:

$$\delta((i, p_j, >)(i', p_{j'}, >)a) = \mathsf{MVR},$$
$$\delta((i, p_j, >)(i', p_{j'}, >)(i'', p_{j''}, >)) = \mathsf{MVR},$$
$$\delta((i, p_j, >)(i', p_{j'}, >)(i'', p_{j''}, <)) = \mathsf{MVR}, \text{ if } p_{j'} \neq p_{j''},$$
$$\delta((i, p_j, >)(i', p_{j'}, <)(i'', p_{j''}, <)) = (i', p_{j'}, >),$$
$$\delta((i, p_j, >)(i', p_{j'}, >)(i'', p_{j''}, <)) = (i+1 \bmod p_j, p_j, <), \text{ if } p_{j'} = p_{j''} \text{ and } i' < l,$$
$$\delta((i, p_j, >)(i', p_{j'}, >)(i'', p_{j''}, <)) = \mathsf{MVR}, \text{ if } p_{j'} = p_{j''} \text{ and } i' = l,$$
$$\delta((i, p_1, >)aa) = (i+1 \bmod p_1, p_1, <).$$

In the above situation there are two possibilities for further rewrite steps. If, for each letter $t = (i, p_j, z)$ it holds that $z = >$, then the previous rewrite just took place at the rightmost of these symbols, and the next rewrite operation has to rewrite the first of the remaining letters a.

The other possibility is that there is exactly one position on the tape where the components $>$ and $<$ are side by side, that is, there is a factor of the form $t_0 t_1$, where $t_0 = (i, p_j, >)$ and $t_1 = (i', p'_j, <)$. Then the next rewrite operation either rewrites t_0 or t_1. If $p_j = p'_j$ and $j < l$, then M is in the process of shifting the current cycle simulations one step to the right, and accordingly, the next rewrite operation is applied to t_0. Otherwise, M starts a new shifting process and so, it must find the right end. Accordingly, the next rewrite operation is applied to t_1. Together with the fact that the previous inscription can be restored from the information in the left and right neigbouring letters this ensures the property of working reversibly. Of course, there must be special transitions for moving from the chain states to the loop states of B, and also the special case of an empty chain must be taken care of.

Finally, when the rewrites of M reach the right end of the tape, then it must be checked whether at least one of these cycles accepts. For this, M sends a signal to the left that tests, for one loop after another, whether it would lead to acceptance at the right end of the input:

$$\delta((i, p_2, >)(i', p_1, >)\triangleleft) = \mathsf{Accept}, \qquad \text{if } (i', p_1) \in F,$$
$$\delta((i, p_2, >)(i', p_1, >)\triangleleft) = (i', p_1, 0), \qquad \text{if } (i', p_1) \notin F,$$
$$\delta(s(i, p_j, >)(i', p_{j'}, r)) = \mathsf{Accept}, \qquad \text{if } (i' + r \bmod p_{j'}, p_{j'}) \in F,$$
$$\delta(s(i, p_j, >)(i', p_{j'}, r)) = (i, p_j, r+1), \text{ if } (i' + r \bmod p_{j'}, p_{j'}) \notin F,$$

where $1 \leq j \leq l$, and $s \in (P \times \{>, <\}) \cup C \cup \{\triangleright\}$.

Again this part is reversible, since the letter (i, p_j, r), where the last rewrite step has been executes, is the first one with a number r. If the input is not in $L(M)$, then none of these tests is successful. It follows that $L(M) = L(B) = L(A)$ holds. □

The main idea of the construction in the proof of Theorem 12 can be also used to get an exponential lower bound for the conversion of a rev-stl-det-ORWW-automaton into a DFA or an NFA. In [2] the simulation costs between DFAs and NFAs and two-way DFAs (2DFAs) are investigated. In many cases an upper bound for the simulation costs is given by the Landau function [8,9]

$$F(n) = \max\{\,\mathrm{lcm}(p_1, p_2 \ldots, p_l) \mid p_1, p_2, \ldots, p_l \geq 1 \text{ and } p_1 + p_2 + \cdots + p_l = n\,\},$$

where lcm denotes the least common multiple. The best known approximation for F is shown in [15]. Bounds derived from this result [3] are

$$F(n) \in \Omega\left(e^{\sqrt{n \cdot \ln(n)}}\right) \text{ and } F(n) \in O\left(e^{\sqrt{n \cdot \ln(n)}(1+o(1))}\right).$$

It can be concluded from the results of [2] that a DFA as well as an NFA needs at least $F(n)$ states for accepting the language $L_n = \{\,a^m \mid m \bmod p_i \equiv 0 \text{ for all } 1 \leq i \leq l\,\}$, where the p_i are chosen such that $p_1, p_2, \ldots, p_l \geq 2$, $p_1 + p_2 + \cdots + p_l \leq n$, and $\mathrm{lcm}(p_1, p_2, \ldots, p_l) = F(n)$.

We now modify the behavior of M from the proof of Theorem 12 so that it accepts L with $O(n)$ symbols. Again M simulates the computation of all loops $P_1, P_2, \ldots, P_l$. It works in the same way as above until the signal of p_1 reaches the right end, but then the modified M checks whether *all* of the l possible loops fit the input. This can be achieved easily by a modification of the accepting transitions. Thus, we have the following lower bound result.

Corollary 13. *For each $n \in \mathbb{N}$, there is a rev-stl-det-ORWW-automaton with $O(n)$ tape symbols that accepts a unary language L such that any DFA or NFA for L needs at least $F(n)$ states.*

6   Conclusion and Open Problems

We have introduced a type of *reversible* stl-det-ORWW-automaton and shown that it characterizes the regular languages. We have studied its descriptional complexity by taking the size of the tape alphabet as the complexity measure for such an automaton, and we have established an exponential (double exponential) trade-off for turning a rev-set-det-ORWW-automaton into an equivalent NFA (DFA). For the converse transformation we have an exponential upper bound in the case of NFAs, and we have presented a transformation that turns any stl-det-ORWW-automaton into an equivalent rev-stl-det-ORWW-automaton at the cost of an exponential increase in size. However, the following questions are still open:

1. What is the trade-off for turning a stl-det-ORWW-automaton into an equivalent stl-det-ORWW-automaton that is reversible? In Theorem 3 an exponential upper bound is given. Can this bound be improved, or is there a matching lower bound?

2. What is the trade-off for turning an NFA into an equivalent rev-stl-det-ORWW-automaton? Based on Theorem 7 we have an exponential upper bound. Can this bound be improved, or is there a matching lower bound?
3. In the unary case we have a quadratic trade-off for turning an NFA into an equivalent rev-stl-det-ORWW-automaton (Theorem 12). Is there a matching lower bound?

References

1. Bennett, C.H.: Logical reversibiliy of computation. IBM J. Res. Dev. **17**, 525–532 (1973)
2. Chrobak, M.: Finite automata and unary languages. Theoretical Computer Science **47**, 149–158 (1986)
3. Ellul, K.: Descriptional complexity measures of regular languages. Master's thesis, University of Waterloo (2004)
4. Jančar, P., Mráz, F., Plátek, M., Vogel, J.: Restarting automata. In: Reichel, H. (ed.) FCT 1995. LNCS, vol. 965, pp. 283–292. Springer, Heidelberg (1995)
5. Kutrib, M., Malcher, A.: Reversible pushdown automata. J. Comput. System Sci. **78**, 1814–1827 (2012)
6. Kutrib, M., Malcher, A., Wendlandt, M.: Reversible queue automata. In: Bensch, S., Freund, R., Otto, F., (eds.) Proc. Sixth Workshop on Non-Classical Models of Automata and Applications (NCMA 2014), books@ocg.at, Band 304, pp. 163–178. Oesterreichische Computer Gesellschaft, Wien (2014)
7. Kwee, K., Otto, F.: On some decision problems for stateless deterministic ordered restarting automata. In: Shallit, J., Okhotin, A. (eds.) DCFS 2015. LNCS, vol. 9118, pp. 165–176. Springer, Heidelberg (2015)
8. Landau, E.: Über die Maximalordnung der Permutationen gegebenen Grades. Archiv. der Math. und Phys. **3**, 92–103 (1903)
9. Landau, E.: Handbuch von der Lehre der Verteilung der Primzahlen, vol. I. Teubner, Leipzig (1909)
10. Mráz, F., Otto, F.: Ordered restarting automata for picture languages. In: Geffert, V., Preneel, B., Rovan, B., Štuller, J., Tjoa, A.M. (eds.) SOFSEM 2014. LNCS, vol. 8327, pp. 431–442. Springer, Heidelberg (2014)
11. Otto, F.: Restarting automata. In: Ésik, Z., Martín-Vide, C., Mitrana, V. (eds.) Recent Advances in Formal Languages and Applications. Studies in Computational Intelligence, vol. 25, pp. 269–303. Springer, Heidelberg (2006)
12. Otto, F.: On the descriptional complexity of deterministic ordered restarting automata. In: Jürgensen, H., Karhumäki, J., Okhotin, A. (eds.) DCFS 2014. LNCS, vol. 8614, pp. 318–329. Springer, Heidelberg (2014)
13. Pin, J.-E.: On reversible automata. In: Simon, I. (ed.) LATIN 1992. LNCS, vol. 583, pp. 401–416. Springer, Heidelberg (1992)
14. Průša, D.: Weight-reducing Hennie machines and their descriptional complexity. In: Dediu, A.-H., Martín-Vide, C., Sierra-Rodríguez, J.-L., Truthe, B. (eds.) LATA 2014. LNCS, vol. 8370, pp. 553–564. Springer, Heidelberg (2014)
15. Szalay, M.: On the maximal order in S_n and S_n^*. Acta Arithmetica **37**, 321–331 (1980)

Reversible Languages

Garbage Collection for Reversible Functional Languages

Torben Ægidius Mogensen$^{(\boxtimes)}$

DIKU, University of Copenhagen, Universitetsparken 5,
DK-2100 Copenhagen O, Denmark
torbenm@diku.dk

Abstract. Reversible languages are programming languages where all programs can run both forwards and backwards. Reversible functional languages have been proposed that use symmetric pattern matching and data construction. To be reversible, these languages require linearity: Every variable must be used exactly once, so no references are copied and all references are followed exactly once. Copying of values must use deep copying. Similarly, equality testing requires deep comparison of trees.

A previous paper describes reversible treatment of reference counts, which allows sharing of structures without deep copying, but there are limitations. Applying a constructor to arguments creates a new node with reference count 1, so pattern matching is by symmetry restricted to nodes with reference count 1. A variant pattern that does not change the reference count of the root node is introduced to allow manipulation of shared data. Having two distinct patterns for shared and unshared data, however, adds a burden on the programmer.

We observe that we can allow pattern matching on nodes with arbitrary reference count if we also allow constructor application to return nodes with arbitrary reference counts. We do this by using maximal sharing: If a newly constructed node is identical to an already existing node, we return a pointer to the existing node (increasing its reference count) instead of allocating a new node with reference count 1.

To avoid searching the entire heap for an identical node, we use hash-consing to restrict the search to a small segment of the heap. We estimate how large this segment needs to be to give a very low probability of allocation failure when the heap is less than half full. Experimentally, we find that overlapping segments gives dramatically better results than disjoint segments.

1 Introduction

A reversible first-order functional language RFUN [16] has been suggested. Steps towards an implementation were made by first implementing a simple heap manager [1] and later [6], a full translation of RFUN to reversible machine language was made. This translation uses linearity and deep copying, so all heap nodes have exactly one reference. Other reversible functional languages that rely on linearity include Theseus [7] and Ψ-Lisp [2].

© Springer International Publishing Switzerland 2015
J. Krivine and J.-B. Stefani (Eds.): RC 2015, LNCS 9138, pp. 79–94, 2015.
DOI: 10.1007/978-3-319-20860-2_5

By extending Axelsen's heap manager [1], a previous paper [12] studied reversible treatment of reference counts, which allows copying of values by pointer sharing. This did, however, not constitute true garbage collection, as the functional language used in this paper required explicit distinction of shared and unshared nodes, so unshared nodes are explicitly deallocated at pattern matching and shared nodes are explicitly preserved at pattern matching, using two different forms of pattern for constructor nodes with one or several references.

In this paper, we will implement a heap manager that does true garbage collection, so high-level languages using this manager do not have to distinguish between shared and unshared nodes and nodes are automatically collected once the last reference is used. In order to make construction and deconstruction symmetric we must, however, make construction use maximal sharing: If a node identical to the node being built exists anywhere in the heap, no new node is built. Instead, a new pointer to the existing node is returned and its reference count is increased. Conversely, deconstructing (by pattern matching) a shared node removes a pointer to the node and deconstructing an unshared node deallocates it. To make searching for existing identical nodes efficient, we will employ hash-consing [4,5], which limits the search space to a small segment of the heap. We estimate how large this segment must be to make the probability of allocation failure very small if the heap is less than half full. We find that a segment that can contain four to eight nodes suffice for a 32-bit address space.

We implement heap operations including a node construction/deconstruction procedure in a low-level reversible intermediate language RIL.

2   The Reversible Intermediate Language RIL

We define a reversible low-level language RIL, similar to a language of the same name in [13]. RIL is inspired by Janus [10], using unstructured jumps in the style of the Janus variant described in [11]. We use RIL instead of Janus because it is closer to a machine language but not specific to any particular machine architecture. RIL can be considered as a reversible alternative to three-address code and is mainly a vehicle for presenting code in a machine-independent form. Its design is in itself not a significant contribution.

A RIL program consists of an unordered set of basic blocks, each consisting of an entry point followed by either updates and exchanges or a subroutine call and is terminated by an exit point. We will describe each of these below.

RIL uses 32-bit words using two's complement number representation. Addresses are to 8-bit bytes, but will be truncated to the nearest 32-bit boundary at memory transfers. We will use an unbounded number of named variables to represent registers, relying on register allocation to map these to a finite set of numbered registers.

2.1   Entry and Exit Points

An entry point has one of the forms

$l \leftarrow$	where l is a label,
$l_1; l_2 \leftarrow c$	where c is a condition and l_1 and l_2 are labels, or
begin l	where l is a label.

An exit point has one of the forms:

$\rightarrow l$	where l is a label,
$c \rightarrow l_1; l_2$	where c is a condition and l_1 and l_2 are labels, or
end l	where l is a label.

Each label in the program must occur in exactly one entry point and exactly one exit point. Furthermore, a label that occurs in a **begin** entry point must also occur in an **end** exit point.

Conditions are of the form $L \bowtie R$, where a left-value L is either a named variable x or of the form $M[x]$, representing the memory location pointed to by a variable x. A right-value R is either a left-value or a signed constant in the range -2^{31} to $2^{31} - 1$, and $\bowtie$ is an operator from the set ==, <, >, !=, <=, >= and &, using notation from the programming language C. We use 0 to represent false and any non-zero value to represent true, so the condition $L \& R$ is true if the result of the bitwise AND is non-zero.

begin and **end** represent beginnings and ends of subroutines. The start and end of the entire program are entry and exit points with the label **main**. An exit point of the form $\rightarrow l$ constitutes an unconditional jump to the (unique) entry point where l occurs. An exit point of the form $c \rightarrow l_1; l_2$ constitutes a conditional jump: If c is true, the jump goes to l_1, otherwise to l_2. An entry point of the form $l \leftarrow$ unconditionally accepts incoming jumps. An entry point of the form $l_1; l_2 \leftarrow c$ conditionally accepts incoming jumps: Jumps to l_1 are accepted if c is true and jumps to l_2 are accepted if c is false. If the incoming jump is not accepted, a run-time error occurs.

2.2   Updates and Exchanges

A basic block can hold a (possibly empty) sequence of updates and exchanges.

An update is of the form $L \oplus= R_1 \odot R_2$, where L is a left-value, R_1 and R_2 are right-values and $\oplus=$ is one of the update assignments +=, -= or ^= with the same semantics as in the programming language C. $\odot$ is an infix arithmetic operation that can be either +, -, ^, &, |, >>, or <<, again with the same semantics as in C. Specifically, & and | are bitwise AND/OR and >> and << are bitwise shifts.

An exchange is of the form $L_1 \leftrightarrow L_2$, where L_1 and L_2 are left-values. The effect is that the values in the two specified locations are swapped.

In order to ensure reversibility, the following restrictions apply to updates and exchanges:

- In an update of the form $L \oplus= R_1 \odot R_2$, the same named variable can not occur both to the left and to the right of the update operator $\oplus=$.

- In an update of the form $L \oplus= R_1 \odot R_2$, memory accesses (left-values of the form $M[x]$) can not be used on both sides of the update operator $\oplus=$.
- In an exchange of the form $L_1 \leftrightarrow L_2$, the same named variable can not occur both to the left and to the right of the exchange operator $\leftrightarrow$.

2.3   Subroutine Calls

Instead of exchanges and updates, a basic block can hold a single subroutine call. A subroutine call is done using the instructions `call` l and `uncall` l. There can be several calls to the same subroutine. We use an implicit stack to store return information.

A subroutine call must be in a basic block of the form $l_1 \leftarrow$ `call` $l \rightarrow l_2$ or $l_1 \leftarrow$ `uncall` $l \rightarrow l_2$.

In such a block, `call` l stores l_2 on the implicit stack and jumps to the entry point `begin` l until it reaches `end` l, at which point it pops the stack and jumps to the label l_2 that is stored on the top of the stack.

RIL (like Janus) also supports running subroutines backwards: `uncall` l stores l_2 on the implicit stack, and then runs the subroutine l backwards, starting from the exit point `end` l and ending with `begin` l, again returning via the stack to l_2.

2.4   Formal Semantics

Figure 1 shows a formal semantics for execution of RIL as rules for state transitions. A state consists of the program P (which never changes), an environment ρ, that maps named variables to integers, a memory store σ, that maps word-aligned addresses to integers, a stack S that stores return labels, and the current label l. A transition of the form $P \ \rho \ \sigma \ S \ l \rightleftharpoons P \ \rho' \ \sigma' \ S \ l'$ states that a state $P \ \rho \ \sigma \ S \ l$ will lead to the state $P \ \rho' \ \sigma' \ S \ l'$ in one or more steps.

The semantics shows how execution of a basic block makes a transition from a label to another while changing the environment and store. The transition is bidirectional, so it describes both forwards and backwards execution. This is used in the rule for `uncall`, where the transition relation is used in the reverse order for executing the subroutine.

We use I to indicate an unspecified instruction (update or exchange), E to indicate an unspecified entry point, X to indicate an unspecified exit point and c to indicate an unspecified condition. Abusing notation, we use $\oplus$, $\odot$ and $\bowtie$ to represent both the syntactic and semantic versions of operators. We use the same rules for evaluating expressions and conditions, using 0 to represent false and any non-zero value to represent true.

2.5   Shorthands

To make code more readable, we introduce a number of shorthands when displaying RIL code in the paper.

We will use $L \oplus= R$ as an abbreviation of $L \oplus= R + 0$.

Basic blocks:

$$\frac{(l_1 \leftarrow \mathtt{call}\ l\ \rightarrow l_2) \in P \quad P\ \rho\ \sigma\ (l_2 : S)\ l \rightleftharpoons P\ \rho'\ \sigma'\ (l_2 : S)\ l}{P\ \rho\ \sigma\ S\ l_1 \rightleftharpoons P\ \rho'\ \sigma'\ S\ l_2}$$

$$\frac{(l_1 \leftarrow \mathtt{uncall}\ l\ \rightarrow l_2) \in P \quad P\ \rho'\ \sigma'\ (l_2 : S)\ l \rightleftharpoons P\ \rho\ \sigma\ (l_2 : S)\ l}{P\ \rho\ \sigma\ S\ l_1 \rightleftharpoons P\ \rho'\ \sigma'\ S\ l_2}$$

$$\frac{(E\ I\ X) \in P \quad E \vdash \rho\ \sigma\ l_1 \quad I \models \rho\ \sigma \rightsquigarrow \rho'\ \sigma' \quad X \dashv \rho'\ \sigma'\ l_2}{P\ \rho\ \sigma\ S\ l_1 \rightleftharpoons P\ \rho'\ \sigma'\ S\ l_2}$$

$$\frac{P\ \rho\ \sigma\ S\ l_1 \rightleftharpoons P\ \rho'\ \sigma'\ S\ l_2 \quad P\ \rho'\ \sigma'\ S\ l_2 \rightleftharpoons P\ \rho''\ \sigma''\ S\ l_3}{P\ \rho\ \sigma\ S\ l_1 \rightleftharpoons P\ \rho''\ \sigma''\ S\ l_3}$$

Entry points:

$$\overline{l' \leftarrow\ \vdash \rho\ \sigma\ l} \qquad \overline{\mathtt{begin}\ l\ \vdash \rho\ \sigma\ l} \qquad \frac{\rho\ \sigma \rhd c \rightsquigarrow 0}{l_1; l_2 \leftarrow c \vdash \rho\ \sigma\ l_2} \qquad \frac{\rho\ \sigma \rhd c \not\rightsquigarrow 0}{l_1; l_2 \leftarrow c \vdash \rho\ \sigma\ l_1}$$

Exit points:

$$\overline{\rightarrow l \dashv \rho\ \sigma\ l} \qquad \overline{\mathtt{end}\ l \dashv \rho\ \sigma\ l} \qquad \frac{\rho\ \sigma \rhd c \rightsquigarrow 0}{c \rightarrow l_1; l_2 \dashv \rho\ \sigma\ l_2} \qquad \frac{\rho\ \sigma \rhd c \not\rightsquigarrow 0}{c \rightarrow l_1; l_2 \dashv \rho\ \sigma\ l_1}$$

Updates and exchanges:

$$\frac{\rho\ \sigma \rhd e \rightsquigarrow v \quad w = u \oplus v}{x \oplus= e \rhd \rho[x \mapsto u]\ \sigma \rightsquigarrow \rho[x \mapsto w]\ \sigma}$$

$$\frac{\rho\ \sigma \rhd e \rightsquigarrow v \quad w = u \oplus v}{M[x] \oplus= e \rhd \rho[x \mapsto a]\ \sigma[a \mapsto u] \rightsquigarrow \rho[x \mapsto a]\ \sigma[a \mapsto w]}$$

$$\overline{x \leftrightarrow y \rhd \rho[x \mapsto u, y \mapsto v]\ \sigma \rightsquigarrow \rho[x \mapsto v, y \mapsto u]\ \sigma}$$

$$\overline{x \leftrightarrow M[y] \rhd \rho[x \mapsto u, y \mapsto a]\ \sigma[a \mapsto v] \rightsquigarrow \rho[x \mapsto v, y \mapsto a]\ \sigma[a \mapsto u]}$$

$$\overline{\models \rho\ \sigma \rightsquigarrow \rho\ \sigma} \qquad \frac{I_1 \models \rho\ \sigma \rightsquigarrow \rho'\ \sigma' \quad I_2 \models \rho'\ \sigma' \rightsquigarrow \rho''\ \sigma''}{I_1\ I_2 \models \rho\ \sigma \rightsquigarrow \rho''\ \sigma''}$$

Expressions and conditions:

$$\frac{k\ \text{is a constant}}{\rho\ \sigma \rhd k \rightsquigarrow k} \qquad \overline{\rho[x \mapsto v]\ \sigma \rhd x \rightsquigarrow v} \qquad \overline{\rho[x \mapsto a]\ \sigma[a \mapsto v] \rhd M[x] \rightsquigarrow v}$$

$$\frac{\rho\ \sigma \rhd R_1 \rightsquigarrow v_1 \quad \rho\ \sigma \rhd R_2 \rightsquigarrow v_2 \quad w = v_1 \odot v_2}{\rho\ \sigma \rhd R_1 \odot R_2 \rightsquigarrow w}$$

$$\frac{\rho\ \sigma \rhd R_1 \rightsquigarrow v_1 \quad \rho\ \sigma \rhd R_2 \rightsquigarrow v_2 \quad w = v_1 \bowtie v_2}{\rho\ \sigma \rhd R_1 \bowtie R_2 \rightsquigarrow w}$$

Fig. 1. Semantics of RIL

Two blocks $E\ I_1\ \rightarrow\ l$ and $l\ \leftarrow\ l\ I_2\ X$, where E in an entry point, X is an exit point and I_1 and I_2 are updates, exchanges or calls, will be abbreviated to a single extended basic block $E\ I_1 I_2\ X$. This abbreviation can be applied repeatedly, so arbitrarily many basic blocks connected by unconditional exit and entry point pairs will be shown as a single extended block. Similarly, when a block with a conditional exit point where the second label (corresponding to a false condition) occurs in an unconditional entry point of another block, these will be merged and the conditional exit point will be shown as a conditional jump with one target (and fall-through when the condition is false). For example, a block ending with $c \rightarrow l_1; l_2$ will be merged to a block starting with $l_2 \leftarrow$ joined by the one-way jump $c \rightarrow l_1$. Symmetrically, a block with an unconditional exit point can be merged with another block with a conditional entry point: $\rightarrow l_2$ and $l_1; l_2 \leftarrow c$ are joined to $l_1 \leftarrow c$.

Additionally, we will at entry and exit points for subroutines, i.e., after **begin** and before **end**, add assertions of the form **assert** c, where c is a condition. Variables occurring in these assertions are the input and output parameters for the subroutine, and they specify preconditions and postconditions for the subroutine and can be seen either as comments that specify an invariant or as conditions that are actively checked at runtime. In the latter case, an assertion **assert** c can be expanded into a conditional jump and a conditional entry point: $c \rightarrow l_1; l2$ and $l_1; l_2 \leftarrow$ **true**, where **true** represents any tautology, e.g., x==x. We will in assertions, additionally, allow conjunction of simple conditions using the && operator. Such conjunctions can be expanded to sequences of simple assertions.

3   Implementation of a Heap Manager

We will now show implementations of a heap manager in RIL, using the short-hands described in Section 2.5. In particular, we use assertions to describe partial pre and post conditions[1]. If code compiled from a high-level language to RIL statically ensures that these assertions are true, they can be omitted.

3.1   Data Representation

Our heap manager will use LISP-like values. A value can be either a symbol, an integer or a pair of two values a and d, written as Cons(a, d). We represent these in the following way on a machine with 32-bit words:

- The value 0 is used for uninitialised variables and heap nodes.
- An integer is represented by a machine word ending in 1. The integer value is given by the first 31 bits.
- A symbol is represented by a machine word that ends in 10.
- Cons(a, d) is represented by a three-word-aligned address A (so ending in 00), where $H \leq a \leq lastH$, where $lastH$ is the address of the last node in the heap. A points to a node consisting of three words: A reference count

---

[1] The assertions are not strong enough to describe full pre and post conditions.

and two fields a and d, representing the elements of a pair Cons(a,d). In an unallocated node, all three words are zero, and in an allocated node, all three words are non-zero.

We assume that the fields a and d in a pair Cons(a,d) can not be destructively updated, which is true in functional languages. This allows us to share identical pairs.

Note that we can test if a value v is a node pointer by checking if the two least significant bits are 00, i.e., that the condition v & 3 is 0, representing false.

3.2 Value Copying

This subroutine copies a value stored in the variable copyP to the variable copyQ, which must initially be zero, while maintaining reference counts if the value is a pointer.

```
begin copy
assert copyP > 0 && copyQ == 0
copyP & 3 → copyNonPointer
M[copyP] += 1
copyNonPointer ← copyP & 3
copyQ += copyP
assert copyP > 0 && copyQ == copyP
end copy
```

Note that only copying of pointer fields update reference counts.

Calling copy in reverse requires that the two values are identical. Though the reference count of the node decreases when calling copy in reverse, it can never reach zero, as the equality assertion implies that there are at least two pointers to the node before the decrement.

3.3 Copying the Fields of a Cons Node

We sometimes want to access the fields of a Cons node while keeping the pointer to the node. This will not change the reference count to the node, but it will increase the reference count to its fields (if they are pointers).

```
begin fields
assert fieldsP >= H && fieldsA == 0 && fieldsD == 0
fieldsP += 4
fieldsA += M[fieldsP]
fieldsA & 3→ nonPointerA
M[fieldsA] += 1
nonPointerA ← fieldsA & 3
fieldsP += 4
fieldsD += M[fieldsP]
fieldsD & 3 → nonPointerD
M[fieldsD] +=1
nonPointerD ← fieldsD & 3
fieldsP -= 8
assert fieldsP >= H && fieldsA > 0 && fieldsD > 0
end fields
```

When called in reverse, it is implicitly assumed that `fieldsA` and `fieldsD` are equal to the fields of `fieldsP`. `fieldsA` and `fieldsD` are cleared by subtracting from these the two fields of `fieldsP` and reducing the reference counts of these (if pointers). If, when `fields` is called in reverse, `fieldsA` and `fieldsD` are *not* equal to the fields of `fieldsP`, the assertion that they are zero after `begin fields` will fail.

3.4   Naive Implementation of Construction / Destruction of Nodes

The above subroutines neither allocate nor free data, as reference counts are non-zero both before and after calling these subroutines.

We now describe a subroutine `cons` that takes two arguments `consA` and `consD` and returns a pointer `consP` to a Cons-node that has the values of `consA` and `consD` as fields, while clearing the contents of these variables.

If there is already such a node in the heap, a new reference to this node is returned. Finding an existing node with the required fields requires a search through the heap. If there is no suitable node to share, a new node is allocated. Allocating a new node requires searching backwards through the heap for a node that has zero reference count (which also implies zeroed fields).

When called in reverse, `cons` takes a pointer `consP` and returns the values of the fields in the variables `consA` and `consD`, while clearing `consP`. If the node pointed to by `consP` is unshared (indicated by reference count 1), it is deallocated by clearing the reference count and the fields to 0. The code for `cons` is shown in Figure 2. For readability, we will use indentation to indicate structure.

The loop `consSearchSame` searches forwards through the heap to find a matching node. If that succeeds, the block `consFoundSame` increases the reference count of the node and decreases the counts of the fields (if they are not symbols) because it clears `consA` and `consD`, that are references to the fields.

If the search for a matching node fails, the loop `consSearchEmpty` searches for an unallocated node. If one such is found, a new Cons-node is created in it.

If no empty node is found, no allocation is possible, and a jump to the label `consFail` is made. This should do some kind of error handling (not shown).

It should be obvious that the naive implementation of `cons` is slow: Whenever a new node is created, the entire heap is walked through to find an existing, identical node, and if that fails, the heap is walked through again to find an unallocated node. Since allocations happen near the top of the heap and searches for existing nodes start from the bottom, the average case is quite bad. So we will, below, describe an optimised implementation of `cons`.

3.5   An Optimised Implementation of Cons

We will use an old idea for effective maximal sharing: Hashing field values to find the address of the node [5]. Rather than searching the entire heap, we search only a small segment of the heap starting at the address given by a hash code calculated from the values of the fields. Since we both add and remove nodes,

```
begin cons
assert consA != 0 && consD != 0 && consP == 0
consP += H
consSearchSame ← consP > H
  M[consP] == 0 → consNext
    consP += 4
    M[consP] != consA → consNotA
      consP += 4
      M[consP] == consD → consFoundSame
      consP -= 4
    consNotA ← M[consP] != consA
    consP -= 4
  consNext ← M[consP] == 0
  consP += 12
consP <= lastH → consSearchSame
consSearchEmpty ← consP <= lastH
  consP -= 12
  consP < H → consFail
M[consP] != 0 → consSearchEmpty
  M[consP] += 1
  consP += 4
  consA ↔ M[consP]
  consP += 4
  consD ↔ M[consP]
  consP -= 8
consEnd ← M[consP] > 1
assert consP >= H && consA == 0 && consD == 0
end cons

consFoundSame ←
  consD & 3 → consNonPointerD
    M[consD] -= 1
  consNonPointerD ← consD & 3
  consD -= M[consP]
  consP -= 4
  consA & 3 → consNonPointerA
    M[consA] -= 1
  consNonPointerA ← consA & 3
  consA -= M[consP]
  consP -= 4
  M[consP] += 1
→ consEnd
```

Fig. 2. Naive reversible implementation of cons

we can not keep searching until we find either a match or a free node, so we need a fixed segment size. For efficiency reasons, we want the segment to be small, but we also want to minimise the risk that the segment we want to allocate into is full while the heap as a whole is mostly empty. It seems reasonable to require that the probability of trying to allocate into an already full segment is very small when less than half the total heap is allocated.

If hashing distributes values uniformly randomly, allocating m Cons-nodes in a heap with n segments of size b is equivalent to randomly throwing m balls into n bins, where no bin holds more than b balls. If $n < m < n \log n$, the maximum number of balls in a bin is [15] with very high probability no more than $\frac{\log n}{\log \frac{n \log n}{m}}$. If the heap is half full, $m = \frac{bn}{2}$, and we get a bound of $\frac{\log n}{\log \frac{2 \log n}{b}}$. We want this not to exceed b, so we want $\frac{\log n}{\log \frac{2 \log n}{b}} \leq b \Leftrightarrow \frac{n}{\log n} \leq \frac{e^b}{b}$. For $b = 12$, we get $n \leq 1.6 \cdot 10^5$, which gives approximately $12 \cdot 1.6 \cdot 10^5 = 1.8 \cdot 10^6$ nodes.

We will assume a subroutine hash exists that takes a cleared variable hashV and the values in consA and consD as arguments and returns in the variable hashV a hash code of consA and consD while preserving the values of consA and consD. If hashV is the hash code for consA and consD, running hash in reverse will clear hashV. The hash code should be the start of a segment, $i.e.$, $H, H+12b, H+24b, \ldots,$ lastH $-(12b-12)$ (the address of the last segment in the heap). We will in Section 4 discuss how the hash procedure can be implemented.

The optimised implementation of cons is shown in Figure 3. We start by computing hashV, which is the address of the start of the segment to search, and segEnd, which is the address of the last node in this segment. We then search as before, but constrained to the interval between hashV and segEnd. When we find the matching or empty node we need, we uncompute hashV and segEnd.

4   Reversible Hashing

We want a procedure hash that expects variables consA and consD to contain non-zero values and hashV to be zero. After the call, consA and consD are unchanged and hashV holds a value between H and $lastH - (12b - 12)$ in increments of $12b$. We will assume that b is a power of 2, as this eases scaling.

We base our hash function, shown in Figure 4, on Jenkins' 96-bit reversible mix function [8] that is well tested and has good statistical properties. This mixes three integers, so we use a constant as the third. The three values are stored in variables hashA, hashB and hashC that are globally initialised to constants k_a, k_b and k_c. hashA and hashB are XOR'ed with consA and consD, Jenkins' mix function is executed, and a scaled version of the resulting hashC is used as the hash code hashV. Uncalling hash resets hashA, hashB and hashC to their original values and hashV to zero.

Since hashV needs to be between H and $lastH - (12b - 12)$ in increments of $12b$ and hashC can be any 32-bit integer, we need to mask and scale this to the right range. We first choose H and $lastH$ so $H = lastH - 12b \cdot 2^m + 12$ for some m. We can then do the scaling by bitwise ANDing hashC with $b \cdot 2^{m+2} - 4b$,

```
begin cons
assert consA != 0 && consD != 0 && consP == 0 && hashV == 0 && segEnd == 0
call hash
consP += hashV
segEnd += hashV + (12b − 12)
consSearchSame ← consP > hashV
  M[consP] == 0 → consNext
    consP += 4
    M[consP] != consA → consNotA
      consP += 4
      M[consP] == consD → consFoundSame
      consP -= 4
    consNotA ← M[consP] != consA
    consP -= 4
  consNext ← M[consP] == 0
  consP += 12
consP <= segEnd → consSearchSame
consSearchEmpty ← consP <= segEnd
  consP -= 12
  consP < H → consFail
M[consP] != 0 → consSearchEmpty
  segEnd -= hashV + (12b − 12)
  uncall hash
  M[consP] += 1
  consP += 4
  consA ↔ M[consP]
  consP += 4
  consD ↔ M[consP]
  consP -= 8
consEnd ← M[consP] > 1
assert consP >= H && consA == 0 && consD == 0 && hashV == 0 && segEnd == 0
end cons

consFoundSame ←
  segEnd -= hashV + (12b − 12)
  uncall hash
  consD & 3 → consNonPointerD
    M[consD] -= 1
  consNonPointerD ← consD & 3
  consD -= M[consP]
  consP -= 4
  consA & 3 → consNonPointerA
    M[consA] -= 1
  consNonPointerA ← consA & 3
  consA -= M[consP]
  consP -= 4
  M[consP] += 1
→ consEnd
```

Fig. 3. Optimised reversible implementation of cons

giving $4b$ times an m-bit integer. We then multiply this by 3 (getting a multiple of $12b$) and add H. The maximum value will, hence, be $3(b \cdot 2^{m+2} - 4b) + H = 12b \cdot 2^m - 12b + lastH - 12b \cdot 2^m + 12 = lastH - (12b - 12)$, as we wanted.

```
begin hash
assert hashV == 0 && hashA == kₐ && hashB == k_b && hashC == k_c
hashA ^= consA
hashB ^= consD
hashA -= hashB + hashC
hashA ^= hashC >> 13
hashB -= hashC + hashA
hashB ^= hashA << 8
hashC -= hashA + hashB
hashC ^= hashB >> 12
hashA -= hashB + hashC
hashA ^= hashC >> 12
hashB -= hashC + hashA
hashB ^= hashA << 16
hashC -= hashA + hashB
hashC ^= hashB >> 5
hashA -= hashB + hashC
hashA ^= hashC >> 3
hashB -= hashC + hashA
hashB ^= hashA << 10
hashC -= hashA + hashB
hashC ^= hashB >> 15
hashV += hashC & (b · 2^{m+2} − 4)
hashV += hashC & (b · 2^{m+2} − 4)
hashV += hashC & (b · 2^{m+2} − 4)
hashV += H
end hash
```

Fig. 4. Reversible `hash` subroutine based on Jenkins' mix function

5   Performance Analysis and Experiments

When analysing the time used by `cons`, we count the number of instructions executed. We do not count `assert` instructions, as these are assumed to be invariants that need not be checked at runtime, and we will count an unconditional jump to an unconditional entry point as free (as code layout can in most cases make it so), but we count a conditional jump to a conditional entry point as two instructions because two conditions are checked. We also count `call` and `uncall` as two instructions each, as we count the cost of the return into the cost of the call, but otherwise we do not distinguish the cost of instructions. This is, admittedly, a gross simplification, but a more precise costs measure depends on the choice of machine that RIL is translated to and the cost model of this.

```
begin hash
assert hashV == 0 && hashT == k_a
hashT ^= consA << 7
hashT += consA >> 1
hashT ^= consD << 5
hashT += consD >> 3
hashV += hashT & (b · 2^{m+2} − 4)
hashV += hashT & (b · 2^{m+2} − 4)
hashV += hashT & (b · 2^{m+2} − 4)
hashV += H
end hash
```

Fig. 5. Simplified hash subroutine

In the best case, a call to cons will have symbols as arguments and find a match in the first node it encounters. This will use 71 instructions, 52 of which are used by the two calls to hash. If the arguments to cons are pointers, add two instructions to update their reference counts. In the worst case, no matching node is found (but consA matches the head of all nodes in the segment) and the only free node is the last searched. This will use $15b + 58$ instructions, 52 of which are, again, used by hash.

We have tested the heap manager with different heap sizes to find how full the heap is when an allocation fails. This is (rather naively) done by adding pseudo-random numbers to a list until allocation fails. For each heap size, we have run the test twenty times using different random numbers (so hashing yields different numbers), and for each heap size we have listed the average and maximum number of free nodes when allocation fails. Our first test uses $b = 8$.

Heap size (nodes)	average free nodes		maximum free nodes		spread	
2^{10}	135	13%	639	62%	177	17%
2^{14}	3139	19%	10291	63%	2891	18%
2^{18}	56373	22%	144783	55%	40769	16%
2^{22}	1014423	24%	2194523	52%	713904	17%

The worst-case utilisation is with all heap sizes under 50%, though the average case is around 80%. Our estimate was that a bin size of 12 would be needed for heaps up to 10^6 nodes, so it is hardly surprising that the results are bad. The reason we have chosen a smaller bin size is to compare the setup above with a variant where the bins overlap: Instead of using hash values that point to the start of disjoint 8-node segments, we change it so hash values can point to any node start in the heap. We still use a bin size of 8, so the changes to the code are minimal: The mask used in the hash subroutine needs changing, so it instead of $b · 2^{m+2} − 4b$ is $b · 2^{m+2} − 4$. Additionally, $b − 1$ extra nodes must be added to the heap, so there are b nodes to search from the largest generated address onwards. The results are shown below

Heap size (nodes)	average free nodes		maximum free nodes		spread	
2^{10}	69	7%	171	17%	52	5%
2^{14}	767	5%	2170	13%	553	3%
2^{18}	13708	5%	34229	13%	12403	5%
2^{22}	384618	9%	974626	23%	239922	6%

The difference is quite dramatic: In none of the tests was more than 23% of the heap unused, and the average heap utilisation is between 91% and 95%, depending on heap size.

Hashing takes a significant fraction of the time for allocating nodes, so using a simpler hashing function might be worthwhile, even if this gives a higher risk of collision. As an experiment, we have replaced the hash function with the very simple function shown in Figure 5 and repeated the above tests. Reducing the body of **hash** from 24 to 8 instructions reduces the number of instructions for executing **cons** by 32 (as **hash** is called twice). The results of using the simplified **hash** function are shown below.

Heap size (nodes)	average free nodes		maximum free nodes		spread	
2^{10}	79	8%	215	21%	73	7%
2^{14}	438	3%	1022	6%	372	2%
2^{18}	10266	4%	24673	9%	7484	3%
2^{22}	215346	5%	597394	14%	168784	4%

The results are not significantly different from the previous, but that may be due to the simplicity of the tests. More testing is required to verify if this or another cheap hash function is adequate for more realistic use.

We have also made experiments using a smaller segment size, i.e., searching only 4 nodes instead of 8 for matching or empty nodes. This will reduce the cost of executing **cons**, but the expectation is that this will make allocation failure happen when a larger fraction of the heap is empty. The table below shows heap utilisation with a segment size of 4 (using the simple hash function).

Heap size (nodes)	average free nodes		maximum free nodes		spread	
2^{10}	107	10%	293	29%	94	9%
2^{14}	1311	8%	6546	40%	1860	11%
2^{18}	15871	6%	43784	17%	12874	5%
2^{22}	802967	19%	1884954	45%	539114	13%

The heap utilisation is, as expected, not as good as with the larger segment size, but it is not below 50% in any of the tests. So if space is not tight, it can be a good choice to reduce the segment size to 4.

6   Conclusion and Discussion

We have presented a reversible intermediate language RIL and implementations in RIL of a reversible heap manager that uses reference counts and hash-consing to achieve garbage collection: The heap manager does all the necessary management of reference counts, and nodes are automatically reclaimed when their reference count becomes zero.

The key insight is that to get symmetric construction and destruction of values, either linearity (no sharing) or maximal sharing is needed. Previous works assume linearity, but we implement maximal sharing by a reversible hash-cons subroutine. This allows copying of values just by copying pointers (and updating reference counts) and structural equality testing by comparison of pointers. This is, we believe, the first real reversible garbage collection method that does not rely on linearity.

Our use of fixed-size segments (bins) to handle hash-code collisions means that a segment can be filled long before the heap is full. We have calculated a segment size that makes this very unlikely before the heap is at least half full. The calculation is based on results from the literature for non-overlapping bins and gives a fairly large segment size. We have also tested overlapping bins, which has not been studied much in the literature, and found that the results are dramatically better when overlapping bins are used. Overlapping bins have proved to be beneficial for cuckoo hashing [9], so it is, perhaps, not so surprising. Experimentally, we have found that a segment size of 8 gives heap utilisation above 75% in the worst case and better than 90% in the average case, while a segment size of 4 gives heap utilisation around 55% in the worst case and better than 80% in the average case.

The hashing and searching used during node construction has a significant cost, so construction and deconstruction of nodes is relatively expensive. This is, however, partially offset by vey cheap equality testing and copying of data.

We have made preliminary tests of two different hash functions and found no significant difference in results, though one is much simpler than the other. Further trials with more realistic allocation/freeing patterns are needed to draw a firm conclusion. Further trials could also investigate more different hash functions.

Our use of a fixed segment/bin size makes reversibility simple at the cost of relatively low heap utilisation. More advanced hashing techniques such as two-way chaining [3] may improve heap utilisation with small segment sizes at the cost of increasing the hashing cost. Cuckoo hashing [9,14] offer high utilisation with short searches, but this (or any other) hash-table technique that moves nodes around after they are allocated are not suitable for our purpose, as changing the address of a node requires modifying pointers globally.

A limitation of the heap manager is that heap nodes can only be pairs. It is easy enough to modify the heap manager to another fixed size of nodes, but mixing nodes of several sizes in the same heap will require all nodes to be padded to the largest size. A simple solution is to have separate heaps for different node sizes, but that can be very wasteful. Larger tuples can be built from pairs, but that requires an average of one node per field in the tuple. A compromise might be to let nodes be four words including reference count. This will waste one word when building pairs but there will be less waste when building larger tuples, as an average of two fields can be stored in each node. A node size that is a power of two can also save some instructions when scaling the hash code to a multiple of the node size.

References

1. Axelsen, H.B., Glück, R.: Reversible representation and manipulation of constructor terms in the heap. In: Dueck, G.W., Miller, D.M. (eds.) RC 2013. LNCS, vol. 7948, pp. 96–109. Springer, Heidelberg (2013)
2. Baker, H.G.: Nreversal of fortune — the thermodynamics of garbage collection. In: Bekkers, Y., Cohen, J. (eds.) Memory Management. Lecture Notes in Computer Science, vol. 637, pp. 507–524. Springer, Berlin Heidelberg (1992)
3. Broder, A.Z., Mitzenmacher, M.: Using multiple hash functions to improve IP lookups. In: Proceedings of the Twentieth Annual Joint Conference of the IEEE Computer and Communications Societies (INFOCOM 2001), vol. 3, pp. 1454–1463. IEEE Comput. Soc. Press (2001)
4. Ershov, A.P.: On programming of arithmetic operations. Communications of the ACM $\mathbf{1}$(8), 3–6 (1958)
5. Goto, E.: Monocopy and associative algorithms in an extended lisp. Technical Report TR 74–03, University of Tokyo (1974)
6. Hansen, J.S.K.: Translation of a reversible functional programming language. Master's thesis, DIKU, University of Copenhagen, December 2014
7. James, R.P., Sabry, A.: Theseus: a high-level language for reversible computation. In: Reversible Computation - Booklet of work-in-progress and short reports (2014). http://www.reversible-computation.org
8. Jenkins, B.: Hash functions. Dr. Dobb's Journal of Software Tools $\mathbf{22}$(7) (1997)
9. Lehman, E., Panigrahy, R.: 3.5-Way cuckoo hashing for the price of 2-and-a-bit. In: Fiat, A., Sanders, P. (eds.) ESA 2009. LNCS, vol. 5757, pp. 671–681. Springer, Heidelberg (2009)
10. Lutz, C.: Janus: a time-reversible language. A letter to Landauer (1986). http://www.tetsuo.jp/ref/janus.pdf
11. Mogensen, T.Æ.: Partial evaluation of janus part 2: assertions and procedures. In: Clarke, E., Virbitskaite, I., Voronkov, A. (eds.) PSI 2011. LNCS, vol. 7162, pp. 289–301. Springer, Heidelberg (2012)
12. Mogensen, T.Æ.: Reference counting for reversible languages. In: Yamashita, S., Minato, S. (eds.) RC 2014. LNCS, vol. 8507, pp. 82–94. Springer, Heidelberg (2014)
13. Oh, C.W.: Reversible intermediate language for the translation of reversibleprogramming languages. Master's thesis, DIKU, University of Copenhagen, November 2009
14. Pagh, R., Rodler, F.F.: Cuckoo hashing. J. Algorithms $\mathbf{51}$(2), 122–144 (2004)
15. Raab, M., Steger, A.: "Balls into bins" - a simple and tight analysis. In: Rolim, J.D.P., Serna, M., Luby, M. (eds.) RANDOM 1998. LNCS, vol. 1518, pp. 159–170. Springer, Heidelberg (1998)
16. Yokoyama, T., Axelsen, H.B., Glück, R.: Towards a reversible functional language. In: De Vos, A., Wille, R. (eds.) RC 2011. LNCS, vol. 7165, pp. 14–29. Springer, Heidelberg (2012)

Reverse Code Generation for Parallel Discrete Event Simulation

Markus Schordan[✉], David Jefferson, Peter Barnes,
Tomas Oppelstrup, and Daniel Quinlan

Lawrence Livermore National Laboratory, Livermore, USA
{schordan1,jefferson6,barnes26,oppelstrup2,dquinlan}@llnl.gov

Abstract. Reverse computation has become a central notion in discrete event simulation over the last decade. It is not just a theoretical line of research, but an immensely practical one that is necessary to achieve high performance for large parallel discrete event simulations (PDES). The models that are implemented for PDES are of increasing complexity and size and require various language features to support abstraction, encapsulation, and composition when building a simulation model. In this paper we focus on parallel simulation models that are written in C++ and present an approach for automatically generating reverse code for C++. The strategy we have adopted for our approach is to first assure that we can correctly handle event methods that use the entire C++ language. Although a significant runtime overhead is introduced with our technique, the assurance that the reverse code is always generated fully automatically is an enormous win that can open the door to routine optimistic simulation with models that can be implemented using the entire C++ language.

1 Introduction

Reverse computation has become a central notion in discrete event simulation over the last decade [1,2]. It is not just a theoretical line of research, but an immensely practical one necessary to achieve high performance for large parallel discrete event simulations. In fact, the most highly parallel and fastest discrete event simulation benchmarks ever executed have made essential use of it [3]. In this paper we will briefly describe the connection between reverse computation and simulation, and then describe how we produce efficient reverse code for simulations written in standard C++.

1.1 Discrete Event Simulation

Discrete event simulation (DES) is a simulation paradigm suitable for systems whose states are modeled as changing *discontinuously* and *irregularly* at discrete moments of simulation time. DES is *event-driven* in that the times at which state changes occur are calculated dynamically rather than statically as

© Springer International Publishing Switzerland 2015
J. Krivine and J.-B. Stefani (Eds.): RC 2015, LNCS 9138, pp. 95–110, 2015.
DOI: 10.1007/978-3-319-20860-2_6

in time-stepped simulations. Example applications include simulations of digital communication networks, vehicular traffic flow, markets and economies, epidemiological models, logistical models, ecological and population models, tactical and strategic military models, and many others. Most systems whose behavior is not describable by continuous equations and that are not suitable for simple time-stepped models are candidates for DES.

The general sequential DES algorithm is very straightforward. It is based on an *event queue*, i.e. a priority queue of *events* (scheduled simulation state changes) in which the priority value is simulation time. The algorithm is simply to repeatedly remove the event with the lowest simulation time from the event queue and execute it. An event execution generally will cause a change in the simulated system state and/or will insert new future events into the event queue. This algorithm guarantees the basic simulation correctness conditions that all events are executed once and only once in increasing (or at least non-decreasing) simulation time order, and that causal relationships between events are directed only forward in simulation time, with no backward-in-time causality.

1.2   Parallel Discrete Event Simulation

Efficient parallel discrete event simulation (PDES) is much more complex than this, however. The general approach is to divide the simulation and its state into semi-independent parallel units called LPs (logical processes) that each have their own event queues and that generally execute concurrently and asynchronously. Each simulated event is now executed within one LP only and affects only that LP's state. An event may also schedule other events for future simulation times, either for the same LP (self) or for others. Events scheduled for other LPs must be transmitted to them as event messages with a timestamp indicating the simulation time when the event should be executed. Arriving event messages get enqueued in the event queues of the receiving LPs in increasing time stamp order.

The fundamental issue that makes PDES so complex is the synchronization problem. Every LP must execute all events from its own event queue in strictly non-decreasing timestamp order despite the fact that it does not generally know which LPs might be sending it events, or how many, or what timestamps they may carry. Furthermore there is no guarantee that event messages will arrive at an LP in increasing timestamp order. The asynchronous concurrent execution of the LPs means that at any hypothetical snapshot taken at a single instant of wall clock time some LPs will be ahead in simulation time and some will be behind. Furthermore, which LPs are ahead or behind may change during execution. As a result, there is a danger of a *causality violation* when an LP that is behind in simulation time, e.g. at t_1, sends an event message with a (future) timestamp $t_2 > t_1$ that arrives at a receiver that has already simulated to time $t_3 > t_2$. In that case the receiver has already simulated past the simulation time when it *should* have executed the event at t_2, and yet it would be incorrect to execute events out of order. This is the essence of the PDES synchronization problem.

There are two broad approaches to resolving the PDES synchronization issue, called *conservative* and *optimistic* [4]. Conservative synchronization uses conventional process blocking primitives along with extra knowledge about the simulation model (called *lookahead* information) to prevent the execution from ever getting into a situation in the first place in which an event message arrives at an LP with a timestamp in its past. This seems like the natural approach, but it is generally model-dependent and surprisingly complex. In many cases it is not the most efficient approach, and in some cases where there is no useful lookahead information it cannot yield good performance at all.

Optimistic synchronization, by contrast, does not try to prevent the simulation from getting into a causality violation situation in which an event arrives at an LP in its past, i.e. with a timestamp $t_2 < t_3$. Whenever that occurs, the simulator rolls back the LP from t_3 to the state it was in at time t_2, executes the arriving event, and the re-executes forward from time t_2 to t_3 and beyond. Another way to look at optimistic synchronization is that all event executions are speculative or provisional, and are always subject to rollback if the simulation gets into local synchronization trouble. Most of the time that does not happen and the simulation proceeds forward in parallel. But occasionally a causality violation occurs that has to be corrected by rollback and, after that minor performance penalty, the simulation continues forward again. There is considerably more to it than we have space to convey here, but that is the basic idea. And it is sufficient to motivate our interest in reverse computation. For more detail see [2].

1.3   Motivation for Reverse Code Generation

So how exactly does reverse computation help with PDES? In this paper we assume the parallel simulation model is written in C++. Each event is the execution of some event method $E()$ that makes changes to the state variables of the simulation. If that event has to be rolled back to deal with a causality violation, then the simulator needs another method $E'()$ that exactly reverses all of the side effects of $E()$ to return the simulation to the exact state it was in before $E()$ was executed.

However, the situation is more complicated because in general a C++ method $E()$ will destroy information during its forward execution. It will usually overwrite or update some state variables, destroy control information (e.g. by forgetting which branch it took at a conditional) and also possibly deallocate data structures on the heap. It is not possible in general to write an $E'()$ that can restore information that was actually destroyed by $E()$. But we can frame the problem differently and achieve our purpose.

Instead, for an event method E() written in C++ (with return type void), we generate *two* derived methods, $E^+()$ and $E^-()$. $E^+()$ is identical to $E()$ except that it is instrumented to save in a side data structure a trace of all of the information that $E()$ would destroy. $E^-()$ uses that saved trace information to undo the side effects of $E^+()$, and also destroys the side data structure that $E^+()$ created. As a result we can write the reverse computation equation

$$\{E^+(); E^-()\} = \{\}$$

(where $\{\}$ is a **skip** or no-op)

If $E()$ does any memory deallocation, we do not actually do the deallocation in $E^+()$ since it cannot be reversed in $E^-()$ if need be. Instead we defer the actual deallocation of an object (but not the call to the destructor) to be done in a *commit method* $E^*()$, which is only called at *commit time* when we can be sure that $E^+()$ will never need to be reversed. Once the entire simulation is progressed (on all nodes) beyond a certain simulation time t, it is guaranteed that no event at a simulation time $< t$ will ever need to be reversed. At this point the commit function is called for all events at simulation times earlier than t. The computation equation involving the commit method is

$$\{E^+(); E^*()\} = \{E()\}$$

The commit method is also used in the handling of I/O and certain other issues, but they are beyond the scope of this paper.

In Section 2 we describe in detail our approach for automatically generating $E^+()$, $E^-()$, and $E^*()$ from an arbitrary C++ function $E()$, and present an evaluation on small benchmarks with dynamic memory allocation. In Section 3 we describe a complete PDES model for which we automatically generate reverse code and evaluate the performance of our generated reverse code running under the parallel discrete event simulator ROSS on LLNL's parallel Blue Gene/Q machine *Vulcan*, and also compare the performance of different compilers. In Section 4 we describe the related work for our approach.

2   Reverse Code Generation

Our approach is a variant of incremental check pointing and the forward-reverse-commit paradigm ([2], Chapter 7.3). This paradigm applies to situations when a program fragment can be executed "ahead of time", but is found to be incorrect, and requires re-execution from a previous state of execution.

In parallel discrete event simulation with optimistic synchronization, we need to reverse events if they turn out to be not on the correct execution path (e.g. because an event that was transmitted on the network arrives with a timestamp that is older than the one that has already been simulated).

Our approach requires only that we generate new code for the forward event. The transformed forward code records additional information in a data structure that is used by the reverse and commit methods. No code is generated for the reverse and commit method. They share the same implementation for all variants of transformed forward event codes. We have implemented our approach in a tool called *Backstroke* as source-to-source transformation based on the compiler infrastructure ROSE [5].

In the following sections we describe the code transformation operations, recorded data at runtime, and how the recorded data is used by the reverse and commit methods in the following sections.

2.1   Code Transformations for Intercepting All Memory Modifying Operations

For our approach it is sufficient to intercept all memory modifying operations. Measured in bits we store more information than necessary, but we do not need to store control flow information, which simplifies the handling of branch constructs, virtual method calls, and exceptions.

We consider three kinds of operations as memory modifying operations: assignment operators, memory allocation, and memory deallocation. C++ offers 15 different assignment operators, which can modify the memory for all built-in types, two operators for memory allocation (single object and arrays) and two operators for memory deallocation (single object and arrays).

In the following section we define the transformations for the C++ operators by specifying its semantics. In subsequent sections we present how concrete C++ code can be generated.

2.2   Forward Code Generation for Assignment Operators

C++ offers 15 assignment operators

1. Assignment: $E_1 = E_2$
2. Assignment with additional operation: E_1 op E_2
   where $op \in \{$ +=, -=, *=, /=, %=, &=, |=, ^=, <<=, >>= $\}$
3. pre/post increment/decrement operators: op E, E op where $op \in \{$ ++,-- $\}$

For Assignment operators we define the transformation α which intercepts all forms of assignments. The transformation is applied to all 15 operators as a unified operation (including pre- and post-increment/decrement operators). The transformation α is introduced as follows for the different kinds of assignment:

1. $E_1 = E_2 \Longrightarrow \alpha(E_1) = E_2$
2. E_1 op $E_2 \Longrightarrow \alpha(E_1)$ op E_2
3. op $E \Longrightarrow op$ $\alpha(E)$, E $op \Longrightarrow \alpha(E_1)$ op

For example, let p be a pointer to an object and x be a data member of this object. Then we introduce for the assignment p->x=y the transformation α such that α(p->x)=y.

2.3   Addressing Dynamic Memory Allocation

To address memory allocation we introduce transformation β and for deallocation we introduce transformation γ.

Let T be a built-in type or a user defined type (class, struct, or union) and n be the size of an array to be allocated or deallocated. Then for every occurrence of the operators **new** and **delete** in a program, we introduce the following transformations

1. **new** T() $\Longrightarrow \beta_1(\text{T})$.
2. **new** T()[E] $\Longrightarrow \beta_2(T,E)$.
3. **delete** $E \Longrightarrow \gamma_1(E)$.
4. **delete[]** $E \Longrightarrow \gamma_2(E)$.

2.4   Semantics of the Transformation Operators

To generate forward code, the transformation operators α, β, γ, are applied and C++ code with function calls to the Backstroke Runtime Library are introduced. Next we specify the semantics of the generated forward code with the functions in Table 1.

Table 1. Functions used for specifying the semantics of transformations α, β, γ

$address(E) \rightarrow a$	computes the address a of the l-value denoted by expression E and returns that address a.
$allocateArray(s_a, s_e) \rightarrow p$	allocates array of size s_a with element type size s_e. Register the pointer to the allocated memory region
$callArrayElemDestrs(T_e, p) \rightarrow p$	calls destructor for each array element of type T_e of array at address p in reverse order and returns p.
$cast(T, E)$	casts the type of expression E to type T.
$dereference(p)$	dereference pointer p.
$etypeof(E) \rightarrow T_e$	determines element type T_e of array denoted by E.
$new\ T() \rightarrow p$	performs C++ operation new and returns pointer p.
$ptr(T)$	denotes a pointer to an object of type T.
$pstore(p) \rightarrow p$	stores pointer p in the state store and returns the same pointer p.
$rdestructor(T)$	calls the reversed destructor for Type T.
$registerAllocation(p) \rightarrow p$	registers the pointer p referring to allocated memory to be deallocated by reverse functions and returns p.
$registerArrayAllocation(p, E) \rightarrow p$	registers the pointer p referring to allocated array memory to be deallocated by reverse functions and returns p. The size of the array is defined by expression E.
$registerArrayDealloc(p)$	registers the pointer p referring to memory to be deleted by commit.
$registerDeallocation(p)$	registers the pointer p referring to memory to be deleted by commit functions and returns p.
$store(a) \rightarrow a$	stores memory address a of a built-in data type (not being a pointer) and returns a.
$typeof(E) \rightarrow T$	determines type T of expression E.

To generate forward code for the C++ **new** and **delete** operators we generate code that involves calls to generated forward-code of constructors and destructors, and the introduced backstroke library function calls perform the recording of allocated memory and the deferred deallocation of memory. Memory deallocation is deferred until an event is committed, and memory allocation is undone with memory deallocation in case an event is reversed.

In Table 2 the transformations α, β, γ are defined. For intercepting assignments, α_1 introduces code that (i) computes the address of expression E. Expression E represents the l-value of an assignment and therefore denotes a memory address to which the address operator can be applied. (ii) This address is passed (as pointer) to a function that stores this pointer. In the C++ Code (described in Section 2.5) the store function corresponds to a Backstroke Run Time Library call. The store function returns the same pointer that was passed to it. (iii) The returned pointer is dereferenced. This produces an l-value to which the right-hand side of the assignment can be assigned. Intercepting assignments in this way allows to perform transformations on expressions source-to-source. This also holds for all other transformations. Therefore the generated forward code remains readable in comparison to the original forward code. Further beautifications are possible by using templated wrapper functions. For α_1 all computed addresses are pointers to built-in types with one level of indirection. For α_2 we pass all pointers that represent more than one level of indirection and those are cast to a pointer of level one to any type. This allows to cover also pointers of arbitrary levels of indirection.

Let *any* denote a pointer to any type, and T, E, as above. We define the required transformations in Table 2. The transformation operators $\alpha_{1,2}$ introduce the transformations required for assignments, $\beta_{1,2}$ introduce the transformations for C++ memory allocation operators, and $\gamma_{1,2}$ for C++ memory deallocation operators.

Table 2. Transformation specification (uses specified functions from Table 1)

$\alpha_1(E)$	$::= dereference(store(address(E)))$
$\alpha_2(E)$	$::= dereference(cast(typeof(E),(pstore(cast(any,address(E))))))$
$\beta_1(T)$	$::= cast(ptr(T),registerAllocation(cast(any,new\ T())))$
$\beta_2(T,E)$	$::= cast(ptr(T),registerArrayAllocation(cast(any,new\ T()),E))$
$\gamma_1(E)$	$::= rdestructor(typeof(E)),registerDeallocation(cast(any,E))$
$\gamma_2(E)$	$::= registerArrayDealloc(cast(any,callArrayElemDestrs(etypeof(E),E)))$

Pointers are cast to *any* because we want to maintain all pointers to allocated memory of a given program in the same data structure. Only level-one pointers are not cast (α_1) because we maintain separate stacks for all built-in data type values, and one stack for all pointer values (of the original program). We therefore cast each pointer value to *any* and cast the return value of the register-functions to its original pointer type. In the following sections we describe in more detail how these pointer values are used in C++ to store and restore program states. For the assignment of objects of user-defined types we assume that the assignment operator is implemented (and thus, can be reversed). Otherwise an implementation of the default assignment operator needs to be generated.

β transformations use the C++ operator **new** and only register the pointer to the allocated memory. The constructors involved are functions that have been reversed as well. In contrast, the γ transformations break up the original C++

delete operator into an explicit call of the reversed constructor and a register function that maintains the pointer to the memory to be deallocated. It is important that the destructor is called but only the actual deallocation of memory is deferred until the event is committed.

Array deallocation has the additional complication that we also need to (i) know the size of the array (which is not explicitly provided in the source code), (ii) apply the destructor for each array element in reverse order (of the array), and finally (iii) deallocate the memory allocated for the array and the memory location storing the size.

Our current implementation utilizes the fact that C++ compilers (to the best of our knowledge) generate code for array allocation/deallocation that stores the array size in a memory word of size `size_t` before the array elements (and the entire size of the allocated memory region is adjusted to the additional size information).

2.5   C++ Code Generation

We generate C++ code for the functions specified in Table 1 and compose them according to Table 2 to implement the introduced transformation operators α, β, and γ. The generated code contains functions that are implemented in the Backstroke Runtime library. The Runtime Library is linked with the transformed forward code. The execution of the forward code computes all data necessary to restore any previous state in the computation of the forward function by calling the reverse function of the runtime library. When the commit function is called, all registered memory deallocations are performed.

In Listings 1.1 and 1.2, we show the original and forward codes for inserting an element into a list. The forward codes show the applied α, β and γ transformations. In Section 2.7 we present an evaluation of benchmarks involving above list manipulating functions.

Listing 1.1: Original Code	Listing 1.2: Forward Code

```
List* insert_sorted(List* head, int k)     class List *insert_sorted(class List *head,int k)
  {                                           {
  List* cur;                                    class List *cur;
  List* tail;                                   class List *tail;
  cur = head;                                   cur = head;
  while (cur->next != 0                         while(cur -> List::next != 0
    && (cur->next->data < k)) {                   && cur -> List::next -> List::data < k){
    cur = cur->next;                              cur = cur -> List::next;
  }                                             }
  tail = cur->next;                             tail = cur -> List::next;
  List *elem = new List(k);                     class List *elem = (List*)
                                                  rtss->registerAllocation((void*)new List(k));
  elem->next = tail;                            (*rtss->avpushptr((void**)&(elem -> next))) = tail;
  cur->next  = elem;                            (*rtss->avpushptr((void**)&(cur -> next))) = elem;

  return head;                                  return head;
}                                             }
```

2.6   Stack vs Heap - The Necessary Check

The Backstroke Runtime Library must ensure that data stored on the runtime stack of the event is not restored in the reverse function because once the event function has been executed, all elements on the event function's runtime stack are popped from the stack by the C++ runtime system. Therefore a compiler/system dependent test is performed with each pointer that is requested to be stored in the Run Time State Storage (RTSS). If the pointer refers to a stack address, then the pointer is not stored in the RTSS. This is necessary, because otherwise we would restore memory (in the reverse function) that is no longer allocated on the runtime stack after the event function has been executed (in the forward-function). On the other hand, if it is a heap pointer, then the pointer is stored in the RTSS and the reverse and commit functions use this information to perform the proper operations to restore the memory state.

The Backstroke Runtime Library is initialized at the beginning of the simulation. It stores the current start address and end address of the thread's stack (currently we use POSIX pthread library function calls to determine the stack's start address and the length of the stack). Using this information we perform this check for every stored pointer whether it is stored on the event's runtime stack or in the heap. Using this check we ensure that only heap pointers are restored.

2.7   Evaluation

We evaluate the performance of the Backstroke generated code with two benchmarks that exercise a specific set of operations, such that we can assess the introduced overhead independent of the impact of the simulator. In Section 3 we also evaluate the performance of a PDES simulation using generated reverse code.

Benchmark Array, performs 0 to 250 array operations per event. The array operation is an addition to one random element of the array. In the very first event the array is allocated, in all subsequent events the array is modified. The List benchmark also performs 0 to 250 operations per event. The list operation is the insertion of an element in a sorted list and the subsequent deletion of the very first element of the list. Similar to the Array benchmark, the list is allocated in the very first event. In subsequent events the list is modified. Thus, both benchmarks also contain a control flow, selecting the very first event by checking whether the container has already been allocated. The size of the array is 100,000 elements and the length of the list is 100 in the benchmarks. In both benchmarks the event function is executed 100,000 times, followed by either 100,000 reverse or commit function calls. Furthermore, we also evaluate the performance difference of two modes of the Backstroke Runtime State Storage (RTSS). Mode A is the default mode, and Mode B performs an object reuse of event records used for storing all required information of an event function call to be able to reverse or commit the event later.

In Fig. 1 we show the penalty factor for generated forward code in comparison to the original code for both benchmarks, Array and List, running in both modes A+B. Mode B reuses allocated event function call records inside the RTSS and avoids re-initialization of this data structures. As shown in Fig. 3,

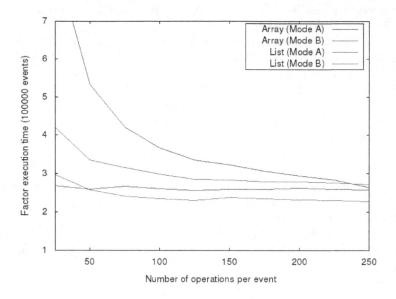

Fig. 1. Shown is the penalty factor for the forward event function $E^+()$ in comparison to the original event function $E()$ for both benchmarks Array and List and both RTSS allocation modes, denoted A and B

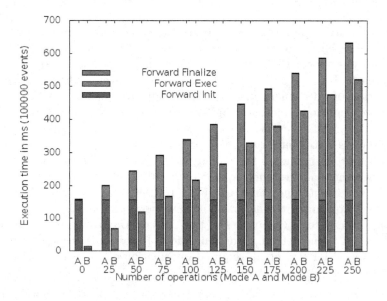

Fig. 2. Comparison of the two RTSS allocation modes (denoted A and B) for the Array Benchmark

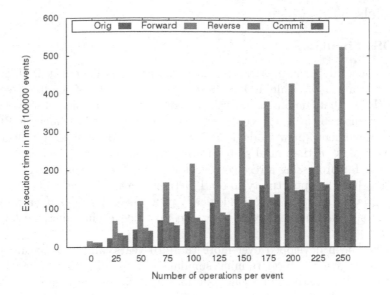

Fig. 3. Array benchmark: comparison of execution times for $E()$, $E^+()$, $E^-()$, $E^*()$

the execution time for the initialization of the internal data structure for an event (Forward Init) in Mode B is only a very small fraction of Mode A. This significantly reduces the initialization cost (Forward Init) and improves the performance comparatively more as fewer operations are performed in a single event. The total execution time for a generated forward event code is the sum of the three execution times, Forward Init, Forward Exec (actual execution of the function), and Forward Finalize, shown in the stacked bars in Fig. 3.

With Mode B the generated forward functions show a penalty factor between 2 and 3 (depicted in Fig. 1). Without this pre-allocation optimization of Mode B, the penalty can go up to 8.6 (Array) and 4.2 (List) for 25 operations. The more operations are performed, the less significant becomes the initialization time. In Fig. 2 we also show the execution times for the Original, Forward (total execution time), Reverse, and Commit functions.

The benchmarks were performed on a system with Intel(R) Core(TM) i7 CPU X 980, 3.46GHz, CPU and 1600 MHz DDR3 memory. The presented results were computed with Backstroke, version 2.0.4, whereas previous versions of Backstroke [6] implemented other approaches requiring to take control flow information into account and turned out to be difficult to apply to full C++ – in particular in the presence of C++ exceptions. Backstroke 2 addresses full C++ but without templates. Future versions will also address templates.

3   Models

3.1   ROSS Simulator

ROSS is a general purpose discrete event simulator developed at RPI by C. Carothers et. al. [7]. Within ROSS, a simulation consists of a set of logical processes (LP's) that communicate with each other through time-stamped event messages. A discrete event process formulated in this way is called a ROSS model. To implement a new model in ROSS one needs to write an initialization function that sets off the initial state of each LP, and an event function which is responsible for processing a received event message for a given LP. The event function also has the opportunity to send further event messages.

After initialization the simulation logically progresses by processing any event messages in simulation time order using the provided event functions for the LP's.

ROSS has been developed over more than 10 years, and is a mature software. It has the capability of running simulation in parallel. The Time Warp mechanism is the versatile and scalable option in ROSS for running simulations in parallel. Time Warp is an optimistic approach, where each processor employs speculative execution to process any event messages it is aware of. Causality conflicts, such as when a previously unknown message which should already have been processed is received, are handled through local roll back. During roll back the effects of messages that were processed in error are undone.

In order to use Time Warp in a ROSS model, a reverse event function must be provided. For a given event message it is responsible for undoing the state changes that the forward event function incurred for the same message.

The power of Backstroke in this context is that it can automatically generate the appropriate reverse event function for a given forward event function. For complicated discrete event models, this greatly increases productivity since less code needs to be written by hand. In addition, it is much less error prone and lessens the code maintenance burden, compared to hand written reverse code. It can not be enough stressed that even a very minute bug in the reverse code, so that it only almost reverses the effect of the forward event code, is disastrous for Time Warp simulations. Small state differences can make the code address out of bounds, cause exceptions, and result in infinite loops.

3.2   Diffusion Model

In order to test the Backstroke concept and its implementation and runtime library, we have written a small ROSS model that simulates a simplistic process of diffusing particles. In this model, particles are sent between LP's, and an event message consists of a set of particles. An event is processed by the receiving LP adding the particles in the event message to its local pool of particles. Then a subset of the local particles are sent to a different LP, scheduled to arrive to the destination at a future time drawn from an exponential distribution.

In Listings 1.3 and 1.4 the original C++ code for the implementation of the model is shown and the generated forward code. The forward code also involves a call at the beginning of the function to obtain the proper instance of the Backstroke Run Time Library event record for the respective LP (function call rossLpMapping(lp)). For the calls to the ROSS random number generators, three calls to the respective reverse function of the random number generator must be performed. We have added those 3 function calls manually to the generated forward code (the next version of Backstroke will allow to mark such a function with a C++ pragma and generate the respective function call automatically).

Listing 1.3: Original Code*	Listing 1.4: Forward Code
| ```
void ctr_event_handler(ctr_state * s,
                       tw_bf * bf,
                       ctr_message * m,
                       tw_lp * lp)
{


    s->npart += m->npart_send;
    s->transit -= m->npart_send;

    tw_lpid destination;
    double event_time;
    long long int nsend;
    ctr_message *msg;
    tw_event *evt;

    destination = tw_rand_integer(lp->rng,
        0, total_no_lps - 1);
    if(destination < 0||destination >= (
        g_tw_nlp* tw_nnodes())){
        tw_error(TW_LOC, "bad dest");
    }
    nsend = tw_rand_integer(lp->rng,0,(s->
        npart+1)/2);
    event_time = tw_rand_exponential(lp->rng
        , mean) + lookahead;


    evt = tw_event_new(destination,
                event_time, lp);
    msg = tw_event_data(evt);
    msg->npart_send = nsend;
    tw_event_send(evt);

    s->npart -= nsend;
    s->transit += nsend;
}
``` | ```
void ctr_event_handler(ctr_state *s,
                       tw_bf *bf,
                       ctr_message *m,
                       tw_lp *lp)
{
    Backstroke::RunTimeStateStorage* rtss
        =rtl->rossLpMapping(lp);
    (*rtss->avpush(&(s -> npart))) += m->npart_send;
    (*rtss->avpush(&(s -> transit))) -= m->npart_send;

    tw_lpid destination;
    double event_time;
    long long nsend;
    ctr_message *msg;
    tw_event *evt;

    destination = tw_rand_integer(lp -> rng,0,
        total_no_lps - 1);
    if (destination < 0||destination >= g_tw_nlp*
        tw_nnodes()) {
        tw_error(TW_LOC,"bad dest");
    }
    nsend = (tw_rand_integer(lp -> rng,0,(s -> npart +
        1) / 2));
    event_time = (tw_rand_exponential(lp -> rng,mean))
        + lookahead;


    evt = (tw_event_new(destination,
                event_time,lp));
    msg = (tw_event_data(evt));
    (*rtss->avpush(&(msg -> npart_send))) = nsend;
    tw_event_send(evt);

    (*rtss->avpush(&(s -> npart))) -= nsend;
    (*rtss->avpush(&(s -> transit))) += nsend;
}
``` |

Employing the Time Warp parallel option in ROSS, we have run simulations with this diffusion model both using hand-written reverse code, and using Backstroke generated code. To study portability and the performance impact of using Backstroke, we run simulations on two different architectures, using two different compilers on each platform. In all cases, the simulation ran correctly.

On the Intel cluster, we observed that in the version with Backstroke code, event processing was about half the speed compared to the original code in the (normal) case where there are few (<5%) rollbacks (i.e. executions of reverse code), and about the same speed to 30% slower when there are lots of rollbacks (>70%). On the IBM BlueGene/Q machine the Backstroke code also processes events about half as fast as the original code in the low rollback case and about 1.5 to 2 times slower for lots of rollbacks. In general, there is less variability in performance impact on the BlueGene/Q machine compared to the Intel cluster. The performance impact ranges are shown in Table 3, with a more detailed graph in Figure 4.

Table 3. Performance impact on gross event processing of using Backstroke to obtain reverse event code, compared to original manually written reverse code

Architecture	Compiler	Impact of Backstroke
Intel x86	Intel icc/icpc	1.05 − 2.20
Intel x86	GNU gcc / g++	1.05 − 2.22
IBM BlueGene/Q	IBM xlc / xlxcxx	1.50 − 1.95
IBM BlueGene/Q	GNU gcc / g++	1.50 − 1.90

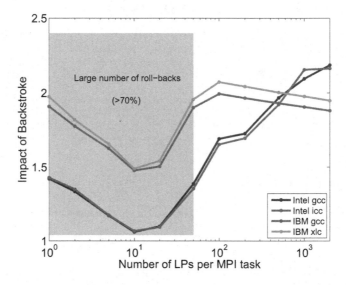

Fig. 4. Performance impact on gross event processing of using Backstroke to obtain reverse event code, compared to original manually written reverse code

4   Related Work

In [8] Jefferson started the subject of rollback-based synchronization in 1984. The paper discusses rollback implemented by restoring a snapshot of an old state, but today we are interested in using reverse computation for that purpose. Also, this paper is written as if discrete event simulation is one of several applications of virtual time, but in fact it was then and is now the primary application. Although the term "virtual time" is used, you can safely read it as "simulation time".

In 1999 Carothers et. al published the first paper [1], that suggests using reverse computation instead of snapshot restoration as the mechanism for rollback. But it does not contemplate using a reversible language. It is written in terms of very simple and conventional programming constructs (C-like rather than C++ -like) and instrumenting the forward code to store near minimal trace information to allow reversing of side effects when needed.

Barnes et. al demonstrated in 2013 [3], how important reverse computation can be in a practical application area. The fastest and most parallel discrete event simulation benchmark ever executed was done at LLNL on one of the world's largest supercomputers using reverse computation as its rollback method for synchronization. But the reverse code was hand-generated, and methodologically we know that this is unsustainable. So we need a way of automatically generating reverse code from forward code, and this is what we address with the work presented in this paper - to have a tool available, Backstroke2, for generating reverse code that can be applied to full C++.

Kalyan Perumalla and Alfred Park discuss the use of Reverse Computation for scalable fault tolerant computations [9]. The paper is limited in a number of ways, but they make a fundamental point, which is that Reverse Computation can be used to recover from faults by mechanisms that are much faster than check pointing mechanisms.

In [10] Justin LaPre et. al discuss reverse code generation for PDES. The presented method is similar to one of our previous approaches in the work on Backstroke [6] as it takes control flow into account and generates code for computing additional information required to reconstruct the execution path that had been take in the forward code. Our presented approach in this paper is different as we do not need to take any control flow information into account, and therefore our approach allows to address full C++ by considering only a small subset of the language constructs, and by regenerating all other constructs unmodified in the forward code. However, the drawback of our approach is that it is likely to generate a higher overhead in the forward code. In specific cases with complicated control flow but only very few updates on the simulation state, our approach can store less information and can be faster - but those are specific cases.

5   Conclusion

We have demonstrated an approach to reverse computation that can be applied to full C++. In contrast to other approaches for generating reverse code, we do not need to explicitly take any control flow information into account, but instead store address-value pairs of modified memory locations and record information about all dynamic memory allocation and deallocation. This information is used in the reverse code to restore the original memory state of the program (in PDES an event method).

The main advantage of our approach is that we need to address only a small number of language constructs, in fact only the memory-manipulating operations in C++. This allows to address full C++ and perform the reverse code generation as a transformation of the original code by only considering forms of assignment and memory allocation and deallocation functions. All other constructs can remain unmodified in the transformation. The drawback is the overhead in the forward code and a higher memory consumption (in most cases) than with approaches that take control flow into account.

Most of the future Backstroke research will be devoted to improving static analysis of the code to eliminate more and more of the runtime checks (though we will never get rid of them all). The strategy is also to incorporate algorithms for reconstructing the initial state variables from the final values where feasible, and for substituting trusted abstract reverse methods for Backstroke-generated ones when we have them, e.g. hand-written reverse number generates as used in ROSS.

In future work we plan to incorporate approaches that address reversible languages into Backstroke, by detecting reversible subsets in event method implementations, and delegate the reconstruction of the program state for those parts of the program to the generated overhead-free reverse code (of reversible code). This may motivate users who implement PDES models, to write more and more parts of their models in reversible subsets of C++ (with possibly some extensions) to achieve better performance. Similar, other approaches, taking control flow into account, may also be applicable to subsets of C++.

Thus, possibly in the long run, some kind of hybrid reversible and conventional language, may turn out to be the best strategy for implementing PDES models in the future, if users can combine both languages. That remains to be seen.

References

1. Carothers, C.D., Perumalla, K.S., Fujimoto, R.M.: Efficient optimistic parallel simulations using reverse computation. ACM Trans. Model. Comput. Simul. **9**(3), 224–253 (1999)
2. Perumalla, K.S.: Introduction to Reversible Computing (2013)
3. Barnes, Jr., P.D., Carothers, C.D., Jefferson, D.R., LaPre, J.M.: Warp speed: executing time warp on 1,966,080 cores. In: Proceedings of the 2013 ACM SIGSIM Conference on Principles of Advanced Discrete Simulation. SIGSIM-PADS 2013, pp. 327–336. ACM, New York (2013)
4. Fujimoto, R.M.: Parallel and Distribution Simulation Systems, 1st edn. John Wiley & Sons Inc, New York (1999)
5. Quinlan, D., Liao, C., Matzke, R., Schordan, M., Panas, T., Vuduc, R., Yi, Q.: ROSE Web Page (2014). http://www.rosecompiler.org
6. Vulov, G., Hou, C., Vuduc, R., Fujimoto, R., Quinlan, D., Jefferson, D.: The backstroke framework for source level reverse computation applied to parallel discrete event simulation. In: Proceedings of the Winter Simulation Conference. WSC 2011, Winter Simulation Conference, pp. 2965–2979 (2011)
7. Holder, A.O., Carothers, C.D.: Analysis of time warp on a 32,768 processor ibm blue gene/l supercomputer. In: Proceedings of the European Modeling and Simulation Symposium (EMSS) (2008)
8. Jefferson, D.R.: Virtual time. ACM Trans. Program. Lang. Syst. **7**(3), 404–425 (1985)
9. Perumalla, K.S., Park, A.J.: Reverse computation for rollback-based fault tolerance in large parallel systems. Cluster Computing **17**(2), 303–313 (2014)
10. LaPre, J.M., Gonsiorowski, E.J., Carothers, C.D.: Lorain: a step closer to the pdes 'holy grail'. In: Proceedings of the 2nd ACM SIGSIM/PADS Conference on Principles of Advanced Discrete Simulation. SIGSIM-PADS 2014, pp. 3–14. ACM, New York (2014)

Towards a Domain-Specific Language for Reversible Assembly Sequences

Ulrik Pagh Schultz[1]([✉]), Johan Sund Laursen[1], Lars-Peter Ellekilde[1], and Holger Bock Axelsen[2]

[1] University of Southern Denmark, Odense, Denmark
ups@mmmi.sdu.dk
[2] University of Copenhagen, Copenhagen, Denmark

Abstract. Programming industrial robots for small-sized batch production of assembly operations is challenging due to the difficulty of precisely specifying general yet robust assembly operations. We observe that as the complexity of assembly increases, so does the likelihood of errors. We propose that certain classes of errors during assembly operations can be addressed using reverse execution, allowing the robot to temporarily back out of an erroneous situation, after which the assembly operation can be automatically retried. Moreover, reversibility can be used to automatically derive a disassembly sequence from a given assembly sequence, or vice versa.

This paper presents the initial design of the RASQ domain-specific language (DSL) for specifying such assembly sequences, based on initial experiments using an industrial case study. The language is defined in terms of a formal semantics corresponding to a realistic execution model currently under implementation. The DSL is used as part of a software framework that aims at tackling uncertainties through a combination of reverse and probabilistic execution.

1 Introduction

Bringing robotics to small-sized batch production is highly important for future industrial development [3,5]. The traditional approach within automation has relied on highly precise and deterministic behavior for avoiding errors during operations. Avoiding operational errors by precision and determinism is however a time-consuming and costly process. For small-sized production, where each automation sequence is only run in small numbers, this is often not a viable option. Moreover, we note that as the complexity of an assembly increases, so does the likelihood of errors.

We observe that certain classes of critical errors occurring during experiments with an industrial case study (described later) could in practice have been solved by backtracking and then repeating part of the assembly sequence. Based on this observation, we hypothesize that certain classes of errors during assembly operations can be addressed using reverse execution of the robot controller, allowing the robot to temporarily back out of an erroneous situation, after which the assembly operation can be automatically retried. Moreover, we hypothesize that

© Springer International Publishing Switzerland 2015
J. Krivine and J.-B. Stefani (Eds.): RC 2015, LNCS 9138, pp. 111–126, 2015.
DOI: 10.1007/978-3-319-20860-2_7

reverse execution can facilitate programming of assembly operations in general: reverse execution could enable automatic derivation of certain required operations from their forwards counterparts, and more generally an entire disassembly sequence could be derived from an assembly sequence, or vice versa. We are however not aiming for a theoretical model; we are interested in physical robots performing realistic and practically useful assembly sequences, which include a mix of reversible operations (moving objects, attaching a bolt to a nut) and non-reversible operations (drilling holes, welding and bending materials).

To explore the above hypotheses further in this setting, in particular through physical experimentation, we are developing a domain-specific language (DSL) for specifying reversible assembly sequences, for control of an industrial robot (a robot arm, as described below.) The underlying principle for reverse execution is statement-level program inversion [14]. However, physical constraints necessitate the ability to explicitly specify the meaning of reverse execution for a subset of operations. Concretely, we propose program inversion as the default mechanism to handle errors and inversion of assembly sequences, while allowing the programmer to override the default program inversion semantics in special cases.

This paper presents the initial design of the DSL, named RASQ (Reversible Assembly SeQuence.) The language is defined in terms of a formal semantics corresponding to a realistic execution model currently under implementation. The RASQ DSL is used as part of a software framework that aims at tackling uncertainties through a combination of reverse and probabilistic execution [2,6]. In general, our approach assumes that operational errors are inevitable and will eventually appear at some point during the assembly. Therefore, instead of trying to avoid errors altogether, the errors are to be managed and rectified. The current paper exclusively concerns the issue of reversible execution. Initial works on probabilistic execution and error recovery were discussed in previous work [2,6], and we return to these issues in the conclusion.

The rest of this paper is organized as follows: First, we discuss the overall concept of what it means to perform reversible execution of assembly operations (Sec. 2). Then follows a presentation of the high-level RASQ language (Sec. 3), its translation to a low-level language (Sec. 4), and the semantics of this low-level language (Sec. 5). Last, we elaborate on a few perspectives and conclude the paper (Sec. 6).

2   The Reversible Assembly Concept

We now present background information on our industrial case study and the use of reversibility in robotics. This is followed by a discussion on the conceptual idea of executing assembly sequences in reverse.

2.1   Robotic Assembly

In the context of this paper, unless otherwise noted, the term *robot* refers to an industrial robot, more precisely a robot arm, as depicted in Fig 1. Usually,

Fig. 1. Our experimental setup: The robot is seen performing a pick-and-place sequence composed of several sub-commands. Commands instruct the robot in where and how to move, as well as controlling the gripper.

general-purpose robot arms consist of 6 or more joints connected in series, and are programmed using a dedicated language containing basic structures for branching and loops as well as a rather limited set of motion and I/O commands. The I/O commands are used to communicate with attached peripheral equipment such as grippers and sensors.

Our experimental setup is shown in Fig. 1, where the robot is seen performing a pick-and-place operation. This operation is a small part of a larger assembly case where several objects have to be placed in a fixture before they are joined together using screws. The case comes from the company VOLA and is an example of a small-sized batch run that includes an assembly case that the company is currently performing manually. In the specific case there is a relatively large number of objects that need to be aligned and placed with high accuracy, plus a number of other requirements and problems that only become apparent when attempting to divide the assembly into smaller steps. A real-world case for demonstration provides real-life complexities and challenges, which otherwise might have been ignored: Humans are good at handling and adapting many of these challenges, but for robots these problems are a significant challenge, since they lack the constant feedback that a human naturally uses when performing such operations.

2.2 Reversibility and Robotics

Robotics represent a real-world application area where computational reversibility has a physical counterpart: Several kinds of actions performed by robots can be physically reversed, for example changing the direction in which a mobile robot is driving, or reversing an industrial assembly process to perform disassembly. Specifically, in this paper we investigate the use of a reversible programming language to control physically reversible robot behavior. We observe that reverse execution is a feature of the mainstream KUKA Robotics Language, but mainly intended as a tool for debugging [7]. Moreover, reversibility is not supported in recent proposals for a revised programming platform, due to the difficulty of integrating reversibility with a general-purpose language [1].

Reversibility has been investigated for the specific case of self-reconfigurable robots. Self-reconfigurable, modular robots are distributed robotic devices that can autonomously change their physical shape [13]. Self-reconfiguration from one shape to another is typically achieved through a specific sequence of actuation operations distributed across the modules of the robot. Automatically reversing the sequence of operations brings the robot back to its initial shape, as has been experimentally demonstrated using the DynaRole reversible language [9]. Dyna-Role however only allows simple sequences of operations to be reversed, such as, e.g., extension or retraction of connectors followed by rotational movement. This capability is suitable for reversing self-reconfiguration sequences, but lacks the generality needed to implement more complex behaviors, such as the assembly operations addressed in this paper.

Initial ideas on generalizing the DynaRole language to support a wider range of modular robot control scenarios retain the possibility of reversing distributed sequences [10,11]. In this paper, reversibility is investigated as a practical feature, reducing the programming task of the programmer, and allowing error recovery by backing out of an error state using reverse execution. We have investigated the generalization using informally specified prototype implementations in limited scenarios, providing preliminary evidence in support of our hypotheses. With the work documented in this paper we give an exact formal semantics for a precisely defined language, providing a basis for a rigorous investigation of reversibility in robotic assembly.

2.3   Executing Assembly Sequences in Reverse

We are interested in reversible programming of assembly sequences for two reasons: (1) Increased robustness through backtracking when certain errors occur, and (2) Increased software reuse through invocation of the same sequence of operations both forwards and backwards. We believe that an appropriately defined concept of reverse execution can be used to fulfill both of these goals. Our approach is similar in principle to the notion of reversible computing from Zuliani [15] and Stoddart et al [12], but where their primary concern is the use of backtracking to search a state space, we use a mix of forwards and reverse execution to deal with unexpected errors in the environment.

We are concerned with controlling physical robots performing realistic and practically useful assembly sequences, which include drilling holes, welding and bending materials, and moving objects in an environment with gravity. Reverse execution of assembly sequences is thus never going to be time-invertible; although certain classes of operations tend to be time-invertible, in practice robotic control seems to require different kinds of operations to implement time-inverse behaviors. For example, removing a peg from a tightly-fitting hole simply requires pulling the peg out of the hole, whereas reinserting the peg into the same hole is most easily done by edging the peg into the hole at an angle [8].

We observe that although the goal is to establish a kind of bidirectional transformation between different robot and world states, similarly to the bidirectional tree transformations of Foster et al [4], the presence of a physical environment

```
object nut
object bolt
sequence attach_nut_bolt {
  state begin_nut_bolt (...tool pos...) bolt:(...pos...) nut:(...pos...)
  moveto (...pos above table...)
  pickup (nut, fixed_gripper, (...pos of nut...))
  moveto (...)
  try 3 (force<1) {
    moveto (...pos on bolt...)
    call apply_and_turn_nut
  }
  release (nut, fixed_gripper, (...))
  moveto (...pos above table...)
}

sequence apply_and_turn_nut { ...commands... }
reverse { ...commands that undo apply_and_turn_nut... }

grip fixed_gripper (nut) { ...commands for gripping a nut... }
```

Fig. 2. Sample RASQ program, vector constants are omitted for clarity, only the body of attach_nut_bolt is shown

and the requirement of dealing with unpredictable errors requires a different kind of semantics where reverse execution of an operation might require a completely different set of operations compared to the forwards execution of the operation. Nevertheless, concepts from bidirectional transformation might eventually prove useful for reasoning about the execution of reversible assembly operations at a higher level of abstraction; this is, however, left as future work.

3   The RASQ Language

We now present the RASQ language. We start by giving a small, expository example of a RASQ program for attaching nuts to bolts, showing the key features of RASQ. We then give a grammar for RASQ in the form of an EBNF, and present our considerations on defining the RASQ semantics.

3.1   RASQ by Example

We now introduce the key features of the RASQ language, using the small example shown in Fig. 2. A RASQ program consists of declarations of *objects*, *sequences* and *grips*. Objects are to be manipulated by sequences of commands, using grips to pick up and release objects (an object is moved by moving the robot while the object is gripped.) The example program declares two objects, named nut and bolt. Object declarations introduce names that serve a dual purpose: they are used to select which gripping operation to use, and they can be used to specify assertions on the current state of the system as a whole.

The program declares two sequences, `attach_nut_bolt` and `apply_and_turn_nut`. The sequence `attach_nut_bolt` only specifies a single (forwards) body for both forwards and reverse execution, so reverse execution will inversely evaluate the forwards body in reverse order, as specified later. The first statement is a state assertion, named `begin_nut_bolt`, specifying the spatial positioning of the tool and the respective positions of the bolt and nut objects:

```
state begin_nut_bolt (...) bolt:(...) nut:(...)
```

The positions of the bolt and nut objects are not known precisely but must be estimated, for example using a vision system. (Its implementation is not specified as part of the semantics of the language.) Should the assertion fail, e.g., by failing to find an object in the asserted location, an error will be triggered, identified by the state assertion name. Triggering an error reverses the direction of execution, up until the boundary of an enclosing try block handling the corresponding error (as defined by using the state assertion name for the restriction of the try block.)

The next statement of the program is a move, which moves the robot to the given position (again, the position is given as a constant, not shown):

```
moveto (...pos above table...)
```

Unlike DynaRole, we do not require the programmer to explicitly provide information to make move operations locally invertible, but we shall see later that the program does provide sufficient detail for reversibility, nonetheless. A move command can be guarded by an enclosing try block that can define the amount of force that is maximally allowed to be exerted to complete the move; exceeding this force triggers an execution-reversing error.

After the move follows a pick up instruction:

```
pickup (nut, fixed_gripper, (...nut pos...))
```

This causes the pickup sequence associated with the name `fixed_gripper` and the object `nut` to be evaluated, using a local frame corresponding to the position given as the last argument. All movement is done relative to a frame defining a position and an orientation. Evaluating a grip or release sequence using a specific local frame allows the commands to be defined relative to the object they are manipulating.

A try block follows the pickup instruction, which specifies to perform the given statements using a force that does not exceed 1N (1 Newton), and to try this at most 3 times:

```
try 3 (force<1) {
  moveto (...pos on bolt...)
  call apply_and_turn_nut
}
```

Should a movement statement in the body of the try (or in any sequence or grip invoked herein) exceed 1N of force, an error will be triggered reversing the direction of execution, until it reaches the boundary of the try block. From there the execution direction will change again to try evaluating the body once more. Exit from the try block can be in either direction of execution, but must either be in the same direction as the block was entered, or in reverse direction once the block has been evaluated 3 times. The try block in the example contains a move and a call of another sequence; calling a sequence is similar to invocation of a procedure, but since a sequence can have different forwards and backwards implementations by specifying a `reverse` block, the appropriate one is called based on the current direction of execution.

After the try block a release statement is used, releasing the object currently being held at the given position:

```
release (nut, fixed_gripper, (...))
```

The release is in this case performed by evaluating the corresponding pickup in reverse direction, since no specific "reverse pickup" implementation is specified for the grip.

The last operation is the declaration of the second sequence `apply_and_turn_nut`, which is not shown in detail, but has both a forwards and a reverse body, so forwards execution evaluates the forwards body in forwards order, and reverse execution evaluates the reverse body in forwards order (i.e., in the order written in the program). The program also declares a single grip, `fixed_gripper`, which only applies to the object `nut` (although it may be defined for other objects, too.) The gripper is defined using a single body consisting of arbitrary commands that can do anything except using other grips. This grip body is used both for forwards evaluation (gripping an object) and reverse evaluation (releasing it.)

3.2 Syntax

The syntax of the RASQ language is given by the grammar shown in Fig. 3. A RASQ program consists of a number of declarations of named objects, a number of command sequences of which one is considered the main sequence, and a number of grip sequences. Named objects O are used to statically decide which grip sequence to use for a given grip operation, and their position can be asserted using the command `state`. Sequences S are lists of commands, sequences can invoke other sequences and make grips, but cannot be recursive. Grips G are named and are defined separately for each specific object similarly to static overloading; grips can invoke arbitrary commands including sequences but excluding other grips (the semantics of gripping during a grip currently results in an error).

The command `moveto` moves the robot to the given position, moving any object that has been gripped. The commands `pickup` and `release` perform grips and releases of objects. The command `call` evaluates the named sequence in the same direction as the current execution direction, whereas the command `uncall` evaluates the named sequence using the opposite direction. The command `io` activates low-level I/O operations, for example for operating the gripper or activating some other tool. Moreover, I/O operations can also activate operations

Program $P ::= (O|S|G)^*$
Object $O ::= \text{object } N_O$
Sequence $S ::= \text{sequence } N_S \ \{ \ C^* \ \} \ (\text{reverse } N_S \ \{ \ C^* \ \})?$
Command $C ::= \text{moveto}(V) \ | \ \text{pickup}(N_O, N_G, V) \ | \ \text{release}(N_O, N_G, V) \ | \ \text{call } N_S$
          $| \ \text{uncall } N_S \ | \ \text{try}(n) \ R^* \ \{ C^* \} \ | \ \text{io } N_I \ (n_0 \ldots n_i; V_0 \ldots V_j)$
          $| \ \text{wait } n \ | \ \text{state } (N_R : V)? \ (N_O : V)^* \ | \ \text{error}$
Grip $G ::= \text{grip } N_G \ (N_O^*) \ \{ \ C^* \ \} \ (\text{reverse } N_G \ \{ \ C^* \ \})? \ \text{where no } C \text{ grips}$
Restriction $R ::= \text{force} < n \ | \ \text{state } N_R$

$N_O, N_S, N_G, N_I, N_R \in$ name space of corresponding construct
$V \in \mathbb{R}^k, n, k \in \mathbb{N}, \mathbb{R}$ real numbers, $\mathbb{N}$ natural numbers.

Fig. 3. EBNF grammar of high-level RASQ programs

from an underlying library of preprogrammed actions that are automatically parameterized and randomized using a probabilistic approach described in earlier work [2], see Sec. 6 for a discussion. Whether an I/O operation is reversible is dependent on its implementation, which is checked dynamically during execution. The command wait waits a number of seconds before proceeding execution. The command state asserts the current state of the system, optionally including the position of the robot and the current estimated position of any of the named objects. The command error terminates the program, and can thus be used to specify the implementation of sequences or grips that can only evaluate in one direction. A forwards-only sequence can for example be implemented by providing a reverse body that only contains the command error.

3.3   RASQ Semantics: High-Level and Low-Level Languages

Rather than defining the semantics in terms of the RASQ language, we describe a translation to a low-level graph-based language, and then provide a semantics for this low-level language. This approach closely mirrors our current implementation of the RASQ language, and the semantics thus serves as a formal specification of this implementation. Moreover, we found that formally expressing the semantics of arbitrary program point execution reversal was more easily done using an explicit graph-based based representation. The translation and low-level semantics are presented in the next two sections.

4   Low-Level Language

Execution of RASQ programs is defined in terms of the low-level language L-RASQ, based on a graph representation. This section defines the language, the translation from RASQ, and a forwards analysis used to annotate movement commands with the position that they move from, used for reverse execution.

4.1   Language Definition

We define an L-RASQ program P^L as a graph with nodes X, each node representing a single command to be executed. Forwards edges F are used for forwards execution of the program, and backwards edges B are used for backwards execution of the program:

$$P^L = (X, F, B), X = \mathcal{L}(G_L) \times \{\overline{F}, \overline{B}\}, F \subseteq X \times X, B \subseteq X \times X$$

Nodes are also annotated with their execution direction: $\overline{F}$ indicating forwards and $\overline{B}$ indicating backwards. Execution of a node in the opposite direction of its indicated direction requires inversion of the command contained within the node (e.g., a movement command from p_1 to p_2 contained in a node will move to p_2 when executed in the direction of the node annotation and move to p_1 when executed in the opposite direction). The operator $\hookleftarrow$ yields the reverse direction, e.g., $\hookleftarrow \overline{F} = \overline{B}$ and $\hookleftarrow \overline{B} = \overline{F}$. The nodes contain commands that are elements of the language defined by the grammar G_L, given by the following EBNF (using definitions from Fig. 3):

$$L ::= l : \texttt{movefromto}(V, V) \mid l : \texttt{trying}(l', n, R) \mid l : \texttt{gripping}(V) \mid l : \texttt{skip}$$
$$\mid \quad l : \texttt{wait}(n) \mid l : \texttt{error} \mid l : \texttt{state} \ N_R : V \ (N_O : V)*$$
$$\mid \quad l : \texttt{io} \ N_I \ (X;Y)$$
$$X \in \mathbb{N}^i, Y \in \mathbb{R}^j, i, j, \in \mathbb{N}$$

During translation each command is annotated with a unique label l, explicitly making distinct values from identical commands. Additional labels are used to match the beginning and end of a try-block.

4.2   Translation from RASQ

The translation from RASQ to L-RASQ is defined by recursive descent on RASQ terms using the function $\mathcal{T}$ that builds the L-RASQ graph according to the RASQ control flow by appending nodes corresponding to each term. With the exception of sequence calls and grips the translation rules generate a chain; for sequence calls and grips separate branches are generated for the forwards and reverse translations. The function $\mathcal{T}$ is defined as follows:

$$\mathcal{T}(f, \Delta)[t] = (x, y, G)$$

Here f is the unique node that should execute immediately before the translation of t in forwards execution, Δ is the current execution direction, t is the term to translate, x is the unique node that should be executed first in forwards execution of the translation of t, y is the unique node that should be executed last (and vice versa for x and y for backwards execution), and lastly, G is a subgraph of the resulting translated program representing the translation of t.

The key translation rules are shown in Fig 4, with similar and trivial rules are omitted for brevity. The rule [T:Mov] translates a single move command

$$\frac{x = (l : \mathtt{movefromto}(\bot, V), \Delta) \quad l \text{ is fresh}}{\mathcal{T}(f, \Delta)[\mathtt{moveto}(V)] = (x, x, (\{x\}, \{(f, x)\}, \{x, f\}))} \; [\mathrm{T:Mov}]$$

$$\frac{\begin{array}{c} x = (l_x : \mathtt{trying}(l, n, r), \Delta) \quad y = (l_y : \mathtt{trying}(l, n, r), \Delta) \\ \mathcal{T}(f, \Delta)[C_1 \dots C_n] = (z_1, z_n, (Z, F, B)) \quad l, l_x, l_y \text{ are fresh} \\ Z' = \{x, y\} \cup Z \\ F' = \{(f, x), (x, z_1), (z_n, y)\} \cup F \quad B' = \{(x, f), (z_1, x), (y, z_n)\} \cup B) \end{array}}{\mathcal{T}(f, \Delta)[\mathtt{try}(n) \; r \; \{C_1 \dots C_n\}] = (x, y, (Z', F', B'))} \; [\mathrm{T:Try}]$$

$$\frac{\begin{array}{c} \xi = \{1, \dots, n\} \quad \mathcal{T}(f_{i-1}, \Delta)[C_i] = (x_i, f_i, (Z_i, F_i, B_i)), i \in \xi \\ Z = \bigcup_{i \in \xi} Z_i \\ F = \{(f_{i-1}, x_i) | i \in \xi\} \cup \bigcup_{i \in \xi} F_i \quad B = \{(x_i, f_{i-1}) | i \in \xi\} \cup \bigcup_{i \in \xi} F_i \end{array}}{\mathcal{T}(f_0, \Delta)[C_1 \dots C_n] = (x_1, f_n, (Z, F, B))} \; [\mathrm{T:Seq}]$$

$$\frac{\begin{array}{c} (\Delta_0, \Delta_1) = (\Delta, \hookleftarrow \Delta) \\ s_0 = (l_0 : \mathtt{skip}, \Delta_0) \quad s_1 = (l_1 : \mathtt{skip}, \Delta_1) \quad l_0, l_1 \text{ are fresh} \\ \mathrm{lookup}_S^{\Delta_0}(z) = C_1^0 \dots C_{n_0}^0 \quad \mathrm{lookup}_S^{\Delta_1}(z) = C_1^1 \dots C_{n_1}^1 \\ \mathcal{T}(s_j, \Delta_j)[C_1^j \dots C_{n_j}^j] = (x_j, y_j, (Z_j, F_j, B_j)), j \in 0, 1 \\ Z = \{s_0, s_1\} \cup Z_0 \cup Z_1 \quad F = \{y_0, s_1\} \cup F_0 \cup F_1 \quad B = \{y_1, s_0\} \cup B_0 \cup B_1 \end{array}}{\mathcal{T}(f, \Delta)[\mathtt{call} \; z] = (s_0, s_1, (Z, F, B))} \; [\mathrm{T:Cal}]$$

$\mathrm{lookup}_S^{\Delta}(z) = $ the direction Δ definition of sequence z

Fig. 4. Translation from RASQ to L-RASQ (selected rules)

into a move node, adding edges to attach this node to the predecessor in the graph. The first argument of the move instruction is left undefined (indicated by $\bot$), and will be defined in a later phase, described in Sec 4.3. The translation rules for wait, io, state and error all work in the same way, adding a single node to the graph that attaches to the predecessor.

The rule [T:Try] basically translates a try block into a sequence of nodes defining the body of the block, delimited by nodes x and y with the same content, that define the borders of the try region. Due to execution symmetry, entering a try region has the same semantics whether execution is forwards or reverse.

The rule [T:Seq] defines how to translate a sequence of statements by translating each statement independently, always attaching a given statement to the predecessor: either the node preceding the whole sequence as a base case, or the translation of the previous statement as the induction case.

The rule [T:Cal] defines the translation of a sequence call into a DAG with common start and end nodes (the s_i skip nodes). From the node s_0 forwards execution leads into the forwards branch, whereas from the node s_1 reverse execution leads into the backwards branch. As all other nodes are fully connected in both directions, this is our reason for separating forwards and backwards edges. The uncall command is defined similarly, except that the backwards definition of the sequence is laid out as the forwards branch, and vice versa. The `pickup` and `release` commands are similar to `call` and `uncall`, except that they use the special `gripping` instruction in the places of the skip nodes. Note that since sequences are non-recursive, it is safe to translate calls by unfolding.

4.3   From-Position Analysis

Both the high-level RASQ and low-level L-RASQ language rely on most statements being reversible. The movement statement `moveto` is translated into the instruction `movefromto`, which explicitly includes the position that the robot is moving from, making statement reversal trivial (e.g., moving from x to y is reversed by moving from y to x). The translation however does not define the from-position; this position can be derived either off-line using a simple static analysis, or on-line using an execution trace.

The off-line static analysis starts with the root node of the L-RASQ graph, at which point the robot position must be known, either by being predefined outside the program or using the `state` assertion to define the state of the robot. The robot position is then simply propagated in a depth-first traversal of the graph and used to annotate all `movefromto` nodes. Since sequence calls and grip invocations are always fully expanded, and there are no conditionals or loops, in a given node in a program the robot position will always be uniquely defined.

The on-line approach simply records the robot positions as the program executes, in principle similar to recording an execution trace and then using it for backtracking, as was done by Stoddart et al [12]. This approach has the advantage that it reverses unexpected behaviors more precisely, for example after collision with an object in the environment. Since assembly sequence executions normally will consist of a relatively limited number of moves, saving such an execution trace only consumes a limited amount of memory.

We are currently implementing the off-line approach for use with our experimental platform, due to its simplicity and the ability to run a program in reverse without first having executed it forwards. We however expect that the on-line approach will be valuable for the error handling case, and plan to eventually use a combination of both.

5   Semantics

The L-RASQ semantics are defined as a small-step operational semantics that uses two sets of evaluation rules: graph evaluation that transfers control between nodes, and node evaluation that evaluates the current node of the graph.

In more detail, graph evaluation steps $\rightarrow$ are of the following form:

$$\langle E, f, l_1 : (\alpha, \delta) \rangle_L^{\Delta} \xrightarrow{\tau} \langle E', f', l_2 : (\beta, \delta') \rangle_{L'}^{\Delta'}$$

Where E is the current environment mapping labels to error-tracking information, f is the current frame for movement commands, $l_1 : (\alpha, \delta)$ is the node

$$\frac{dir(\Delta, \delta), E, f, L \vdash \alpha \Rightarrow (E', f', \mathbf{continue}, \tau, L')}{\langle E, f, l_1 : (\alpha, \delta) \rangle_L^\Delta \overset{\tau}{\to} \langle E', f', next^\Delta(l_1) \rangle_{L'}^\Delta} \quad [\text{G:Con}]$$

$$\frac{dir(\Delta, \delta), E, f, L \vdash \alpha \Rightarrow (E', f', \mathbf{reverse}, \tau, L') \quad \Delta' = \hookleftarrow \Delta}{\langle E, f, l_1 : (\alpha, \delta) \rangle_L^\Delta \overset{\tau}{\to} \langle E', f', back^\tau(\Delta', l_1 : (\alpha, \delta)) \rangle_{L'}^{\Delta'}} \quad [\text{G:Rev}]$$

$$dir(\Delta, \delta) = \begin{cases} \Delta, & \Delta = \delta \\ \hookleftarrow \Delta, & \text{otherwise} \end{cases}$$

$$next^{\overline{F}}(l_1) = l_2 : (\beta, \delta'), \text{ where } (l_1 : (\alpha, \delta), l_2 : (\beta, \delta')) \in F \text{ for } P^L = (X, F, B)$$

$$next^{\overline{B}}(l_1) = l_2 : (\beta, \delta'), \text{ where } (l_1 : (\alpha, \delta), l_2 : (\beta, \delta')) \in B \text{ for } P^L = (X, F, B)$$

$$back^\tau(\Delta, l : (\alpha, \delta)) = \begin{cases} next^\Delta(l), & \tau = [\text{none}] \\ l : (\alpha, \delta), & \text{otherwise} \end{cases}$$

Fig. 5. Graph evaluation rules

to evaluate with instruction α and translation direction δ, Δ is the execution direction, L is the current set of error-condition labels used for the **try** command, τ is the effect of the command in the node (e.g., moving the robot), E' is the resulting environment, f' is the resulting frame, $l_2 : (\beta, \delta')$ is the next node to evaluate, Δ' is the execution direction in which this next node should be evaluated, and L' is the resulting set of error-condition labels.

Program execution is defined by iterated graph evaluation, which starts with an empty environment E, an undefined frame f (meaning to use the global frame in which the robot operates), either the head or tail node of the program graph as $l_1 : \alpha$ with the appropriate corresponding execution direction Δ ($\overline{F}$ when starting with the head node, $\overline{B}$ when starting with the tail node), and an empty set of labels L.

Node evaluation rules $\Rightarrow$ are of the following form:

$$\Delta, E, f, L \vdash \alpha \Rightarrow (E', f', r, \tau, L')$$

Where Δ is the execution direction, E is the current environment, f is the current frame for movement commands, L is the current set of error-condition labels, α is the term of the node being evaluated, E' is the resulting environment, f' is the resulting movement frame, r is the result of the evaluation (whether to continue execution, reverse execution, or fail), τ is the effect of the command, and L' is the resulting set of error-condition labels.

5.1   Graph Evaluation

The graph-level evaluation strategy is defined using the two rules in Fig. 5. In both cases, the direction in which the statement of a node is evaluated depends on the current execution direction and the direction annotation of the node, as expressed by the function *dir:* if these match the current direction is used, otherwise the reverse direction is used (i.e., executing a reverse body in forwards execution mode inverts each statement). The rule [G:Con] defines the reaction to a statement that succeeded and resulted in "continue": execution continues in the same direction with the next node according to this direction. The rule [G:Rev] defines the reaction to a statement that failed in a controlled way and resulted in "reverse": the direction of execution is reversed, and if there was no effect we continue with the next node, otherwise the current node is repeated but with reverse execution semantics (this potentially allows undoing the effect of a halfway-completed operation.) The reaction to a statement that fails is simply to stop evaluation of the program.

5.2   Node Evaluation

Node evaluation rules are defined in Fig. 6. All rules are symmetric in the execution direction Δ. Some of these rules are defined in terms of *primitives:* functions that correspond to operating the robot and reading the result; primitive names are always underlined.

Movement is defined using the three rules [Mov:Con], [Mov:Rev], and [Mov:Fail]. These rules all select their goal position according to the current execution direction Δ, using the select function:

$$select^{\overline{F}}(p_1, p_2) = p_1, \ select^{\overline{B}}(p_1, p_2) = p_2$$

All movement rules make use of the movement primitive $\underline{move}(p, E, f)$ which moves the robot to position p while observing any restrictions in E and moving relative to the frame f if defined (otherwise the global frame of the robot is used.) The return value of $\underline{move}$ either indicates success with $\underline{ok}$, the label l of an exceeded restriction, or severe failure (e.g., robot shutdown) with $\underline{fail}$.

The try statement is defined using three rules. The rule [Try:Begin] describes first entering a try block with the unique label l, in this case the repetition counter from the try block is stored in the environment. The rule [Try:End] describes finishing a try block, either because the maximum number of attempts has been reached, or because it is being exited in the same execution direction as it was entered. Last, the rule [Try:Rev] describes reaching the boundary of a try block, but with the opposite execution direction from which it was entered; in this case the direction is reversed and the block is retried with a decreased attempts counter value.

Gripping is defined using the two rules [Grip:On] and [Grip:Off], that simply define and undefine the local frame. When defined, the movement primitive is relative to this local frame, otherwise the movement primitive is relative to the global frame.

I/O is defined according to the three rules [IO:Con], [IO:Rev], and [IO:Fail]. These rules all make use of the primitive $\underline{io}(\Delta, op, x, y)$: This primitive invokes the corresponding I/O function in direction Δ with the parameters x and y, depending on whether the primitive succeeds execution either continues (I/O success), reverses (I/O failure), or stops if the primitive is undefined for the given execution direction (indicated by a return value of $\perp$).

$$\frac{p = select^\Delta(p_1, p_2) \quad \underline{\text{move}(p, E, f) = \text{ok}}}{\Delta, E, f, L \vdash \text{movefromto}(p_1, p_2) \Rightarrow (E, f, \textbf{continue}, [\text{move} : p], L)} \text{ [Mov:Con]}$$

$$\frac{p = select^\Delta(p_1, p_2) \quad \underline{\text{move}(p, E, f) = l}, l \text{ is a label}}{\Delta, E, f, L \vdash \text{movefromto}(p_1, p_2) \Rightarrow (E, f, \textbf{reverse}, [\text{move:fail}], L \cup \{l\})} \text{ [Mov:Rev]}$$

$$\frac{p = select^\Delta(p_1, p_2) \quad \underline{\text{move}(p, E, f) = \text{fail}}}{\Delta, E, f, L \vdash \text{movefromto}(p_1, p_2) \Rightarrow (E, f, \textbf{fail}, [\text{move:fail}], L)} \text{ [Mov:Fail]}$$

$$\frac{E(l) = \bot}{\Delta, E, f, L \vdash \text{trying}(l, n, r) \Rightarrow (E[l \mapsto (\Delta, r, n)], f, \textbf{continue}, [\text{none}], L)} \text{ [Try:Begin]}$$

$$\frac{E(l) = (\Delta', r, n') \quad (\Delta = \Delta' \vee n' = 1)}{\Delta, E, f, L \vdash \text{trying}(l, n, r) \Rightarrow (E[l \mapsto \bot], f, \textbf{continue}, [\text{none}], L \backslash \{l\})} \text{ [Try:End]}$$

$$\frac{l \in L \quad E(l) = (\Delta', r, n') \quad (\Delta \neq \Delta' \wedge n' > 1)}{\Delta, E, f, L \vdash \text{trying}(l, n, r) \Rightarrow (E[l \mapsto (\Delta', r, n' - 1)], f, \textbf{reverse}, [\text{none}], L \backslash \{l\})} \text{ [Try:Rev]}$$

$$\frac{f = \bot}{\Delta, E, f, L \vdash \text{gripping}(v) \Rightarrow (E, v, \textbf{continue}, [\text{none}], L)} \text{ [Grip:On]}$$

$$\frac{f \neq \bot}{\Delta, E, f, L \vdash \text{gripping}(v) \Rightarrow (E, \bot, \textbf{continue}, [\text{none}], L)} \text{ [Grip:Off]}$$

$$\frac{\underline{\text{io}}(\Delta, \text{op}, x, y) = \underline{\text{ok}}}{\Delta, E, f, L \vdash \text{io op } (x; y) \Rightarrow (E, f, \textbf{continue}, [\text{io} : \text{op}, x, y], L)} \text{ [IO:Con]}$$

$$\frac{\underline{\text{io}}(\Delta, \text{op}, x, y) = \underline{\text{fail}}}{\Delta, E, f, L \vdash \text{io op } (x; y) \Rightarrow (E, f, \textbf{reverse}, [\text{none}], L)} \text{ [IO:Rev]}$$

$$\frac{\underline{\text{io}}(\Delta, \text{op}, x, y) = \bot}{\Delta, E, f, L \vdash \text{io op } (x; y) \Rightarrow (E, f, \textbf{fail}, [\text{io:fail}], L)} \text{ [IO:Fail]}$$

$$\frac{\underline{\text{state}}(x, E, v_0, \{(o_1, v_1), \ldots, (o_n, v_n)\}) = \underline{\text{ok}}}{\Delta, E, f, L \vdash \textbf{state } x : v_0 \ o_1 : v_1 \ldots o_n : v_n \Rightarrow (E, f, \textbf{continue}, [\text{none}], L)} \text{ [St:OK]}$$

$$\frac{\underline{\text{state}}(x, E, v_0, \{(o_1, v_1), \ldots, (o_n, v_n)\}) = l, l \text{ is a label}}{\Delta, E, f, L \vdash \textbf{state } x : v_0 \ o_1 : v_1 \ldots o_n : v_n \Rightarrow (E, f, \textbf{reverse}, [\text{none}], L \cup \{l\})} \text{ [St:Fail]}$$

$$\Delta, E, f, L \vdash \text{wait}(n) \Rightarrow (E, f, \textbf{continue}, [\text{wait} : n], L) \text{ [Wait]}$$

$$\Delta, E, f, L \vdash \text{error} \Rightarrow (E, f, \textbf{fail}, [\text{none}], L) \text{ [Error]}$$

Fig. 6. Node evaluation rules

The state assertion is defined according to the two rules [St:OK] and [St:Fail] that use the primitive $\underline{\text{state}}(x, E, v_0, OV)$: This primitive uses sensors to check the assertion that the robot position (if given) is v_0 and that the object positions given by OV are correct (the precision of this assertion is not defined by the language semantics). If the assertion fails, a label l from E mapping to a tuple holding a restriction named x is returned (if the assertion fails and no such label exists, the behavior is undefined). The rule [ST:OK] describes an assertion that succeeds (and hence has no effect). The rule [ST:FAIL] describes a failed assertion that causes the execution to switch direction. The label corresponding to the state assertion is added to the set of error-signaling labels, so that a try restricting the same name can catch the error condition.

Last, waiting is defined as an effect using the rule [WAIT], and unrecoverable errors are defined using the rule [ERROR].

6   Conclusion and Future Work

We have presented the formal definition of the RASQ language, a DSL for describing reversible execution of assembly scenarios. RASQ is unique in being a reversible language that incorporates inversion as the default error handling mechanism, but allows the programmer to override the default with an explicit reverse implementation of selected operations. In general, we believe that robotics is an interesting application area for reversible computing, and that implementing reversible languages for robotic control can contribute to a better understanding of reversible computing, reversible programming languages, and, in general, reversible phenomena in nature.

In terms of future work, we are currently implementing L-RASQ as execution engine for the CARMEN platform [2]. A key goal is determining the degree of reversibility required in practice. For example, the current semantics allow the execution direction to change at any point, even while performing backtracking using reverse execution: the robot can be backtracking due to an error when another error happens, causing the robot to move forwards again. However, in practice this situation may be so rare that it is not relevant to support in the semantics of the language. The CARMEN platform incorporates a library of probabilistic actions that are optimized in simulation, essentially allowing I/O operations (such as insertion of a rod into a hole) to be varied every time, using an optimized range of randomized parameters. We believe that combining this probabilistic approach with error recovery based on reverse execution has potential for significantly improving the robustness of loosely specified assembly operations, since actions can execute differently every time they are retried.

Acknowledgments. This work was initiated at Schloss Dagstuhl Seminar 15062 on Domain-Specific Languages. Thanks to William Cook and Matthew Flatt for help in the early stages of the work, and to Henrik Gordon Petersen and Robin Kaarsgaard for constructive comments on the paper. This work was partly supported by The Danish Council for Strategic Research through the CARMEN project, and The Danish Council for Independent Research | Natural Sciences through the Foundation of Reversible Computing (FoRC) project.

References

1. Angerer, A., Hoffmann, A., Schierl, A., Vistein, M., Reif, W.: Robotics API: Object-oriented software development for industrial robots. Journal of Software Engineering in Robotics 4(1), 1–22 (2013)

2. Buch, J.P., Laursen, J.S., Sørensen, L.C., Ellekilde, L.-P., Kraft, D., Schultz, U.P., Petersen, H.G.: Applying simulation and a domain-specific language for an adaptive action library. In: Brugali, D., Broenink, J.F., Kroeger, T., MacDonald, B.A. (eds.) SIMPAR 2014. LNCS, vol. 8810, pp. 86–97. Springer, Heidelberg (2014)
3. EU Robotics AISBL: Robotics 2020 multi-annual roadmap for robotics in europe (2014)
4. Foster, J.N., Greenwald, M.B., Moore, J.T., Pierce, B.C., Schmitt, A.: Combinators for bi-directional tree transformations: A linguistic approach to the view update problem. ACM Transactions on Programming Languages and Systems **29**(3), Article 17 (2007)
5. Haegele, M., Skordas, T., Sagert, S., Bischoff, R., Brogardh, T., Dresselhaus, M.: White paper - Industrial Robot Automation (2005). http://www.euron.org/miscdocs/docs/euron2/year2/dr-14-1-industry.pdf
6. Laursen, J.S., Buch, J.P., Sørensen, L.C., Kraft, D., Petersen, H.G., Ellekilde, L.P., Schultz, U.P.: Towards Error Handling in a DSL for Robot Assembly Tasks (2014), DSLRob 2014. arXiv:1412.4538
7. Muhe, H., Angerer, A., Hoffmann, A., Reif, W.: On reverse-engineering the KUKA Robot Language (2010), DSLRob 2010. arXiv:1009.5004
8. Savarimuthu, T.R., Liljekrans, D., Ellekilde, L.P., Ude, A., Nemec, B., Krüger, N.: Analysis of human peg-in-hole executions in a robotic embodiment using uncertain grasps. In: Robot Motion and Control (RoMoCo 2013), pp. 233–239. IEEE (2013)
9. Schultz, U., Bordignon, M., Stoy, K.: Robust and reversible execution of self-reconfiguration sequences. Robotica **29**, 35–57 (2011). http://www.youtube.com/watch?v=SYizuooEs7s
10. Schultz, U.: Poster: programming language abstractions for self-reconfigurable robots. In: Systems, Programming, and Applications: Software for Humanity (SPLASH 2012), pp. 69–70. ACM, New York (2012)
11. Schultz, U.P.: Towards a general-purpose, reversible language for controlling self-reconfigurable robots. In: Glück, R., Yokoyama, T. (eds.) RC 2012. LNCS, vol. 7581, pp. 97–111. Springer, Heidelberg (2013)
12. Stoddart, B., Lynas, R., Zeyda, F.: A virtual machine for supporting reversible probabilistic guarded command languages. Electronic Notes in Theoretical Computer Science **253**(6), 33–56 (2010). Reversible Computation (RC 2009)
13. Yim, M., Shen, W.M., Salemi, B., Rus, D., Moll, M., Lipson, H., Klavins, E., Chirikjian, G.S.: Modular Self-Reconfigurable Robot Systems [Grand Challenges of Robotics]. IEEE Robotics and Automation Magazine **14**(1), 43–52 (2007)
14. Yokoyama, T., Axelsen, H.B., Glück, R.: Principles of a reversible programming language. In: Computing Frontiers (CF 2008), pp. 43–54. ACM, New York (2008)
15. Zuliani, P.: Logical reversibility. IBM Journal of Research and Development **45**(6), 807–818 (2001)

Design and Verification
of Quantum Circuits

Reversibility in Extended Measurement-Based Quantum Computation

Nidhal Hamrit[1,3] and Simon Perdrix[2,3]([✉])

[1] Telecom ParisTech, Paris, France
[2] CNRS, Villers-lès-Nancy, France
[3] LORIA, UMR 7503, CNRS, Inria, Université de Lorraine, Nancy, France
simon.perdrix@loria.fr

Abstract. When applied on some particular quantum entangled states, measurements are universal for quantum computing. In particular, despite the fondamental probabilistic evolution of quantum measurements, any unitary evolution can be simulated by a measurement-based quantum computer (MBQC). We consider the extended version of the MBQC where each measurement can occur not only in the $\{X, Y\}$-plane of the Bloch sphere but also in the $\{X, Z\}$- and $\{Y, Z\}$-planes. The existence of a gflow in the underlying graph of the computation is a necessary and sufficient condition for a certain kind of determinism. We extend the focused gflow (a gflow in a particular normal form) defined for the $\{X, Y\}$-plane to the extended case, and we provide necessary and sufficient conditions for the existence of such normal forms.

1 Introduction

Performing one-qubit measurements on an initially entangled state called *graph state* [8] is a universal model for quantum computation introduced by Raussendorf and Briegel [14,15]. This model is very promising for the physical implementation of a quantum computer [13,16]. The measurement-calculus [4,5] is a formal framework for measurement-based quantum computation. In the original model introduced by Briegel and Raussendorf, all measurements are applied in the so called $\{X, Y\}$-plane of the Bloch sphere, however the model can be extended to other planes, namely $\{X, Z\}$- and $\{Y, Z\}$-planes. For instance, measurements in the $\{X, Z\}$-planes are universal [12] for quantum computation, with the particular property that only real numbers are used in this case. The Extended Measurement-Calculus [5] is an extension of the Measurement-Calculus in which the three possible planes of measurement are available.

The question of the reversibility is central in measurement-based quantum computation since the key ingredient of this model – the quantum measurement – has a fundamentally probabilistic evolution. Reversibility is essential for the simulation of quantum circuits, and as a consequence for the universality of the model. For deciding whether an initial resource (a graph state) can be used to implement a reversible evolution, a graphical condition called *gflow* has been introduced [2,3].

© Springer International Publishing Switzerland 2015
J. Krivine and J.-B. Stefani (Eds.): RC 2015, LNCS 9138, pp. 129–138, 2015.
DOI: 10.1007/978-3-319-20860-2_8

Gflow is not unique in general. In the non-extended case a focused gflow [10] is nothing but a gflow in some normal form. We consider three natural extensions of the focused gflow for the extended measurement based quantum computation and we study in which cases these normal forms exist.

2   Extended Measurement-Based Quantum Computation

In this section, a brief description of the extended measurement-based quantum computation is given, a more detailed introduction can be found in [4,5]. A measurement-based quantum computation (MBQC) is:

(i) **Initialisation.** An *open graph* (G, I, O) which describes the initial entanglement $(G = (V, E)$ is a simple undirected graph), the inputs $(I \subseteq V)$ and outputs $(O \subseteq V)$ of the computation. The initial entanglement is obtained by applying the following preparation map N which associates with every arbitrary input state located on the input qubits the initial entangled state of the MBQC:

$$N : \mathbb{C}^{\{0,1\}^I} \to \mathbb{C}^{\{0,1\}^V}$$
$$|x\rangle \mapsto \frac{1}{\sqrt{2^{|I^c|}}} \sum_{y \in \{0,1\}^{I^c}} (-1)^{|G[x,y]|} |x, y\rangle$$

where $G[x, y]$ denotes the subgraph of G induced by the supports of x and y and $|G[x, y]|$ its size. In other words $|G[x, y]|$ is the number of edges $(u, v) \in E$ such that $(x(u){=}1 \vee y(u){=}1) \wedge (u(v){=}1 \vee y(v){=}1)$;

(ii) **Measurements.** For every non output qubit $u \in O^c$, $\alpha(u) \in [0, 2\pi)$ and two distinct Pauli operators $\lambda_1(u), \lambda_2(u) \in \{X, Y, Z\}$ describe the *plane* $\{\lambda_1(u), \lambda_2(u)\}$ and the *angle* $\alpha(u)$ according to which the qubit u is measured i.e., u is measured according to the observable

$$\cos(\alpha(u))\lambda_1(u) + \sin(\alpha(u))\lambda_2(u)$$

Measurement of qubit u produces a classical outcome $(-1)^{s_u}$ where $s_u \in \{0, 1\}$ is called *signal*, or simply *classical outcome* with a slight abuse of notation;

(iii) **Corrections.** Two maps $\mathbf{x}, \mathbf{z} : O^c \to 2^V$ called *corrective maps*. Corrections work as follows: for every non output qubit u, the measurement of qubit u is followed by the application of X^{s_u} on the qubits in $\mathbf{x}(u)$ and Z^{s_u} on the qubits in $\mathbf{z}(u)$. A vertex $v \in \mathbf{x}(u) \cup \mathbf{z}(u)$ is called a *corrector* of u. The maps $\mathbf{x}, \mathbf{z}$ should be *extensive* in the sense that there exists a partial order $\prec$ over the vertices of the graph s.t. any corrector v of a vertex u is larger than u, i.e. $v \in \mathbf{x}(u) \cup \mathbf{z}(u)$ implies $u \prec v$. The extensivity of $\mathbf{x}$ and $\mathbf{z}$ guarantees that the corrections are applied on qubits which are no yet measured.

The *extended* variant of MBQC refers to the possibility to perform measurements in the three possible planes $\{X, Y\}$, $\{X, Z\}$ and $\{Y, Z\}$ of the Bloch sphere, whereas all measurements are performed in the $\{X, Y\}$-plane in the original measurement-based quantum computation.

3   Reversibility, Determinism, and Generalized Flow

Despite of the probabilistic evolution of quantum measurements, the correction mechanism can be used to make the overall evolution of an MBQC reversible which means that there exists an isometry U ($U^{\dagger} U = \mathbb{I}$) from the input to the output qubits such that, whatever the classical outcomes of the measurements during the computation are, the evolution implemented by the MBQC is U. In the context of measurement-based quantum computation this form of reversibility is called *determinism* [3]. Determinism is an essential feature which is used for instance for proving that any quantum circuit can be simulated by an MBQC. Thus, this is a key ingredient for the universality of the model for quantum computing. The existence of a correction strategy that makes an MBQC deterministic crucially depends on the initial entangled state, i.e. on the open graph (G, I, O) and the planes of measurement: given $\lambda : O^c \rightarrow \{\{X, Y\}, \{X, Z\}, \{Y, Z\}\}$ a map which associates with every non output qubit its plane of measurement, an *extended open graph* (G, I, O, λ) is *uniformly deterministic* if for any measurement angles $\alpha : O^c \rightarrow [0, 2\pi)$, there exist two corrective maps $\mathbf{x}$ and $\mathbf{z}$ such that the corresponding MBQC is deterministic.

Significant efforts have been made to characterize the open graphs that guarantees uniform determinism. Flow [3], and generalised flow (*gflow*) [2] are graphical conditions which are sufficient for uniform determinism. Gflow can be defined as follows for the extended open graphs:

Definition 1 (GFlow). *An extended open graph (G, I, O, λ) has a gflow if there exists $g : O^c \rightarrow 2^{I^c}$ s.t. $u \mapsto g(u) \cup Odd(g(u))$ is extensive and for any $u \in O^c$,*

$$\lambda(u) = \{X, Y\} \Rightarrow u \in Odd(g(u)) \setminus g(u)$$
$$\lambda(u) = \{X, Z\} \Rightarrow u \in g(u) \cap Odd(g(u))$$
$$\lambda(u) = \{Y, Z\} \Rightarrow u \in g(u) \setminus Odd(g(u))$$

where $Odd(A) = \{w \in V \mid |N(w) \cap A| = 0 \mod 2\}$ is the odd neighbourhood *of A and a map $f : O^c \rightarrow 2^V$ is extensive if there exists a partial order $\prec$ such that for any $u \in O^c$, u is smaller than its image by f i.e., $\forall v \in V \setminus \{u\}, v \in f(u) \Rightarrow u \prec v$.*

Concretely, if an extended open graph (G, I, O) has a gflow g then for any measurement angles $\alpha : O^c \rightarrow [0, 2\pi)$ the corrective maps defined as $\forall u \in O^c, \mathbf{x}(u) := g(u) \setminus \{u\}$ and $\mathbf{z}(u) := Odd(g(u)) \setminus \{u\}$ guarantees that the corresponding MBQC is deterministic [2].

With some additional assumptions gflow is not only sufficient but also necessary for determinism in measurement-based quantum computing. More precisely, there are mainly two cases to consider, depending on the number of inputs and outputs of the computation. When there are as many inputs as outputs, determinism corresponds to the notion of unitary evolution (evolution U s.t. $U^\dagger U = UU^\dagger = \mathbb{I}$). In this particular case, the gflow condition is necessary for strong – i.e., all measurements occur with the same probability – uniform determinism [10]. In the general case, when the number of inputs and outputs may differ, determinism corresponds to isometries (also called *unitary embedding*). In this general case, gflow characterizes *stepwise* strong uniform determinism (roughly speaking the additional stepwise condition means that any partial computation is also deterministic) [2]. Notice that it is not known whether the strong and stepwise conditions are required: there is no known example of uniformly deterministic MBQC which corresponding open graph does not have a gflow.

Notice that if an extended open graph has a gflow then all the input qubits must be measured in the $\{X, Y\}$-plane:

Property 1. If an extended open graph (G, I, O, λ) has a gflow then $\forall u \in I \cap O^c$, $\lambda(u) = \{X, Y\}$.

Proof. Let g be a gflow for (G, I, O, λ), and $u \in I \cap O^c$, since for any $u \in O^c$, $g(u) \subseteq I^c$, $u \notin g(u)$, thus according to the definition of gflow, $\lambda(u) \neq \{X, Z\}$ and $\lambda(u) \neq \{Y, Z\}$.   □

4   Focused Gflow and Normal Forms

The gflow of an (extended) open graph is not unique in general. In the non extended case i.e., when all measurements are performed in the $\{X, Y\}$-plane several classes of gflow have been identified: the *maximally delayed gflow* which depth is minimal and which is produced by a polytime algorithm [11]; and the focus gflow which guarantees that the z corrective map acts only on the output qubits. The definition of focused gflow is as follows: Given an open graph (G, I, O), a gflow g is *focused* [10] if $\forall u \in O^c$, $Odd(g(u)) \cap O^c = \{u\}$. Since any gflow can be transformed into a focused gflow by means of signal shifting [4] for instance, focused gflow can be used to characterize the open graphs that have a gflow:

Property 2. An open graph (G, I, O) has a gflow if and only if there exists $g : O^c \to 2^{I^c}$ extensive such that $\forall u \in O^c$,

$$Odd(g(u)) \cap O^c = \{u\}$$

Focused gflow is a simpler but equivalent variant of gflow, which can be used for instance as a tool for quantum circuits translation and optimisation [1, 6, 7].

So far, there is no definition of 'focused' gflow in the context of the extended MBQC. By symmetry, there are three natural kinds of 'focused' extended gflow: those for which $Odd(g(u)) \cap O^c \subseteq \{u\}$; those for which $g(u) \cap O^c \subseteq \{u\}$; and finally those for which $g(u) \oplus Odd(g(u)) \cap O^c \subseteq \{u\}$, $\oplus$ denotes the *symmetric difference*. We define the corresponding three normal forms (NF for short) for extended gflows:

Definition 2 (Normal forms). *A gflow g of an extended open graph (G, I, O, λ) is*

- *X-NF if $\forall u \in O^c$,*

$$Odd(g(u)) \subseteq \{u\} \cup O$$

- *Y-NF if $\forall u \in O^c$,*

$$(Odd(g(u)) \oplus g(u)) \subseteq \{u\} \cup O$$

- *Z-NF if $\forall u \in O^c$,*

$$g(u) \subseteq \{u\} \cup O$$

Intuitively a σ-NF, for $\sigma \in \{X, Y, Z\}$, guarantees that in the corresponding MBQC all the correctors applied on the non output qubits are Pauli-σ operators. For instance, given a Z-NF gflow, in the corresponding MBQC $\forall u \in O^c, \mathbf{x}(u) = g(u) \setminus \{u\} \subseteq O$ which implies that all Pauli correctors applied on non output qubits are Z operators. Given a Y-NF gflow, in the corresponding MBQC $\forall u \in O^c, \mathbf{x}(u) \cap O^c = \mathbf{z}(u) \cap O^c$ which means that all the Pauli correctors applied on non output qubits are products of X and Z which is nothing but Pauli-Y operators (up to a global phase). Notice that given an open graph (G, I, O), g is a focused gflow of (G, I, O) if and only if g is a X-NF gflow of $(G, I, O, u \mapsto \{X, Y\})$.

5   Existence of Normal Forms

In this section we consider the problem of the existence of gflow in normal forms. First notice that some extended open graphs have a gflow but no Z-NF gflow for instance. The following extended open graph (G, I, O, λ) where $G = (\{1, 2, 3\}, \{(1, 2), (2, 3)\})$, $I = \{1\}$, $O = \{3\}$ and $\lambda(1) = \lambda(2) = \{X, Y\}$ admits exactly two gflows g and g' ($g(1) = \{1\}$, $g'(1) = \{2, 3\}$, and $g(2) = g'(2) = \{3\}$), none of them is in the Z-normal form.

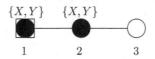

This simple example points out a crucial difference with respect to the non-extended case for which any gflow can be turned into a focused gflow. A sufficient condition for the existence of a σ-NF gflow for an extended open graph with gflow is that every non-input measurement plane contains σ:

Theorem 1. *If an extended open graph (G, I, O, λ) has a gflow then, for any $\sigma \in \bigcap_{u \in I^c \cap O^c} \lambda(u)$, (G, I, O, λ) has a σ-NF gflow.*

Proof. Let g be a gflow for (G, I, O, λ), and $\sigma \in \bigcap_{u \in I^c \cap O^c} \lambda(u)$. We define $g_\sigma : O^c \to 2^{I^c}$ as follows, depending on σ:

$$g_X(u) := g(u) \oplus \left(\bigoplus_{v \in Odd(g(u)) \backslash (O \cup \{u\})} g_X(v) \right)$$

$$g_Y(u) := g(u) \oplus \left(\bigoplus_{v \in (g(u) \oplus Odd(g(u))) \backslash (O \cup \{u\})} g_Y(v) \right)$$

$$g_Z(u) := g(u) \oplus \left(\bigoplus_{v \in g(u) \backslash (O \cup \{u\})} g_Z(v) \right)$$

Extensivity of $u \mapsto g(u) \cup Odd(g(u))$ guarantees that g_σ is well-defined. In the following we prove that g_σ is a gflow, and then that g_σ is in σ-NF.

[gflow] Let $\prec$ a partial order according to which $u \mapsto g(u) \cup Odd(g(u))$ is extensive, we show that $u \mapsto g_\sigma(u) \cup Odd(g_\sigma(u))$ is also extensive according to $\prec$. Indeed, for any $u \in O^c$ and any $w \in V \setminus \{u\}$, s.t. $w \in g_\sigma(u) \cup Odd(g_\sigma(u))$, by induction if there is no larger elements in O^c then $g_\sigma(u) = g(u)$, so $u \prec w$. Otherwise, $w \in g(u) \cup Odd(g(u)) \cup (\bigcup_{v \in g(u) \cup Odd(g(u)) \backslash (O \cup \{u\})} g_\sigma(v) \cup Odd(g_\sigma(v)))$, so either (i) $w \in g(u) \cup Odd(g(u))$ which implies $u \prec w$, or (ii) $\exists v \in g(u) \cup Odd(g(u))$ s.t. $w \in g_\sigma(v) \cup Odd(g_\sigma(v))$, so $u \prec v$ and, by induction, $v \prec w$ which implies $u \prec w$. Regarding the remaining gflow conditions, notice that the extensivity of g and g_σ guarantees that for any $u \in O^c$, $g_\sigma(u) \cap \{u\} = g(u) \cap \{u\}$ and $Odd(g_\sigma(u)) \cap \{u\} = Odd(g(u)) \cap \{u\}$ (the linearity of Odd is also used in this second case: $Odd(A \oplus B) = Odd(A) \oplus Odd(B)$). Thus g_σ is a gflow.

[σ-NF] In the following we prove that g_σ is in a σ-NF. W.l.o.g. assume $\sigma = Y$ (the other two cases are similar). We actually prove by induction that $\forall u \in O^c$, $Odd(g_Y(u) \oplus g_Y(u)) \cap O^c = \{u\}$. Let $u \in O^c$.

- If there is no larger element according to $\prec$ (the partial order induced by g and g_Y) in O^c, then $Odd(g_Y(u)) \oplus g_Y(u) \subseteq Odd(g_Y(u)) \cup g_Y(u) \subseteq \{u\} \cup O$ by extensivity of g_Y, moreover since $Y \in \lambda(u)$, $u \in Odd(g_Y(u)) \oplus g_Y(u)$, so $(Odd(g_Y(u)) \oplus g_Y(u)) \cap O^c = \{u\}$.
- Otherwise, $(Odd(g_Y(u)) \oplus g_Y(u)) \cap O^c =$

$$\left(Odd(g(u)) \oplus g(u) \oplus \left(\bigoplus_{v \in (g(u) \oplus Odd(g(u))) \backslash (O \cup \{u\})} Odd(g_Y(v)) \oplus g_Y(v) \right) \right) \cap O^c$$

$$= (Odd(g(u)) \oplus g(u)) \cap O^c \oplus \left(\bigoplus_{v \in (g(u) \oplus Odd(g(u))) \backslash (O \cup \{u\})} (Odd(g_Y(v)) \oplus g_Y(v)) \cap O^c \right)$$

$$= (Odd(g(u)) \oplus g(u)) \cap O^c \oplus \left(\bigoplus_{v \in (g(u) \oplus Odd(g(u))) \backslash (O \cup \{u\})} \{v\} \right)$$

$$= (Odd(g(u)) \oplus g(u)) \cap O^c \oplus ((g(u) \oplus Odd(g(u))) \setminus (O \cup \{u\}))$$

$$= (Odd(g(u)) \oplus g(u)) \cap \{u\}$$

Moreover, since $Y \in \lambda(u)$, $u \in Odd(g(u)) \oplus g(u)$, so $(Odd(g_Y(u)) \oplus g_Y(u)) \cap O^c = \{u\}$.   □

As a corollary, any (non extended) open graphs with gflow, admits both X- and Y-NF gflows. More generally, any extended open graph (G, I, O, λ) with gflow such that λ is constant over $I^c \cap O^c$ admits both σ- and σ'-NF gflows where $I^c \cap O^c \subseteq \lambda^{-1}(\{\sigma, \sigma'\})$

Theorem 1 provides a sufficient condition for the existence of a σ-normal form. The following example points out that this condition is not necessary: in this extended open graph $\lambda(2) = \{X, Z\}$ however it admits the following Y-NF gflow $1 \mapsto \{4\}; 2 \mapsto \{2, 3, 4\}$.

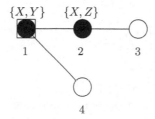

Notice that in this counter example there are strictly more outputs than inputs. Indeed, we show that the existence of a σ-NF gflow with $\sigma \in \{Y, Z\}$, implies that the number non-input measurement-planes which do not contain σ is upper bounded by the *input defect* i.e., the difference between the number of outputs and inputs:

Theorem 2. *Given $\sigma \in \{Y, Z\}$ and an extended open graph (G, I, O, λ), if (G, I, O, λ) has a σ-NF gflow then*

$$|\{u \in I^c \cap O^c \mid \sigma \notin \lambda(u)\}| \leq |O| - |I|.$$

Proof. Given (G, I, O, λ) with a σ-NF gflow g where $\sigma \in \{Y, Z\}$, we show that any non-input vertex which is measured in a plane which does not contain σ can be, roughly speaking, turned into an input vertex. The proof is by induction on $|\{u \in I^c \cap O^c \mid \sigma \notin \lambda(u)\}|$. If $|\{u \in I^c \cap O^c \mid \sigma \notin \lambda(u)\}| = 0$ the property is satisfied since determinism implies $|I| \leq |O|$. Otherwise, let $u_0 \in I^c \cap O^c$ s.t. $\sigma \notin \lambda(u_0)$ and let $g'(u) := \begin{cases} g(u) & \text{if } u = u_0 \text{ or } u_0 \notin g(u) \\ g(u) \oplus g(u_0) & \text{otherwise} \end{cases}$. g' is a σ-NF gflow s.t. $\forall u \in O^c \setminus \{u_0\}$, $u_0 \notin g'(u)$.

[Z-NF] If $\sigma = Z$, $\lambda(u_0) = \{X, Y\}$, so $u_0 \notin g'(u_0)$. As a consequence $\forall u \in O^c, g'(u) \in (I \cup \{u_0\})^c$, and g' is a Z-NF gflow of $(G, I \cup \{u_0\}, O, \lambda)$: in this new extended open graph the number of measurement-planes which do not contain Z is decreased by one, as well as the input defect i.e., the difference between the number of outputs and inputs.

[Y-NF] If $\sigma = Y$, a new degree-one vertex u_1 is connected to u_0, and let $g'' : O^c \to 2^{(I \cup \{u_0\})^c}$ be defined as follows

$$g''(u) := \begin{cases} \{u_1\} & \text{if } u = u_0 \\ g'(u_0) \oplus \{u_0, u_1\} & \text{if } u = u_1 \\ g'(u) & \text{otherwise} \end{cases}$$

g'' is a Y-NF gflow for $(G', I \cup \{u_0\}, O, \lambda')$, where G' is the graph G augmented with the dangling vertex u_1, and $\lambda'(u) = \begin{cases} \{X, Y\} & \text{if } u = u_0 \\ \{Y, Z\} & \text{if } u = u_1 \\ \lambda(u) & \text{otherwise} \end{cases}$. In this new open graph the number of inputs is increased by one, so the input defect decreases by one, moreover the number of measurement planes which do not contain Y also decreases by one since u_1 is measured in the $\{Y, Z\}$-plane in this new open graph. $\square$

Corollary 1. *Given* $\sigma \in \{Y, Z\}$ *and an extended open graph* (G, I, O, λ) *with gflow such that* $|I| = |O|$, (G, I, O, λ) *has a* σ-*NF gflow if and only if for any* $u \in I^c \cap O^c$, $\sigma \in \lambda(u)$.

Theorem 2 shows that in a Z-NF gflow, when a non-input is measured in the $\{X, Y\}$-plane, this non-input somehow behaves as an input. Regarding the Y-NF gflow when a non-input qubit is measured in the $\{X, Z\}$-plane, this qubit cannot be seen as an input qubit mainly because all inputs have to be measured in the $\{X, Y\}$-plane (Property 1). However, up to a transformation of the graph, it can be turned into an input (see proof of Theorem 2). One can wonder whether such a transformation exists for X-NF gflow? Surprisingly, Theorem 2 cannot be extended to the X-NF case as illustrated by the following counter example where the number of inputs is equal to the number of outputs and which has a X-NF gflow $(1 \mapsto \{3\}; 2 \mapsto \{2, 3\})$ despite of the measurement of a non-input qubit in the $\{Y, Z\}$-plane:

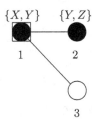

6   Conclusion

We have introduced three kinds of normal forms for extended gflows: X-, Y- and Z-normal forms: a σ-normal form guarantees that all the corrections are done by means of σ unitary transformations. These normal forms generalise the notion of 'focused' gflow. Contrary to the non-extended case not every gflow can be turned into a normal form gflow. We show that if σ appears in every plane of measurement, then a σ-normal form is possible. This sufficient condition is not necessary in general. Indeed, it strongly relies on the input defects i.e., on the difference between the numbers of inputs and outputs: when $\sigma \in \{Y, Z\}$, if a σ-normal form exists then the number of measurement planes which do not include σ is at most the input defect. Surprisingly, the X-normal form case behaves quite differently: there exist X-normal form gflows with no input defect and measurements in the $\{Y, Z\}$-plane. This result breaks the symmetries between the three Pauli operators X, Y and Z which are used to define the measurement planes: whereas the Z is known to plays a particular role mainly because the input qubits must be measured in the $\{X, Y\}$-plane, the present result on the X-normal form is the first result, up to our knowledge, which breaks the symmetries between the X and the Y directions. It sheds some new light on the interesting question of the choice of the measurement planes in measurement-based quantum computation.

References

1. Broadbent, A., Kashefi, E.: Parallelizing quantum circuits. Theoretical computer science **410** (26), 2489–2510
2. Browne, D.E., Kashefi, E., Mhalla, M., Perdrix, S.: Generalized flow and determinism in measurement-based quantum computation. New J. Phys. **9**, 250 (2007)
3. Danos, V., Kashefi, E.: Determinism in the one-way model. Physical Review A **74** (2006)
4. Danos, V., Kashefi, E., Panangaden, P.: The measurement calculus. J. ACM **54**, 2 (2007)
5. Danos, V., Kashefi, E., Panangaden, P., Perdrix, S.: Extended measurement calculus. In: Chapter in Semantic Techniques in quantum Computation. Cambridge University Press (2010)
6. Duncan, R., Perdrix, S.: Rewriting measurement-based quantum computations with generalised flow. In: Abramsky, S., Gavoille, C., Kirchner, C., Meyer auf der Heide, F., Spirakis, P.G. (eds.) ICALP 2010. LNCS, vol. 6199, pp. 285–296. Springer, Heidelberg (2010)
7. Dias da Silva, R., Pius, E., Kashefi, E.: Global Quantum Circuit Optimization. arXiv:1301.0351
8. Hein, M., Eisert, J., Briegel, H.J.: Multi-party entanglement in graph states. Phys. Rev. A **69**, 062311 (2004)
9. Kashefi, E., Markham, D., Mhalla, M., Perdrix, S.: Information flow in secret sharing protocols. In: Developments in Computational Models (DCM 2009), EPTCS **9**, pp. 87–97 (2009)
10. Mhalla, M., Murao, M., Perdrix, S., Someya, M., Turner, P.S.: Which graph states are useful for quantum information processing? In: Bacon, D., Martin-Delgado, M., Roetteler, M. (eds.) TQC 2011. LNCS, vol. 6745, pp. 174–187. Springer, Heidelberg (2014)
11. Mhalla, M., Perdrix, S.: Finding optimal flows efficiently. In: Aceto, L., Damgård, I., Goldberg, L.A., Halldórsson, M.M., Ingólfsdóttir, A., Walukiewicz, I. (eds.) ICALP 2008, Part I. LNCS, vol. 5125, pp. 857–868. Springer, Heidelberg (2008)
12. Mhalla, M., Perdrix, S.: Graph States, Pivot Minor, and Universality of (X, Z)-measurements. IJUC **9**(1–2), 153–171 (2013)
13. Prevedel, R., Walther, P., Tiefenbacher, F., Bohi, P., Kaltenbaek, R., Jennewein, T., Zeilinger, A.: High-speed linear optics quantum computing using active feed-forward. Nature **445**(7123), 65–69 (2007)

14. Raussendorf, R., Briegel, H.: A one-way quantum computer. Phys. Rev. Lett. **86**, 5188 (2001)
15. Raussendorf, R., Browne, D.E., Briegel, H.J.: Measurement-based quantum computation with cluster states. Physical Review A **68**, 022312 (2003)
16. Walther, P., Resch, K.J., Rudolph, T., Schenck, E., Weinfurter, H., Vedral, V., Aspelmeyer, M., Zeilinger, A.: Experimental one-way quantum computing. Nature **434**(7030), 169–176 (2005)

A Fully Fault-Tolerant Representation
of Quantum Circuits

Alexandru Paler[1]($\boxtimes$), Ilia Polian[1], Kae Nemoto[4], and Simon J. Devitt[2,3,4]

[1] University of Passau, Innstr. 43, 94032 Passau, Germany
alexandru.paler@uni-passau.de
[2] Ochanomizu University, 2-1-1 Otsuka, Bunkyo-ku, Tokyo 112-8610, Japan
[3] Graduate School of Media and Governance, Keio University,
Fujisawa, Kanagawa 252-0882, Japan
[4] National Institute of Informatics, 2-1-2 Hitotsubashi, Chiyoda-ku, Tokyo, Japan

Abstract. We present a quantum circuit representation consisting entirely of qubit initialisations (I), a network of controlled-NOT gates (C) and measurements with respect to different bases (M). The ICM representation is useful for optimisation of quantum circuits that include teleportation, which is required for fault-tolerant, error corrected quantum computation. The non-deterministic nature of teleportation necessitates the conditional introduction of corrective quantum gates and additional ancillae during circuit execution. Therefore, the standard optimisation objectives, gate count and number of wires, are not well-defined for general teleportation-based circuits. The transformation of a circuit into the ICM representation provides a canonical form for an exact fault-tolerant, error corrected circuit needed for optimisation prior to the final implementation in a realistic hardware model.

1 Introduction

Quantum computing promises speed-ups for a number of relevant computational problems. Building a scalable and reliable quantum computer is one of the challenges of modern science. As the size of quantum computers increases, the focus of interest shifts from their basic physical principles to structured design methodologies that will allow us to realise large-scale systems.

In general, quantum circuit optimisation methods are used to minimise the implementation costs like the number of gates or the number of wires [29]. Classical circuit optimisation assumes fixed gate lists even in the presence of gate errors, but classical circuits are more robust towards errors, whereas quantum information is fragile [24, Ch. 8]. Classical gate failures are usually solved either by hardening the circuit (e.g. modifying transistor sizes), or by introducing various types of information redundancies that mitigate the failures. Gate hardening is not considered realistic in quantum computing architectures, and a feasible solution requires quantum error-correcting codes (QECC) [11]. The structure and design of QECC allows encoded quantum gates to be applied directly to the encoded quantum data.

© Springer International Publishing Switzerland 2015
J. Krivine and J.-B. Stefani (Eds.): RC 2015, LNCS 9138, pp. 139–154, 2015.
DOI: 10.1007/978-3-319-20860-2_9

In contrast to the classical case, the most practical implementations of QECC and fault-tolerant quantum circuits are composed of gates which are *non-deterministic* even in the absence of errors [14]. They either work correctly or require a correction, which is only determined during the execution of the circuit. Most such correction gates do not need to be dynamically included into the executing circuit, because their effect can be classically tracked through the subsequent gates [26]. This is not true for all possible corrections occurring during the execution of a quantum circuit and some need to be actively applied to the quantum data[14]. This means that the overall circuit is dynamic, because its gate list needs to be modified during its execution based on certain measurement results. Reducing the incidence of such gates is difficult because when a fully error-corrected, fault-tolerant circuit is examined, it is exactly these measurement based corrections that appear to give quantum computing its power [15]. In general, fault-tolerant quantum circuits are constructed from Clifford and T (Section 1.1) gates, and the T gate is the main source of the complications [4] for which dynamic corrections cannot be avoided.

The separation of circuit gates into Clifford and T gates is generally performed at the higher level circuit design layer in order to make fault-tolerant error constructions more amenable to practical implementation. The physical mapping of these circuits to an actual error corrected architecture is then done with a specific QECC and hardware architecture in mind, preserving fault-tolerance. Fault-tolerance is understood as the set of procedures by which the cascade of quantum errors (bit and phase flips) caused by the circuit [11] is restricted allowing the underlying QECC to be effective when mapped to actual operations in a hardware model. In standard fault-tolerant constructions (those that are widely used in state-of-the-art hardware models [10,20,23,31]), the only dynamic corrections needed are when we implement logical layer corrections for T gates. These correctional gates are constructed using ancillae initialised into high-fidelity states (see Section 1.5) and gate teleportation protocols [14]. Our results are quite similar to those present in Ref. [9], however this work focuses on producing a representation that is compatible with fault-tolerant error correction protocols.

The solution to having all the required corrections into the logical layer of the computation is to translate circuits into a regular representation that replaces correctional gate dynamics with the dynamics of reading and interpreting the circuit outputs. Such an approach is similar to the model of measurement based quantum computing (MBQC) [7], where a computation is solely described by the interpretation of the measurements performed on a specifically initialised quantum state. A circuit is described in this work as an ICM sequence, where the I part contains qubit initialisations, the C part is a sub-circuit consisting entirely of CNOT gates, and the qubits are measured in the M part. This work represents a separate and distinct approach from the work of [21], where NCV (reversible) circuits were mapped into Clifford and T gate circuits, because the ICM representation is regular and consists entirely of ancillae, CNOTs and measurements.

The ICM representation is the extension of the methods presented in [15] to fit into the measurement based paradigm [7]. The presented algorithmic formulation will output the ICM representation for arbitrary quantum and reversible circuits. Such a formulation, although it requires an increased number of ancillae, allows us to directly synthesise fully fault-tolerant error corrected circuits for an underlying higher level circuit (including all required ancillary protocols), represents the realistic resource requirements of fault-tolerant quantum computations for state-of-the-art quantum architectures [12,17] and provides an elegant form for further circuit optimisation techniques for QECC models such as topological codes [13,25].

The paper is organised as follows: Section 1.1 offers a short introduction to quantum computing, illustrates the concepts of controlled and rotational gates, discusses the reversibility aspects of computing and the applications of information and gate teleportations. Section 2 details the non-deterministic resource requirements of arbitrary quantum circuits, introduces the ICM representation and presents the algorithm used for achieving it. The algorithm is benchmarked using circuits from the RevLib library and the results are discussed in Section 3. Finally, conclusions and future work are formulated.

1.1   Quantum and Reversible Computing

Quantum circuits represent and manipulate information in *qubits* (quantum bits). The *quantum state* of a qubit is the vector $|\psi\rangle = (\alpha_0, \alpha_1)^T = \alpha_0 |0\rangle + \alpha_1 |1\rangle$. Here, $|0\rangle = (1,0)^T$ and $|1\rangle = (0,1)^T$ are quantum analogues of classical logic values 0 and 1, respectively. α_0 and α_1 are complex numbers called *amplitudes* with $|\alpha_0|^2 + |\alpha_1|^2 = 1$.

A state may be modified by applying single-qubit *quantum gates*. Each quantum gate corresponds to a complex unitary matrix, and gate function is given by multiplying that matrix with the quantum state. The application of X gate to a state results in a *bit flip*: $X(\alpha_0, \alpha_1)^T = (\alpha_1, \alpha_0)^T$. The application of the Z gate results in a *phase flip*: $Z(\alpha_0, \alpha_1)^T = (\alpha_0, -\alpha_1)^T$. The matrices of the Pauli gates I, X, Y, Z are:

$$I = \begin{pmatrix} 1 & 0 \\ 0 & 1 \end{pmatrix} \ Y = \begin{pmatrix} 0 & -i \\ i & 0 \end{pmatrix} \ X = \begin{pmatrix} 0 & 1 \\ 1 & 0 \end{pmatrix} \ Z = \begin{pmatrix} 1 & 0 \\ 0 & -1 \end{pmatrix}$$

Further important single-qubit quantum gates in the context of this work are H, P, T, where $T^2 = P$ and $P^2 = Z$.

$$H = \frac{1}{\sqrt{2}} \begin{pmatrix} 1 & 1 \\ 1 & -1 \end{pmatrix} \ P = \begin{pmatrix} 1 & 0 \\ 0 & i \end{pmatrix} \ T = \begin{pmatrix} 1 & 0 \\ 0 & e^{i\frac{\pi}{4}} \end{pmatrix}$$

Quantum measurement is defined with respect to a basis and yields one of the basis vectors with a probability related to the amplitudes of the quantum state. Of importance in this work are Z- and X-measurements. Z-measurement is defined with respect to basis $(|0\rangle, |1\rangle)$. Applying a Z-measurement to a qubit in state $|\psi\rangle = \alpha_0 |0\rangle + \alpha_1 |1\rangle$ yields $|0\rangle$ with probability $|\alpha_0|^2$ and $|1\rangle$ with probability

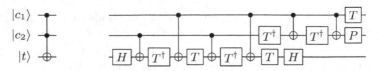

Fig. 1. Toffoli gate using CNOT, T, $T^\dagger$ and H gates [24, Ch. 4]

$|\alpha_1|^2$. Moreover, the state $|\psi\rangle$ *collapses* into the measured state (i.e. only the components of $|\psi\rangle$ consistent with the measurement result remains). X-measurement is defined with respect to the basis $(|+\rangle, |-\rangle)$, where $|+\rangle = \frac{1}{\sqrt{2}}(|0\rangle + |1\rangle)$ and $|-\rangle = \frac{1}{\sqrt{2}}(|0\rangle - |1\rangle)$.

1.2   Rotational Gates

The exponentiation of the Pauli matrices results in the rotational gates R_x, R_y, R_z parametrised by the angle of the rotation [24, Ch. 4]. Hence the bit flip is a rotation by π around the X-axis, implying that $X = R_x(\pi)$, and the phase-flip is a rotation by π around the Z-axis, such that $Z = R_z(\pi)$. Furthermore, $P = R_z(\pi/2)$ and $T = R_z(\pi/4)$. The V and $V^\dagger$ gates are parametrised X-rotations, $V = R_x(\pi/2)$. The Hadamard gate is $H = R_z(\pi/2)R_x(\pi/2)R_z(\pi/2) = PVP$.

$$R_x(\theta) = \begin{bmatrix} \cos\frac{\theta}{2} & -i\sin\frac{\theta}{2} \\ -i\sin\frac{\theta}{2} & \cos\frac{\theta}{2} \end{bmatrix} \quad R_y(\theta) = \begin{bmatrix} \cos\frac{\theta}{2} & -\sin\frac{\theta}{2} \\ \sin\frac{\theta}{2} & \cos\frac{\theta}{2} \end{bmatrix}$$

$$R_z(\theta) = \begin{bmatrix} e^{-i\theta/2} & 0 \\ 0 & e^{i\theta/2} \end{bmatrix} \quad CNOT = \begin{bmatrix} 1 & 0 & 0 & 0 \\ 0 & 1 & 0 & 0 \\ 0 & 0 & 0 & 1 \\ 0 & 0 & 1 & 0 \end{bmatrix}$$

1.3   Controlled Gates

An n-qubit circuit processes states represented by 2^n amplitudes, α_y, with $y \in \{0,1\}^n$ and $\sum_y |\alpha_y|^2 = 1$. Measuring all qubits of the circuit results in one basis vector with the probability given by the corresponding amplitude, $|\alpha_y|^2$. Quantum gates may act on several qubits simultaneously. A gate operating on n qubits is represented by a $2^n \times 2^n$ complex unitary matrix. One important two-qubit gate is the *controlled-not* $CNOT(c,t)$ gate, where the c qubit conditionally flips the state of the t qubit when set to $|1\rangle$. In general, any quantum gate can be used in a controlled manner, and other versions are controlled-Z (CPHASE), controlled-V (C-V) and controlled-$V^\dagger$ (C-$V^\dagger$), where $V^2 = X$.

Similarly to how arbitrary classical Boolean functions can be constructed entirely from NAND gates, universal quantum computations can be constructed using a discrete set of gates. The universal gate set has to contain at least one coupling operation, and the most often used one is CNOT. A commonly used gate set in fault-tolerant quantum computing is $UGS_{ft} = \{CNOT, H, T\}$ [24, Ch. 4]. There are gate sets that are not universal, an example is the Clifford gate group,

(a)   (b)

Fig. 2. a) Toffoli gate using CNOT, controlled-V and controlled-$V^\dagger$ gates [24, Ch. 4]. b) The decomposition of the controlled-V using CNOT, T, $T^\dagger$ and H gates

generated by the gates $\{CNOT, H, P\}$. Circuits comprised of gates exclusively from the Clifford group can be efficiently simulated on a classical computer [16], but the Clifford group together with the T gate is quantum universal. The T gate is one of the most expensive quantum gates to implement when QECC and fault-tolerant computation is taken into account [12,17]. Thus, there is ongoing research into reducing the T gate count of synthesised quantum circuits [4,19,21].

1.4 Reversibility

The linearity of quantum mechanics has the effect that information can not be erased, therefore, for an arbitrary computation, the number of input qubits equals the number of output qubits. *Reversible circuits*, as presented in [27,29], are the result of enforcing this requirement on classical Boolean circuits. The interest in classical reversible computing was initially motivated by Landauer's principle, which states that the erasure of information is dissipating energy [22]. The hope was that computers might become more energy-efficient if classical computations would be reversible. Therefore, FANINs and FANOUTs are not allowed into the circuits. The majority of the classical gates are not linear maps. For example the inputs a and b of the $AND(a,b) = c$ gate are impossible to infer from the output c. However, the NOT gate is reversible because its output is the negation of the input, and no information is erased.

The reversibility of classical circuits is achieved by the *Toffoli* gate (Fig. 1), operating on three bits, where two of them control the bit-flip of the third: $toffoli(a,b,c) = (a,b,c \oplus ab)$. Arbitrary classical circuits can be completely constructed using Toffoli gates [24, Ch. 3]. While a quantum Toffoli performs effectively the same transformation on qubits, the key difference between quantum and reversible circuits is that the Toffoli gate is not universal for quantum computations because universality also require at least the H gate [2]. Reversible circuits can be considered restricted quantum circuits operating only on computational basis states. However, it is possible to decompose the Toffoli gate into quantum gates (Fig. 1 and Fig. 2a). One decomposition (the quantum version) uses the gate set $\{CNOT, H, T\}$ ($T^\dagger = T^7$), while a second decomposition uses the gates $\{CNOT, V, V^\dagger\}$. The second representation will be called *the reversible version* (although the V gate is quantum), because its lower gate cost makes it widely used in the designs of reversible circuits [27,29], although these costs generally don't account for the true nature of error corrected quantum circuits.

Fig. 3. Circuits for teleporting the state of a source qubit to a neighbouring destination qubit

1.5   Information and Gate Teleportation

Quantum information (qubit states) cannot be copied [30], but there are ways to *move* information from one qubit to another through quantum state *teleportation* (Fig. 3) [5]. The most general teleportation technique [24, Ch. 4] is implemented using a slightly different mechanism, but quantum computing models and architectures like [10,14,20,23,31] use the two circuits presented herein.

Each of the circuits requires an ancilla initialised into either $|0\rangle$ or $|+\rangle$. For the first circuit, after applying the CNOT on the states $|\psi\rangle = a|0\rangle + b|1\rangle$ and $|0\rangle$, the two-qubit state will be $a|00\rangle + b|11\rangle$. The measurement of the input qubit, in the X-basis is probabilistic, and depending on its result the final state of the ancilla will be either $|\psi_1\rangle = a|0\rangle + b|1\rangle$ if $|+\rangle$ is measured, or $|\psi_2\rangle = a|0\rangle - b|1\rangle$ for $|-\rangle$. The execution of the second circuit, where instead a Z-basis measurement is used, will result in the state of the ancilla being $|\psi_3\rangle = a|0\rangle + b|1\rangle$ after measuring $|0\rangle$, or $|\psi_4\rangle = a|1\rangle + b|0\rangle$ after measuring $|1\rangle$. For both teleportations the final state is the desired one with 50% probability ($|\psi_1\rangle$ and $|\psi_2\rangle$), while otherwise correctional gates are required, because $|\psi_1\rangle = Z|\psi_2\rangle$ and $|\psi_3\rangle = X|\psi_4\rangle$. The corrections are a direct result of the measurements being probabilistic. The correction mechanism is illustrated in the circuit diagrams by the double vertical lines connecting the measurements to the X/Z gates, indicating a classically controlled gate of either X or Z.

Information teleportation is a linear transformation of the destination qubit, such that its state is exactly the state of the source, but quantum gates are linear transformations, too. It follows that it is possible to construct teleported versions for single-qubit quantum gates. Such constructs are commonly used in the fault-tolerant implementation of quantum gates. The teleportation-based gate circuits for the V, T and P gates are shown in Fig. 4. The teleportations are again probabilistic and the output state requires corrections (derived in [26]). Gate teleportations are based on *magic states* [6] like $|Y\rangle = \frac{1}{\sqrt{2}}(|0\rangle + i|1\rangle)$ and $|A\rangle = \frac{1}{\sqrt{2}}(|0\rangle + e^{i\frac{\pi}{4}}|1\rangle)$. The utilization of magic states and the above teleportation circuits is that they can be implemented using fault-tolerant QECC through a process known as state distillation [6,14], which accounts for the majority of resources necessary for a large-scale error corrected algorithm [11].

The $R_z(\pi/4)^\dagger = T^\dagger = R_z(-\pi/4)$ rotation is implemented using the same circuit as the gate T, the only difference being the interpretation of the measurement result in terms of any subsequent correction. Because the $T, T^\dagger, V$ and

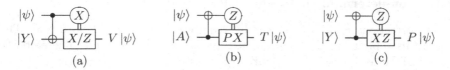

Fig. 4. Teleported rotational gates using the magic states $|A\rangle, |Y\rangle$. a) The teleported V gate; b) The teleported T gate; c) The teleported P gate.

$V^\dagger$ gates can be implemented by teleportations, it follows that the Toffoli gate (in both its quantum and reversible versions) can be decomposed into teleportation sub-circuits.

The magic states in the construction of fault-tolerant gates are assumed to be high-fidelity (As high as the fidelity of the underlying quantum information protected by the QECC). Otherwise, high-fidelity instances are obtained after *distilling* multiple low-fidelity states using circuits consisting entirely of CNOTs and measurements [6]. For example, the distillation of a single $|Y\rangle$ state from low-fidelity $|Y\rangle$ ancillae is reported in [6], reducing the infidelity, p, of the output from $O(p)$, $p < 1$, of the seven inputs to $O(p^3)$ on the output.

2   The ICM Representation

In state-of-the-art fault-tolerant quantum circuits, two sources of non-determinism can be distinguished. First, errors can occur during calculation due to undesired interaction with the environment. The errors are handled by quantum error-correcting codes [11]. Second, as mentioned above, the realisation of gates by teleportation is inherently probabilistic. The outcome of the gate application is correct with 50% probability and requires a correction with 50% probability even in absence of errors.

Circuit gate dynamics, as presented in Section 1, is the consequence of applying specific quantum gates (e.g. T) by teleportation. Correctional gates may or may not be required, depending on the outcome of a measurement that is only available when the circuit is being executed. A further source of non-determinism is error-correction, which is not considered herein and is handled at a lower level in the overall design stack of a quantum circuit [14].

A circuit with a dynamic gate list is difficult to execute on a quantum computer, and is furthermore difficult to optimise. This section introduces the ICM representation, which replaces the non-deterministic gate dynamics with an exact gate list. The resulting circuit still contains correctional mechanisms, but these are controlled by measurement results of introduced ancillae and active feedforward determining subsequent measurement choices. We essentially fan-out using extra ancillae to remove the complication of dynamic circuit construction with fault-tolerant and reversible quantum circuits.

2.1 Non-deterministic Resource Requirements

Gate corrections may or may not be required after each teleportation. They consist in applying X, Y, Z or P gates to the calculated result. Therefore, the total number of gates in the circuit depends on the number of corrections, and this number is not known *a priori* because the need for corrections is determined only during circuit execution (each individual teleportation has a 50:50 chance of each ancilla measurement result, so the possibilities grow exponentially in the number of teleported gates). Moreover, corrections require an introduction of additional ancillae qubits, thus making the computation total number of qubits unpredictable as well.

It can be shown that X, Y and Z corrections (Pauli corrections) do not have to be addressed immediately in a quantum way after an unsuccessful gate application. Instead they can be postponed to the end of calculation using *Pauli tracking* [26] and instead of applying an active quantum gate to the data, we simply reinterpret the meaning of the classical measurement results. However, this technique does not apply to P corrections necessary for implementing the T gate (Section 1.5). This is because the P correction does not commute through either the H gate of the target of a $CNOT$ gate in a straightforward manner and changes the probability distribution of subsequent X-basis measurements.

For example, in the teleported T gate (Fig. 4b), applying a CNOT on two qubits $|t\rangle = \frac{1}{\sqrt{2}}(|0\rangle + r|1\rangle)$ (where $r = e^{\frac{i \cdot \pi}{4}}$) and $|q\rangle = a|0\rangle + b|1\rangle$ results in $|qt\rangle = (a|00\rangle + ar|11\rangle + b|10\rangle + br|01\rangle)/\sqrt{2}$. The $|0\rangle$ result of the first qubit's Z-measurement will result in the second qubit's state as if it were directly rotated by T: $a|0\rangle + br|1\rangle$. If the measurement result is $|1\rangle$, the state is $ar|1\rangle + b|0\rangle$, which after a PX correction is required [26], and it can be applied using the circuit from Fig. 4c.

The P correction requires us to dynamically change the circuit being executed as this correction cannot be classically tracked. A second ancilla is introduced in the $|Y\rangle = |0\rangle + i|1\rangle$ state, a CNOT applied between the ancilla and the state to be corrected, and the input is measured according to Fig. 4c. For an n-qubit circuit C with a gate list $GL(C)$, each probabilistic P correction increments the number of qubits by one, and inserts a P gate into the gate list.

The problem of applying the P gate dynamically is solved by introducing into the circuit the possibility to operate both a teleported identity gate, used when no correction is needed, and a teleported P gate. Similarly to a classical demultiplexer the measurement result of the teleported T gate is used to decide, at run-time, whether I or P gate is applied. Finally, after performing either the I or P correction, the corresponding state has to be routed to a single qubit. This is realised by classically controlled teleportations in a manner similar to a classical multiplexer with the select signal being the measurement result of the teleported T gate. Classically controlled teleportations were described in [15], and a circuit using these mechanisms will have a fixed number of qubits and a determined gate list. Compared to a dynamically changing circuit, these are larger, but the predictability of these parameters is useful for circuit optimisation.

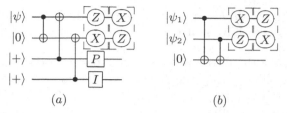

Fig. 5. Teleportations: a) Selective destination; b) Selective source [15]

For *selective destination teleportation* (Fig. 5) the first group of measurements (Z_1X_2 where the subscripts indicate the qubit's number) will teleport $|\psi\rangle$ on the third qubit where it will be corrected by P. The second group of measurements (X_1Z_2) will teleport the state to the fourth qubit where the trivial correction I is applied, thus leaving the state unchanged. In the *selective source teleportation* the X_1Z_2 measurements will select $|\psi_1\rangle$ for teleportation on the third qubit, while the second measurement group (Z_1X_2) will teleport $|\psi_2\rangle$ [15]. The selective teleportation circuits require only Pauli corrections, which are not shown in the diagrams, because their application can be postponed to the end of the computation and classically tracked.

As a consequence, Pauli tracking can reduce but not completely eliminate the non-determinism of fault-tolerant circuits. This implies that standard synthesis methods which optimise gate count and/or number of qubits are not applicable to teleportation-based quantum circuits because these numbers are not well-defined. It is possible to circumvent the non-determinism by using "conditional-identity construction" which results in the maximal possible number of gates. The initial gate dynamics of a circuit, with all the classically controlled corrections replaced by classically controlled teleportations, is interpreted as the dynamics of the measurements.

2.2   ICM Correctness and Construction

The role played by the structured representation of circuits was recognised in [1], where stabiliser circuits were decomposed into a canonical sequence of sub-circuits constructed from a single type of gates. In the context of fault-tolerant quantum computing, the systematic derivations of the circuits [32] uses teleportation sub-circuits, too. However, the combination of the fault-tolerant constructions with the regular gate decompositions [28], required for efficient synthesis algorithms, is limited by the realistic requirements of future quantum computing architectures. Nevertheless, structured mapping techniques between various architectures were investigated in [8, 18]. These approaches were targeted at specific quantum hardware properties, such as nearest-neighbour interaction between qubits, but fault-tolerant constructions were not specifically addressed.

ICM is a structured representation, which consists in the regular representation of arbitrary quantum and reversible circuits using the UGS_{ft} gate set, where the single-qubit rotational gates are teleportation-based. Circuits are transformed into the ICM representation after decomposing all non-UGS_{ft} gates into $UGS_{ft} = \{CNOT, H, T\}$ component gates, and simultaneously introducing, where necessary, selective source and destination teleportation circuits into the resulting circuit.

The correctness of the ICM representation is based on the observation that the teleported gate circuits (Figs. 4c,4b and 4a) and the selective teleportation circuits (Fig. 5) consist entirely of qubit initialisations, CNOT gates and qubit measurements. Thus, decomposing an arbitrary circuit into elements that can be expressed entirely using the above mentioned sub-circuits, will consist only of initialisations, CNOTs and measurements. The circuit from Fig. 5a can be rewritten, such that the P gate will not be directly applied: in general, R_z rotations (e.g. the P gate) commute with the control of CNOT gates [24, Ch. 4]. As a result, the P gate can be moved on the left side of the CNOT, and $P|+\rangle = |Y\rangle$. The third qubit from Fig. 5a will be initialised into $|Y\rangle$ instead of $|+\rangle$.

The ICM representation of an arbitrary quantum circuit is the result of applying algorithm presented in this paper. The algorithm is taking a circuit composed of gates from the set $\{Toffoli, CNOT, C\text{-}V \text{ and } C\text{-}V^\dagger, H, P, T\}$, and performs pattern replacements resulting in the circuit $CICM$ (Line 1) consisting of gates from UGS_{ft}. The Toffoli gates are decomposed into single qubit rotations (either $\{V, V^\dagger\}$ or $\{H, T, T^\dagger\}$) and CNOT gates. The Hadamard gates are replaced with the series of Z- and X-axis rotational gates (P and V gates). Afterwards, each P and V gate is replaced using the corresponding teleportation-based gate implementations from Figs. 4c,4b,4a. The effect of replacing a gate G acting on qubit i is that an ancilla is introduced on the position $i+1$. Thus, all the gates following the initial application of G on i are moved to $i + 1$ (Line 20).

The ICM representation is obtained by *moving* all the single-qubit measurements to the end of the circuit, and all the ancillae initialisations to the beginning of the circuit. The middle part of the resulting circuit consists entirely of CNOT gates. The single qubit measurements are then temporally staggered (e.g. Fig. 6), such that the results of previous measurements determine the basis choices for subsequent measurements to teleport data to pre-prepared ancillae. In the case of the teleported T gate, this procedure dictates to either apply P gate corrections or not, as required.

2.3   Resource Analysis

Transforming arbitrary quantum and reversible circuits into the ICM representation requires the introduction of supplemental ancillae, CNOT gates and measurements. The obtained representation is an augmented version of the initial circuit, and there is a constant resource overhead associated with each gate transformation. In the following the gate cost of implementing a sub-circuit (gate) S is represented by $gc(S)$, and the ancilla cost is denoted $ac(S)$.

Theorem: The ICM representation of a quantum circuit C with n_T T gates, n_P P gates, n_V V gates, n_H Hadamard gates and n_{Tf} Toffoli gates requires $ac(C) = 5n_T + n_P + n_V + 3n_H + 42n_{Tf}$ ancillae and $gc(C) = 6N_T + n_P + n_V + 3n_H + 55n_{Tf}$ additional gates.

Proof: The central quantum gate is T, which requires $ac(T) = 5$ ancillae and $gc(T) = 6$ CNOTs. One of the ancillae is the one initialised into $|A\rangle$, three other ancillae are used for the selective destination teleportation sub-circuit, and, finally, the fifth ancilla is introduced for the selective source teleportation and represents the output of the teleported T gate.

The P and the V gates introduce a single ancilla $ac(P) = ac(V) = 1$ initialised into the $|Y\rangle$ state, and because the teleportation circuits require a single CNOT $gc(P) = gc(V) = 1$. The Hadamard gate being implemented as a sequence of P and V gates generates a gate cost of $gc(H) = 3gc(P) = 3$, and an ancilla cost of $ac(H) = 3ac(P) = 3$.

The quantum version of the Toffoli gate (denoted $Toffoli_q$) decomposition contains 6 CNOTs, 7 T gates, one P and two H gates (Fig. 1), and thus $gc(Toffoli_q) = 6 + 7gc(T) + (1 + 2 \times 3)gc(P) = 55$ and $ac(Toffoli_q) = 7ac(T) + (1 + 2 \times 3)ac(P) = 42$.

Note: The Theorem was formulated for the ICM decomposition of quantum Toffoli gates, but can easily be updated to include the reversible version of these gates (in the following denoted $Toffoli_2$). These gates are decomposed into quantum gates, and the initial version contains 2 CNOT gates and 3 controlled-V gates (denoted by CV), which are further decomposed (Fig. 2b) into 2 Hadamard gates, 3 T and 2 CNOTs. Therefore, because $gc(CV) = 2gc(H) + 3gc(T) + 2 = 26$ and $ac(CV) = 2ac(H) + 3ac(T) = 21$, the gate cost of the reversible Toffoli is $gc(Toffoli_2) = 3gc(CV) + 2 = 80$ and the ancilla cost $ac(Toffoli_2) = 3ac(CV) = 63$.

State distillation (see Section 1.5) is not analysed here, as it is an intrinsic requirement for any type of computation where magic states are required. An exhaustive and complete analysis of the distillation circuits overhead is presented in [12] and, as a consequence, the present ICM resource analysis is a continuation of that work.

3 Discussion

The ICM representation of an arbitrary circuit prepared into a fault-tolerant manner will not affect its properties. Therefore, fault-tolerance statistics will not be discussed. The results of executing the implementation of Algorithm 1 on circuits from the RevLib benchmark are presented in Table 1. The EQ circuits consisted of gates from the set $\{CNOT, C\text{-}V, C\text{-}V^\dagger\}$ and the NCT circuits from the set $\{Toffoli, CNOT, X\}$. The best-case non-ICM representation consists of the teleportation-based gate construction where no P corrections is required for the T gate. The worst-case non-ICM scenario assumed that all the T gates require the P correction. For other types of gates the corrections can be tracked through the circuit [26], but tracking is not possible for the probabilistic P-correction (see Section 2.1). In order to illustrate the benefit of the ICM representation the time required for executing the critical path of the decomposed

Require: Circuit C composed from $\{Toffoli, CNOT, H, P, T\}$
1: Circuit $CICM \leftarrow C$
2: Replace in $CICM$ the Toffoli gates with their decomposition (Figure 1 or Figure 2a)
3: Replace in $CICM$ the H gates with PVP
4: **forall** P gates in $CICM$
5:    Introduce the ancilla a_p below the qubit having P
6:    Construct the circuit for the teleported P gate
7:    Move all the gates following the initial P onto a_p
8: **endfor**
9: **forall** V gates in $CICM$
10:    Introduce the ancilla a_v below the qubit having V
11:    Construct the circuit for the teleported V gate
12:    Move all the gates following the initial V onto a_v
13: **endfor**
14: **forall** T gates in $CICM$
15:    Introduce the ancilla a_c below the qubit having T
16:    Construct the circuit for the teleported T gate
17:    Introduce 4 ancillae below the previous ancilla
18:    Construct the selective destination circuit where a_c corresponds to the first qubit,
and s_3 and s_4 are the third and fourth qubits respectively
19:    Construct the selective source circuit where s_3 corresponds to the first qubit,
s_4 to the second qubit, and a_{out} is the third qubit
20:    Move all the gates following the initial T onto the ancilla a_{out}
21: **endfor**
22: **return** $CICM$

circuits was computed. The model presumed a time cost of 10 for initialisations, and a cost of 1 for the CNOTs and the measurements.

It can be seen that the time required by ICM circuits is predictable and better than the worst-case time of circuits before transformation. Note that longer time translates to higher decoherence and more stringent requirements on quantum error-correction.

3.1   Example

The systematic transformations of the T gate and of the controlled-V gate decomposition from Fig. 2b are presented after applying Algorithm 1 and obtaining a circuit composed from UGS_{ft} (see Section 1.3). The ICM representation of the T gate (Fig. 6) takes the $|in_0\rangle$ qubit, and after performing the CNOT with the $|A\rangle$ ancilla, selectively teleports (the leftmost group of gates) the intermediary state to either the fourth or the fifth qubit.

The measurement of the first qubit (Z_1) is followed by either the measurement pattern Z_2X_3 if the result of the teleported T needs a P correction, or the measurement pattern X_2Z_3 if the result was correct up to Pauli corrections. The correctness of the teleported gate application is indicated by the measurement result. Applying the Z_2X_3 pattern teleports the intermediary state on the output

Table 1. Comparison betweeen non-ICM and ICM representation

| | Original circuit | | | | | | Fault-tolerant circuit | | | | | | | | |
| | | | | | | | Best-Case Non-ICM | | | Worst-Case Non-ICM | | | ICM | | |
Circuit	Qub.	X	C-X	Toff.	C-V	C-V†	Ancilla	CNOT	Time	Ancilla	CNOT	Time	Ancilla	CNOT	Time
EQ/0410184_170	14	8	33	0	17	16	297	396	255	297	495	736	693	891	435
EQ/3_17_15	3	1	3	0	2	4	54	69	56	54	87	177	126	159	100
EQ/add16_175	49	0	32	0	48	16	576	736	287	576	928	1013	1344	1696	551
EQ/add32_185	97	0	64	0	96	32	1152	1472	543	1152	1856	1973	2688	3392	1063
EQ/add64_186	193	0	128	0	192	64	2304	2944	1055	2304	3712	3893	5376	6784	2087
EQ/add8_173	25	0	16	0	24	8	288	368	159	288	464	533	672	848	295
EQ/c2_182	35	15	121	0	116	53	1521	1980	366	1521	2487	1172	3549	4515	661
EQ/decod24-v0_40	4	1	5	0	2	1	27	38	40	27	47	95	63	83	60
EQ/decod24-v1_42	4	1	5	0	2	1	27	38	41	27	47	87	63	83	59
EQ/decod24-v2_44	4	1	5	0	1	2	27	38	41	27	47	95	63	83	60
EQ/decod24-v3_46	4	0	6	0	1	2	27	39	42	27	48	96	63	84	61
EQ/fredkin_5	3	0	4	0	1	2	27	37	41	27	46	94	63	82	59
EQ/graycode6_48	6	0	5	0	0	0	0	5	16	0	5	16	0	5	16
EQ/miller_12	3	0	5	0	1	2	27	38	42	27	47	95	63	83	60
EQ/peres_8	3	0	1	0	1	2	27	34	38	27	43	92	63	79	57
EQ/toffoli_1	3	0	2	0	2	1	27	35	38	27	44	92	63	80	57
EQ/toffoli_double_3	4	0	4	0	2	1	27	37	38	27	46	94	63	82	59
NCT/0410184_169	14	8	27	11	0	0	297	412	248	297	511	788	693	907	431
NCT/add16_174	49	0	32	32	0	0	864	1152	440	864	1440	1514	2016	2592	807
NCT/add32_183	97	0	64	64	0	0	1728	2304	840	1728	2880	2938	4032	5184	1559
NCT/add64_184	193	0	128	128	0	0	3456	4608	1640	3456	5760	5786	8064	10368	3063
NCT/add8_172	25	0	16	16	0	0	432	576	240	432	720	802	1008	1296	431
NCT/c2_181	35	18	35	63	0	0	1701	2240	345	1701	2807	1177	3969	5075	631
NCT/cnt3-5_180	16	0	5	10	0	0	270	355	60	270	445	186	630	805	102
NCT/graycode6_47	6	0	5	0	0	0	0	5	16	0	5	16	0	5	16
NCT/ham7_106	7	0	19	6	0	0	162	229	145	162	283	441	378	499	245

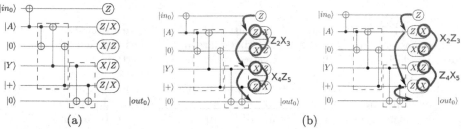

(a)   (b)

Fig. 6. a) The ICM version of the T gate [15]; b) The arrows sketch the information flow between the ancillas: a P gate correction is the result of the $Z_2X_3X_4Z_5$ measurement pattern, and the $X_2Z_3Z_4X_5$ measurement pattern is used if the teleported T gate application was correct

qubit marked by $|out_0\rangle$, and the fourth and fifth qubits are measured using X_4Z_5. Otherwise, the measurement Z_4X_5 will result in teleporting the state of the fifth qubit on the sixth qubit. The measurement of specific qubit groups depends on the results of previous measurements.

The controlled-V gate ICM representation (Fig. 7 after applying Algorithm 1) has the input states c_{in} (control) and t_{in} (target) and outputs c_{out} and t_{out}. The individual decomposition of the single-qubit gates from Fig. 2b is highlighted by the dashed bounding boxes. The boxes containing three CNOTs are implementations of the Hadamard gate where for each constituent sub-gate a CNOT and a $|Y\rangle$-qubit are used. The ancillae introduced by the ICM transformation are affecting the distance between the control and the target of the initial CNOTs (not marked by bounding boxes). The order of the measurements is dictated

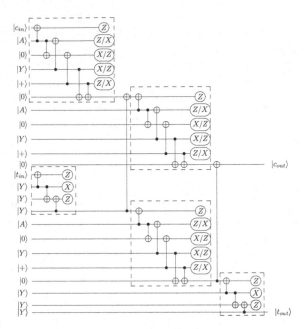

Fig. 7. The ICM representation of the controlled-V gate. There are three ICM T-gate applications (see Fig. 6) and two ICM Hadamard applications (marked by bounding boxes in which three ancillae are measured using the ZXZ pattern)

by the temporal order of the bounding boxes, meaning that the measurements implementing the leftmost T and H can be applied in parallel. Afterwards, the measurements associated to the middle bounding boxes can be again executed in parallel. Finally, the last Hadamard gate from the initial circuit is applied by measuring the last three qubits.

4   Conclusion

The usual assumptions made for quantum optimisation techniques do not necessarily hold for the fault-tolerant circuits because of their inherent dynamicity. A regular representation of quantum and reversible circuits was presented starting from the fault-tolerant implementation of quantum circuits. The ICM representation is a consequence of the results presented in [15, 26] and has the potential, when combined with the synthesis method from [3, 4], to be used for future circuit optimisation techniques.

The results indicate that, while making a quantum circuit fault-tolerant significantly increases its gate count and the number of required ancilla qubits, the ICM representation outperforms direct mapping without enforcing the ICM condition with respect to both predictability and worst-case execution time. The major advantage of this representation is that it produces a deterministic circuit description for a higher level circuit. A deterministic description is essential to allow for more global circuit optimisations in various error corrected implementations. Future work will investigate quantum circuit synthesis, optimisation and validation techniques based on the ICM representation.

Acknowledgments. SJD acknowledges support from the JSPS Grant-in-aid for Challenging Exploratory Research, NICT, Japan and JSPS KAKENHI Kiban B 25280034.

References

1. Aaronson, S., Gottesman, D.: Improved simulation of stabilizer circuits. Physical Review A **70**(5), 052328 (2004)
2. Aharonov, D.: A simple proof that Toffoli and Hadamard are quantum universal. arXiv preprint quant-ph/0301040 (2003)
3. Amy, M., Maslov, D., Mosca, M.: Polynomial-time t-depth optimization of clifford+t circuits via matroid partitioning. IEEE Transactions on Computer-Aided Design of Integrated Circuits and Systems **33**(10), 1476–1489 (2014)
4. Amy, M., Maslov, D., Mosca, M., Roetteler, M.: A meet-in-the-middle algorithm for fast synthesis of depth-optimal quantum circuits. IEEE Transactions on Computer-Aided Design of Integrated Circuits and Systems **32**(6), 818–830 (2013)
5. Bennett, C.H., Brassard, G., Crépeau, C., Jozsa, R., Peres, A., Wooters, W.K.: Teleporting an Unknown quantum state via dual classical and Einstein-Podolsky-Rosen channels. Phys. Rev. Lett. **70**, 1895 (1993)
6. Bravyi, S., Kitaev, A.: Universal quantum computation with ideal Clifford gates and noisy ancillas. Physical Review A **71**(2), 022316 (2005)
7. Briegel, H.J., Browne, D.E., Dür, W., Raussendorf, R., Van den Nest, M.: Measurement-based quantum computation. Nature Physics **5**(1), 19–26 (2009)
8. Cheung, D., Maslov, D., Severini, S.: Translation techniques between quantum circuit architectures. In: Workshop on Quantum Information Processing. Citeseer (2007)
9. Danos, V., Kashefi, E., Panangaden, P.: The measurement calculus. Journal of the ACM (JACM) **54**(2), 8 (2007)
10. Devitt, S.J., Fowler, A.G., Stephens, A.M., Greentree, A.D., Hollenberg, L.C.L., Munro, W.J., Nemoto, K.: Architectural design for a topological cluster state quantum computer. New Journal of Physics **11**(8), 083032 (2009)
11. Devitt, S.J., Munro, W.J., Nemoto, K.: Quantum error correction for beginners. Reports on Progress in Physics **76**(7), 076001 (2013)
12. Devitt, S.J., Stephens, A.M., Munro, W.J., Nemoto, K.: Requirements for fault-tolerant factoring on an atom-optics quantum computer. Nature communications **4** (2013)
13. Devitt, S.J.: The Mequanics game (2013). www.mequanics.com
14. Fowler, A.G., Mariantoni, M., Martinis, J.M., Cleland, A.N.: Surface Codes, Towards practical large-scale quantum computation. Phys. Rev. A. **86**, 032324 (2012)
15. Fowler, A.G.: Time-optimal quantum computation. arXiv preprint arXiv:1210.4626 (2012)
16. Gottesman, D.: The Heisenberg Representation of Quantum computers. quant-ph/9807006 (1998)
17. Gottesman, D.: What is the overhead required for fault-tolerant quantum computation? arXiv preprint arXiv:1310.2984 (2013)

18. Hirata, Y., Nakanishi, M., Yamashita, S., Nakashima, Y.: An efficient conversion of quantum circuits to a linear nearest neighbor architecture. Quantum Information & Computation 11(1), 142–166 (2011)
19. Jones, C.N.: Novel constructions for the fault-tolerant Toffoli gate. arXiv preprint arXiv:1212.5069 (2012)
20. Cody Jones, N., Van Meter, R., Fowler, A.G., McMahon, P.L., Kim, J., Ladd, T.D., Yamamoto, Y.: A Layered Architecture for Quantum Computing Using Quantum Dots. Phys. Rev. X., 2(031007) (2012)
21. Miller, D.M., Soeken, M., Drechsler, R.: Mapping NCV circuits to optimized clifford+T circuits. In: Yamashita, S., Minato, S. (eds.) RC 2014. LNCS, vol. 8507, pp. 163–175. Springer, Heidelberg (2014)
22. Moore, S.K.: Computing's power limit demonstrated. Spectrum, IEEE 49(5), 14–16 (2012)
23. Nemoto, K., Trupke, M., Devitt, S.J., Stephens, A.M., Buczak, K., Nobauer, T., Everitt, M.S., Schmiedmayer, J., Munro, W.J.: Photonic architecture for scalable quantum information processing in NV-diamond. Phys. Rev. X. 4, 031022 (2014)
24. Nielsen, M.A., Chuang, I.L.: Quantum computation and quantum information. Cambridge University Press (2010)
25. Paetznik, A., Fowler, A.G.: Quantum circuit optimization by topological compaction in the surface code. arXiv preprint arXiv:1304.2807 (2013)
26. Paler, A., Devitt, S., Nemoto, K., Polian, I.: Software-based Pauli tracking in fault-tolerant quantum circuits. In: Design, Automation and Test in Europe Conference and Exhibition (DATE), 2014, pp. 1–4. IEEE (2014)
27. Saeedi, M., Markov, I.L.: Synthesis and optimization of reversible circuits - a survey. ACM Computing Surveys (CSUR) 45(2), 21 (2013)
28. Shende, V.V., Bullock, S.S., Markov, I.L.: Synthesis of quantum-logic circuits. IEEE Transactions on Computer-Aided Design of Integrated Circuits and Systems 25(6), 1000–1010 (2006)
29. Wille, R., Drechsler, R.: Towards a design flow for reversible logic. Springer (2010)
30. Wooters, W.K., Zurek, W.H.: A Single Quantum Cannot be Cloned. Nature (London) 299, 802 (1982)
31. Yao, N.Y., Jiang, L., Gorshkov, A.V., Maurer, P.C., Giedke, G., Cirac, J.I., Lukin, M.D.: Scalable Architecture for a Room Temperature Solid-State Quantum Information Processor. Nature Communications 3, 800 (2012)
32. Zhou, X., Leung, D.W., Chuang, I.L.: Methodology for quantum logic gate construction. Physical Review A 62(5), 052316 (2000)

Equational Reasoning About Quantum Protocols

Simon J. Gay[1] and Ittoop V. Puthoor[1,2](✉)

[1] School of Computing Science, University of Glasgow, Glasgow, UK
1006132p@student.gla.ac.uk
[2] School of Physics and Astronomy, University of Glasgow, Glasgow, UK

Abstract. Communicating Quantum Processes (CQP) is a quantum process calculus that applies *formal* techniques from classical computer science to concurrent and communicating systems that combine quantum and classical computation. By employing the theory of *behavioural equivalence* between processes, it is possible to verify the correctness of a system in CQP. The *equational theory* of CQP helps us to analyse quantum systems by reducing the need to explicitly construct *bisimulation* relations. We add three new equational axioms to the existing equational theory of CQP, which helps us to analyse various quantum protocols by proving that the implementation and specification are equivalent. We summarise the necessary theory and demonstrate its application in the analysis of quantum secret sharing. Also, we illustrate the approach by verifying other interesting and important practical quantum protocols such as superdense coding, quantum error correction and remote CNOT.

Keywords: Quantum Computing · Formal methods · Quantum process calculus · Verification · Operational semantics · Equational reasoning

1 Introduction

Quantum computing is believed to be the next computing revolution as it promises to offer a very high degree of improvement over its classical counterpart by using the principles of quantum mechanics. On the other hand, quantum cryptography and quantum communication have made rapid progress already with the commercial deployment of the first secure cryptography systems [12,13]. It has been mathematically proven that quantum cryptographic systems are unconditionally secure [14] but this doesn't provide a formal assurance to the security when these systems are implemented as a whole unit which may also include classical components. Therefore, there is still the need to develop techniques that verify the correctness of these systems. This was the prime motivation of using *process calculus* (a specialised area in *formal methods*) in modelling and analysing quantum information processing (QIP) systems that can be implemented.

Supported by a Lord Kelvin/Adam Smith Scholarship from the University of Glasgow.

© Springer International Publishing Switzerland 2015
J. Krivine and J.-B. Stefani (Eds.): RC 2015, LNCS 9138, pp. 155–170, 2015.
DOI: 10.1007/978-3-319-20860-2_10

Quantum process calcululi provide the techniques which help us to formally define the structure and behaviour of systems that are a combination of both quantum and classical subsystems. We use a particular quantum process calculus called Communicating Quantum Processes (CQP) [8], developed by Gay and Nagarajan. The other quantum process calculus which has been established is qCCS by Feng et al.[4]. The property of *behavioural equivalence* of processes in quantum process calculus helps to verify the correctness of a system. The *congruence* property of equivalence makes it more powerful by preserving the equivalence in any environment. This has been developed for CQP [2] and qCCS [5].

Equational reasoning is essential in mathematics and logics, and plays an important role in many applications of formal methods in theoretical computer science. With the use of theorem provers for equational logic, it is possible to perform automated analysis. The equational axioms reduce the need to explicitly construct bisimulation relations, which is reported in [2] for CQP with an analysis of the quantum teleportation protocol (*Teleport*).

Our Contributions. In this paper, we demonstrate the use of the equational theory of CQP [2] and introduce three new axioms that helps us to take a step further to analyse various quantum protocols that include: *quantum secret sharing* (*QSS*), *superdense coding* (*SDC*), *quantum error correction code* (*QECC*) and *Remote CNOT* (*RCNOT*). Our results show that the protocols, *QSS* and *QECC* are equivalent to the specification process *Identity*. We provide a similar reasoning for other protocols. Using the *transitivity* property of equivalence, we also prove that $QSS \leftrightarrow^c QECC \leftrightarrow^c Teleport$.

The structure of the paper is as follows. First, in Section 2 we provide in brief the fundamentals of quantum computing. We review the language of CQP in Section 3 and illustrate it with a model of quantum secret sharing. Section 4 provides a brief summary on the theory of behavioural equivalence of CQP. Section 5 summarises the equational theory of CQP, which has not previously been published other than in Davidson's thesis, and applies it to quantum secret sharing and other protocols. Section 6 concludes with an indication of directions of future work.

Related Work. Previous work on automated analysis is based on exhaustive simulation based on stabiliser formalism. Model checking tools like the QMC [10] and the equivalence checker [1] were developed for the verification of quantum protocols. Since the tool uses stabilizer formalism, it is restricted to use only the operators in the Clifford group. The equational theory of CQP is not based on the stabilizer formalism and hence is not restricted to Clifford group operations.

2   Preliminaries

We recall briefly the aspects of quantum computing that are relevant for this paper. For more detailed information we refer to [16]. A *qubit* is an information unit comprising two states ($|0\rangle$ and $|1\rangle$) which are called the *standard* basis.

The *state space* $\mathbb{H}$ (or Hilbert space) of a qubit is a vector space that consists of all *superpositions* of the basis states: $|\psi\rangle = \alpha|0\rangle + \beta|1\rangle$ where α and β are complex amplitudes such that $|\alpha|^2 + |\beta|^2 = 1$. The states can be represented by column vectors:

$$\begin{pmatrix} \alpha \\ \beta \end{pmatrix} = \alpha \begin{pmatrix} 1 \\ 0 \end{pmatrix} + \beta \begin{pmatrix} 0 \\ 1 \end{pmatrix} = \alpha|0\rangle + \beta|1\rangle$$

A system can consist of many qubits (say n qubits) and the Hilbert space is a 2^n dimensional space whose standard basis is $|00\ldots0\rangle \ldots |11\ldots1\rangle$. This is represented by *tensor product* of unit vectors which is denoted as $|0\rangle \otimes |0\rangle \cdots \otimes |0\rangle$. The evolution of the quantum state of a system can be described by quantum operations called *unitary transformations*. If the state of a qubit is represented by a column vector, then a unitary transformation is represented by a matrix. Some unitary transformations which are commonly used are the *Hadamard* (H) and the *Pauli* transformations, denoted by either I, X, Z, Y:

$$H = \frac{1}{\sqrt{2}} \begin{pmatrix} 1 & 1 \\ 1 & -1 \end{pmatrix}, I = \begin{pmatrix} 1 & 0 \\ 0 & 1 \end{pmatrix}, X = \begin{pmatrix} 0 & 1 \\ 1 & 0 \end{pmatrix}, Y = \begin{pmatrix} 0 & -i \\ i & 0 \end{pmatrix}, Z = \begin{pmatrix} 1 & 0 \\ 0 & -1 \end{pmatrix}$$

The *measurement* operation changes the quantum state permanently and measuring the above quantum state $|\psi\rangle$ gives a result 0 with probability $|\alpha|^2$ and result 1 with probability $|\beta|^2$. We will be using the *controlled Not* transformation (or CNOT) on a pair of qubits. The action of this operation is that it flips the second qubit (target qubit) if and only if the first qubit (control qubit) is 1. We have $CNOT|0x\rangle = |0x\rangle$ and $CNOT|1x\rangle = |1y\rangle$ where $x, y \in \{0, 1\}$ and $y = x \oplus 1$ with $\oplus$ denoting addition modulo 2. *Entanglement* is an important phenomenon in quantum computing which is observed in a system that comprises of two or more qubits. This means that the states of the qubits are not *separable*. For example, a three qubit state $\frac{1}{\sqrt{2}}(|000\rangle + |111\rangle)$ (also called *GHZ* state) is said to be *entangled* and cannot be decomposed into single qubit states. Measurement of one of the qubits will fix the state of the others even if the entangled qubits are physically separated.

3   Communicating Quantum Processes (CQP)

CQP is based on the π-calculus [15] with primitives for quantum information. The language uses the concept that a system can be considered to be made up of independent components or *processes*. The *processes* can communicate by sending and receiving data along *channels* and these data are qubits, or classical bits. A distinctive feature of CQP is its static type system [9], the purpose of which is to classify classical and quantum data and also to enforce the no-cloning property of quantum information. In our recent work, we have extended CQP to describe and verify linear optical quantum computing (LOQC) [6,7].

3.1   Syntax and Semantics of CQP

The syntax of CQP is defined by the grammar as shown in Figure 1. We use the notation $\tilde{e} = e_1, \ldots, e_n$, and write $|\tilde{e}|$ for the length of a tuple. The syntax

$$T ::= \mathsf{Int} \mid \mathsf{Qbit} \mid \mathsf{Bit} \mid \widehat{\ \widetilde{T}\ } \mid \mathsf{Op}(1) \mid \mathsf{Op}(2) \mid \cdots$$
$$v ::= 0 \mid 1 \mid \cdots \mid \mathsf{H} \mid \cdots$$
$$e ::= v \mid \mathsf{measure}\ \tilde{e} \mid \tilde{e} *= e \mid e + e' \mid (e, e)$$
$$P ::= \mathbf{0} \mid (P|P) \mid P + P \mid e?[\tilde{x} : \widetilde{T}].P \mid e![\tilde{e}].P \mid \{e\}.P \mid (\mathsf{qbit}\ x)P \mid (\mathsf{new}\ x : \widehat{\ \widetilde{T}\ })P$$

(i)

$$v ::= \ldots \mid q \mid c$$
$$E ::= [] \mid \mathsf{measure}\ E, \tilde{e} \mid \mathsf{measure}\ v, E, \tilde{e} \mid \ldots \mid \mathsf{measure}\ \tilde{v}, E \mid E + e \mid v + E$$
$$F ::= []?[\tilde{x}].P \mid []![\tilde{e}].P \mid v![[].\tilde{e}].P \mid v![v, [], \tilde{e}].P \mid \cdots \mid v![\tilde{v}, []].P \mid \{[]\}.P$$

(ii)

Fig. 1. (i) Syntax of CQP and (ii) Internal syntax of CQP

consists of types T, values v, expressions e (including quantum measurements and the conditional application of unitary operators $\tilde{e} *= e$), and processes P. Values v consist of variables (x,y,z etc), channel names c, literal values of data types $(0,1,..)$, unitary operators such as the Hadamard operator H. Expressions e consist of values, measurements $\mathsf{measure}\ e_1, \ldots, e_n$, applications $e_1, \ldots, e_n *= e$ of unitary operators and expressions involving data operators such as $e + e'$ and a pair of values (e, e). Processes include the nil process $\mathbf{0}$, parallel composition $P|P$, inputs $e?[\tilde{x}:\widetilde{T}].P$, outputs $e![\tilde{e}].P$, actions $\{e\}.P$ (typically a unitary operation or measurement), typed channel restriction $(\mathsf{new}\ x : \widehat{\ \widetilde{T}\ })P$ and qubit declaration $(\mathsf{qbit}\ x)P$. In order to define the operational semantics we provide the *internal syntax* in Figure 1(ii). We assume a countably infinite set of qubit names, ranging over $q, r, \ldots$ and similarly channel names c. Values are supplemented with qubit names q which are generated at run-time and substituted for the variables used in qbit declaration. Evaluation contexts for expressions $(E[])$ and processes $(F[])$ are used to define the operational semantics [19].

The complete formal semantics are provided in [2] and we explain briefly in this paper. In CQP, the execution of a system is described by the process term (which is the case for classical process calculus) and the quantum state. Hence, the operational semantics are defined using *configurations*.

Definition 1. *A configuration is a tuple $(\sigma; \omega; P)$ where σ is a mapping from qubit names to the quantum state and ω is a list of qubit names associated with the process P*

The semantics of CQP consists of labelled transitions between configurations. For example, the configuration $([q, r \mapsto |\psi\rangle]; q; c![q].P)$, means that the global quantum state consists of two qubits, q and r, in the specified state $(|\psi\rangle)$; that the process term under consideration has access to qubit q but not to qubit r; and that the process itself is $c![q].P$.

Example 1. $([q, r \mapsto |\psi\rangle]; q; c![q].P) \xrightarrow{c![q]} ([q, r \mapsto |\psi\rangle]; \emptyset; P).$

The example illustrates an output transition where the quantum state ($|\psi\rangle =$ $\frac{1}{\sqrt{2}}(|00\rangle + |11\rangle)$) is not changed by this output transition. Since qubit q is given as output, the continuation process P no longer has access to it; the final configuration has an empty list of owned qubits.

3.2   Quantum Secret Sharing

In this paper, we describe a quantum secret sharing [11] protocol that consists of three users represented by the processes: *Alice*, *Bob* and *Charlie*. *Alice* would like to send a message to *Bob* and *Charlie*. We analyse a scenario in which *Charlie* ends up with the original qubit. *Alice* encodes her message in a way such that *Bob* and *Charlie* must cooperate with each other to retrieve it. The protocol begins by applying a Hadamard and CNOT operations to qubits x, y and z in order to generate the GHZ state as described in previous section. The qubits are shared between the three users. *Alice* also possesses the qubit labelled q which is in some unknown state $|\psi\rangle$; this is the qubit she wishes to send. The CQP definitions of *Alice*, *Bob* and *Charlie* are as follows

$Alice(c, e, x) = c?[q : \mathsf{Qbit}] . \{q, x \mathrel{*=} \mathsf{CNOT}\} . \{q \mathrel{*=} \mathsf{H}\} . e![\text{measure } q, \text{measure } x] . \mathbf{0}$
$Bob(f, y) = \{y \mathrel{*=} \mathsf{H}\} . f![\text{measure } y] . \mathbf{0}$
$Charlie(e, f, d, z) = e?[i : \mathsf{Bit}, j : \mathsf{Bit}] . f?[k : \mathsf{Bit}] . \{z \mathrel{*=} \mathsf{Z}^k\} . \{z \mathrel{*=} \mathsf{X}^j\} . \{z \mathrel{*=} \mathsf{Z}^i\} .$
$d![z] . \mathbf{0}$

Alice receives the qubit q from the environment through her channel c and performs unitary operations (CNOT and H) before measuring her qubits. She sends the outcomes which are classical bits i and j through channel e to *Charlie*. *Charlie* cannot retrieve the information without the help of *Bob*. *Bob* performs an Hadamard operation on his qubit y before measuring it. Then, he sends the outcome to *Charlie*. Using the classical bits from *Alice* and *Bob*, *Charlie* performs the necessary unitary operations on his qubit z in order to recover the original state $|\psi\rangle$. The complete system is defined as:

$$QSS(c, d) = (\mathsf{qbit}\ x, y, z)(\{x \mathrel{*=} \mathsf{H}\} . \{x, y \mathrel{*=} \mathsf{CNOT}\} . \{y, z \mathrel{*=} \mathsf{CNOT}\} .$$
$$(\mathsf{new}\ e, f)(Alice(c, e, x) \mid Bob(f, y) \mid Charlie(e, f, d, z)))$$

QSS process consists of *Alice*, *Bob* and *Charlie* in parallel. That is the outputs on e and f in *Alice* and *Bob* respectively synchronise with the inputs on e and f in *Charlie*. Channel e and f are designated as a private local channels. This is specified by ($\mathsf{new}\ e, f$), which is a construct from pi-calculus to dynamically create fresh channels. The first term, ($\mathsf{qbit}\ x, y, z$) in *QSS*, allocates three fresh qubits, each in state $|0\rangle$, and gives them the local names x, y and z. The next three terms create the GHZ state with qubits x, y and z. The aim is to prove that *QSS* is equivalent to its specification process given by the following definition:

$$Identity(c : \widehat{\ }[\mathsf{Qbit}], d : \widehat{\ }[\mathsf{Qbit}]) = c?[x : \mathsf{Qbit}] . d![x] . \mathbf{0}.$$

4   Probabilistic Branching Bisimulation of CQP

The equivalence for CQP is a form of *probabilistic branching bisimilarity* [18], adapted to the situation in which probabilistic behaviour comes from quantum measurement. A key point is that when considering matching of input or output transitions involving qubits, it is the reduced density matrices of the transmitted qubits that are required to be equal. Here, we summarise the essential definitions in [2]. Let $\xrightarrow{\tau}{}^+$ denote zero or one τ transitions; let $\Longrightarrow$ denote zero or more τ transitions; and let $\xRightarrow{\alpha}$ be equivalent to $\Longrightarrow\xrightarrow{\alpha}\Longrightarrow$.

Definition 2 (Probabilistic Branching Bisimulation). *An equivalence relation $\mathcal{R}$ on configurations is a* probabilistic branching bisimulation *on configurations if whenever $(s,t) \in \mathcal{R}$ the following conditions are satisfied.*

> I. *If $s \in \mathcal{S}_n$ and $s \xrightarrow{\tau} s'$ then $\exists t', t''$ such that $t \Longrightarrow t' \xrightarrow{\tau}{}^+ t''$ with $(s, t') \in \mathcal{R}$ and $(s', t'') \in \mathcal{R}$.*
>
> II. *If $s \xrightarrow{c![V,\widetilde{q}_1]} s'$ where $s' = \boxplus_{j\in\{1...m\}} p_j s'_j$ and $V = \{\widetilde{v}_1, \ldots, \widetilde{v}_m\}$ then $\exists t', t''$ such that $t \Longrightarrow t' \xrightarrow{c![V,\widetilde{q}_2]} t''$ with*
> > a) *$(s, t') \in \mathcal{R}$,*
> > b) *$t'' = \boxplus_{j\in\{1...m\}} p_j t''_j$,*
> > c) *for each $j \in \{1, \ldots, m\}$, $\rho_E(s'_j) = \rho_E(t''_j)$.*
> > d) *for each $j \in \{1, \ldots, m\}$, $(s'_j, t''_j) \in \mathcal{R}$.*
>
> III. *If $s \xrightarrow{c?[\widetilde{v}]} s'$ then $\exists t', t''$ such that $t \Longrightarrow t' \xrightarrow{c?[\widetilde{v}]} t''$ with $(s, t') \in \mathcal{R}$ and $(s', t'') \in \mathcal{R}$.*
>
> IV. *If $s \in \mathcal{S}_p$ then $\mu(s, D) = \mu(t, D)$ for all classes $D \in \mathcal{S}/\mathcal{R}$.*

Here, μ is the probabilistic function that is defined in the style of [18], which is necessary when calculating the total probability of reaching a terminal state. This is needed to ensure the matching of probabilistic configurations.

Definition 3 (Probabilistic Branching Bisimilarity). *Configurations s and t are* probabilistic branching bisimilar, *denoted $s \leftrightarrow t$, if there exists a probabilistic branching bisimulation $\mathcal{R}$ such that $(s, t) \in \mathcal{R}$.*

Definition 4 (Full Probabilistic Branching Bisimilarity). *Processes P and Q are* full probabilistic branching bisimilar, *denoted $P \leftrightarrow^c Q$, if for all substitutions κ and all quantum states σ, $(\sigma; \widetilde{q}; P\kappa) \leftrightarrow (\sigma; \widetilde{q}; Q\kappa)$.*

In order to state the *congruence* theorem, we need an assumption that processes are typable. Due to space constraints, we have not presented the type system in this paper but the idea is to associate each qubit with a unique owning component of the process.

Theorem 1 (Full Probabilistic Branching Bisimilarity is a Congruence [2]). *If $P \leftrightarrow^c Q$ then for any context $C[]$, if $C[P]$ and $C[Q]$ are typable then $C[P] \leftrightarrow^c C[Q]$.*

$$M \mid N = \Sigma_{i=1}^{m}\alpha_i.(P_i \mid N) + \Sigma_{j=1}^{n}\beta_j.(M \mid Q_j) + \Sigma_{\alpha_i C\beta_j}\tau.(P_i \mid Q_j) \qquad \text{(E1)}$$

where $M = \Sigma_{i=1}^{m}\alpha_i.P_i, N = \Sigma_{j=1}^{n}\alpha_j.Q_j$ and $\alpha_i C\beta_j$ if α_i is $c![\tilde{e}]$ and β_j is $c?[\tilde{x}]$

$$\{\tilde{x} *= V\}.\{\tilde{x} *= W\}.P = \{\tilde{x} *= U\}.P \qquad \text{if } U = WV \qquad \text{(QI1)}$$

$$\{\tilde{y} *= U^{\text{measure } x}\}.P = \{x, \tilde{y} *= \text{CU}\}.\{\text{measure } x\}.P \qquad \text{(QI2)}$$

$$\{\tilde{y} *= U^{\text{measure } x.\text{measure } z}\}.P = \{(x, z), \tilde{y} *= \text{CU}\}.\{\text{measure } x\}.\{\text{measure } z\}.P \quad \text{(QI3)}$$

$$\{\tilde{x} *= U\}.\{\tilde{y} *= V\}.P = \{\tilde{y} *= V\}.\{\tilde{x} *= U\}.P \quad \text{if } \tilde{x} \cap \tilde{y} = \emptyset \qquad \text{(Qc1)}$$

$$\{\tilde{x} *= U\}.\{\text{measure } \tilde{y}\}.P = \{\text{measure } \tilde{y}\}.\{\tilde{x} *= U\}.P \quad \text{if } \tilde{x} \cap \tilde{y} = \emptyset \qquad \text{(Qc2)}$$

$$\{\tilde{x} *= U\}.(\text{qbit } \tilde{y}).P = (\text{qbit } \tilde{y}).\{\tilde{x} *= U\}.P \quad \text{if } \tilde{x} \cap \tilde{y} = \emptyset \qquad \text{(Qc3)}$$

$$\{\text{measure } \tilde{x}\}.\{\text{measure } \tilde{y}\}.P = \{\text{measure } \tilde{y}\}.\{\text{measure } \tilde{x}\}.P \quad \text{if } \tilde{x} \cap \tilde{y} = \emptyset \qquad \text{(Qc4)}$$

$$\{\text{measure } \tilde{x}\}.(\text{qbit } \tilde{y}).P = (\text{qbit } \tilde{y}).\{\text{measure } \tilde{x}\}.P \quad \text{if } \tilde{x} \cap \tilde{y} = \emptyset \qquad \text{(Qc5)}$$

$$(\text{qbit } \tilde{x}).(\text{qbit } \tilde{y}).P = (\text{qbit } \tilde{y}).(\text{qbit } \tilde{x}).P \quad \text{if } \tilde{x} \cap \tilde{y} = \emptyset \qquad \text{(Qc6)}$$

$$\alpha.\{\tilde{y} *= U\}.c?[\tilde{x}].P = \alpha.c?[\tilde{x}].\{\tilde{y} *= U\}.P \quad \text{if } \tilde{y} \subseteq \mathbf{n}(\alpha), \tilde{x} \cap \tilde{y} = \emptyset \qquad \text{(Qc7)}$$

$$\alpha.\{\tilde{y} *= U\}.c![\tilde{x}].P = \alpha.c![\tilde{x}].\{\tilde{y} *= U\}.P \quad \text{if } \tilde{y} \subseteq \mathbf{n}(\alpha), \tilde{x} \cap \tilde{y} = \emptyset \qquad \text{(Qc8)}$$

$$\alpha.\{\text{measure } \tilde{y}\}.c?[\tilde{x}].P = \alpha.c?[\tilde{x}].\{\text{measure } \tilde{y}\}.P \quad \text{if } \tilde{y} \subseteq \mathbf{n}(\alpha), \tilde{x} \cap \tilde{y} = \emptyset \qquad \text{(Qc9)}$$

$$\alpha.\{\text{measure } \tilde{y}\}.c![\tilde{x}].P = \alpha.c![\tilde{x}].\{\text{measure } \tilde{y}\}.P \quad \text{if } \tilde{y} \subseteq \mathbf{n}(\alpha), \tilde{x} \cap \tilde{y} = \emptyset \qquad \text{(Qc10)}$$

$$(\text{qbit } \tilde{x}).c?[\tilde{y}].P = c?[\tilde{y}].(\text{qbit } \tilde{x}).P \quad \text{if } \tilde{x} \cap \tilde{y} = \emptyset \qquad \text{(Qc11)}$$

$$(\text{qbit } \tilde{x}).c![\tilde{y}].P = c![\tilde{y}].(\text{qbit } \tilde{x}).P \quad \text{if } \tilde{x} \cap \tilde{y} = \emptyset \qquad \text{(Qc12)}$$

$$\{\text{measure } x\}.0 = 0 \qquad \text{(Qs1)}$$

$$\{\tilde{x} *= U\}.0 = 0 \qquad \text{(Qs2)}$$

$$(\text{qbit } x).0 = 0 \qquad \text{(Qs3)}$$

$$\alpha.\tau.P = \alpha.P \qquad \text{(Tau1)}$$

$$\alpha.\{\tilde{x} *= \Pi\}.P\{\pi(\tilde{q})/\tilde{x}\} = \alpha.P \quad \text{if } \tilde{x} \subseteq \mathbf{n}(\alpha) \qquad \text{(QP1)}$$

$$(\text{qbit } x).\{\tilde{y}, x *= U\}.P = (\text{qbit } x).\{\tilde{y}, x *= V\}.P \qquad \text{if } U(I_{\tilde{y}} \otimes |0\rangle) = V(I_{\tilde{y}} \otimes |0\rangle) \qquad \text{(QD1)}$$

$$c?[x : \text{Bit}].P(x) = c?[x : \text{Bit}].Q(x) \text{ if } P(x) = Q(x) \text{ for all } x \in \{0, 1\} \qquad \text{(Cv1)}$$

$$(\text{new } c)(P + Q) = (\text{new } c)P + (\text{new } c)Q \qquad \text{(R1)}$$

$$(\text{new } c)\alpha.P = 0 \quad \text{if } \alpha \in \{c?[\cdot], c![\cdot]\} \qquad \text{(R2)}$$

$$(\text{new } c)\alpha.P = \alpha.(\text{new } c)P \quad \text{if } \alpha \notin \{c?[\cdot], c![\cdot]\} \qquad \text{(R3)}$$

Fig. 2. Axioms for full probabilistic branching bisimilarity

5 Equational Theory of CQP

The congruence property of behavioural equivalence guarantees that equivalent processes remain equivalent in any context, which is the foundation for equational reasoning. The axioms for full probabilistic branching bisimilarity are shown in Figure 2 and have been proved sound in [2]. The axioms were used in the analysis of the quantum teleportation protocol which is reported in [2] but does not help us to verify other quantum protocols like $SDC, QECC$ etc.

In this paper, we demonstrate the usefulness of the equational theory of CQP by introducing additional three new axioms Cv1, Qı3 and Tau1, that helps us to take a step further to analyse various other important quantum protocols.

$$c?[x : \text{Bit}] . P(x) = c?[x : \text{Bit}] . Q(x) \text{ if } P(x) = Q(x) \text{ for all } x \in \{0,1\} \quad (\text{Cv1})$$

The *classical value* rule Cv1 enables us to compare processes that are controlled by the classical bit, say x. This rule will be used when we analyse the *SDC* protocol. Rule Qı3 introduced in this paper is an extension of the identity rule Qı2. This rule, expresses the *principle of deferred measurement* [16] and helps us to analyse *QECC* protocol, where the unitary operator U is controlled by the measurement of more than one qubit

$$\{\widetilde{y} *= \text{U}^{\text{measure } x.\text{measure } z}\}.P = \{(x, z), \widetilde{y} *= \text{CU}\}.\{\text{measure } x\} . \{\text{measure } z\}.P$$
$$(\text{Qı3})$$

The correctness of *QECC* has been proved by creating bisimulation relations [3] and in this paper, we show that we can analyse *QECC* by not creating bisimulation relations explicitly. Finally, we define the Tau1 rule that helps to remove the unnecessary τ which arise during the elimination of parallel composition.

$$\alpha . \tau . P = \alpha . P \quad (\text{Tau1})$$

The new axioms introduced in the paper are proved to be sound [17].

5.1   Analysing Quantum Secret Sharing

Now, we present the use of an axiomatic approach for proving that the processes are equivalent with respect to full probabilistic branching bisimilarity that is defined earlier. We begin by applying the expansion law E1 to the definition of *QSS*, to get:

$$\begin{aligned}
&(\text{qbit } x, y, z) . \{x *= \text{H}\} . \{x, y *= \text{CNOT}\} . \{y, z *= \text{CNOT}\} . (\text{new } e, f) \\
&(c?[q] . (Alice' \mid Bob \mid Charlie) + \{y *= \text{H}\} . (Alice \mid Bob' \mid Charlie) + \\
&e?[i, j] . (Alice \mid Bob \mid Charlie'))
\end{aligned} \quad (1)$$

where $Alice = c?[q] . Alice'$, $Bob = \{y *= \text{H}\} . Bob'$ and $Charlie = e?[i, j] . Charlie'$. Using the rules R1 and R2 on Eq. 1, the third term of the sum vanishes to give:

$$\begin{aligned}
&(\text{qbit } x, y, z) . \{x *= \text{H}\} . \{x, y *= \text{CNOT}\} . \{y, z *= \text{CNOT}\} . (\text{new } e, f) \\
&(c?[q] . (Alice' \mid Bob \mid Charlie) + \{y *= \text{H}\} . (Alice \mid Bob' \mid Charlie))
\end{aligned} \quad (2)$$

Expanding Eq. 2 as before, we get:

$$\begin{aligned}
&(\text{qbit } x, y, z) . \{x *= \text{H}\} . \{x, y *= \text{CNOT}\} . \{y, z *= \text{CNOT}\} . (\text{new } e, f)(c?[q] . \{y *= \text{H}\} . \\
&(Alice' \mid Bob' \mid Charlie) + \{y *= \text{H}\} . c?[q] . (Alice' \mid Bob' \mid Charlie) + \{y *= \text{H}\} . \\
&f![\text{measure } y] . (Alice \mid \mathbf{0} \mid Charlie) + c?[q] . \{q, x *= \text{CNOT}\} . (Alice' \mid Bob \mid Charlie))
\end{aligned}$$
$$(3)$$

Using restriction rules R1 – R3 and commutative identities, QC7 and QC8, we can commute between the process terms which leads to the first two terms in Eq. 3 essentially the same and the third term is eliminated to give:

$$(\text{qbit } x, y, z) . \{x *= \mathsf{H}\} . \{x, y *= \mathsf{CNOT}\} . \{y, z *= \mathsf{CNOT}\} . c?[q] .$$
$$(\{y *= \mathsf{H}\} . (\text{new } e, f)(Alice' \mid Bob' \mid Charlie) + \{q, x *= \mathsf{CNOT}\} . \quad (4)$$
$$(\text{new } e, f)(Alice' \mid Bob \mid Charlie))$$

Repeating the procedure of expansion and using the reduction rules, we get:

$$(\text{qbit } x, y, z) . \{x *= \mathsf{H}\} . \{x, y *= \mathsf{CNOT}\} . \{y, z *= \mathsf{CNOT}\} . c?[q] . \{q, x *= \mathsf{CNOT}\} .$$
$$\{q *= \mathsf{H}\} . \{y *= \mathsf{H}\} . (0 + 0 + (\text{new } e, f) . \tau . f![\text{measure } y] . 0 \mid f?[k : \text{Bit}] .$$
$$\{z *= \mathsf{Z}^k\} . \{z *= \mathsf{X}^{\text{measure } r}\} . \{z *= \mathsf{Z}^{\text{measure } q}\} . d![z] . 0$$

$$(5)$$

where τ represents the communication between *Alice* and *Charlie*, which happens internally. Similarly, the communication between *Bob* and *Charlie* gives:

$$(\text{qbit } x, y, z) . \{x *= \mathsf{H}\} . \{x, y *= \mathsf{CNOT}\} . \{y, z *= \mathsf{CNOT}\} . c?[q] .$$
$$\{q, x *= \mathsf{CNOT}\} . \{q *= \mathsf{H}\} . \{y *= \mathsf{H}\} . (\text{new } e, f) . \tau . \tau . \quad (6)$$
$$\{z *= \mathsf{Z}^{\text{measure } y}\} . \{z *= \mathsf{X}^{\text{measure } r}\} . \{z *= \mathsf{Z}^{\text{measure } q}\} . d![z] . 0$$

After several iterations using R3 and followed by $(\text{new } e, f) . 0 = 0$, we get:

$$(\text{qbit } x, y, z) . \{x *= \mathsf{H}\} . \{x, y *= \mathsf{CNOT}\} . \{y, z *= \mathsf{CNOT}\} . c?[q] .$$
$$\{q, x *= \mathsf{CNOT}\} . \{q *= \mathsf{H}\} . \{y *= \mathsf{H}\} . \tau . \tau . \{z *= \mathsf{Z}^{\text{measure } y}\} . \quad (7)$$
$$\{z *= \mathsf{X}^{\text{measure } r}\} . \{z *= \mathsf{Z}^{\text{measure } q}\} . d![z] . 0$$

Finally, we remove the two τ transitions by using the TAU1 rule and thereby arrive at the sequentialised definition of *QSS*.

Proposition 1. $QSS(c, d) \leftrightarrow^c Identity(c, d)$

Proof. We will now simplify Eq. 7 and transform it into the *Identity* process by using the axioms in Figure 2. Rule QI1 allows us to manipulate quantum operators by combining the unitary actions into a single operation:

$$(\text{qbit } x, y, z) . \{x, y, z *= \mathsf{CNOT}_{yz} . \mathsf{CNOT}_{xy} . \mathsf{H}_x\} . c?[q] . \{q, x, y *= \mathsf{H}_y . \mathsf{H}_q . \mathsf{CNOT}_{qx}\} .$$
$$\{z *= \mathsf{Z}^{\text{measure } y}\} . \{z *= \mathsf{X}^{\text{measure } x}\} . \{z *= \mathsf{Z}^{\text{measure } q}\} . d![z] . 0$$

The subscripts on the unitary operators indicates to which qubits they are applied. Applying rule QI2 to the measurement operations in the above process and noting that $\mathsf{CX} = \mathsf{CNOT}$, we get:

$$(\text{qbit } x, y, z) . \{x, y, z *= \mathsf{CNOT}_{yz} . \mathsf{CNOT}_{xy} . \mathsf{H}_x\} . c?[q : \text{Qbit}] .$$
$$\{q, x, y *= \mathsf{H}_y . \mathsf{H}_q . \mathsf{CNOT}_{qx}\} . \{y, z *= \mathsf{CZ}\} . \{\text{measure } y\} . \{x, z *= \mathsf{CNOT}\} .$$
$$\{\text{measure } x\} . \{q, z *= \mathsf{CZ}\} . \{\text{measure } q\} . d![z] . 0$$

We can swap the operators around due to commutativity provided that the operators are not acting on the same qubits. For example, we swap the order of the measurement on z and the controlled-Z operator on x and y because the qubits are independent; mathematically, this is due to the use of the tensor product. The commutativity of internal operators are expressed by the rules QC1-QC6. Using QC2 on the above process, we can move the measurements, and then using QI1, the unitary operators are combined to give:

$$(\text{qbit } x, y, z).\{x, y, z *= \text{CNOT}_{yz}.\text{CNOT}_{xy}.\text{H}_x\}.c?[q:\text{Qbit}].$$
$$\{q, x, y *= \text{H}_y.\text{H}_q.\text{CNOT}_{qx}\}.\{q, x, y, z *= \text{CZ}_{qz}.\text{CNOT}_{xz}.\text{CZ}_{yz}\}.$$
$$\{\text{measure } y\}.\{\text{measure } x\}.\{\text{measure } q\}.d![z].\mathbf{0}$$

The rules QC7-QC10 consider the commutativity of unitary operations with input and output actions by applying certain conditions if $\widetilde{y} \subseteq \mathbf{n}(\alpha)$ and $\widetilde{x} \cap \widetilde{y} = \emptyset$. The first condition is important as it ensures that there is no blocking behaviour. We are also able to commute qubit declarations with input and output actions since a qubit declaration is never blocking. This is expressed by the rules QC11 and QC12. We use these rules to bring the input action to the top and move the measurement operations after the output to give:

$$c?[q].(\text{qbit } x, y, z).\{x, y, z *= \text{CNOT}_{yz}.\text{CNOT}_{xy}.\text{H}_x\}\{q, x, y *= \text{H}_y.\text{H}_q.\text{CNOT}_{qx}\}.$$
$$\{q, x, y, z *= \text{CZ}_{qz}.\text{CNOT}_{xz}.\text{CZ}_{yz}\}.d![z].\{\text{measure } y\}.\{\text{measure } x\}.\{\text{measure } q\}.\mathbf{0}$$

With the help of the principle of deferred measurement, we were able to swap classical control for quantum control. Now we consider the *principle of implicit measurement* [16] which states that, any qubits at the end of a circuit may be assumed to be measured. This is provided by the rule Qs1. Applying this rule to eliminate the measurements and combining the remaining quantum operators with QI1, we obtain:

$$c?[q].(\text{qbit } x, y, z).$$
$$\{q, x, y, z *= \text{CZ}_{qz}.\text{CNOT}_{xz}.\text{CZ}_{yz}.\text{H}_y.\text{H}_q.\text{CNOT}_{qx}.\text{CNOT}_{yz}.\text{CNOT}_{xy}.\text{H}_x\}.d![z].\mathbf{0}$$

In a similar way, the unitary operators and qubit declarations are removed by using the rules Qs2 and Qs3. We see that the qubits y, q and x will each finish in the state $\frac{1}{\sqrt{2}}(|0\rangle + |1\rangle)$. So, we apply the Hadamard operator to each using the rule Qs2 which allows these operations to be added. Combining these operators to a single unitary action by using QC8 and QI1; we get

$$c?[q].(\text{qbit } x, y, z).$$
$$\{q, x, y, z *= \text{H}_y.\text{H}_q.\text{H}_x.\text{CZ}_{qz}.\text{CNOT}_{xz}.\text{CZ}_{yz}.\text{H}_y.\text{H}_q.\text{CNOT}_{qx}.\text{CNOT}_{yz}.\text{CNOT}_{xy}.\text{H}_x\}.$$
$$d![z].\mathbf{0}$$

Next, we insert a permutation in order to swap the output qubit z with q. Rule QP1 defines this action where π is the permutation of qubits and the corresponding permutation on the quantum state is given by Π. Applying this rule and followed by QI1, we get

$$c?[q].(\text{qbit } x, y, z).\{q, x, y, z *= U\}.d![q].\mathbf{0} \tag{8}$$

where $\pi(q) = z, \pi(z) = q, \pi(x) = x, \pi(y) = y$ and $U = \Pi.\text{H}_y.\text{H}_q.\text{H}_x.\text{CZ}_{qz}.$ CNOT_{xz}.

$Alice(c,e,x,y) = c?[a:\mathsf{Bit}, b:\mathsf{Bit}] . \{x \mathrel{*=} \mathsf{X}^b\} . \{y \mathrel{*=} \mathsf{Z}^a\} . e![x] . \mathbf{0}$

$Bob(e,d,y) = e?[x:\mathsf{Qbit}] . \{x,y \mathrel{*=} \mathsf{CNOT}\} . \{x \mathrel{*=} \mathsf{H}\} . d![\mathsf{measure}\ x, \mathsf{measure}\ y] . \mathbf{0}$

$SDC(c,d) = (\mathsf{qbit}\ x,y)(\{x \mathrel{*=} \mathsf{H}\} . \{x,y \mathrel{*=} \mathsf{CNOT}\} . (\mathsf{new}\ e)(Alice(c,e,x,y) \mid Bob(e,d,y))$

$CIdent(c,d) = c?[a:\mathsf{Bit}, b:\mathsf{Bit}] . d![a,b] . \mathbf{0}$

(i)

$Elsa(a,c,d) = (\mathsf{qbit}\ x,y)a?[q:\mathsf{Qbit}, r:\mathsf{Qbit}] . \{x \mathrel{*=} \mathsf{H}\} . \{x,y \mathrel{*=} \mathsf{CNOT}\} . c![q,x] . d![r,y] . \mathbf{0}$

$Anna(c,e,f,g) = c?[q,x] . \{x,q \mathrel{*=} \mathsf{CNOT}\} . e?[j:\mathsf{Bit}] . \{x \mathrel{*=} \mathsf{X}^{\mathsf{measure}\ q}\} . f![\mathsf{measure}\ q] .$
$\{x \mathrel{*=} \mathsf{Z}^j\} . g![x] . \mathbf{0}$

$Iven(d,f,e,h) = d?[r,y] . \{r,y \mathrel{*=} \mathsf{CNOT}\} . \{r \mathrel{*=} \mathsf{H}\} . e![\mathsf{measure}\ r] . f?[i:\mathsf{Bit}] . \{y \mathrel{*=} \mathsf{X}^i\} .$
$\{y \mathrel{*=} \mathsf{Z}^{\mathsf{measure}\ r}\} . h![y] . \mathbf{0}$

$Bob(g,h,b) = g?[x] . h?[y] . b![x,y] . \mathbf{0}$

$RCNOT(a,b) = (\mathsf{new}\ c,d,e,f,g,h)(Elsa(a,c,d) \mid Anna(c,e,f,g) \mid Iven(d,f,e,h) \mid Bob(g,h,b))$

$SCNOT(a,b) = a?[q:\mathsf{Qbit}, r:\mathsf{Qbit}] . \{r,q \mathrel{*=} \mathsf{CNOT}\} . b![q,r] . \mathbf{0}$

(ii)

$Alice(a,b) = (\mathsf{qbit}\ y,z)a?[x:\mathsf{Qbit}] . \{x,z \mathrel{*=} \mathsf{CNot}\} . \{x,y \mathrel{*=} \mathsf{CNot}\} . b![x,y,z] . \mathbf{0}$

$NoiseRnd(p) = (\mathsf{qbit}\ u,v)\{u \mathrel{*=} \mathsf{H}\} . \{v \mathrel{*=} \mathsf{H}\} . p![\mathsf{measure}\ u, \mathsf{measure}\ v] . \mathbf{0}$

$NoiseErr(b,p,c) = b?[x:\mathsf{Qbit}, y:\mathsf{Qbit}, z:\mathsf{Qbit}] . p?[j:\mathsf{bit}, k:\mathsf{bit}] . \{x \mathrel{*=} \mathsf{X}^{jk}\} . \{y \mathrel{*=} \mathsf{X}^{j\bar{k}}\} .$
$\{z \mathrel{*=} \mathsf{X}^{\bar{j}k}\} . c![x,y,z] . \mathbf{0}$

$Noise(b,c) = (\mathsf{new}\ p)(NoiseRnd(p) \mid NoiseErr(b,p,c))$

$BobRec(c,p) = (\mathsf{qbit}\ s,t)c?[x,y,z] . \{x,s \mathrel{*=} \mathsf{CNot}\} . \{y,s \mathrel{*=} \mathsf{CNot}\} . \{x,t \mathrel{*=} \mathsf{CNot}\} .$
$\{z,t \mathrel{*=} \mathsf{CNot}\} . p![x,y,z, \mathsf{measure}\ s, \mathsf{measure}\ t] . \mathbf{0}$

$BobCorr(p,d) = p?[x,y,z,j:\mathsf{bit}, k:\mathsf{bit}] . \{x \mathrel{*=} \mathsf{X}^{jk}\} . \{y \mathrel{*=} \mathsf{X}^{j\bar{k}}\} . \{z \mathrel{*=} \mathsf{X}^{\bar{j}k}\} .$
$\{x,y \mathrel{*=} \mathsf{CNot}\} . \{x,z \mathrel{*=} \mathsf{CNot}\} . d![x] . \mathbf{0}$

$Bob(c,d) = (\mathsf{new}\ p)(BobRec(c,p) \mid BobCorr(p,d))$

$QECC(a,d) = (\mathsf{new}\ b,c)(Alice(a,b) \mid Noise(b,c) \mid Bob(c,d))$

(iii)

Fig. 3. CQP definitions of quantum protocols: (i) Superdense coding (SDC), (ii) Remote CNOT (RCNOT) and (iii) Quantum error correction (QECC)

$\mathsf{CZ}_{yz}.\mathsf{H}_y.\mathsf{H}_q.\mathsf{CNOT}_{qx}.\mathsf{CNOT}_{yz}.\mathsf{CNOT}_{xy}.\mathsf{H}_x$. Now, we have the qubit declaration (qbit x,y,z) which introduces three qubits in the combined state $|000\rangle$. We can define a linear map Q for which the action of teleportation on the single qubit q is given by UQ. Based on QI1, we use a similar rule QD1 to deal with quantum operators that appear under qubit declarations.

We have $UQ = I_{qxyz}Q$ where I_{qxyz} is the identity operator on qubits q, x, y, z. Then by applying QD1 to Eq. 8, we get $c?[q] . \{q, x, y, z \mathrel{*=} I\} . d![q] . \mathbf{0}$. We can now apply Q$I$1, Q$C$8 and Q$S$3 to give

$$c?[q] . \{q \mathrel{*=} I\} . d![q] . \mathbf{0}$$

This is a special case of QP1 where we consider identity permutation that results in the process which we are aiming for: $c?[q] . d![q] . \mathbf{0}$ □

5.2   Other Quantum Protocols

In this section, we will discuss the analysis of three essential quantum protocols using our axioms. The CQP definitions of all the protocols are given in Figure 3. We have omitted the types of channels in our definitions for brevity.

(qbit $x, y)a?[q: \text{Qbit}, r: \text{Qbit}] . \{x *= \mathsf{H}\} . \{x, y *= \mathsf{CNOT}\} . \{x, q *= \mathsf{CNOT}\} . \{r, y *= \mathsf{CNOT}\} .$
$\{r *= \mathsf{H}\} . \{x *= \mathsf{X}^{\text{measure } q}\} . \{y *= \mathsf{X}^{\text{measure } q}\} . \{x *= \mathsf{Z}^{\text{measure } r}\} . \{y *= \mathsf{Z}^{\text{measure } r}\} . b![x, y] . \mathbf{0}$

Applying QI1 and QI2 to combine the unitary operations, we get:
(qbit $x, y)a?[q, r] . \{q, r, x, y *= \mathsf{H}_r.\mathsf{CNOT}_{ry}.\mathsf{CNOT}_{xq}.\mathsf{CNOT}_{xy}.\mathsf{H}_x\} . \{q, x, y *= \mathsf{CNOT}_{qy}.\mathsf{CNOT}_{qx}\} .$
$\{\text{measure } q\} . \{r, x, y *= \mathsf{CZ}_{ry}.\mathsf{CZ}_{rx}\} . \{\text{measure } r\} . b![x, y] . \mathbf{0}$
Applying QC2, QC10, and QS1 to remove the measurements:
(qbit $x, y)a?[q, r] . \{q, r, x, y *= \mathsf{H}_r.\mathsf{CNOT}_{ry}.\mathsf{CNOT}_{xq}.\mathsf{CNOT}_{xy}.\mathsf{H}_x\} . \{q, x, y *= \mathsf{CNOT}_{qy}.\mathsf{CNOT}_{qx}\} .$
$\{r, x, y *= \mathsf{CZ}_{ry}.\mathsf{CZ}_{rx}\} . b![x, y] . \mathbf{0}$

Applying QC11 and QI1,to move the input action in the front and combining the unitary operations:
$a?[q, r] . (\text{qbit } x, y) . \{q, r, x, y *= \mathsf{CZ}_{ry}.\mathsf{CZ}_{rx}.\mathsf{CNOT}_{qy}.\mathsf{CNOT}_{qx}.\mathsf{H}_r.\mathsf{CNOT}_{ry}.\mathsf{CNOT}_{xq}.\mathsf{CNOT}_{xy}.\mathsf{H}_x\}$
$. b![x, y] . \mathbf{0}$
Applying QS2, QC8 and QI1, to add a Hadamard operation on qubit r to give:
$a?[q, r] . (\text{qbit } x, y) . \{q, r, x, y *= \mathsf{H}_r.\mathsf{CZ}_{ry}.\mathsf{CZ}_{rx}.\mathsf{CNOT}_{qy}.\mathsf{CNOT}_{qx}.\mathsf{H}_r.\mathsf{CNOT}_{ry}.\mathsf{CNOT}_{xq}.\mathsf{CNOT}_{xy}.$
$\mathsf{H}_x\} . b![x, y] . \mathbf{0}$
Applying QP1 a permutation operator to perform $\pi(q) = x$ and $\pi(x) = q$, we get:
$a?[q, r] . (\text{qbit } x, y) . \{q, r, x, y *= \Pi.\mathsf{H}_r.\mathsf{CZ}_{ry}.\mathsf{CZ}_{rx}.\mathsf{CNOT}_{qy}.\mathsf{CNOT}_{qx}.\mathsf{H}_r.\mathsf{CNOT}_{ry}.\mathsf{CNOT}_{xq}.\mathsf{CNOT}_{xy}.$
$\mathsf{H}_x\} . b![q, y] . \mathbf{0}$

Applying QS2, QC8 and QI1 to add a Hadamard operation on qubit x to give:
$a?[q, r] . (\text{qbit } x, y) . \{q, r, x, y *= \mathsf{H}_x.\Pi.\mathsf{H}_r.\mathsf{CZ}_{ry}.\mathsf{CZ}_{rx}.\mathsf{CNOT}_{qy}.\mathsf{CNOT}_{qx}.\mathsf{H}_r.\mathsf{CNOT}_{ry}.\mathsf{CNOT}_{xq}.$
$\mathsf{CNOT}_{xy}.\mathsf{H}_x\} . b![q, y] . \mathbf{0}$
Applying QP1 a permutation operator as before to perform $\pi(r) = y$ and $\pi(y) = r$, we get:
$a?[q, r] . (\text{qbit } x, y) . \{q, r, x, y *= \Pi.\mathsf{H}_x.\Pi.\mathsf{H}_r.\mathsf{CZ}_{ry}.\mathsf{CZ}_{rx}.\mathsf{CNOT}_{qy}.\mathsf{CNOT}_{qx}.\mathsf{H}_r.\mathsf{CNOT}_{ry}.\mathsf{CNOT}_{xq}.$
$\mathsf{CNOT}_{xy}.\mathsf{H}_x\} . b![q, r] . \mathbf{0}$
Applying QD1, we get: $a?[q, r] . (\text{qbit } x, y) . \{r, q *= \mathsf{CNOT}\} . \{x, y *= \mathsf{I}\} . b![q, r] . \mathbf{0}$
Applying QC8, QS2, QC3 and QS3, we get: $a?[q, r] . \{r, q *= \mathsf{CNOT}\} . b![q, r] . \mathbf{0}$

Fig. 4. Reasoning about Remote CNOT

Superdense Coding (*SDC*): It involves two users (*Alice* and *Bob*) sharing a pair of entangled qubits. In this protocol, two classical bits are communicated by exchanging a single qubit. Alice is in possession of the first qubit, while Bob has possession of the second qubit. By sending the single qubit in her possession to Bob, it turns out Alice can communicate two classical bits to Bob. The specification process for this protocol is *CIdent*.

Proposition 2. $SDC(c, d) \leftrightarrow^c CIdent(c, d)$

Proof. We begin by eliminating the parallel composition in the process *SDC* as we had done earlier for *QSS*. By applying the expansion law E1 to the definition of *SDC*, to get:

$$(\text{qbit } x, y) . \{x *= \mathsf{H}\} . \{x, y *= \mathsf{CNOT}\} . (\text{new } e)(c?[a, b] .$$
$$(Alice' \mid Bob) + e?[x] . (Alice \mid Bob')) \tag{9}$$

where $Alice' = c?[a, b] . Alice$ and $Bob' = e?[x] . Bob$. Using the rules $R1 - R3$ on Eq. 9, the second term of the sum vanishes and rearranging the terms, we get:

$$(\text{qbit } x, y) . \{x *= \mathsf{H}\} . \{x, y *= \mathsf{CNOT}\} . c?[a, b] . (\text{new } e)(\{x *= \mathsf{X}^b\} . \{y *= \mathsf{Z}^a\} .$$
$$e![x] . \mathbf{0} \mid e?[x] . \{x, y *= \mathsf{CNOT}\} . \{x *= \mathsf{H}\} . d![\text{measure } x, \text{measure } y] . \mathbf{0})$$
$$\tag{10}$$

Expanding Eq. 10 as before and doing similar manipulations, we arrive at:

$$(\text{qbit } x, y) . \{x \mathrel{*}= \mathsf{H}\} . \{x, y \mathrel{*}= \mathsf{CNOT}\} . c?[a, b] . \{x \mathrel{*}= \mathsf{X}^b\} . \{y \mathrel{*}= \mathsf{Z}^a\} . (\text{new } e)$$
$$(e![x] . \mathbf{0} \mid e?[x] . \{x, y \mathrel{*}= \mathsf{CNOT}\} . \{x \mathrel{*}= \mathsf{H}\} . d![\text{measure } x, \text{measure } y] . \mathbf{0})$$

$$(11)$$

The next is a τ transition that happens internally and then performing several iterations using R3 and followed by $(\text{new } e) . \mathbf{0} = \mathbf{0}$, we get:

$$(\text{qbit } x, y) . \{x \mathrel{*}= \mathsf{H}\} . \{x, y \mathrel{*}= \mathsf{CNOT}\} . c?[a, b] . \{x \mathrel{*}= \mathsf{X}^b\} . \{y \mathrel{*}= \mathsf{Z}^a\} .$$
$$\tau . \{x, y \mathrel{*}= \mathsf{CNOT}\} . \{x \mathrel{*}= \mathsf{H}\} . d![\text{measure } x, \text{measure } y] . \mathbf{0}$$

$$(12)$$

Then using Tau1 in Eq. 12, we arrive at the sequentialised form of definition of SDC:

$$(\text{qbit } x, y) . \{x \mathrel{*}= \mathsf{H}\} . \{x, y \mathrel{*}= \mathsf{CNOT}\} . c?[a, b] . \{x \mathrel{*}= \mathsf{X}^b\} . \{y \mathrel{*}= \mathsf{Z}^a\}$$
$$\{x, y \mathrel{*}= \mathsf{CNOT}\} . \{x \mathrel{*}= \mathsf{H}\} . d![\text{measure } x, \text{measure } y] . \mathbf{0}$$

$$(13)$$

Using the rule Qi1 on Eq. 13 to combine the unitary actions to give:

$$(\text{qbit } x, y) . \{x, y \mathrel{*}= \mathsf{CNOT}_{xy}.\mathsf{H}_x\} . c?[a, b] . \{xy \mathrel{*}= \mathsf{H}_x.\mathsf{CNOT}_{xy}.\mathsf{Z}_y^a\,\mathsf{X}_x^b\}$$
$$d![\text{measure } x, \text{measure } y] . \mathbf{0}$$

$$(14)$$

To move the input actions to the top, we apply Qc7 and Qc11 on Eq. 14 to give:

$$c?[a, b] . (\text{qbit } x, y) . \{x, y \mathrel{*}= \mathsf{CNOT}_{xy}.\mathsf{H}_x\}\{xy \mathrel{*}= \mathsf{H}_x.\mathsf{CNOT}_{xy}.\mathsf{Z}_y^a\,\mathsf{X}_x^b\}$$
$$d![\text{measure } x, \text{measure } y] . \mathbf{0}$$

$$(15)$$

Applying Qi1 on Eq. 15, we arrive at the sequential definition of SDC.

$$c?[a, b] . (\text{qbit } x, y) . \{x, y \mathrel{*}= \mathsf{H}_x.\mathsf{CNOT}_{xy}.\mathsf{Z}_y^a\,\mathsf{X}_x^b.\mathsf{CNOT}_{xy}.\mathsf{H}_x\} . d![\text{measure } x, \text{measure } y] . \mathbf{0}$$

Then by applying the rules Qi1 to combine the unitary operations into a single action and using Qc7 and Qc11 to move the input action to the beginning of the process, we get:

$$c?[a:\mathsf{Bit}, b:\mathsf{Bit}] . (\mathsf{Qbit} : x, y) . \{xy \mathrel{*}= U^{ab}\} . d![\text{measure } x, \text{measure } y] . \mathbf{0} \quad (16)$$

Here, $U^{ab} = \mathsf{H}_x.\mathsf{CNOT}_{xy}.\mathsf{Z}_y^a.\mathsf{X}_x^b.\mathsf{CNOT}_{xy}.\mathsf{H}_x$, is a unitary operator which depends on the classical bits a and b. Now, let $P(a, b) = (\mathsf{Qbit} : x, y) . \{xy \mathrel{*}= U^{ab}\} . d![\text{measure } x, \text{measure } y] . \mathbf{0}$ and $Q(a, b) = d![a, b] . \mathbf{0}$ be two processes that are parameterised by the classical bits a and b. It can be proven easily that $P(a, b) \leftrightarrow^c Q(a, b)$ for all possible values of a and b. Hence using Cv1, Eq. 16 $\leftrightarrow^c c?[a, b] . d![a, b] . \mathbf{0}$, which is the specification process $CIdent$. $\square$

Remote CNOT ($RCNOT$): The protocol [20] demonstrates the concept of teleporting a quantum logic gate. Our definitions for the protocol are shown in Figure 3(ii) consisting of four users. *Anna* and *Iven* have in their possession qubits q and r respectively, which they have received from *Elsa*. Also, *Elsa*

$(\text{qbit } y,z)a?[x] . \{x,y,z *= \text{CNOT}_{xy}.\text{CNOT}_{xz}\} . (\text{qbit } u,v)\{u,v *= H_v.H_u\}.$
$\{x *= X^{\text{measure } u.\text{measure } v}\} . \{y *= X^{\text{measure } u.\text{measure } v}\} . \{z *= X^{\text{measure } u.\text{measure } v}\} . (\text{qbit } s,t).$
$\{x,y,z,s,t *= \text{CNOT}_{zt}.\text{CNOT}_{xt}.\text{CNOT}_{ys}.\text{CNOT}_{xs}\} . \{x *= X^{\text{measure } s.\text{measure } t}\}.$
$\{y *= X^{\text{measure } s.\text{measure } t}\} . \{z *= X^{\text{measure } s.\text{measure } t}\} . \{x,y,z *= \text{CNOT}_{xz}.\text{CNOT}_{xy}\} . d![x] . 0$

Applying QI3, QC2, QS1 and QC3, we get:$(\text{qbit } y,z) . a?[x] . (\text{qbit } u,v) . (\text{qbit } s,t) .$
$\{x,y,z,u,v *= \text{CNOT}_{(uv)z}.\text{CNOT}_{(uv)y}.\text{CNOT}_{(uv)x}.H_v.H_u.\text{CNOT}_{xy}.\text{CNOT}_{xz}\}.$
$\{x,y,z,s,t *= \text{CNOT}_{xz}.\text{CNOT}_{xy}.\text{CNOT}_{(st)z}.\text{CNOT}_{(st)y}.\text{CNOT}_{(st)x}.\text{CNOT}_{zt}.\text{CNOT}_{xt}.\text{CNOT}_{ys}.\text{CNOT}_{xs}\}$
$. d![x] . 0$

Applying QC11 and QI1, we get:
$a?[x] . (\text{qbit } y,z,u,v,s,t) . \{x,y,z,u,v,s,t* = \text{CNOT}_{xz}.\text{CNOT}_{xy}.\text{CNOT}_{(st)z}.\text{CNOT}_{(st)y}.\text{CNOT}_{(st)x}.$
$\text{CNOT}_{zt}.\text{CNOT}_{xt}.\text{CNOT}_{ys}.\text{CNOT}_{xs}.\text{CNOT}_{(uv)z}.\text{CNOT}_{(uv)y}.\text{CNOT}_{(uv)x}.H_v.H_u.\text{CNOT}_{xy}.$
$\text{CNOT}_{xz}\} . d![x] . 0$

Applying QS2, QI1 and QD1, we get: $a?[x] . (\text{qbit } y,z,u,v,s,t) . \{x,y,z,u,v,s,t *= I\} . d![x] . 0$
Applying QI1, we get: $a?[x] . (\text{qbit } y,z,u,v,s,t) . \{x *= I\} . \{y,z,u,v,s,t *= I\} . d![x] . 0$
Applying QC10, QS1, QC12 andQS3, we get: $a?[x] . d![x] . 0$

Fig. 5. Reasoning about quantum error correction

has prepared an EPR pair with qubits x and y before sharing it with *Anna* and *Iven*. The objective of the protocol is that *Anna* and *Iven* would like to perform a CNOT operation with their qubits q and r, without communicating any quantum information between them. *Anna* entangles her qubits q and x by performing a CNOT and *Iven* performs the same with his qubits in addition to a H operation on r before measuring it. He then sends the result to *Anna*. She measures her qubit q and performs certain unitary operations on x based on the outcome of her's and *Iven*'s measurements. Also, she sends her measurement outcome to *Iven*. Hence, *Anna* and *Iven* communicate only their classical results between them, which are used to perform unitary operation on their EPR pair. Essentially *Iven*'s qubit y is a CNOT operation of q and r and they communicate their EPR pair qubits (x and y) to *Bob*. The specification of $RCNOT$ is $SCNOT$.

Proposition 3. $RCNOT(a,b) \leftrightarrow^c SCNOT(a,b)$

Proof. The proof is provided in Figure 4.   □

Quantum Error Correction $(QECC)$: $QECC$ consists of three processes: *Alice*, *Bob* and *Noise*. *Alice* wishes to send a qubit to *Bob* over a noisy channel, represented by *Noise*. She uses a error correcting code based on threefold repetition [16]. The code is able to correct single bit-flip error in each block of three transmitted qubits, so for the purpose of this example, in each block of three qubits, *Noise* either applies X to one of them or does nothing. *Bob* uses the appropriate decoding procedure to recover *Alice*'s original qubit. The CQP definitions are provided in Figure 3 (iii) and this system is equivalent to *Identity*.

Proposition 4. $QECC(a, d) \leftrightarrow^c Identity(a, d)$

Proof. The proof is provided in Figure 5 and alternatively given in [3] by constructing a bisimulation. In Figure 5, we begin with the sequentialised definition of $QECC$ which is obtained in the same way as we had done for the previous protocols. □

Proposition 5. $Teleport \leftrightarrow^c QSS \leftrightarrow^c QECC$

Proof. Quantum teleportation (*Teleport*) is a protocol which allows two users who share an entangled pair of qubits to exchange an unknown quantum state by communicating only two classical bits. The CQP definition of *Teleport* protocol and the proof that $Teleport \leftrightarrow^c Identity$ are provided in [2]. We prove the proposition easily using the *transitivity* of $\leftrightarrow^c$ as we have seen that $QECC$ and QSS are equivalent to *Identity* through Propositions 1 and 4. □

The congruence property helps to analyse a combination of systems. For example, if we consider a process defined as $System\ (c, d) = (\text{new } a)\ Teleport(c, a) \mid QECC(a, d)$. We can consider this equivalent to a process $(\text{new } a)\ Teleport(c, a) \mid Identity(a, d)$ by using Proposition 4. This is also equivalent to $(\text{new } a)Identity(c, a) \mid Identity(a, d)$ which is equivalent to $Identity(c, d)$.

6   Conclusion and Future Work

We have explained the use of the quantum process calculus CQP in analysing various quantum protocols. We have summarised the theory of equational axioms based on the concept of behavioural equivalence which is presented in full detail in [2]. We present the analysis of QSS by using the equational axioms and have verified the correctness of QSS and other quantum protocols.

Verification of the quantum protocols using the bisimulation relations requires hard work. First, we need to perform the computation of the *System* (that models the system of interest) and the *Specification*, which expresses the desired behaviour of *System*, and then we need to establish a bisimulation relation. Because of equational reasoning, we show that we can reduce the need to explicitly construct bisimulation relations. The next step for this line of research is to prove the completeness of these laws. The axioms provide the additional advantage for automated reasoning which is our long-term goal following the recent work on automated equivalence checking [1].

References

1. Ardeshir-Larijani, E., Gay, S.J., Nagarajan, R.: Verification of concurrent quantum protocols by equivalence checking. In: Ábrahám, E., Havelund, K. (eds.) TACAS 2014 (ETAPS). LNCS, vol. 8413, pp. 500–514. Springer, Heidelberg (2014)
2. Davidson, T.A.S.: Formal Verification Techniques using Quantum Process Calculus. Ph.D thesis, University of Warwick (2011)

3. Davidson, T.A.S., Gay, S.J., Nagarajan, R., Puthoor, I.V.: Analysis of a quantum error correcting code using quantum process calculus. In: Proceedings of the International Workshop on QPL, vol. 95, pp. 67–80. EPTCS (2011)
4. Feng, Y., Duan, R., Ji, Z., Ying, M.: Probabilistic bisimilarities between quantum processes (2006). arXiv:cs.LO/0601014
5. Feng, Y., Duan, R., Ying, M.: Bisimulation for quantum processes. In: ACM Symposium on Principles of Programming Languages, pp. 523–534. ACM (2011)
6. Franke-Arnold, S., Gay, S.J., Puthoor, I.V.: Quantum process calculus for linear optical quantum computing. In: Dueck, G.W., Miller, D.M. (eds.) RC 2013. LNCS, vol. 7948, pp. 234–246. Springer, Heidelberg (2013)
7. Franke-Arnold, S., Gay, S.J., Puthoor, I.V.: Verification of linear optical quantum computing using quantum process calculus. In: Proceedings of the Combined International Workshop on Expressiveness in Concurrency and Structural Operational Semantics (EXPRESS/SOS), vol. 160, pp. 111–129. EPTCS (2014)
8. Gay, S., Nagarajan, R.: Communicating Quantum Processes. In: ACM Symposium on Principles of Programming Languages, pp. 145–157. ACM (2005)
9. Gay, S.J., Nagarajan, R.: Types and Typechecking for Communicating Quantum Processes. Mathematical Structures in Computer Science **16**(3), 375–406 (2006)
10. Gay, S.J., Nagarajan, R., Papanikolaou, N.: QMC: a model checker for quantum systems. In: Gupta, A., Malik, S. (eds.) CAV 2008. LNCS, vol. 5123, pp. 543–547. Springer, Heidelberg (2008)
11. Hillery, M., Buzek, V., Berthiaume, A.: Quantum secret sharing. Phys. Rev. A **59**, 1829–1834 (1999)
12. IDQ. http://www.idquantique.com/company/presentation.html
13. MagiQ. http://www.magiqtech.com/magiq/home.html
14. Mayers, D.: Unconditional security in quantum cryptography. Journal of the ACM **48**(3), 351–406 (2001)
15. Milner, R.: Communicating and Mobile Systems: the Pi-Calculus. Cambridge University Press (1999)
16. Nielsen, M.A., Chuang, I.L.: Quantum Computation and Quantum Information. Cambridge University Press (2000)
17. Puthoor, I.V.: Theory and applications of quantum process calculus. Ph.D thesis, University of Glasgow (2015)
18. Trčka, N., Georgievska, S.: Branching bisimulation congruence for probabilistic systems. Electronic Notes in Theoretical Computer Science **220**(3), 129–143 (2008)
19. Wright, A.K., Felleisen, M.: A syntactic approach to type soundness. Information and Computation **115**(1), 38–94 (1994)
20. Zhou, X., Leung, D.W., Chuang, I.L.: Methodology for quantum logic gate construction. Phys. Rev. A **62** (2000)

Design of Reversible Circuits

Design and Fabrication of a Microprocessor Using Adiabatic CMOS and Bennett Clocking

Ismo K. Hänninen[1], César O. Campos-Aguillón[2], Rene Celis-Cordova[2], and Gregory L. Snider[1(✉)]

[1] Department of Electrical Engineering, University of Notre Dame,
Notre Dame, IN 46556, USA
snider.7@nd.edu
[2] Department of Electrical and Computer Engineering,
Tecnológico de Monterrey, Monterrey, Mexico

Abstract. This paper will describe the design and implementation of a MIPS-based microprocessor using Bennett clocking to implement reversible logic. In Bennett clocking the clock signals form a "cascade" that moves information forward through logic gates in the compute phase, and then recovers energy during a decompute phase, forming a reversible logic circuit. New logic design and verification tools were developed, using structural Verilog and extensions to ModelSim to address the issues of adiabatic clocking, tools that are currently unavailable in commercial packages. The microprocessor is based on a simplified version of the MIPS architecture. After verification by our design tools it was then implemented using CMOS standard cells based on split-level charge recovery logic. The final design contains approximately 5700 transistors, and is currently being fabricated at MOSIS.

Keywords: Reversible microprocessor · Adiabatic CMOS · Bennett clocking

1 Introduction

In the 1960s computers dissipated a large amount of power and required significant cooling, so they were located in rooms with dedicated air conditioning units. This large power dissipation helped drive the transition in the 1970s from BJT-based computers to ones based on MOSFETs. BJTs were faster, but FETs produced less heat. Likewise power dissipation drove the transition in the early 1980s from NMOS to CMOS. NMOS was faster but CMOS produced less heat. In the 1980s and early 1990s the power requirements of computers were relatively low and significant computing resources could be placed in a closet with minimal cooling. During this time the need for processing speed was the paramount issue, and the exponential increases in power dissipation and heat each year were minor concerns. But by the late 1990s progress in devices had led to systems where power dissipation was again becoming a significant problem, and charts extrapolating the exponential increase in dissipation showed the heat production per unit area of a processor surpassing that of the sun, ~6 kW/cm², by 2017.

© Springer International Publishing Switzerland 2015
J. Krivine and J.-B. Stefani (Eds.): RC 2015, LNCS 9138, pp. 173–185, 2015.
DOI: 10.1007/978-3-319-20860-2_11

Clearly something had to change. Because of power dissipation the progress in device size that underlies Moore's Law could not immediately be translated into a performance increase, undermining the business models of semiconductor manufactures. Unlike previously there was no new device or circuit primitive that could immediately offer lower dissipation. The solution needed to be at the system level, and the approach decided upon was multi-core architectures. Here, the clock frequency was held nearly constant to control power dissipation, but splitting up the computing task and spreading it among parallel computing cores produced overall performance gains. Through the 2000s the most important processor design constraint was to keep the power dissipation below 200 W/cm^2, the practical limit of air-cooling. To meet this constraint, it became necessary to turn off parts of the chip at certain times to reduce power, a practice known as Dark Silicon. It has been projected that by the 8 nm node 50-80% of a chip will be "dark" at any given time [1], which begs the question: why have that many transistors if they can't be used?

Today, high-performance computers are back to requiring huge amounts of power and cooling. A number of data centers are being built where the waste heat can be used to heat buildings. Facebook recently opened a data center in Lulea Sweden, near the Arctic Circle, located in part to take advantage of the low ambient temperature for cooling. Data Centers consumed approximately 91 billion kilowatt-hours, 2-3% of electrical power in the US in 2013, a number that is expected to grow to 140 billion kW-hr by 2020 [2].

There are a number of factors contributing to the power dissipation in computation, but processing chips themselves contribute a significant fraction, and the power density is limiting chip development and utilization. Processor clock frequencies have not increased in a decade although the transistors used are nearly an order of magnitude faster. Without a significant change in the underlying approach to computation the rate of increase in computing performance will slow significantly. Moving forward requires an approach that combines devices and system architectures.

Today's computers encode information with charge stored on capacitors, the CMOS gate and interconnect capacitors. Power dissipation for standard CMOS logic is given by the equation

$$P_{Total} = N\left(\alpha C V_{DD}^2 f + P_{Passive}\right) \qquad (1)$$

where V_{DD} is the supply voltage, C is the load capacitance at the output of each logic gate, N is the number of gates, α is the activity factor, and f is the operating frequency. The first term represents the active power dissipation, *i.e.*, the power dissipated in processing information. The second term, the passive power dissipation, is power that is simply wasted because a voltage is applied to the circuit.

Even modest projections of future device density and switching speed highlight the severity of the power issue. By lowering the supply voltage and using ideal switches with no leakage it may be possible to lower the switching energy to 100 k_BT, considered a practical limit for error-free computing. However, a device density of 10^{11} cm^{-2} and a clock frequency of 100 GHz with $\alpha=1$ will give an active power of 4 kW/cm^2, close to that of the surface of the sun. Approaches to increase device density such as 3D integration will only exacerbate the power density problem.

Clearly, lowering the power dissipated per switching event needed, but is there a minimum energy that *must* be dissipated in computation? In 1961 Landauer [3] postulated that energy must be dissipated as heat only when information is destroyed, an idea that has come to be known as the Landauer principle (LP). The minimum amount of energy that must be dissipated is related to a quantity known as the Ultimate Shannon Limit [4], $k_B T \ln(2)$, the minimum energy needed to make a bit of information distinguishable from noise. According to LP, if information is not destroyed there is no fundamental lower limit to dissipation in computation, just practical limits. In the last decade there have been suggestions that the Landauer principle is incorrect, or at best applicable only in special situations, not in realistic systems [5, 6]. Recent experiments at the University of Notre Dame [7, 8]} have experimentally shown that the Landauer principle is correct and the dissipation to heat in simple, charge-based systems, can be much less than $k_B T \ln(2)$ if information is not destroyed, which requires reversible logic.

2   Reversible Circuit Design

A challenge in reversible circuit design is the overhead associated with reversibility. In general this can be viewed as the need to retain enough information about the state of the circuit as the computation runs forward, so that in the de-compute phase the energy in the circuit can be pushed back to its origin, rather than let it dissipate to heat. In one scheme this overhead is in circuit complexity [9], using reversible gates and implementing the additional circuitry to control the de-compute phase. Another way to implement a reversible computation is to use Bennett clocking, also known as a retractile cascade [10, 11]. As explained in more detail below, the inputs to a logic block are held until the de-compute phase, and this information is used for energy recovery. This has the advantage of simple implementation, since the design can map easily onto a reversible design. For this reason we chose to use Bennett clocking in our design.

2.1   Bennett Clock

In Bennett Clocking power clocks are used to sequentially energize successive levels of logic in the compute phase, and then to sequentially de-energize logic in the reverse fashion during the de-compute phase. The timing of a three-level, positive going Bennett clock is shown in Fig. 1(a).

When combined with adiabatic CMOS logic such as split-rail charge recovery logic [12], using both positive and negative going clocks, Fig. 1(b), Bennett clocking can be used to simply convert conventional combinational logic to reversible logic. This is accomplished by retaining the inputs during the de-compute phase, as illustrated in Fig. 1(c). In the energizing phase an input is applied to the first gate, and then the first level Bennett clock, CLK 1, is ramped up and held. The output from this first gate can then be used as the input to the next gate and then the second level Bennett clock is ramped, and so on. In the de-compute phase the last Bennett level, e.g. CLK 3 in Fig. 1, is ramped down first, and since the inputs from previous

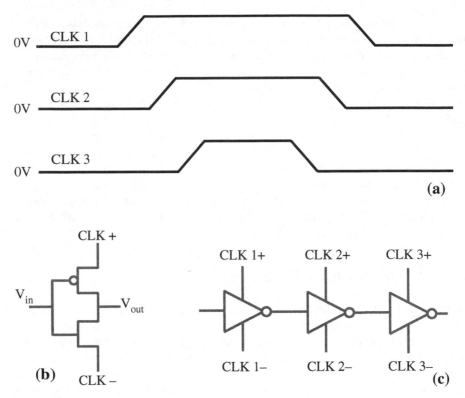

Fig. 1. (a) Timing diagram of three-level Bennett clocking. (b) Schematic diagram of a split-rail charge recovery inverter. (c) Simplified schematic showing the Bennett clock connections to a three-inverter chain.

levels are held, the energy stored in the gate is recovered by the clock as it ramps down. This repeats until the first Bennett level is ramped down. At this point the inputs to the Bennett clocked logic block can be changed and the ramping begun for the next computation. In effect Bennett clocking creates temporal reversibility overhead, since the inputs to the logic block must be held throughout, limiting the scope of pipelining.

2.2 Microprocessor Architecture

A general-purpose microprocessor based on the Bennett clocking scheme was designed to obtain an understanding of the challenges related to the organization and timing of relatively complex retractile circuits. The chosen specification follows a standard textbook RISC MIPS subset with an 8-bit data word length and a multicycle microarchitecture [13], which can be considered as a real-world worst-case scenario for the Bennett clocking scheme.

The processor instruction set and its microarchitecture are not optimized for the Bennett clocked implementation, which can recover only the energy in combinatorial logic blocks. Since the microarchitecture uses about 60% of the total number of transistors in sequential elements, only the signal energy associated with 40% of the transistors is amenable to adiabatic recovery. However, the sequential elements generally have much lower activity rates than the combinatorial blocks, which leads to a better rate of energy recovery than suggested by the simple transistor number ratio.The microprocessor designed is based on a simplified, fully functional, MIPS architecture. The instruction word length is 32 bits as in a full modern-day MIPS, but the adiabatic processor implements only a subset of the instructions and the datapath word length is limited to 8 bits. Only ten instructions are implemented: addition, subtraction, bitwise and, bitwise or, set less than, add immediate, branch if equal, jump, load byte and store byte; but these enable universal computation. There are eight 8-bit registers in the register file. These instructions conform to the standard MIPS instructions, details of which can be found elsewhere [13].

The instruction set is embodied in a relatively straight-forward RISC multicycle microarchitecture with the top-level block diagram in Fig. 2. The datapath includes an external memory, while internally the datapath has three stages separated by registers: register file stage, ALU stage, and memory stage. The stages correspond to Bennett clocking blocks with adiabatically clocked combinational logic. A 13 state controller state machine, with an additional init state, controls the operation of the datapath.

In the datapath, the partially adiabatic processor simply replaces each combinatorial block with a corresponding Bennett clocked block, and the timing constraints are satisfied with standard clocking of the interspersed sequential elements. During the cycle of the standard clock, the Bennett clocked combinatorial levels run through a full cycle of energization and de-energization. The sequential elements sample their input when all Bennett levels are fully energized (all signals valid) and change their output when all Bennett levels are fully relaxed.

The controller block provides the multiplexer select and register enable signals, which in standard static logic would practically instantaneously have valid logic values. However, since the adiabatic controller module computes these signals using Bennett clocked logic, the energization state of the controls changes according to the

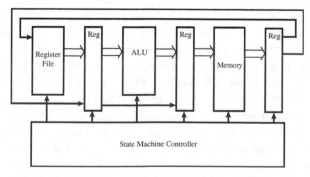

Fig. 2. Simplified top-level diagram of the microprocessor

power-clocks. A relaxed or ramping control signal cannot be fed into an energized datapath block, which would leak current (or produce other erratic behavior) and consequently lose energy. This brings an essential timing constraint into play: the controls must be computed before the controlled block can be energized.

In our prototype processor, both the control module and the datapath share the same set of 12 power-clock pairs. The aforementioned timing constraint can be enforced by careful design, taking into account the control dependencies according to Fig. 4. With this limited number of Bennett levels, some of the control signals could not meet the deadlines if they were computed by Bennett logic from the control state, but those controls had to be directly represented by specific bits in the state register. The alternatives would have been to include more Bennett levels (more power-clock pairs) or implement the control computation partially in standard static logic.

3   Adiabatic CMOS Design Tools

Several computer tools were developed for the logic design, design verification, and design automation of adiabatic CMOS circuits. While the software tools are applicable to some other styles of energy-recovery logic, they were aimed at and tested with Bennett Clocked Adiabatic CMOS.

Industry standard logic level design tools were extended to enable the faithful structural modeling and semi-timing simulation of the Bennett clocked adiabatic circuits. The hardware design language (HDL) of choice for the development platform was *SystemVerilog* and the utilized simulation environment *Mentor Graphics Model-Sim*.

The signal/circuit models are discrete-level and discrete-time, while still capturing the important timing constraints of the retractile circuits. The environment extension is divided into two components: Bennett Wrappers Package, and Bennett Gate Model Library.

Bennett Wrappers Package. contains the ramp logic signal type definition and extensive signal generator and conversion functions. While the standard Verilog/SystemVerilog logic signal type has four states {1, 0, X, Z}, the adiabatic circuits require verification using a model which includes the transitional states. The ramp logic signal type has nine states {X, RLXD, ACT1, ACT0, REN1, RDE1, REN0, RDE0, Z}, including a relaxed (often called "null") state and separate energization/de-energization transition states for both logic 1 and 0. In semi-timing simulation, each signal explicitly transitions through the intermediate states when there is a switching event. This enables behaviorally-accurate tracking of the structural component energization levels.

Bennett Gate Model Library. contains modules describing the behavior of the 45 logic gates in a standard CMOS library with Bennett power-rail modifications. While a minimal standard logic gate model defines only the logical mappings between the input and output signal spaces, the Bennett gate model explicitly takes as input also the power-clocks and defines the behavior based on the energization level of the data inputs and the power-clocks, which are both modeled using the 9-state ramp logic type. This ensures that a gate model will produce the valid logical output only if also the relative timing and the energization of the inputs and the power-clocks are legal, which is a real concern in the retractile cascade circuit having components that turn on and off regularly.

Figure 3 shows a screenshot of the beginning of a simulation run of the Bennett MIPS RISC microprocessor. The sawtooth pattern is the repeating activation sequence of 12 Bennett levels.

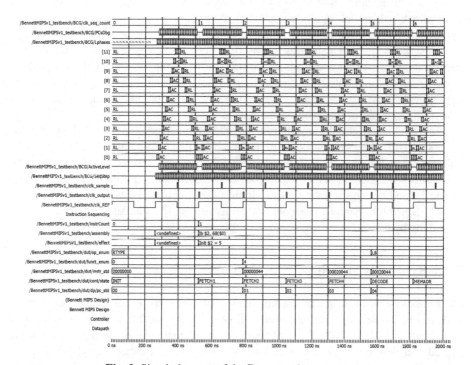

Fig. 3. Simulation run of the Bennett microprocessor

Bennett Energization Sequence Checker

The Bennett standard gate model library (part of the environment) ensures that the logical function of a design is well-specified (and based on the designer effort, also correct), but it does not guarantee that the circuit has been connected to the power-clocks in such a way that it incorporates the desired adiabatic signal energy-recovery. It is allowed and often useful to include circuit parts that have the power-clocks tied to static V_{DD} and V_{SS} rails, which enables standard CMOS operation with the associated loss of all signal energy. However, the main goal of the design effort is to maximize the adiabatic recovery and use as few standard statically powered blocks as possible. To this extent, the semi-timing simulation should perform automatic checking of the correct adiabatic energization sequence in every node that the designer intends to achieve energy-recovery.

The Bennett Energization Sequence Checker is a package containing SystemVerilog assertion functions/tasks and compiler macros to enforce the adiabatic charging and discharging of the desired circuits nodes as defined by the logic designer. The macros are typically called in the definition of a new adiabatic module, where they check the desired signals and generate debug output as necessary. Each new adiabatic module should contain at least the following assertions: 1. all incoming power-clocks for internal consistency, and 2. all incoming data signals for validity during specified time interval.

The power-clock consistency checker has a vector input port for all positive power-clocks and all negative power-clocks. The checker produces an assertion error if any power-clock pair is not legally complementary or any power-clock below the current highest active level has a transition (since all lower levels should be stable active).

The signal sequence assertions are used to check that a given set of signals energizes in a specific order and there are no transitions or illegal states below the highest active level. For example, it is typical that an adiabatic module requires that all data input signals must have a stable active logic value (not relaxed or ramping), before the lowest power-clock of that module starts to activate.

Bennett clocked circuits using split-rail charge recovery logic can be synthesized using standard CMOS to with only minor modifications. We developed a stand-alone netlist parsing program, still in its early stages, that can extract the structural netlist and identify the Bennet levels. This tool essentially reads the netlist from the logic synthesis, and tags each gate with the logic row (Bennett) level in which it must be placed. Since full synthesis tool are not yet available, the standard cells in the library were done by hand.

4   Synthesis and Spice Simulations

The transistor-level and layout implementation of the microprocessor are based on the HDL model. To verify proper operation of logic gates and modules, electrical simulations were conducted using a SPICE engine. For each individual gate, an electric schematic was created and verified in simulation before designing the corresponding physical layout. Finished layouts underwent netlist extraction including parasitics to ensure equivalence between circuit design and physical implementation; and to obtain a closer estimate of their real operation.

To simulate adiabatic operation a testbench that generates the necessary power clock waveforms was written using SPICE directives. Figure 4 (c) shows a sample waveform for a single power clock phase operating at a frequency of 100 kHz. Electrical simulations showed that all components work as intended and follow the behavioral model. Figure 4 shows typical operation for a minimum size inverter with NMOS size 8λ and PMOS size 16λ. For this simulation, the netlist was extracted from layout including parasitics for the MOSIS 0.5 μm C5 process [14].

A frequency-domain analysis was performed for the inverter described above. Since the circuit topology is similar to a standard CMOS inverter, the same cell can be used in adiabatic or static CMOS mode by connecting it to the power clocks or the DC power supplies respectively. Both operation modes were simulated in LTspice at various frequencies between 100 kHz and 5 GHz. Figure 5 compares power dissipation as a function of frequency for the standard CMOS and adiabatic operation modes of the inverter. The inverter was loaded with 20 fF for both cases. A square input with half the operating frequency was fed into the inverter. Rail-to-rail voltage is 5V in both cases, well above the threshold value for the 500 nm process.

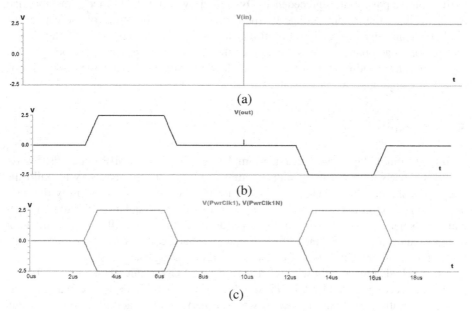

Fig. 4. Typical operation for an adiabatic minimum size inverter running at 100 kHz. (a) Input waveform. (b) Output waveform. (c) Power clock waveforms.

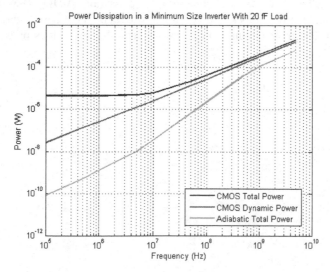

Fig. 5. Frequency-domain analysis of power dissipation for adiabatic and static CMOS operation modes in a minimum size inverter

In CMOS mode total power dissipation was found by multiplying the rail-to-rail voltage and the power supply current. At low frequencies the main contributor to total dissipation is static (leakage) power and consequently it remains roughly constant until dynamic power takes precedence. Dynamic power in CMOS mode was obtained by multiplying the output voltage by the current flowing in or out of the capacitive load. Dynamic dissipation is proportional to the operating frequency. Total power dissipation in adiabatic mode is the sum of the products of each power clock voltage and their corresponding drawn current. For lower frequencies adiabatic dissipation is orders of magnitude lower than static CMOS.

5   Layouts

A fully custom IC layout was created to implement the Bennett MIPS microprocessor. As no synthesis tools currently support adiabatic logic, it was necessary to build the entirety of the design by hand. The layout follows the HDL design closely down to the bottom-up modular structure. We decided to use the standard cell technique because it helps lay complex circuits in an orderly fashion, is well-suited to modular designs, and is ideal for Bennett-clocked systems. Each cell row must contain a single logic level and thus, single power clock phase, minimizing routing issues.

All standard cells comply with the design rules of ON Semiconductor's C5 0.5 μm process, as recommended by MOSIS. In addition to this foundry, the design is undergoing fabrication at Notre Dame's own Nanofabrication Facility using a custom process with no additional design rules and a minimum feature size of 1 μm. The same design is used for both processes.

Cells have a height of 75λ and contain four power rails: VDD, VSS and the positive and negative power clock sources for a single Bennett clock phase. Rails run horizontally through the circuit and each row shares the same clock phase. Therefore,

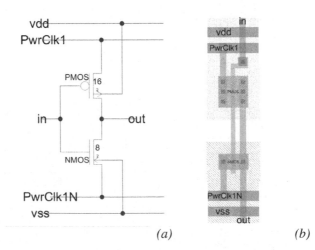

(a)   *(b)*

Fig. 6. Adiabatic minimum size inverter. (a) Electrical schematic. (b) Physical layout.

all cells in a row need to have the same logic depth in logic design. Data flows from the top to the bottom of the circuit, with the only exception of non-buffered multiplexers. Because of this directionality, it was decided to have inputs above each cell and outputs below. Interconnections were made on a metal layer on top of the cells to optimize transistor density. All layouts were drawn in the L-Edit software from the Tanner Tools suite. Figure 6 shows a minimum size inverter layout 6(b) displaying all design choices described herein and its corresponding electrical schematic 6(a).

The custom adiabatic standard cells were organized in a library that contains all adiabatic gate definitions from the HDL model. This library includes inverters, NAND gates from 2 to 8 inputs, 2-input NOR, 2-input AND, 2-input OR, 2-input XOR, transfer gate (TG)-based multiplexers, a TG-based conditional inverter and a few complex logic modules. Additional to this library, conventional CMOS sequential elements such as SRAMs and flip-flops were used in the microprocessor.

The microprocessor layout was assembled by hand using the cells from this library. Since it was decided to have each row correspond to a single power clock phase, physical placement became tied to logic design. Consequently it was not possible to follow the traditional standard cell approach strictly throughout the circuit. Two deviations were permitted: logic levels with too many components were split into multiple physical rows to maintain a reasonable width; and the layout process progressed in a vertical direction. This method aims to optimize routing space around the power clocks, which amount to a large number of signals for Bennett-clocked systems. The trade-off is higher complexity in the layout process and some areas of suboptimal

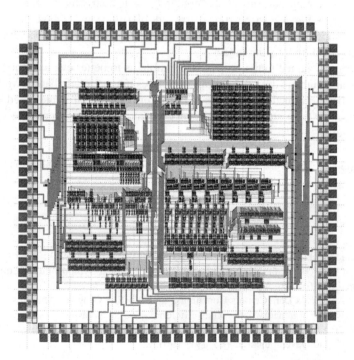

Fig. 7. Final layout for the adiabatic MIPS microprocessor

transistor density. Static CMOS elements within the circuit have no timing requirements and can be placed in any convenient space. Throughout the layout design they
were used to fill gaps and improve transistor density.

The final layout for the adiabatic MIPS microprocessor is shown in Fig. 7. The
chip is approximately 2.3 x 2 mm, using 1 µm design rules, excluding the bondpads.
Combinatorial logic is fully adiabatic and is located in the mid and lower portion of
the layout. The upper section is dominated by the register and SRAM memory banks.
Registers that are closely tied to a combinatorial section (e.g. the state register for the
state machine) are located near their corresponding logic to optimize routing. The
total transistor count is 5,766 of which approximately 40% are adiabatic.

6   Conclusions

A complete microprocessor for adiabatic computing was designed and synthesized
using Bennett Clocking and adiabatic CMOS. While simplified the processor is ca-
pable of general computing and simulations show that it should yield significant power savings. In the course of the project we have developed a number of tools that will
be applicable to a broad range of adiabatic CMOS circuits. These tools can be used as
extensions of existing tools, and begin to define and address the specific needs of
reversible adiabatic circuits.

Testing of the chip will begin as soon as the fabrication is complete. In addition
we are also fabricating portions of the processor as test structures. Since a Bennett
clocked logic block can also be run in irreversible mode by connecting the power
clocks to DC supplies, we will be able to evaluate the dissipation in the subcircuits in
both reversible and irreversible modes.

The experience gained in the project will enable us to better evaluate the trade-offs
necessary in an adiabatic design. Several challenges unique to adiabatic CMOS circuit
design have been outlined and addressed in the project. Future automated synthesis
tools will need to take some of these concerns into account to produce optimized
adiabatic circuits.

Acknowledgments. This work was supported by the National Science Foundation grant CHE
1124762.

References

1. Esmaeilzadeh, H., Blem, E., Amant, R., Sankaralingam, K., Burger, D.: ``Dark silicon and
   the end of multicore scaling''. In: 38th Annual International Symposium on Computer Architecture. pp. 365–376. ACM (2011)
2. NRDC, "America's Data Centers Consuming and Wasting Growing Amounts of Energy".
   http://www.nrdc.org/energy/data-center-efficiency-assessment.asp
3. Landauer, R.: Irreversibility and Heat Generation in the Computing Process. IBM Journal
   of Research and Development **5**, 183–191 (1961)

4. Costello, D.J., Forney, G.D.: Channel coding: The road to channel capacity. Proceedings of the IEEE **95**, 1150–1177 (2007)
5. Cavin, R.K., Zhirnov, V.V., Hutchby, J.A., Bourianoff, G.I.: Energy barriers, demons, and minimum energy operation of electronic devices. Fluctuation and Noise Letters **5**, C29–C38 (2005)
6. Zhirnov, V.V., Cavin, R.K., Hutchby, J.A., Bourianoff, G.I.: Limits to binary logic switch scaling - A Gedanken model. Proceedings of the IEEE **91**, 1934–1939 (2003)
7. Orlov, A.O., Lent, C.S., Thorpe, C.C., Boechler, G.P., Snider, G.L.: Experimental Test of Landauer's Principle at the Sub-kBT Level. Jpn. J. Appl. Phys **51**, 06FE10-1–06FE10-5 (2012)
8. Berut, A., Arakelyan, A., Petrosyan, A., Ciliberto, S., Dillenschneider, R., Lutz, E.: Experimental verification of Landauer's principle linking information and thermodynamics. Nature **483**, 187–189 (2012)
9. Vieri, C.J.: "Reversible Computer Engineering and Architecture" Massachusets Institute of Technology, Ph.D Thesis, (1999)
10. Lent, C.S., Liu, M., Lu, Y.H.: Bennett clocking of quantum-dot cellular automata and the limits to binary logic scaling. Nanotechnology **17**, 4240–4251 (2006)
11. Valiev, K.A., Starosel'skii, V.I.: A Mondel and Properties of a Thermodynamically Reversible Logic Gate. Russian Microelectronics **29**, 83–98 (2000)
12. Younis, S.: "Asymptotically Zero Energy Computing Using Split-Level Charge Recovery Logic". Massachusets Institute of Technology, Ph.D. Thesis (1994)
13. Weste, N., Harris, D.: CMOS VLSI Design: A Circuits and Systems Perspectives. 4th ed. Addison-Wesley (2010)
14. MOSIS, "MOSIS, Wafer Electrical Test". https://www.mosis.com/cgi-bin/params/ami-c5/v3bm-params.txt

Improved Algorithms for Debugging Problems on Erroneous Reversible Circuits

Yuma Inoue[1][(✉)] and Shin-ichi Minato[1,2]

[1] Graduate School of Information Science and Technology,
Hokkaido University, Sapporo-shi, Japan
`yuma@ist.hokudai.ac.jp`
[2] JST ERATO MINATO Discrete Structure Manipulation System Project,
Sapporo-shi, Japan

Abstract. Reversible circuits and their synthesis methods have been actively studied in order to realize reversible computation. However, there are few known ways to debug erroneous reversible circuits. In this paper, we propose new algorithms for debugging problems. For single gate error, we improve the theoretical efficiency of previous methods, which use worst case exponential time algorithms such as SAT or decision diagrams. We also propose an algorithm debugging multiple gate error circuits by using πDDs, decision diagrams for permutation sets. We evaluate our algorithms theoretically and experimentally, and confirm significant improvement.

Keywords: Reversible computation · Circuit design · Permutations · Algorithms · Decision diagrams · Dynamic programming

1 Introduction

Reversible computation is a fundamental technology for next generation computation such as quantum computation [11] and optical computing [3]. Computation is reversible if we can determine an input pattern for a given output pattern. This means reversible computation is information-lossless. Therefore, reversible computation is also used for low power design [1,8].

Due to the reversible property, a reversible logic circuit has neither fanout nor feedback, i.e. formed as a cascade of reversible logic gates. This distinguishes synthesis of reversible circuits from irreversible ones, and attracts many researchers to study synthesis approaches [2,4,9,13,16].

On the other hand, there are few results concerning debugging such circuits, which is another important process to analyze reversible circuits. Wille et al. [17] proposed the first algorithm to debug reversible circuits using SAT formulation and solvers based on debugging techniques for irreversible circuits. Frehse et al. [6] gave a simulation-based approach and combined it with the SAT-based approach. Since their methods consider only a single gate error, Jung et al. [7] proposed an extended approach for multiple gate errors.

© Springer International Publishing Switzerland 2015
J. Krivine and J.-B. Stefani (Eds.): RC 2015, LNCS 9138, pp. 186–199, 2015.
DOI: 10.1007/978-3-319-20860-2_12

Tague et al. [14] provided another approach for a single gate error using πDDs [10], decision diagrams for permutation sets. However, there are two problems to be considered:

- These algorithms use exponential algorithms or data structures, i.e. they are intractable in the worst case.
- These algorithms only detect error positions, i.e. cannot fix errors efficiently.

In this paper, we address these tasks with different approaches for a single error and multiple errors, respectively. For a single error, we propose a theoretically improved debugging algorithm. This algorithm uses the lemma in [17], which states correction is determined by function composition, and valid gate checking algorithms. For multiple errors, we provide a dynamic programming approach using πDDs. Although this algorithm has worst-case complexity similar to the approach for a single error of Tague et al. [14], it can fix multiple errors and debug them.

We evaluate the efficiency of our algorithms using computational experiments. For single error circuits, our algorithm achieves a significant improvement compared with previous approaches. For multiple error circuits, our algorithm succeeds to fix errors with minimal corrections in circuits with few lines.

The remainder of this paper is organized as follows. Section 2 briefly reviews reversible circuits and πDDs, which are used in our algorithm. In Section 3, we define the problem of debugging single error circuits, review previous work, and introduce our algorithm for debugging single error circuits. In Section 4, we extend the debugging problem of single error circuits to multiple errors, and provide our πDD-based debugging method. Experimental results to evaluate the practical performance of our algorithms are in Section 5 and Section 6 concludes this paper.

2   Preliminary

In this section, we review reversible functions and circuits before proceeding to πDDs, which are used in both previous work and our proposed method.

2.1   Reversible Functions and Permutations

A function $f : \{0,1\}^n \rightarrow \{0,1\}^n$ is *reversible* if it is bijective, i.e., we can determine an input from the corresponding output. Hence, a function f is considered as a permutation on $\{0, 1, \ldots, 2^n - 1\}$.

We define notations of permutations. A permutation on $\{0, 1, \ldots, m - 1\}$, m-permutation for short, is written in a one-line form $\pi = \pi(0)\pi(1)\ldots\pi(m-1)$. The identity m-permutation is denoted by e_m, which satisfies $e_m(i) = i$ for each $0 \leq i \leq m-1$. We denote by π^{-1} the inverse permutation of π, which satisfies $\pi * \pi^{-1} = \pi^{-1} * \pi = e_m$, where $*$ means composition of permutations: $p = q * r$ means $p(i) = r(q(i))$ for all i.

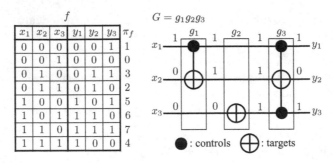

x_1	x_2	x_3	y_1	y_2	y_3	π_f
0	0	0	0	0	1	1
0	0	1	0	0	0	0
0	1	0	0	1	1	3
0	1	1	0	1	0	2
1	0	0	1	0	1	5
1	0	1	1	1	0	6
1	1	0	1	1	1	7
1	1	1	1	0	0	4

Fig. 1. Truth table of a reversible function f and a reversible circuit G realizing f

We denote by π_f the permutation corresponding to f such that we consider input and output bit vectors as binary representations of integers. For example, π_f corresponding to the reversible function f on the left of Fig. 1 is $\begin{pmatrix} 0\ 1\ 2\ 3\ 4\ 5\ 6\ 7 \\ 1\ 0\ 3\ 2\ 5\ 6\ 7\ 4 \end{pmatrix}$, which is briefly written as $\pi_f = 10325674$.

2.2   Reversible Circuits and Gates

Reversible circuits realize reversible functions and consist of reversible gates. A reversible circuit for an n-bit Boolean function has n lines as shown on the right of Fig. 1. Reversible circuits have no fan-out or feedback due to their reversible properties. Therefore, a reversible circuit is a cascade of reversible gates. Several reversible gates have been invented to synthesize reversible circuits, such as Toffoli [15], Fredkin [5], and Peres [12] gates. In this paper, we focus on Toffoli gates.

Let $L = \{1, \ldots, n\}$ be a set of lines. *Toffoli gates* have multiple (possibly zero) *control lines* $C = \{c_1, \ldots, c_k\} \subset L$ and one *target line* $t \in L \setminus C$. For example, the Toffoli gate g_3 in Fig. 1 has the control lines $C = \{1, 3\}$ and the target line $t = 2$. A Toffoli gate inverts the target line when all control lines are 1. Let x_i and y_i be the i-th line's input and output of a Toffoli gate, respectively. Then, we formally define Toffoli gates as follows:

$$y_t = x_t \oplus x_{c_1} \cdots x_{c_k},$$
$$y_i = x_i \quad \text{if } i \neq t.$$

Since a Toffoli gate itself represents a reversible function, we can represent the function corresponding to a Toffoli gate as a permutation. We denote by π_g the permutation corresponding to a gate g as well as a reversible function. Then the permutation representation π_G of the function realized by a reversible circuit $G = g_1 \cdots g_d$ equals $\pi_{g_1} * \cdots * \pi_{g_d}$.

2.3 πDD

First, we define a *transposition* $\tau_{i,j}$ as the permutation such that $\tau_{i,j}(i) = j$ and $\tau_{i,j}(j) = i$, but $\tau_{i,j}(k) = k$ for other k. Any n-permutation can be uniquely

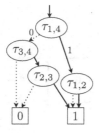

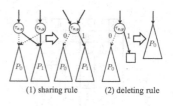

(1) sharing rule   (2) deleting rule

Fig. 2. The πDD representing $\{2431, 4231, 1423\}$ = $\{\tau_{1,2}$ * $\tau_{1,4}, \tau_{1,4}, \tau_{2,3}$ * $\tau_{3,4}\}$

Fig. 3. Two reduction rules of πDDs

decomposed into a composition of at most $n-1$ transpositions by the following algorithm: we start with e_n and repeat swaps to move $\pi(k)$ to the k-th position in its one line form, where k runs from right to left.

A πDD is a rooted directed graph representing a set of permutations compactly, and has efficient set operations for permutation sets [10]. πDDs consist of five components: labeled internal nodes, 0-edges, 1-edges, the 0-sink, and the 1-sink. Fig. 2 shows an example of a πDD. Each internal node has exactly two edges, a 0-edge and a 1-edge. Each path to the 1-sink in a πDD represents a permutation in the set represented: if a 1-edge originates from a node with label $\tau_{x,y}$, the decomposition of the permutation contains $\tau_{x,y}$, while a 0-edge means that the decomposition excludes $\tau_{x,y}$.

A πDD becomes a compact and canonical form by fixing its transposition order and applying the following two reduction rules (Fig. 3):

(1) sharing rule: share all nodes which have the same labels and child nodes.
(2) deleting rule: delete all nodes whose 1-edge points to the 0-sink.

In many practical cases, πDDs demonstrate high compression ratio, although πDD size (i.e. the number of nodes) in the worst case is exponential in the length of permutations.

In addition, πDDs support efficient set operations such as union and intersection on permutation sets. In particular, Cartesian product operation $P \times Q$, which returns the union set of compositions of all pairs $p \in P$ and $q \in Q$, is important and useful for our algorithm to be described later. Since the computation time of these operations depends on the size of πDDs, compactness helps to speed-up πDD operations.

3   Debugging Single Error

We define the single error debugging problem of reversible circuits. Let f : $\{0,1\}^n \to \{0,1\}^n$ be a reversible function and $G = g_1 \cdots g_d$ be a reversible circuit with n lines such that $\pi_G = \pi_f$. We define G' to be a single error circuit for f if $\pi_{G'} \neq \pi_f$ and G' has:

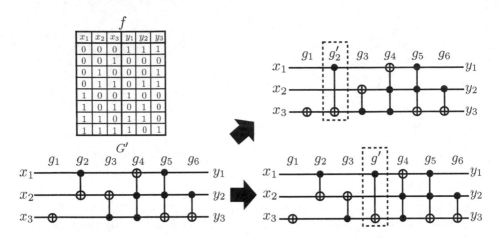

Fig. 4. An erroneous circuit G' and two fixed circuits realizing f

– a replaced error: there is a gate $g' \neq g_i$ s.t. $G' = g_1 \cdots g_{i-1} g' g_{i+1} \cdots g_d$,
– an inserted error: there is a gate g' s.t. $G' = g_1 \cdots g_{i-1} g' g_i g_{i+1} \cdots g_d$, and
– a removed error: $G' = g_1 \cdots g_{i-1} g_{i+1} \cdots g_d$.

The goal of the single error debugging problems is to find the position of an error in an erroneous circuit G' and fix it in order to realize f correctly. We note that even if the number of embedded errors is only one, sometimes there are several ways to debug the circuit. For example, Fig. 4 describes an erroneous circuit G' and an objective function f. At this instance, we have the two ways to debug G': replacing g_2 with g'_2 or inserting g' between g_3 and g_4. In general, we cannot determine which of them the original error is. Therefore, we set our goal to list all ways to debug G'.

3.1   Related Work

Wille et al. proposed a debugging method using SAT solvers [17]. They used SAT (Boolean satisfiability) formulation for debugging problems and solved it with SAT solvers. This method has three problems to be overcome:

– There are $O(nd)$ variables in SAT formula. Though state-of-the-art SAT solvers work practically fast, solving SAT is believed to require exponential time in the worst case. This is therefore not scalable for a large d.
– Their method can find only error candidates, which may include non-errors.
– Their method can debug only a replaced error.

We also note that this method requires verification preprocess to obtain some counterexamples.

Frehse et al. provided a simulation-based debugging algorithm [6]. Their method eliminates error candidates based on the fact that an error gate must be activated (i.e. all the inputs of control lines are 1) for all counterexamples. This method is fast because it runs in linear time with respect to the number of gates and lines. However, outputs of this method also can contain non-errors, since the activation property is a necessary condition but not a sufficient condition.

Tague et al. gave a debugging method using πDDs for a removed error [14]. They considered a gate as a permutation, and used πDDs to represent the set of gates. They insert a πDD into an erroneous circuit G' as an arbitrary gate, and calculate the compositions by Cartesian product operations. If the compositions contain π_f, it means G' has a removed error. This method also has two problems:

- The size of πDDs for a set of N-permutations is $O(2^{N^2})$, and now $N = 2^n$. It is not scalable for even small n.
- Their method can detect an error but cannot find its position and fix it.

In the next subsection, we provide an algorithm overcoming these problems. More precisely, we propose a worst-case $O(n2^n d)$ time algorithm, which can find and fix all the three types of errors.

3.2   Proposed Method for Single Error

Our method is based on Lemma 3 in [17]:

Theorem 1 (Lemma 3 in [17]). *Let F be an error-free circuit of a reversible function and $G = G_1 g_i G_2$ be an erroneous circuit of F. Then G can be fixed by replacing any gate g_i of G with a cascade of gates $G_i^{fix} = G_1^{-1} F G_2^{-1}$.*

This theorem states that, if G_i^{fix} can be represented by a Toffoli gate, the i-th gate is a replaced error and we can fix it by replacing it with the Toffoli gate corresponding to G_i^{fix}. Hereafter, we assume the objective function f and each gate g_i are represented as permutations, and a cascade of gates means the composition of permutations. Then the single replaced error circuit problem can be solved as follows: checking whether $G_i^{rep} = g_{i-1}^{-1} \cdots g_1^{-1} f g_d^{-1} \cdots g_{i+1}^{-1}$ can be represented as a single Toffoli gate for all $1 \leq i \leq d$. Similarly, debugging problems for other types of errors can be solved too:

- an inserted error: checking whether $G_i^{ins} = g_{i-1}^{-1} \cdots g_1^{-1} f g_d^{-1} \cdots g_{i+1}^{-1}$ can be represented as an identity permutation e_{2^n} for all $1 \leq i \leq d$.
- a removed error: checking whether $G_i^{rem} = g_i^{-1} \cdots g_1^{-1} f g_d^{-1} \cdots g_{i+1}^{-1}$ can be represented as a single Toffoli gate for all $0 \leq i \leq d$.

Note that the position of a removed error is between two gates or two ends. We say a removed error occurs at the 0-th position if the error position is the left g_1, and at the i-th position if the error position is the right of g_i.

We let $N = 2^n$ for brevity. If we had an $O(h(n))$ time algorithm checking whether a given permutation represents a Toffoli gate, we could solve the single error circuit problem in $O(d(Nd + h(n)))$ by calculating the products G_i^{rep}, G_i^{ins}, and G_i^{rem} of $O(d)$ N-permutations and running a checking algorithm for all $0 \leq i \leq d$. We can improve this complexity by using the following properties:

$$- \ G_i^{rep} = G_i^{ins},$$
$$- \ G_i^{rem} = g_i^{-1} G_i^{ins},$$
$$- \ G_i^{ins} = G_{i-1}^{rem} g_i.$$

That is, incremental calculation of G_i^x from G_{i-1}^y costs only $O(N)$ time, hence we can solve a single error circuit problem in $O(d(N + h(n)))$. Algorithm 1 gives the entire procedure.

Algorithm 1. Debugging single error circuits

1: **procedure** DEBUGSINGLEERROR(f, G)
2:      $G_0^{rem} \leftarrow f g_d^{-1} g_{d-1}^{-1} \cdots g_1^{-1}$
3:      **if** ISTOFFOLI(G_0^{rem}) **then**
4:          Report a removed error: the gate G_0^{rem} is removed at the 0-th position.
5:      **end if**
6:      **for** $i = 1$ to d **do**
7:          $G_i^{ins} \leftarrow G_{i-1}^{rem} g_i$
8:          **if** $G_i^{ins} = e_N$ **then**
9:              Report an inserted error: g_i is an extra gate.
10:         **else if** ISTOFFOLI(G_i^{ins}) **then**
11:             Report a replaced error: g_i should be replaced by G_i^{ins}.
12:         **end if**
13:         $G_i^{rem} \leftarrow g_i^{-1} G_i^{ins}$
14:         **if** ISTOFFOLI(G_i^{rem}) **then**
15:             Report a removed error: the gate G_i^{rem} is removed at the i-th position.
16:         **end if**
17:     **end for**
18: **end procedure**

The Toffoli gate checking problem is also solved in $O(nN)$ time by Algorithm 2. A permutation representing a Toffoli gate works as a transposition between integers a and b if a and b differ exactly a target bit and their bits in a control bit set are all 1. Lines 3–22 of Algorithm 2 identify control lines and a target line, eliminating cases not satisfying necessary conditions. Lines 24–31 check whether control lines and a target line work as an expected Toffoli gate. This algorithm works as not only a check but also an identification of the corresponding Toffoli gate. That is, we can directly debug G' using the Toffoli gate. It costs $O(nN)$ time and therefore we can solve the single error circuit problem in $O(nNd)$ time.[1]

We can design checking algorithms for Fredkin gates and Peres gates similarly. Generally speaking, given a set of gates, we can solve the single error circuit problem in $O(d(N + h(n)))$ time if we have an $O(h(n))$ time checking algorithm for the gates. We also can easily adapt to deal with negative control

---

[1] If we assume w-bit word RAM model, we can improve it to $O(\lfloor \frac{n}{w} \rfloor N d)$ by adopting bit parallel techniques to manage control lines C.

lines. A Toffoli gate with positive and negative control lines inverts its output of the target line when the inputs of the positive controls are all 1 and the negative controls are all 0.

Algorithm 2. Checking whether a given permutation represents a Toffoli gate.

```
 1: procedure ISTOFFOLI(π)
 2:     C ← {1,...,n}, T ← φ
 3:     for i = 0 to N − 1 do
 4:         if π_{π_i} ≠ i then              ▷ π_i is neither i nor swapped with π_{π_i}
 5:             return False
 6:         end if
 7:         if i and π_i are swapped then
 8:             if i and π_i differ only the j-th bit in binary then
 9:                 T ← T ∪ {j}
10:                 if |T| > 2 then    ▷ there are two or more candidates of target lines
11:                     return False
12:                 end if
13:             else                   ▷ there are two or more candidates of target lines
14:                 return False
15:             end if
16:             for j = 1 to n do
17:                 if the j-th bit of i in binary is 0 then
18:                     C ← C \ {j}            ▷ eliminate candidates of control lines
19:                 end if
20:             end for
21:         end if
22:     end for
23:     ▷ The Toffoli gate corresponding to π must have controls C and a target t ∈ T
24:     for i = 0 to N − 1 do
25:         if ∀j ∈ C, the j-th bit of π_i in binary is 1, but π_i = i then
26:             return False          ▷ all controls are 1 but the target is not inverted
27:         end if
28:         if ∃j ∈ C, the j-th bit of π_i in binary is 0, but π_i ≠ i then
29:             return False          ▷ some controls are 0 but the target is inverted
30:         end if
31:     end for
32:     return True
33: end procedure
```

---

4 Debugging Multiple Errors

We extend single error circuit problems to multiple error circuit problems. We define that k-error circuits are circuits including k errors. Note that k errors can consist of different kinds of errors; replaced errors, inserted errors, and removed errors can be mixed together. We also note that k-error circuits may be debugged by less than k corrections. For example, two inserted errors of a same Toffoli gate at adjacent positions need not to be debugged, in other words these can be debugged by 0 corrections. In multiple error circuit problems, we set our goal to find minimum corrections.

4.1 Related Work

Jung et al. [7] proposed a SAT based debugging algorithm for multiple errors, which is an extension of [6]. They used pruning based on hitting set problems and encoded it into SAT formulation. Although their method can process large circuits, it has two problems to be considered:

- Their method can debug only replaced errors.
- Their method can detect only error candidates, which includes non-errors and cannot fix them directly.

In this section, we try to overcome these problems.

4.2 Naïve Extension of Existing Method

Our proposed method for k-error circuits is derived from Tague's πDD-based approach for single error circuits [14]. For an inserted error, this approach tries to insert a πDD representing usable gates into all possible positions. It can be easily extend to replaced errors and removed errors. If we insert (or replace, remove) k πDDs as sets of usable gates at all possible positions for each, we can detect all error positions and error types. However, there are the following problems:

- The number of all combinations of k positions are $\binom{d}{k} = O(d^k)$. Furthermore, we consider 3 types of errors for each position, i.e. there are 3^k ways of combinations of error types. That is, this algorithm requires $O(3^k d^{k+1})\,\pi$DD operations.
- All error positions are can be detected, but correct gates for replaced errors and removed errors cannot be determined.

We attack these problems with our algorithm proposed in the next subsection.

4.3 Proposed Method for Multiple Errors

We propose a debugging algorithm requiring only $O(dk)\,\pi$DD operations[2] for k-error circuits. Our approach uses dynamic programming calculating $S_{i,j}$, defined as a set of permutations representing functions which can be realized by the first j gates with i errors. The minimum x such that $\pi_f \in S_{x,d}$ is the size of minimum corrections. We can calculate $S_{i,j}$ by the following recurrence relations:

$$S_{0,0} := \phi,$$
$$S_{i,j} := (S_{i,j-1} \times \{g_j\}) \cup (S_{i-1,j-1} \times L) \cup (S_{i-1,j} \times L) \cup S_{i-1,j-1},$$

---

[2] Note that each πDD operation costs exponential time in N^2 in the worst case.

where L is a set of usable gates, which are Toffoli gates in this paper. The first term represents non-error, the second one represents a replaced error, the third one represents an inserted error, and the last one represents a removed error.

Since each $S_{i,j}$ is a set of permutations, we can use πDDs to represent them. Further, calculation of recurrence relations requires only permutation set algebra such as union and Cartesian product, which are supported by πDDs. Each calculation of $S_{i,j}$ requires at most a constant number (i.e. 6) of operations. Hence this algorithm takes only $O(dk)$ πDD operations. In addition, we can calculate this recurrence relation by incrementing k. This means if the minimum corrections of a given k-error circuit is k', this algorithm only costs $O(dk')$ πDD operations, instead of $O(dk)$.

This algorithm can determine the minimum corrections, but cannot identify error positions and types yet. Error identification can be realized by starting from $S_{k',d}$ with π_f and reversely traversing to $S_{0,0}$. For example, if we now consider $S_{i,j}$ with π_x and $(\{\pi_x\} \times L^{-1}) \cap S_{i-1,j-1} \neq \phi$, an replaced error is detected at position j. Furthermore, let $\pi_y \in (\{\pi_x\} \times L^{-1}) \cap S_{i-1,j-1}$, we identify the original gate is $\pi_x * \pi_y^{-1}$. We then restart reverse traversal from $S_{i-1,j-1}$ with π_y until the first index is not 0.

5   Experiments

We implemented all algorithms in C++[3] and carried out experiments on a 3.20GHz CPU machine with 64GB memory. We randomly generate d Toffoli gates with n lines and concatenate them to make correct reversible circuits G. We prepare objective functions f for each circuit by simulating the circuit. Next, we generate erroneous reversible circuits G' with k errors based on correct circuits: we randomly select a position and replace with a random gate, insert a random gate, or remove a gate k times.

Our implementation uses f and G' as inputs. For single error circuits, our implementation detects all corrections but only outputs the number of ways of corrections in order to reduce I/O time. For multiple error circuits, since the way of minimum corrections can be huge, our implementation detects only one way of minimum corrections and outputs it.

5.1   Experiments for Single Error

Computation time of Algorithm 1 for single error circuits (i.e. k=1) is shown in Table 1. This table shows that our algorithm is linear with the number of gates d and almost exponential with the number of lines n. It agrees with the theoretical complexity of our algorithm analyzed in Section 3.

In [17], the SAT solver-based algorithm takes about 2000 seconds or more for $n \geq 8$ and $d \geq 5000$ circuits. On the other hand, our algorithm takes under

---

[3] Note that our implementation of Algorithm 2 uses bitwise operations of 64-bit integer (unsigned long long int in C++) to manage control lines C.

Table 1. Computation time (seconds) for single error circuits

		d								
		10	50	100	500	1000	5000	10000	50000	100000
n	2	0.00	0.00	0.00	0.00	0.00	0.01	0.02	0.05	0.10
	4	0.00	0.00	0.00	0.00	0.00	0.01	0.02	0.09	0.17
	6	0.00	0.00	0.00	0.00	0.00	0.02	0.02	0.12	0.24
	8	0.00	0.00	0.00	0.00	0.00	0.02	0.04	0.21	0.41
	10	0.00	0.00	0.01	0.01	0.01	0.05	0.11	0.54	1.08
	12	0.00	0.00	0.01	0.03	0.04	0.21	0.40	2.05	3.99
	14	0.01	0.02	0.04	0.20	0.38	1.90	3.78	8.83	17.64
	16	0.03	0.10	0.19	0.89	1.75	8.78	17.61	87.71	149.00
	18	0.16	0.52	1.03	4.81	9.46	48.37	97.47	493.42	987.10
	20	0.60	1.87	3.88	18.28	35.90	187.28	377.66	—	—

1 second for circuits of such scale. Further, in [14], the πDD-based algorithm takes more than 100 seconds for $n \geq 4$ and $d \geq 1000$ cases, while our algorithm takes under 0.01 seconds for these cases. This significant improvement is likely due to the theoretical improvement of our algorithm, and not simply to hardware and test case differences.

The simulation-based approach proposed by Frehse et al. in [6] seems to be faster than or equal to our algorithm: Their method completed simulation to detect error candedates in 20 seconds for the $n = 15$ and $d = 716934$ circuit. However, their method output over 30000 error candidates, which is impractical to check manually. In contrast, our algorithm returned only one correction for the $n = 16$ and $d = 100000$ erroneous circuit embedded a replaced error.

5.2 Experiments for Multiple Errors

We also carried out experiments for multiple error circuits. We randomly embedded k errors in circuits consisting of d gates with n lines. Figs. 5–8 show experimental results for 1-, 2-, 3-, and 4-error circuits, respectively.

For 1-error circuits in Fig. 5, i.e. single error circuits, our πDD-based algorithm can perform in 1000 seconds for $n = 5$ and $d = 600$ circuits. For 2-error circuits in Fig. 6, however, all cases with $n = 5$ are time-outs even at $d = 50$. Almost all $n = 4$ cases also time-out; the algorithm can debug up to 100-gate circuits. Results in [7] show that the SAT based method is more scalable: e.g. this method can process $n = 8$ and $d = 637$ circuits in about 300 seconds. However, outputs of this method can include non-errors, and cannot fix them automatically. On the other hand, our method can fix them. For sufficiently small circuits, our method can provide richer debugging information.

Results of 3- and 4-error circuits in Figs. 7 and 8. Our algorithm seems to be enough scalable for the circuits with $n \leq 3$. Debugging time for 3-errors and one of 4-errors seems similar. This is because in random circuits we prepared, the minimum correction of $n = 2$ circuits is usually 1, and for $n = 3$ circuits is

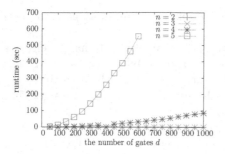

Fig. 5. Runtime for debugging 1-error circuits

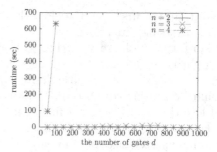

Fig. 6. Runtime for debugging 2-error circuits

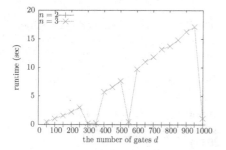

Fig. 7. Runtime for debugging 3-error circuits

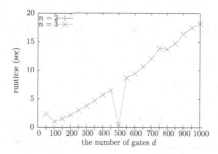

Fig. 8. Runtime for debugging 4-error circuits

usually 2, regardless of the number of embedded errors. In Fig. 8, $d = 50$ and $d = 500$ in $n = 3$ cases seem to be somehow outliers. It is true; the minimum correction size of the $d = 50$ circuit is 3, and for $d = 500$ circuit it is 1.

These results indicate that the minimum correction and the number of lines exponentially affect computation time. On the other hand, the number of gates seems to affect linearly for small gates ($n = 2, 3$), but affect quadratically or exponentially for slightly larger gates ($n = 4, 5$).

6   Concluding Remarks

For debugging erroneous reversible circuits, we propose two kinds of algorithms. The first one is an efficient method for circuits having at most one error. This method uses permutation properties of reversible gates and gate checking algorithms. This method can handle more general gate library by designing gate checking algorithms. The efficient performance of this method is shown theoretically and experimentally, comparing with existing methods. The second algorithm can debug multiple error circuits based on a dynamic programming approach and πDDs. Although the scalability of this algorithm is exponentially worse than the first one, the algorithm enables us to debug more general erroneous reversible circuits.

For future work, we would like to modify the first algorithm to handle circuits with garbage output lines. Garbage lines can output arbitrary values, i.e. multiple permutations can realize desired behavior. This means that multiple G_i's should be considered. Of course πDDs can handle this, but such an algorithm will lose the efficiency of our first approach.

For multiple errors, more scalable algorithms are desirable. We are also interested in expected sizes of minimum corrections for circuits with n lines, d gates, and k randomly-embedded errors. From experimental results, we guess that minimum correction tend to become relatively small with the number of embedded errors. If we show that the size is sufficiently small with high probability, perhaps we need not to consider debugging circuits with a large number of errors.

Acknowledgments. We would like to thank Dr. Mathias Soeken and Dr. Robert Wille for valuable discussion and feedback to write this paper.

References

1. Bérut, A., Arakelyan, A., Petrosyan, A., Ciliberto, S., Dillenschneider, R., Lutz, E.: Experimental verification of Landauer's principle linking information and thermodynamics. Nature **483**(7388), 187–189 (2012)
2. Chattopadhyay, A., Majumder, S., Chandak, C., Chowdhury, N.: Constructive reversible logic synthesis for boolean functions with special properties. In: Yamashita, S., Minato, S. (eds.) RC 2014. LNCS, vol. 8507, pp. 95–110. Springer, Heidelberg (2014)
3. Cuykendall, R., Andersen, D.R.: Reversible optical computing circuits. Optics Letters **12**(7), 542–544 (1987)
4. Donald, J., Jha, N.K.: Reversible logic synthesis with Fredkin and Peres gates. ACM Journal on Emerging Technologies in Computing Systems (JETC) **4**(1), 2 (2008)
5. Fredkin, E., Toffoli, T.: Conservative logic. International Journal of Theoretical Physics 219–253 (1982)
6. Frehse, S., Wille, R., Drechsler, R.: Efficient simulation-based debugging of reversible logic. In: the 40th IEEE International Symposium on Multiple-Valued Logic (ISMVL), pp. 156–161 (2010)
7. Jung, J.C., Frehse, S., Wille, R., Drechsler, R.: Enhancing debugging of multiple missing control errors in reversible logic. In: the 20th symposium on Great Lakes symposium on VLSI (GLVLSI), pp. 465–470. ACM (2010)
8. Landauer, R.: Irreversibility and heat generation in the computing process. IBM Journal of Research and Development **5**(3), 183–191 (1961)
9. Maslov, D., Dueck, G.W., Miller, D.M.: Techniques for the synthesis of reversible toffoli networks. ACM Transactions on Design Automation of Electronic Systems (TODAES) **12**(4), 42 (2007)
10. Minato, S.: πDD: a new decision diagram for efficient problem solving in permutation space. In: Sakallah, K.A., Simon, L. (eds.) SAT 2011. LNCS, vol. 6695, pp. 90–104. Springer, Heidelberg (2011)

11. Nielsen, M.A., Chuang, I.L.: Quantum Computation and Quantum Information. Cambridge University Press (2010)
12. Peres, A.: Reversible logic and quantum computers. Physical Review A **32**(6), 3266 (1985)
13. Rahman, M.Z., Rice, J.E.: Templates for positive and negative control toffoli networks. In: Yamashita, S., Minato, S. (eds.) RC 2014. LNCS, vol. 8507, pp. 125–136. Springer, Heidelberg (2014)
14. Tague, L., Soeken, M., Minato, S., Drechsler, R.: Debugging of reversible circuits using πDDs. In: the 43rd IEEE International Symposium on Multiple-Valued Logic (ISMVL), pp. 316–321. IEEE (2013)
15. Toffoli, T.: Reversible Computing. Springer (1980)
16. Wille, R., Große, D., Dueck, G.W., Drechsler, R.: Reversible logic synthesis with output permutation. In: the 22nd International Conference on VLSI Design, pp. 189–194. IEEE (2009)
17. Wille, R., Große, D., Frehse, S., Dueck, G.W., Drechsler, R.: Debugging of Toffoli networks. In: The Conference on Design. Automation and Test in Europe (DATE), pp. 1284–1289. European Design and Automation Association, IEEE (2009)

Ricercar: A Language for Describing and Rewriting Reversible Circuits with Ancillae and Its Permutation Semantics

Michael Kirkedal Thomsen[1]([⊠]), Robin Kaarsgaard[2], and Mathias Soeken[1]

[1] Group of Computer Architecture, University of Bremen, Bremen, Germany
{kirkedal,msoeken}@informatik.uni-bremen.de
[2] DIKU, Department of Computer Science,
University of Copenhagen, Copenhagen, Denmark
robin@di.ku.dk

Abstract. Previously, Soeken and Thomsen presented six basic semantics-preserving rules for rewriting reversible logic circuits, defined using the well-known diagrammatic notation of Feynman. While this notation is both useful and intuitive for describing reversible circuits, its shortcomings in generality complicates the specification of more sophisticated and abstract rewriting rules.

In this paper, we introduce *Ricercar*, a general textual description language for reversible logic circuits designed explicitly to support rewriting. Taking the not gate and the identity gate as primitives, this language allows circuits to be constructed using control gates, sequential composition, and ancillae, through a notion of *ancilla scope*. We show how the above-mentioned rewriting rules are defined in this language, and extend the rewriting system with five additional rules to introduce and modify ancilla scope. This treatment of ancillae addresses the limitations of the original rewriting system in rewriting circuits with ancillae in the general case.

To set Ricercar on a theoretical foundation, we also define a permutation semantics over symmetric groups and show how the operations over permutations as transposition relate to the semantics of the language.

Keywords: Reversible logic · Term rewriting · Ancillae · Circuit equivalence · Permutation

1 Introduction

In [14] two of the authors presented six elementary rules for rewriting reversible circuits using mixed-polarity multiple-control Toffoli gates. Building on this,

M.K. Thomsen—This work was partly funded by the *European Commission* under the *7th Framework Programme*.
M.K. Thomsen—A preliminary version of Ricercar was presented as work-in-progress at *6th Conference on Reversible Computation, 2014*.

J. Krivine and J.-B. Stefani (Eds.): RC 2015, LNCS 9138, pp. 200–215, 2015.
DOI: 10.1007/978-3-319-20860-2_13

more complex rules, such as moving and deletion rules, can be derived. Rewriting using such rules can be used not just to reduce the size and cost of reversible circuits, but also to analyse and explain other optimisation approaches for reversible circuits. As one example, the templates presented in [12] are all derivable from these rewriting rules.

The rewriting rules in [14] are based on the diagrammatic notation first introduced by Feynman. This notation gives a very intuitive description of reversible circuits and the presented rewriting rules inherit this benefit. However, one goal with rewriting is to provide computer aid to the design of reversible circuits, and just as intuitive as diagrammatic notation is to understand for humans, just as hard it is to model for computers. In particular, representing the more general rules poses a problem.

In this paper we introduce *Ricercar*, a description language for reversible logic circuits (Sect. 3.) inspired by work on a *reversible combinator language* [18] and the *logic of reversible structures* [11]. Its only basic atoms are the not gate and the identity gate (both with named wires) from which other circuits are constructed using control gates and sequential composition. After describing the syntax and semantics of the language, we show how to define the graphical rewriting rules of [14] as textual rewriting rules for Ricercar descriptions (Sect. 4.) To give a theoretical foundation for Ricercar, we also define a permutation semantics over symmetric groups (Sect. 2) and show how the operations over permutations as transposition relate to the semantics of the language (Sect. 3.3).

A notable feature of the language is that it directly supports ancillae. Since reversible circuit logic does not support arbitrary fan-out, ancillae are often used to store partial results from computations by means of reversible duplication. The concept of ancillae have, however, been used in many different ways, but in this work we take the most strict possible definition. By ancillae we mean a variable (or a line) that are, for all possible assignments of other defined variables, guaranteed to be unchanged over the execution of a circuit.

This definition is much more strict than what is normally characterised by temporary storage, but it *is* needed if one wants to ensure that information is leaked and, thus, the backwards semantics of the circuits can be used directly. It is, however, still very useful in both high-level programs as well as reversible circuit constructs. As an example, an n-bit binary adder of linear depth can be implemented without ancillae, but it requires the use of reversible gates that have n inputs. However, using just one ancilla line the linear depth V-shaped adder [5,20] is implemented using only gates with a constant number of inputs. Furthermore, all current designs for implementing sub-linear depth adders require a larger number of ancilla lines that is dependent on the input size [7,17,19]. Using a similar definition, the *restore* model [4] has been investigated with respect to is computational complexity limits.

In Sect. 5 we discuss the *ancilla scope* construct of Ricercar and show five basic rewriting rules for inserting and modifying ancilla wires (Sect. 5.1). This is interesting given that deciding if a wire is indeed an ancilla wire is difficult; it can generally be done using equivalence checking, which for reversible circuits has been shown to be coNP-complete [10]. Furthermore, we show how to derive more general rules (Sect. 5.2), and show a non-trivial and useful example of how these can be used to create reversible circuits with ancilla wires from ancilla-free circuits (Sect. 5.3). As a result, the proposed rewriting language can serve as a framework to formally analyse the trade-off between gate count and number of ancilla lines in reversible circuits. Such trade-offs have so far been investigated theoretically for Turing machines in *e.g.* [2,3] and experimentally for reversible circuit synthesis in [21]. We discuss further related work in Sect. 6.

The main contributions of the paper are the following:

1. An extension of the rewriting rules with rules for circuit rewriting using ancillae.
2. A textual language to describe rewriting which is more concise than the diagrammatic notation.
3. Semantics for the rewrite rules based on permutations that is useful to show soundness of the rules and to formally argue over them.

2   Symmetric Groups as a Theory of Reversible Logic

Every reversible function f computed by a reversible circuit of n input lines $x_1, \ldots, x_n$ and n output lines $y_1, \ldots, y_n$ can be represented by an element π_f of the symmetric group S_{2^n}, *i.e.*, a permutation of the set $\{0, \ldots, 2^n - 1\}$. We have $\pi_f(x) = y$ whenever $f(x_1, \ldots, x_n) = (y_1, \ldots, y_n)$, where x and y denote the natural number representations of the bits $x_1, \ldots, x_n$ and $y_1, \ldots, y_n$, respectively. This duality has been used for reversible logic synthesis in the last decade [6,13], but has also seen use as a theoretical foundation for the analysis of reversible circuit logic [15,16].

Unlike the usual formulation of the symmetric group S_n, we will consider its elements to be permutations of the set $\{0, \ldots, n - 1\}$ rather than $\{1, \ldots, n\}$. However, we will use the standard notation of writing explicit permutations using square brackets, *e.g.* $\pi = [0\,1\,3\,2]$, cycles using parentheses, *e.g.* $\pi = (2, 3)$, and π_e for the identity permutation. Under this interpretation, composition of gates corresponds to multiplication (*i.e.*, composition) of permutations.

The gate library we consider consists of only single-target gates, which are characterised by changing one circuit line based on a control function that argues over the variables of the remaining lines. Since all single-target gates are self-inverse, their respective permutations are involutions with cycle representations consisting of only transpositions and fixpoints. As pointed out in [15], all such transpositions are of the form (a, b) where the hamming distance of a and b is 1, *i.e.*, their binary expansions differ in exactly one position. We refer to the set of all such transpositions as

$$H_n = \{(a, b) \mid \nu(a \oplus b) = 1\} \tag{1}$$

where ν denotes the sideways sum. Note that each transposition (a, b) in H_n corresponds to one fully controlled Toffoli gate with positive and negative control lines, acting on line i, where i is the single index for which $a_i \neq b_i$. The polarity of the controls is chosen according to the other bits. Based on this observation, we partition the set H_n into n sets $H_{n,1}, H_{n,2}, \ldots, H_{n,n}$ such that

$$H_{n,i} = \{(a,b) \in H_n \mid a \oplus b = 2^{i-1}\} \tag{2}$$

contains all transpositions in which the components differ in their i-th bit. Single-target gates that act on the target line i are all permutations that consist of a subset of transpositions in $H_{n,i}$.

We call $g_n(f) \in S_{2^n}$ a *transposition generation function* which takes as argument an injective function $f : \{0, \ldots, 2^n - 1\} \hookrightarrow \{0, \ldots, 2^n - 1\}$ and returns the permutation

$$(0, f(0))(1, f(1)) \cdots (2^n - 1, f(2^n - 1)). \tag{3}$$

3 Ricercar: A Description Language for Reversible Logic

In this section, we will explain the description language, Ricercar, that is used to formulate the rewriting rules. We will first explain the syntax (Fig. 1) and then show two ways to describe the semantics.

3.1 Syntax

Circuit wires (denoted by lower case Latin letters in the end of the alphabet: $\ldots, x, y, z$) are defined over a set of names Σ that includes both input/output wires and ancilla wires currently in scope. (For wires without specific names, we will use lower case Latin letters starting from a.) We define a circuit (denoted by upper case Latin letters) to be one of the following five forms:

- The identity gate on a wire x, written $\mathsf{Id}(x)$, where $x \in \Sigma$.
- The not gate applied to a wire x, written $\mathsf{Not}(x)$, where $x \in \Sigma$.
- Sequential composition of two circuits, written using the operator " ; ".

$A, B, C ::= \mathsf{Id}(x) \mid \mathsf{Not}(x)$	Identity and not gate
$\mid A \; ; \; B$	Sequence of circuits
$\mid \phi \bullet\!\!- A$	Controlled circuit
$\mid \alpha x.A$	Scope of ancilla variable α; α is part of the syntax
$\phi, \psi, \pi ::= x \mid \neg\phi \mid \phi \wedge \phi$	Boolean formulas
$\mid \top \mid \bot \mid \phi \vee \phi \mid \phi \oplus \phi$	Derivable Boolean operators

Fig. 1. Syntax of Ricercar. Note that this grammar does not guarantee reversibility in itself. By x we mean that variables occurring in Boolean formulas must be elements from a predefined set of input/output wires or ancilla wires in scope.

$(a \wedge b \wedge c) \bullet\!\!- \mathsf{Not}(d)$

(a) Three-controlled
Toffoli gate

$\alpha e.((a \wedge b) \bullet\!\!- \mathsf{Not}(e) \; ; \; (c \wedge e) \bullet\!\!- \mathsf{Not}(d) \; ; \; (a \wedge b) \bullet\!\!- \mathsf{Not}(e))$

(b) Sequence of Toffoli gates

Fig. 2. Two (weakly) equivalent reversible circuits and their descriptions in Ricercar. Here, e denotes an arbitrary ancilla wire.

$$
\begin{array}{ll}
\mathsf{inv}(\mathsf{Id}(x)) = \mathsf{Id}(x) & \mathsf{inv}(A \; ; \; B) = \mathsf{inv}(B) \; ; \; \mathsf{inv}(A) \\
\mathsf{inv}(\mathsf{Not}(x)) = \mathsf{Not}(x) & \mathsf{inv}(\phi \bullet\!\!- A) = \phi \bullet\!\!- \mathsf{inv}(A)
\end{array}
\qquad \mathsf{inv}(\alpha x.A) = \alpha x. \mathsf{inv}(A)
$$

Fig. 3. The syntactic function $\mathsf{inv}(\cdot)$ that defines the inverse of a Ricercar description

- A controlled circuit, denoted with the binary "$\bullet\!\!-$" operator, which contains a control function ϕ and a controlled circuit A.[1] The control function can be any Boolean formula.
- An ancilla scope for a circuit A, denoted with a functional lambda-style notation using the symbol α, and a variable denoting a wire which *must* be false both before and after A. Without loss of generality, we will assume that ancillae scopes always introduces fresh variable names.

For readability, we define control gates ($\bullet\!\!-$) to bind tighter than sequence (;) and the unary ($\alpha x.$).

Figure 2 shows two example circuits, defined using multiply controlled Toffoli gates, represented in the usual diagram notation due to Feynman, as well as in Ricercar.

As Ricercar should be reversible, we will define the straight-forward inverse of all the syntactic constructs. We have chosen *not* to include inversion as a basic construct, but will define it as a syntactic function; this simplifies both the language and the following rewriting rules. Figure 3 shows the inversion function $\mathsf{inv}(\cdot)$.

3.2   Ancillae and Reversibly Well-Formed Properties

Ancillae hold a central place in Ricercar. We follow the idea that there are always as many ancilla wires available as needed. Consequently ancilla lines do not need to be declared in advance, but can be introduced on-the-fly. This is not an unrealistic assumption: remember that we define ancillae to be constant (false) at both input and output, which permits a large degree of reuse. Furthermore,

---

[1] The "$\bullet\!\!-$" notation is borrowed from [11], although with a different semantics.

$$\begin{array}{ll} \mathrm{rwf}(\mathsf{Id}(x)) = \{x\} & \mathrm{rwf}(A \; ; \; B) = \mathrm{rwf}(A) \cup \mathrm{rwf}(B) \\ \mathrm{rwf}(\mathsf{Not}(x)) = \{x\} & \mathrm{rwf}(\phi \bullet\!\!- A) = \mathrm{dom}(\phi) \uplus \mathrm{rwf}(A) \end{array} \qquad \mathrm{rwf}(\alpha x.A) = \mathrm{rwf}(A) \backslash \{x\}$$

Fig. 4. A reversible circuit, A, is reversibly well-formed iff $\mathrm{rwf}(A)$ evaluates to a set. Here, $\uplus$ is the disjoint union and $\mathrm{dom}(\phi)$ is the domain of the Boolean function ϕ. We assume that the disjoint union is undefined whenever the operands are not disjoint.

the actual number of ancilla lines used is limited by the depth of the circuit, and cannot grow unboundedly. As an example, given that we know the upper bound of the depth to implement a reversible circuit without ancillae (*cf.* [1]), this also gives an upper bound on the number of (useful) ancilla any circuit with smaller depth can have.

The syntax presented in Fig. 1 does not guarantee reversibility by itself. One problem comes from the control gate, where we must enforce that the wires of the control function are disjoint from wires of the circuit being controlled. This is similar to the concept used in the reversible updates in Janus [22]. Figure 4 shows a function $\mathrm{rwf}(\cdot)$ that implements this check; we say that the circuit is *reversibly well-formed* if it upholds this restriction. Given a circuit description A, it returns the set of all used variable names *if and only if* A is reversibly well-formed. If a circuit A is *not* reversibly well-formed, the disjoint union operation will fail on the control gate operator, and the result of $\mathrm{rwf}(A)$ will thus be undefined.

However, even a reversibly well-formed circuit is not necessarily reversible.[2] To ensure that an ancilla variable within an ancilla scope does indeed have ancilla behaviour (guaranteed false at both input and output), we need a additional semantic check. However, a circuit *without* ancillae is reversibly well-formed if and only if it is reversible. In Sect. 5, we will show how this can be exploited to introduce ancillae in a way that guarentees reversibility.

3.3 Operational Semantics

The straightforward semantics of Ricercar is shown in Fig. 5; they follow, but also extend, the logic by Fredkin and Toffoli, and describe the mapping from a circuit description to a reversible circuit using the well-known gates. More concretely, this semantics can be used to show that Ricercar is actually reversible.

Theorem 1 (Reversibility). *For all mappings σ and circuits A there exists a mapping σ' and a circuit B such that*

$$\sigma \vdash A \to \sigma' \iff \sigma' \vdash B \to \sigma.$$

This theorem and the following two lemmas are easily proven by structural induction over the circuit A and reference to the operational semantics of Ricercar (Fig. 5).

---

[2] The other direction holds: all reversible circuits are reversibly well-formed.

$$\sigma : \Sigma \rightharpoonup \mathbb{B}$$

$$\overline{\sigma \vdash \mathsf{Id}(x) \rightarrow \sigma}$$

$$\frac{\sigma \vdash \neg x \rightarrow b}{\sigma \vdash \mathsf{Not}(x) \rightarrow \sigma[x \mapsto b]}$$

$$\frac{\sigma \vdash A \rightarrow \sigma'' \qquad \sigma'' \vdash B \rightarrow \sigma'}{\sigma \vdash A \; ; \; B \rightarrow \sigma'}$$

$$\frac{\sigma \vdash \phi \rightarrow 1 \qquad \sigma \vdash A \rightarrow \sigma'}{\sigma \vdash \phi \bullet\!\!- A \rightarrow \sigma'}$$

$$\frac{\sigma \vdash \phi \rightarrow 0}{\sigma \vdash \phi \bullet\!\!- A \rightarrow \sigma}$$

$$\frac{\sigma \vdash x \rightarrow b \qquad \sigma[x \mapsto 0] \vdash A \rightarrow \sigma' \qquad \sigma' \vdash x \rightarrow 0}{\sigma \vdash \alpha x.A \rightarrow \sigma'[x \mapsto b]}$$

Fig. 5. The semantics of Ricercar. Here, σ is a partial function mapping variable names to Boolean values; any variable name that is not part of the input is assumed to be undefined in σ. The semantics uses two judgment forms, $\sigma \vdash A \rightarrow \sigma'$ for evaluating circuits, and $\sigma \vdash \phi \rightarrow b$ for evaluating Boolean formulae, both with respect to σ. The rules for judgments of the latter form are not shown, but are completely standard.

To ensure that the previously defined inversion (with sequence as composition function) is indeed inversion, we show the following.

Lemma 1 (Inversion). *For all circuits A and states σ,*

$$\sigma \vdash A \; ; \; \mathrm{inv}(A) \rightarrow \sigma \quad and \quad \sigma \vdash \mathrm{inv}(A) \; ; \; A \rightarrow \sigma.$$

Later it will also be useful to know that the inversion function respects involution symmetry.

Lemma 2 (Involution Symmetry). *For all circuits A, and states σ and σ',*

$$\sigma \vdash A \rightarrow \sigma' \iff \sigma \vdash \mathrm{inv}(\mathrm{inv}(A)) \rightarrow \sigma'.$$

3.4   Permutation (Denotational) Semantics

In order to ease the formal analyses using this language, we also express the functional semantics in terms of permutations. The counterparts to Id, Not, and '$\bullet\!\!-$' are provided for this purpose. In contrast to the language, the permutation description requires an order of variables and therefore we assume a strict total order '$>$' on the variables in Σ for the following equations. If $x > y$, it means that the variable x corresponds to a more significant bit than y. For the identity and the not gate we have

$$\mathsf{Id}(x) = \pi_e \quad and \quad \mathsf{Not}(x) = (0,1) \qquad \text{if } \Sigma = \{x\}. \tag{4}$$

For the following four equations, let $G(\pi, f)$ be the commutator $g_n(f) \circ \pi \circ g_n^{-1}(f)$ for a permutation $\pi \in S_{2^n}$ and a function f as in (3). Note that G is an endomorphism with respect to composition, since

$$G(\pi_1 \circ \pi_2, f) = g_n(f) \circ \pi_1 \circ \pi_2 \circ g_n^{-1}(f)$$
$$= g_n(f) \circ \pi_1 \circ g_n^{-1}(f) \circ g_n(f) \circ \pi_2 \circ g_n^{-1}(f)$$
$$= G(\pi_1, f) \circ G(\pi_2, f).$$

For some circuit A, let π_A be its permutation representation. Then one can "add a control line from the bottom," expressed as

$$\neg x \bullet\!\!- A = G(\pi_A, x \mapsto x) \quad \begin{array}{l} \text{if } \Sigma = \mathrm{rwf}(A) \cup \{x\} \\ \text{and } x > y \text{ for all } y \in \mathrm{rwf}(A) \end{array} \qquad (5)$$

and

$$x \bullet\!\!- A = G(\pi_A, x \mapsto x + 2^n) \quad \begin{array}{l} \text{with } n = |\,\mathrm{rwf}(A)|, \text{ if } \Sigma = \mathrm{rwf}(A) \cup \{x\} \\ \text{and } x > y \text{ for all } y \in \mathrm{rwf}(A). \end{array} \qquad (6)$$

Similarly, one can "add a control line from the top," expressed as

$$\neg x \bullet\!\!- A = G(\pi_A, x \mapsto 2x) \quad \begin{array}{l} \text{if } \Sigma = \mathrm{rwf}(A) \cup \{x\} \\ \text{and } x < y \text{ for all } y \in \mathrm{rwf}(A) \end{array} \qquad (7)$$

and

$$x \bullet\!\!- A = G(\pi_A, x \mapsto 2x + 1) \quad \begin{array}{l} \text{if } \Sigma = \mathrm{rwf}(A) \cup \{x\} \\ \text{and } x < y \text{ for all } y \in \mathrm{rwf}(A). \end{array} \qquad (8)$$

The above denotational semantics is not complete. Circuit sequence (;) can be defined by permutation composition after extending the two permutations to the same symmetric group, and scoped ancillae can be accommodated by imposing restrictions on the permutation for the more general circuit (*i.e.*, where the ancilla is considered as any other input line.) It is then not hard to prove equivalence between the operational and denotational semantics. The denotational semantics is reversible by construction.

4   Rewriting in Ricercar

In this section, we will recap the rewriting rules from [14], and define the rules with respect to Ricercar, as well as show soundness based on the permutation semantics.

First, however, note that gate composition is associative; that is, in a cascade of gates, the order in which we look at the gates does not matter, so in, *e.g.* Fig. 2(b), we are free to either look at the two first gates and perform rewriting on these, or start with the last two gates instead. The identity gate is the identity element for sequences:

$$A = \mathsf{Id}(x) \; ; \; A = A \; ; \; \mathsf{Id}(x) \qquad (\mathrm{ID})$$

Furthermore, note that we can always rewrite the controlling Boolean functions and, *e.g.* use identities from AND-EXOR decomposition:

$$\phi \bullet\!\!\!- \psi \bullet\!\!\!- A = (\phi \wedge \psi) \bullet\!\!\!- A \qquad \text{and}$$
$$\phi \bullet\!\!\!- A \ ; \ \psi \bullet\!\!\!- A = (\phi \oplus \psi) \bullet\!\!\!- A \qquad \text{if } A = \text{inv}(A).$$

Finally, implicit to rules is that the circuits must always be reversibly well-formed both before and after a rewriting, and that in any given circuit we can rewrite any sub-circuit we like.

The first rule presented in [14] is for introducing and eliminating not gates, and states that we can always rewrite the identity function to two not gates.

$$x \ \underline{\hspace{2cm}} \ = \ -\oplus\!-\oplus- \qquad\qquad \text{Id}(x) = \text{Not}(x) \ ; \ \text{Not}(x) \qquad \text{(R1)}$$

Soundness trivially follows from $\pi_e = (0, 1) \circ (0, 1)$.

The second rule states that we can "move" a not gate over a control if we negate the control line.

$$x \ \overset{\bullet\ \oplus}{\underset{\oplus}{\rule{0pt}{1em}}} y \quad = \quad \overset{\oplus\ \circ}{\underset{\oplus}{\rule{0pt}{1em}}} \qquad\qquad \begin{aligned} x \bullet\!\!\!- \text{Not}(y) \ ; \ \text{Not}(x) = \\ \text{Not}(x) \ ; \ \neg x \bullet\!\!\!- \text{Not}(y) \end{aligned} \quad \text{(R2)}$$

Similar to [14], we notice that its dual rule with negative control can be derived using this rule in combination with Rule R1:

$$\neg x \bullet\!\!\!- \text{Not}(y) \ ; \ \text{Not}(x) \overset{\text{(R1)}}{=} \text{Not}(x) \ ; \ \text{Not}(x) \ ; \ \neg x \bullet\!\!\!- \text{Not}(y) \ ; \ \text{Not}(x)$$

$$\overset{\text{(R2)}}{=} \text{Not}(x) \ ; \ x \bullet\!\!\!- \text{Not}(y) \ ; \ \text{Not}(x) \ ; \ \text{Not}(x)$$

$$\overset{\text{(R1)}}{=} \text{Not}(x) \ ; \ x \bullet\!\!\!- \text{Not}(y). \qquad\qquad\qquad \text{(R2')}$$

Soundness follows from Eqs. (5)–(8) and the identity $(a, b)(b, c) = (a, c)(a, b) = (a, c)(b, c)$.

Third, we can extend a gate by copying it and adding once a positive and once a negative control line to it.

$$x \ \overset{\underline{\hspace{2cm}}}{\underset{\oplus}{\rule{0pt}{1em}}} y \quad = \quad \overset{\bullet\ \circ}{\underset{\oplus\ \oplus}{\rule{0pt}{1em}}} \qquad\qquad \begin{aligned} \text{Id}(x) \ ; \ \text{Not}(y) = \\ x \bullet\!\!\!- \text{Not}(y) \ ; \ \neg x \bullet\!\!\!- \text{Not}(y) \end{aligned} \quad \text{(R3)}$$

Soundness follows from Eqs. (7) and (8). In fact, in permutation notation, both controlled not gates are represented by a single transposition, and combining them results in the (permutation corresponding to the) not gate. Also, combining the equation of adding a negative and positive control yields an equation for adding an empty line.

Next, two arbitrary adjacent gates can be interchanged whenever they have a common control line with different polarities. Notice how Ricercar captures the fact that two controlled circuits can have *any* circuit structure; something that is not well captured by the diagrammatic notation in [14].

$$x \bullet\!\!- A \; ; \; \neg x \bullet\!\!- B =$$
$$\neg x \bullet\!\!- B \; ; \; x \bullet\!\!- A \qquad \text{(R4)}$$

The permutation equations also reveal this property, since the transpositions resulting from $\neg x \bullet\!\!- A$ and $x \bullet\!\!- A$ are disjoint.

Whenever two gates share the same control variable with the same polarity, these two gates can be grouped together, where the group is controlled by that control line. Again, Ricercar allows for a precise formulation of the idea, compared to the diagrammatic notation.

$$x \bullet\!\!- A \; ; \; x \bullet\!\!- B = x \bullet\!\!- (A \; ; \; B) \quad \text{(R5)}$$

This property follows from G being an endomorphism. Finally, we have the rule for introducing and eliminating groups of wires.

$$x \bullet\!\!- \mathsf{Id}(y) = \mathsf{Id}(x) \; ; \; \mathsf{Id}(y) \qquad \text{(R6)}$$

4.1 A Note on Completeness

A question raised in [14] regards the *completeness* of the above rules, in the sense that every circuit can be rewritten, in a finite number of steps, to any other equivalent circuit. In this strict sense, the rules are *not* complete. The counter example is the two-line swap gate, which can be represented in the following two ways:

Given the six rules, it is not possible to rewrite one to the other. This is, of course, not satisfactory, and a shortcoming that must be solved. The easy solution would be to add the above equation as a seventh rule, but the extent to which there exist other counter examples related to this problem is unknown, and the solution is only an incremental extension that will not add any interesting new insights.

However, this counter example is restricted in that it does not generalise to more lines. If we have a third line available (no matter its value), it can be used as an auxiliary line and thereby enable rewriting between the two swap gates. The question is now if the six rules are complete for circuits of more than two lines. But there is a possibility that two similar three line circuits exist and we need to assume a fourth auxiliary line to rewrite between them. The better solution, that we will follow in the next section, is thus to extend with rules for ancilla lines.

5   Ancillae and Rewriting

As mentioned earlier, ancillae is a powerful extension to a reversible language, but the power comes at a cost. Checking that some defined ancillae are indeed unchanged for all possible input vectors of an arbitrary description is hard; in general, one has to test all possible input vectors, which is undesirable. For a reversible programming language such as Janus [22], this is therefore implemented as a runtime check that checks the reversibility of a program *only* in relation to the executing input vector. This is also the case for the syntax described in Fig. 1.

For this reason, we will pursue a different approach. Given a description without ancillae, we can statically check reversibility using the rwf-function shown in Fig. 4. From a reversible description without ancillae, we will now define rewriting rules that can extend the given description with ancilla wires. Hence, instead of showing reversibility of a description with ancillae (which is hard), we only have to show that the rewriting rules do not interfere with the ancilla-property of the wires, and thereby with the reversibility of the circuit; this is much easier.

5.1   The Rewriting Rules

To be able to introduce and remove ancilla wires from a circuit, we have identified the need for five basic rules.

The first rule is for introducing and removing an ancilla scope. It states that we can always introduce a scope containing the identity circuit with a fresh (unused) ancilla wire name.

$$x \text{ ————— } = \text{ [ ]}_y \qquad\qquad \mathsf{Id}(x) = \alpha y.\mathsf{Id}(x) \qquad (A1)$$

The second rule states that a circuit in an ancilla scope can be removed (or added) if it is controlled by the ancilla wire. Recall that the ancilla variable is assumed to be assigned false outside of the ancilla scope, so the control is never active. For now, the gate must be the only gate within the scope, but we will show how this can be generalised later.

$$\alpha y.(y \bullet\!\!-\!\! A) = \alpha y.\mathsf{Id}(x), \qquad x \in \mathrm{rwf}(A) \qquad (A2)$$

The third rule considers the case in which the controlling wire is not the ancilla wire of the scope. In this case, the control can be pulled out of the ancilla scope, and thereby control the scope containing the controlled circuit.

$$\alpha y.(x \bullet\!\!-\!\! A) = x \bullet\!\!-\!\! \alpha y.A, \qquad x \neq y \quad (A3)$$

The fourth rules states that a not gate on a non-ancilla wire that is positioned to the immediate left of a circuit it shares a scope with can be pulled out of the ancilla scope.

$$\alpha y.(\mathsf{Not}(x) \; ; \; A) = \\ \mathsf{Not}(x) \; ; \; \alpha y.A, \qquad x \neq y \quad (A4)$$

In the case where the not gate is on the right, a similar rule can be derived from the Involution Symmetry Lemma with Rule A4.

$$\alpha y.(A \; ; \; \mathsf{Not}(x)) = \\ (\alpha y.A) \; ; \; \mathsf{Not}(x), \qquad x \neq y \quad (A4')$$

The fifth and final rule states that if (and only if) an ancilla scope contains a sequence of two circuits where the first is positively controlled, and the second is negatively controlled by the same wire, then this scope can be divided into two; or, in the other direction, merged. Note that x *can* be equal to y. This rule is likely the most powerful of the five, and it shows up in the proofs that extend and generalise the previous rules.

$$\alpha y.(x \bullet\!\!- A \; ; \; \neg x \bullet\!\!- B) = \\ (\alpha y.x \bullet\!\!- A) \; ; \; (\alpha y.\neg x \bullet\!\!- B) \quad (A5)$$

That the first four rules (A1 to A4) do not interfere with the ancilla-property of a wire is clear, but the last rule (A5) requires an argument. Only either A or B (but not both) is performed as the control on x is exclusive. Thus assuming that $x \neq y$, any usage of y in A must have uncomputed y to zero again; similarly any usage of y in B must have assumed it to be zero. Therefore, we can divide the ancilla scope of y. If $x = y$ then y will always be unchanged (zero) as y is not used in B.

5.2   Generalisation of Ancilla Rules

Rule A2 has a twin-rule for the case where the gate is negatively controlled by the ancilla wire. We can derive that this is equal to the controlled gate in the following way:

$$\alpha y.(\neg y \bullet\!\!- A) \overset{(ID)}{=} \mathsf{Id}(x) \; ; \; (\alpha y.\neg y \bullet\!\!- A) \qquad\qquad \overset{(A1)}{=} (\alpha y.\mathsf{Id}(x)) \; ; \; (\alpha y.\neg y \bullet\!\!- A)$$

$$\overset{(A2)}{=} (\alpha y.y \bullet\!\!- A) \; ; \; (\alpha y.\neg y \bullet\!\!- A) \qquad \overset{(A5)}{=} \alpha y.(y \bullet\!\!- A \; ; \; \neg y \bullet\!\!- A)$$

$$\overset{(R3)}{=} \alpha y.A. \qquad\qquad\qquad\qquad\qquad\qquad\qquad\qquad (A2')$$

This twin-rule can now be used to show the more general rule that if an ancilla wire controls a circuit in the beginning of a scope it can be removed entirely:

$$\alpha y.(y \bullet\!\!- A \ ; \ B) \overset{(R3)}{=} \alpha y.(y \bullet\!\!- A \ ; \ y \bullet\!\!- B \ ; \ \neg y \bullet\!\!- B)$$
$$\overset{(R5)}{=} \alpha y.(y \bullet\!\!- (A \ ; \ B) \ ; \ \neg \alpha \bullet\!\!- .B)$$
$$\overset{(A5)}{=} (\alpha y.y \bullet\!\!- (A \ ; \ B)) \ ; \ (\alpha y.\neg y \bullet\!\!- B)$$
$$\overset{(A2)}{=} (\alpha y.\mathsf{Id}(x)) \ ; \ (\alpha y.\neg y \bullet\!\!- B) \overset{(A2')}{=} (\alpha y.\mathsf{Id}(x)) \ ; \ (\alpha y.B)$$
$$\overset{(A1)}{=} \mathsf{Id}(x) \ ; \ \alpha y.B \qquad\qquad \overset{(ID)}{=} \alpha y.B. \tag{D8}$$

Similarly, we can also generalise A3 to the case where the circuit in the ancilla scope contains more than one gate. Assuming that $x \neq y$, to extract x from the ancilla scope of y we can do

$$\alpha y.x \bullet\!\!- A \ ; \ B \overset{(R3)}{=} \alpha y.(x \bullet\!\!- A \ ; \ x \bullet\!\!- B \ ; \ \neg x \bullet\!\!- B)$$
$$\overset{(R5)}{=} \alpha y.(x \bullet\!\!- (A \ ; \ B) \ ; \ \neg x \bullet\!\!- B)$$
$$\overset{(A5)}{=} (\alpha y.x \bullet\!\!- (A \ ; \ B)) \ ; \ (\alpha y.\neg x \bullet\!\!- B)$$
$$\overset{(A3)}{=} x \bullet\!\!- (\alpha y.(A \ ; \ B)) \ ; \ \neg x \bullet\!\!- \alpha y.B. \tag{D9}$$

This duplicates B such that it is performed both when x is true, and when it is false. Assuming that the ancilla wire y does not occur in A (*i.e.* $y \notin \mathrm{rwf}(A)$), we can then use D9 to show by induction on the depth of the control that

$$\alpha y.(A \ ; \ B) = A \ ; \ \alpha y.B, \qquad y \notin \mathrm{rwf}(A). \tag{D10}$$

As a special case of this rule, specifically when $B = \mathsf{Id}(x)$ for any choice of $x \in \mathrm{rwf}(A) \cup \{y\}$, we get that

$$\alpha y.A = A, \qquad y \notin \mathrm{rwf}(A). \tag{D11}$$

As a closing derived rule, we will show how ancilla wires can be introduced to perform computations that were otherwise performed by an input wire. In other words, we can use the rules to introduce ancilla wires that are then used to control what was previously controlled by x.

$$x \bullet\!\!- A \overset{(D11)}{=} \alpha y.(x \bullet\!\!- A \ ; \ \mathsf{Id}(y))$$
$$\overset{(D1)}{=} \alpha y.(x \bullet\!\!- A \ ; \ x \bullet\!\!- y \ ; \ x \bullet\!\!- y)$$
$$\overset{(D8)}{=} \alpha y.(y \bullet\!\!- A \ ; \ x \bullet\!\!- A \ ; \ x \bullet\!\!- y \ ; \ x \bullet\!\!- y)$$
$$\overset{(D6)}{=} \alpha y.(x \bullet\!\!- A \ ; \ y \bullet\!\!- A \ ; \ x \bullet\!\!- y \ ; \ x \bullet\!\!- y)$$
$$\overset{(D7)}{=} \alpha y.(x \bullet\!\!- y \ ; \ y \bullet\!\!- A \ ; \ x \bullet\!\!- y). \tag{D12}$$

Here D1, D6, and D7 refer to derived rules from [14]. This example increases the size and depth of the circuit, but if x controls several gates this can be used to reduce the depth of the circuit considering that gates can be put in parallel.

5.3 Practical Example of Application of Ricercar

As a final example we show how to derive the circuit depicted in Fig. 2(b) from the one in Fig. 2(a) using the rewriting rules. Again D1 and D7 refer to derived rules from [14].

$(a \wedge b \wedge c) \bullet\!\!- \mathsf{Not}(d)$

$\qquad \overset{(D11)}{=} \alpha e.((a \wedge b \wedge c) \bullet\!\!- \mathsf{Not}(d))$

$\qquad \overset{(D8)}{=} \alpha e.((c \wedge \beta) \bullet\!\!- \mathsf{Not}(d) \; ; \; (a \wedge b \wedge c) \bullet\!\!- \mathsf{Not}(d))$

$\qquad \overset{(D1)}{=} \alpha e.((a \wedge b) \bullet\!\!- \mathsf{Not}(e) \; ; \; (a \wedge b) \bullet\!\!- \mathsf{Not}(e) \; ; \; (c \wedge e) \bullet\!\!- \mathsf{Not}(d) \; ;$
$\qquad\qquad (a \wedge b \wedge c) \bullet\!\!- \mathsf{Not}(d))$

$\qquad \overset{(D7)}{=} \alpha e.((a \wedge b) \bullet\!\!- \mathsf{Not}(e) \; ; \; (c \wedge e) \bullet\!\!- \mathsf{Not}(d) \; ; \; (a \wedge b) \bullet\!\!- \mathsf{Not}(e) \; ;$
$\qquad\qquad (a \wedge b \wedge c) \bullet\!\!- \mathsf{Not}(d) \; ; \; (a \wedge b \wedge c) \bullet\!\!- \mathsf{Not}(d))$

$\qquad \overset{(D1)}{=} \alpha e.((a \wedge b) \bullet\!\!- \mathsf{Not}(e) \; ; \; (c \wedge e) \bullet\!\!- \mathsf{Not}(d) \; ; \; (a \wedge b) \bullet\!\!- \mathsf{Not}(e)).$

6 Related Work

This is not the first language that has been designed to describe the concepts of reversible logic; there exist description languages for both reversible and quantum circuits.

The closest related work is the *Reversible Combinator Language* (RCL) [18] that was also made to describe reversible logic; though it is more general than our work, there are still some common ideas. Taking inspiration from RCL, we use a similar sequence operator, and the conditional in RCL is (in its semantics) comparable to our control operator. However, being a combinator language, RCL does not have variables, but rather a type system in which circuits of arbitrary size with a given structure can be defined. Also it has more general combinators, such as a ripple circuit and parallel composition, as basic constructs. RCL also admits a number of rewriting rules, but compared to Ricercar, RCL's type system and larger set of atomic gates makes rewriting more cumbersome.

Although aiming to describe quantum circuits, it is worth mentioning *Quipper* [8,9]. Though Quipper also supports ancilla scopes, in order to uphold the ancilla-property, the Quipper synthesis results in a symmetric compute-use-uncompute "Bennett-style" structure of the ancilla wires. In contrast, the ancilla scopes in Ricercar are more general, but have to be built from the bottom up with rewriting to uphold the property. The interested reader can find further references for quantum description languages in the works above.

7 Conclusion

In this paper we have presented *Ricercar*, a language designed to describe reversible circuits. A main focus during the design process of the language has been rewriting, specifically that rewriting rules should be easy to both define and apply in the language. The previous approach to rewriting of reversible circuits was shown for the standard diagrammatic notation, but this notation neither captures the full intent of all of the six original rules, nor does it provide an optimal setting for a future computer aided system. Ricercar, with its simple symbolic description, both captures the complete intent of the original rules, and has a syntax that is directly implementable.

In addition, Ricercar has support for ancillae as a basic circuit construct in the form of a *scope*. Using this construct, we have extended the six original rules with five basic rules that applies when rewriting ancillae. We have shown how it is possible to use these rules to derive more general ones that also apply to ancillae, and as a final example, how to derive a rule that moves the control of a gate from an input wire to an ancilla wire.

Determining reversibility of a circuit that contains ancillae is generally hard, but with the presented rewriting rules, it is possible to take an ancillae-free circuit (for which it is easy to show reversibility) and rewrite it into a circuit that contains ancillae, and is guaranteed to be reversible. The key here is that the basic rules (and all of the derived rules) cannot break the ancilla-property of a wire and, thus, the reversibility of the circuit.

We hope that this approach can further help in the understanding of the trade-off between ancillae on the one hand, and the size and depth of a reversible circuit on the other.

Acknowledgments. The authors thank the anonymous reviewers from RC'14 for their useful comments on a preliminary version of this paper, presented as work-in-progress at *6th Conference on Reversible Computation, 2014* and the anonymous reviewers from RC'15 on the current version. Finally, we thank Holger Bock Axelsen for several discussion on work in this paper.

References

1. Abdessaied, N., Soeken, M., Thomsen, M.K., Drechsler, R.: Upper bounds for reversible circuits based on Young subgroups. Information Processing Letters **114**(6), 282–286 (2014)
2. Bennett, C.H.: Time/Space Trade-Offs for reversible computation. SIAM Journal on Computing **18**(4), 766–776 (1989)
3. Buhrman, H., Tromp, J., Vitányi, P.: Time and space bounds for reversible simulation. Journal of Physics A: Mathematical and General **34**(35), 6821–6830 (2001)
4. Chan, T., Munro, J.I., Raman, V.: Selection and sorting in the "restore" model. In: Proceedings of the Twenty-Fifth Annual ACM-SIAM Symposium on Discrete Algorithms, pp. 995–1004 (2014)
5. Cuccaro, S.A., Draper, T.G., Kutin, S.A., Moulton, D.P.: A new quantum ripple-carry addition circuit. arXiv:quant-ph/0410184v1 (2005)
6. De Vos, A., Rentergem, Y.V.: Reversible computing: from mathematical group theory to electronical circuit experiment. In: Proceedings of the Second Conference on Computing Frontiers, 2005, Ischia, Italy, May 4–6, 2005, pp. 35–44 (2005)

7. Draper, T.G., Kutin, S.A., Rains, E.M., Svore, K.M.: A logarithmic-depth quantum carry-lookahead adder. arXiv:quant-ph/0406142 (2008)
8. Green, A.S., Lumsdaine, P.L.F., Ross, N.J., Selinger, P., Valiron, B.: An introduction to quantum programming in quipper. In: Dueck, G.W., Miller, D.M. (eds.) RC 2013. LNCS, vol. 7948, pp. 110–124. Springer, Heidelberg (2013)
9. Green, A.S., Lumsdaine, P.L., Ross, N.J., Selinger, P., Valiron, B.: Quipper: a scalable quantum programming language. In: Conference on Programming Language Design and Implementation, PLDI 2013, pp. 333–342. ACM (2013)
10. Jordan, S.P.: Strong equivalence of reversible circuits is coNP-complete. Quantum Information & Computation **14**(15–16), 1302–1307 (2014)
11. Kaarsgaard, R.: Towards a propositional logic for reversible logic circuits. In: de Haan, R. (ed.) Proceedings of the ESSLLI 2014 Student Session, pp. 33–41 (2014). http://www.kr.tuwien.ac.at/drm/dehaan/stus2014/proceedings.pdf
12. Miller, D.M., Maslov, D., Dueck, G.W.: A transformation based algorithm for reversible logic synthesis. In: Design Automation Conference, DAC, pp. 318–323 (2003)
13. Shende, V.V., Prasad, A.K., Markov, I.L., Hayes, J.P.: Synthesis of reversible logic circuits. IEEE Trans. on CAD of Integrated Circuits and Systems **22**(6), 710–722 (2003)
14. Soeken, M., Thomsen, M.K.: White dots *do* matter: rewriting reversible logic circuits. In: Dueck, G.W., Miller, D.M. (eds.) RC 2013. LNCS, vol. 7948, pp. 196–208. Springer, Heidelberg (2013)
15. Soeken, M., Thomsen, M.K., Dueck, G.W., Miller, D.M.: Self-inverse functions and palindromic circuits. arXiv 1502.05825 (2015)
16. Storme, L., De Vos, A., Jacobs, G.: Group theoretical aspects of reversible logic gates. J. UCS **5**(5), 307–321 (1999)
17. Takahashi, Y., Kunihiro, N.: A fast quantum circuit for addition with few qubits. Quantum Info. Comput. **8**(6), 636–649 (2008)
18. Thomsen, M.K.: Describing and optimising reversible logic using a functional language. In: Gill, A., Hage, J. (eds.) IFL 2011. LNCS, vol. 7257, pp. 148–163. Springer, Heidelberg (2012)
19. Thomsen, M.K., Axelsen, H.B.: Parallelization of reversible ripple-carry adders. Parallel Processing Letters **19**(1), 205–222 (2009)
20. Vedral, V., Barenco, A., Ekert, A.: Quantum networks for elementary arithmetic operations. Physical Review A **54**(1), 147–153 (1996)
21. Wille, R., Soeken, M., Miller, D.M., Drechsler, R.: Trading off circuit lines and gate costs in the synthesis of reversible logic. Integration, the VLSI Journal **47**(2), 284–294 (2014)
22. Yokoyama, T., Axelsen, H.B., Glück, R.: Principles of a reversible programming language. In: Conference on Computing Frontiers, CF, pp. 43–54. ACM Press (2008)

Circuit Synthesis

Technology Mapping for Single Target Gate Based Circuits Using Boolean Functional Decomposition

Nabila Abdessaied[1]([✉]), Mathias Soeken[1,2], and Rolf Drechsler[1,2]

[1] Cyber-Physical Systems, DFKI GmbH, Bremen, Germany
[2] Institute of Computer Science, University of Bremen, Bremen, Germany
{nabila,msoeken,drechsle}@informatik.uni-bremen.de

Abstract. Quantum computing offers a promising emerging technology due to the potential theoretical capacity of solving many important problems with exponentially less complexity. Since most of the known quantum algorithms include Boolean components, the design of quantum computers is often conducted by a two-stage approach. In a first step, the Boolean component is realized in reversible logic and then mapped to quantum gates in a second step. This paper describes a new mapping flow for determining quantum gate realizations for single-target gates (ST). Since each ST gate contains a Boolean control function, our method attempts to find a decomposition based on its BDD representation. It consists on breaking large ST gate into smaller ones using additional lines. Experiments show that we obtain smaller realizations when comparing to standard mapping.

1 Introduction

Quantum computers are one of the most promising emerging technologies, generating interest from the corporate sector and attracting government investment. Quantum computers exploit the often counter-intuitive rules of quantum physics to perform computations in a substantially different and often much more efficient way than classical computers, enabling computational solutions to problems that are considered intractable for classical systems [1]. The design and fabrication of these machines has progressed rapidly in the past decade, with many research groups now routinely fabricating and operating small quantum computers in multiple physical systems.

Quantum computing does not only provide challenges for physicists but also offers a variety of challenging and interesting problems to the field of computer science. Large parts of quantum computers perform classical computations which can be described in terms of classical Boolean functions instead of arbitrary unitary operations as they are used for general quantum computing. However, since all quantum computers need to be reversible, also the classical computations need to be described in terms of reversible Boolean functions [2]. In order to create a quantum circuit from such a Boolean function, a first intermediate step

© Springer International Publishing Switzerland 2015
J. Krivine and J.-B. Stefani (Eds.): RC 2015, LNCS 9138, pp. 219–232, 2015.
DOI: 10.1007/978-3-319-20860-2_14

synthesizes a reversible circuit description. The most common gate library for this step consists of mixed-polarity multiple-controlled Toffoli gates. Toffoli gates offer a convenient representation to model the functionality of a reversible circuit but are still too abstract to be used as quantum operations. Many aspects, particularly those considering fault tolerance and error correction properties, cannot effectively be considered on that abstraction level. For the latter, quantum gate libraries are used that consist of a few quantum gates that typically act on at most 2 qubits: one of the currently prominent libraries is the Clifford$+T$ gate library [3]. Technology mapping is performed in order to map Toffoli gates to gates from the quantum gate library and the majority of methods that have been presented so far originate from [4].

Albeit providing a high-level representation for reversible circuits, the lower bound of the size of a reversible circuit consisting of Toffoli gates is exponential [5], i.e., for every number of variables there exists a reversible function for which the size of the minimal circuit is exponential. In order to avoid this complexity when addressing large reversible functions and circuits, recently single-target gates are considered as a representation for reversible circuits. They are a generalization of Toffoli gates and a linear upper bound for reversible circuits composed of these gates has been shown in [6]. Besides that, synthesis approaches presented in [6] and [7] are based on this gate representation. However, for technology mapping into quantum circuits, so far single-target gates are mapped into cascades of Toffoli gates which are then independently mapped using the techniques described in [4].

In this paper, we present a technology mapping approach that is directly based on single-target gates and makes use of Boolean decomposition and a constant number of ancillary lines. Working on the higher level abstraction allows significant cost reductions as shown by our experimental evaluations. In the best case, we were able to reduce the costs of the quantum circuit by 75% and in the average by about 20% for the Clifford$+T$ gate library.

2   Preliminaries

To keep the paper self-contained, this section reviews definitions and notations from Boolean functions, function decomposition, reversible circuits, and reversible synthesis.

2.1   Boolean Functions

Let $\mathbb{B} \stackrel{\text{def}}{=} \{0, 1\}$ denote the *Boolean values*. Then we refer to $\mathcal{B}_{n,m} \stackrel{\text{def}}{=} \{f \mid f \colon \mathbb{B}^n \to \mathbb{B}^m\}$ as the set of all *Boolean multiple-output functions* with n inputs and m outputs. There are 2^{m2^n} such Boolean functions. We write $\mathcal{B}_n \stackrel{\text{def}}{=} \mathcal{B}_{n,1}$ and assume that each $f \in \mathcal{B}_n$ is represented by a propositional formula over the variables $x_1, \ldots, x_n$. Furthermore, we assume that each function $f \in \mathcal{B}_{n,m}$ is represented as a tuple $f = (f_1, \ldots, f_m)$ where $f_i \in \mathcal{B}_n$ for each $i \in \{1, \ldots, m\}$ and hence $f(\boldsymbol{x}) = (f_1(\boldsymbol{x}), \ldots, f_m(\boldsymbol{x}))$ for each $\boldsymbol{x} \in \mathbb{B}^n$. If we emphasize on the domain of the function we write $f(X)$ where X refers to the set of input variables.

2.2 Exclusive Sum of Products

Exclusive sum-of-products (ESOPs, cf. [8]) are two-level descriptions for Boolean functions in which a function is composed of k *product terms* that are combined using the exclusive-OR (XOR, $\oplus$) operation. A product term is the conjunction of l_i *literals* where a literal is either a propositional variable $x^1 \overset{\text{def}}{=} x$ or its negation $x^0 \overset{\text{def}}{=} \bar{x}$. ESOPs are the most general form of two-level AND-XOR expressions:

$$f = \bigoplus_{i=1}^{k} x_{i_1}^{p_{i_1}} \wedge \cdots \wedge x_{i_{l_i}}^{p_{i_{l_i}}} \tag{1}$$

Several restricted subclasses have been considered in the past, e.g., *positive polarity Reed-Muller expressions* (PPRM [8]) in which all literals are positive. There are further subclasses and most of them can be defined based on applying one of the following decomposition rules. An arbitrary Boolean function $f(x_1, x_2, \ldots, x_n)$ can be expanded with respect to a variable x_i as

$$f = \bar{x}_i f_{\bar{x}_i} \oplus x_i f_{x_i} \qquad \text{(Shannon)}$$
$$f = f_{\bar{x}_i} \oplus x_i (f_{\bar{x}_i} \oplus f_{x_i}) \qquad \text{(positive Davio)}$$
$$f = f_{x_i} \oplus \bar{x}_i (f_{\bar{x}_i} \oplus f_{x_i}) \qquad \text{(negative Davio)}$$

with *co-factors* $f_{\bar{x}_i} = f(x_1, \ldots, x_{i-1}, 0, x_{i+1}, \ldots, x_n)$ and $f_{x_i} = f(x_1, \ldots, x_{i-1}, 1, x_{i+1}, \ldots, x_n)$.

2.3 Boolean Function Decomposition

Boolean function decomposition describes the problem of finding, for a Boolean function, two or more simpler functions that being composed are functionally equivalent. Several types of Boolean function decomposition have been found in the last decades with the most important ones being:

1. Ashenhurst decomposition [9]: A function $f \in \mathcal{B}_n$ is decomposed into $f(X) = h(g(X_1), X_2)$ with $g \in \mathcal{B}_{|X_1|}$, $h \in \mathcal{B}_{|X_2|+1}$, and $X = X_1 \cup X_2$. If $X_1 \cap X_2 = \emptyset$, then the decomposition is called *disjoint*, otherwise it is called a *non-disjoint* decomposition. The set X_1 is called *bound set* and the set X_2 is called *free set*.
2. Curtis decomposition [10] is a generalization of the Ashenhurst decomposition with several inner functions of which each can have multiple outputs, i.e., $f(X) = h(g_1(X_1), g_2(X_2), \cdots, g_k(X_k), X_{k+1})$ with $g_i \in \mathcal{B}_{|X_i|, m_i}$, $h \in \mathcal{B}_{|X_{k+1}|+m_1+\cdots+m_k}$, and $X = X_1 \cup X_2 \cup \cdots \cup X_{k+1}$.
3. Factorization [11]: The function is decomposed as $f(X) = g(X_1) \wedge h(X_2) \vee c(X_3)$, with $g \in \mathcal{B}_{|X_1|}$, $h \in \mathcal{B}_{|X_2|}$, $c \in \mathcal{B}_{|X_3|}$ and $X = X_1 \cup X_2 \cup X_3$.

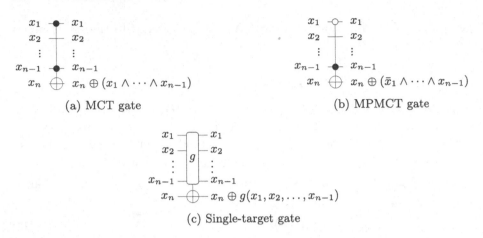

(a) MCT gate

(b) MPMCT gate

(c) Single-target gate

Fig. 1. Examples of reversible gates

4. Bi-decomposition [12] is also known as *simple decomposition*. The function is decomposed into two sub-functions $f(X) = g(X_1) \odot h(X_2)$, with $g \in \mathcal{B}_{|X_1|}$, $h \in \mathcal{B}_{|X_2|}$ and $X = X_1 \cup X_2$. The '$\odot$' is any binary Boolean operation (typically $\vee$, $\wedge$, $\oplus$, or $\leftrightarrow$).

When X_1, X_2, and X_3 are disjoint, the decomposition is called *algebraic*, otherwise *Boolean* or *functional*. Functional decomposition is much more powerful because the majority of Boolean functions are likely to have a functional decomposition rather than an algebraic one. Much work has been presented on decomposition algorithms based on truth tables [13] or binary decision diagrams (BDDs) [14–16].

2.4   Reversible Circuits

Reversible functions of n variables can be realized by reversible circuits that consist of at least n lines and are constructed as cascades of reversible gates that belong to a certain universal gate library. Although the Toffoli gate library is the most common gate library, single-target gates are of interest as they can lead to better circuits, e.g., lower quantum cost [7] and better circuit complexity [17].

Definition 1 (Single-Target Gate). *Given a set of variables* $X = \{x_1, \ldots, x_n\}$, *a single-target gate (ST)* $\mathrm{T}_g(C, t)$ *with control lines* $C = \{x_{i_1}, \ldots, x_{i_k}\} \subset X$, *a target line* $t \in X \setminus C$, *and a control function* $g \in \mathcal{B}_k$ *inverts the variable on the target line if and only if* $g(x_{i_1}, \ldots, x_{i_k})$ *evaluates to true. All other variables remain unchanged.*

Definition 2 (Toffoli Gate). *Mixed-polarity multiple control Toffoli (MPMCT) gates are a subset of the single-target gates in which the control function* g *can be represented with one product term or* $g = \bigwedge_{k=i}^{j} x_i^p = 1$. *Multiple-control*

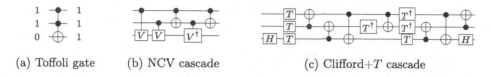

$$x_1 = 0 \quad \oplus \quad 1 \quad \bullet \quad 1 \quad \bullet \quad 1 \quad \quad y_1 = 1$$
$$x_2 = 1 \quad 1 \quad \bullet \quad 1 \quad \oplus \quad 0 \quad \oplus \quad y_2 = 1$$
$$x_3 = 0 \quad 0 \quad \oplus \quad 1 \quad 1 \quad \bullet \quad y_3 = 1$$
$$g_1 \quad g_2 \quad g_3 \quad g_4$$

Fig. 2. Reversible circuit

(a) Toffoli gate   (b) NCV cascade   (c) Clifford+T cascade

Fig. 3. Quantum mapping of a Toffoli gate

Toffoli gates (MCT) *in turn are a subset from MPMCT gates in which the product terms can only consist of positive literals.*

Following from synthesis algorithm implementations, it can easily be shown that any reversible function $f \in \mathcal{B}_{n,n}$ can be realized by a reversible circuit with n lines when using MCT gates. That is, it is not necessary to add any temporary lines (ancilla) to realize the circuit. This can be the case if the MCT (or MPMCT) gates are restricted to a given size, e.g., three bits. For drawing circuits, we follow the established conventions of using the symbol $\oplus$ to denote the target line, solid black circles to indicate positive controls, and white circles to indicate negative controls.

Example 1. Figure 1a shows a Toffoli gate with positive controls, Figure 1b shows a Toffoli gate with mixed-polarity control lines, and Figure 1c shows the representation of a single-target gate based on Feynman's notation. Figure 2 shows different Toffoli gates in a cascade forming a reversible circuit. The annotated values demonstrate the computation of the gate for a given input assignment.

2.5   Cost Metrics

To compare quantum circuits, we define metrics which depend on the gate library. For the NCV gate library, the *quantum cost* of a circuit is used while for the Clifford+T gate library, the T-*depth* is used. The motivation for that cost measure origins from the fact that the T gate is significantly larger compared to the other gates in the circuit.

Definition 3 (NCV-Cost). *The* NCV-cost *is the total number of elementary gates used in a quantum circuit.*

Definition 4 (T-Depth). *The* T-depth *is the number of T-stages in a quantum circuit where each stage consists of one or more T or $T^\dagger$ gates that can be performed concurrently on separate qubits. The total number of incorporated T or $T^\dagger$ gates in the whole circuit is denoted by T-count.*

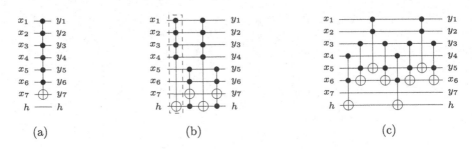

Fig. 4. Mapping from [4]

Example 2. The NCV-cost of the circuit shown in fig. 2 is equal to 8 since the total number of the elementary gates that realize a Toffoli gate is equal to 5. The circuit has a *T-count* of 7 and *T-depth* of 3.

2.6   Young Subgroup Synthesis

The young subgroup based synthesis approach makes use of the following property. Given a variable x, every reversible function $f \in \mathcal{B}_{n,n}$ can be decomposed into three functions $f = g_2 \circ f' \circ g_1$ such that $f' \in \mathcal{B}_{n,n}$ is a reversible function that does not change in x, and $g_1, g_2 \in \mathcal{B}_{n,n}$ are reversible functions that can be realized as single-target gates that act on x. By recursively applying the decomposition on the inner function f', one obtains $2n$ single-target gates that realize f. After at most n recursive applications f' represents the identity function, i.e., it does not change in any variable anymore. Details of the proof can be found in [18]. A synthesis algorithm based on the idea has initially been proposed in [6] that takes as input a reversible function represented by its truth table. The synthesis algorithm has been extended to work symbolically using binary decision diagrams in [7], which allows for handling larger functions.

3   Motivation

As mentioned above, a quantum circuits are described in terms of a reversible Boolean function. In order to derive a quantum circuit for the reversible function, a two step approach is usually applied: first a circuit description in terms of reversible gates is derived, which in the second step is mapped to a quantum circuit composed of gates from a given library. In these steps, reversible gates are very general; e.g., often MCT gates are used for which the number of controls is not restricted. More recently, also the use of MPMCT gates became common practice. Quantum gate libraries are much smaller and usually consist of a few gates which can act on at most 2 qubits. Two prominent quantum gate libraries are the NCV gate library and the Clifford+T gate library. In particular, the latter library is of significant interest in the design of quantum computers due to its good properties in fault tolerant quantum computing. Minimal quantum circuit realizations are known for the 2-controlled Toffoli gate and are shown in Figure 3.

For larger Toffoli gates a procedure from [4] is applied which, according to Lemma 7.3 in [4], maps a reversible Toffoli gate with $c \geq 3$ controls to a network consisting of two identical gates with m controls and two other identical gates with $c - m + 1$ controls, where $m \in \{2, \ldots, c - 2\}$ and each of them are placed alternately. If no free line is available for the gate, a new helper line must be added to the circuit. Its value is restored and hence can be reused afterwards. Finally, each obtained gate is mapped according to Lemma 7.2 in [4]. As a result, all Toffoli gates have at most 2 control lines. At this point, the mapping given in Figure 3 can be applied.

Example 3. The procedure is illustrated in Figure 4 for a Toffoli gate with six control lines. The first circuit depicts the result after the application of Lemma 7.2 in [4], while the second network sketches the obtained circuit from the decomposition of the first gate in the dashed rectangle after applying Lemma 7.3 in [4].

So far, there is no mapping approach into quantum circuits that directly targets the single-target gates as it is done for the MPMCT gates. To map single-target gates, we aim to decompose them into MPMCT gates so that we can afterwards map each obtained MPMCT gate using the approach explained above.

The mapping of a single-target gate to an MPMCT cascade is so far done by computing the XOR decomposition of its controlling function, then each cube in the obtained expression is represented by an MPMCT gate.

Many other Boolean decompositions do exist and have shown good efficiency [14]. Motivated by this, we want to study the impact of applying different kinds of Boolean decompositions while mapping single-target gates to MPMCT gates, i.e., unlike the standard mapping, we will not restrict the decomposition to XOR but also to bi-decomposition, Ashenhurst, and Curtis decomposition.

4 Mapping of Single-Target Gates

This section describes how Boolean decomposition can be applied to map reversible circuits composed of single-target gates into quantum circuits. Only the Young subgroup synthesis, for both the truth table based variant [6] and the BDD-based variant [7], makes use of single-target gates, however, due to the complexity of reversible circuits based on Toffoli gates (see, e.g., [17]) single-target gates are a preferable choice especially for large circuits.

Figure 5 shows how the functional decomposition of a single-target gate's control function can be used to generate less complex circuits. In the following we assume that the control function of the single-target gate that should be mapped depends on the variables $x_1, \ldots, x_{n-1}$. Figure 5(a) shows the mapping approach for a disjoint Ashenhurst-Curtis decomposition. The variables are partitioned into four sets of variables represented as bit-vectors $\boldsymbol{x}_1$, $\boldsymbol{x}_2$, $\boldsymbol{x}_3$, and $\boldsymbol{x}_4$. First, the inner functions g_1, g_2, and g_3 are computed and each of their results is

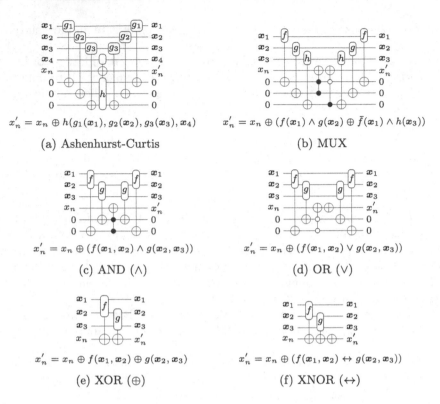

$$x'_n = x_n \oplus h(g_1(x_1), g_2(x_2), g_3(x_3), x_4)$$

(a) Ashenhurst-Curtis

$$x'_n = x_n \oplus (f(x_1) \wedge g(x_2) \oplus \bar{f}(x_1) \wedge h(x_3))$$

(b) MUX

$$x'_n = x_n \oplus (f(x_1, x_2) \wedge g(x_2, x_3))$$

(c) AND ($\wedge$)

$$x'_n = x_n \oplus (f(x_1, x_2) \vee g(x_2, x_3))$$

(d) OR ($\vee$)

$$x'_n = x_n \oplus f(x_1, x_2) \oplus g(x_2, x_3)$$

(e) XOR ($\oplus$)

$$x'_n = x_n \oplus (f(x_1, x_2) \leftrightarrow g(x_2, x_3))$$

(f) XNOR ($\leftrightarrow$)

Fig. 5. Different types of decomposition

stored on an additional helper line that is initialized with a constant 0 value. Having the resulting values on these lines the outer function can be computed and afterwards the constant values on the helper lines are restored by reapplying the inner functions.

Figures 5(b) and (c) show non-disjoint bi-decompositions based on the AND and OR operation, respectively. The sub-function f depends on variables in x_1 and x_2 and the sub-function g depends on variables in x_2 and x_3. As can be seen, the construction follows the representation of the Ashenhurst-Curtis decomposition in Figure 5(a). Whether a decomposition is disjoint or non-disjoint does not have an effect on the circuit construction but only on the size of the single-target gates in terms of their support. Also, a decomposition based on the MUX operation can analogously be performed by adding an extra helper line (see Figure 5(d)).

When using bi-decomposition based on the XOR and XNOR operator, one can update the target line directly as can be seen in Figures 5(e) and (f).

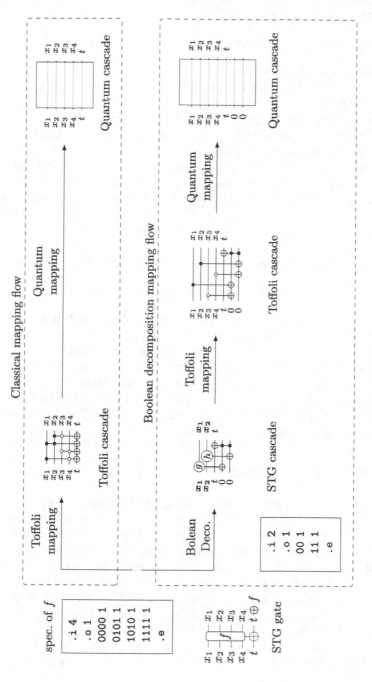

Fig. 6. Example for the mapping flow

The remainder of this section discusses an example application of the approach illustrated in Figure 6. The starting point is a single-target gate that is controlled by a control function

$$f(x_1, x_2, x_3, x_4) = \bar{x}_1 \bar{x}_2 \bar{x}_3 \bar{x}_4 \vee \bar{x}_1 x_2 \bar{x}_3 x_4 \vee x_1 \bar{x}_2 x_3 \bar{x}_4 \vee x_1 x_2 x_3 x_4$$

as also illustrated in its specification.

Decomposing the single-target gate using the standard mapping requires finding an ESOP representation of the function. Since f is given in terms of its minterms, it already resembles an ESOP representation. However, one can obtain a smaller one in terms of literals by applying ESOP minimization techniques finally resulting in the Toffoli gate cascade depicted in the upper box of Figure 6. The circuit consists of 4 Toffoli gates each having 2 controls. Mapping it into quantum circuits using the algorithm presented in [4] gives quantum costs of 21 for the NCV gate library (see Figure 3b and note that a Toffoli gate with two negative controls requires at most 6 NCV gates) and a T-depth of 12 when using the Clifford+T gate library. Each Toffoli gate has a T-depth of 3 as it is depicted in Figure 3c.

Applying our proposed flow will first find a disjoint bi-decomposition

$$f(x_1, x_2, x_3, x_4) = g(x_1, x_3) \wedge h(x_2, x_4)$$

with $g(x_1, x_3) = x_1 \leftrightarrow x_3$ and $h(x_2, x_4) = x_2 \leftrightarrow x_4$. Next, each of the resulting single-target gates controlled by g and h are mapped to Toffoli cascades as it is shown in the reversible circuit, each ST gate has two Toffoli gates with only one control while the last gate computes the AND of both sub-functions using a Toffoli gate with two controls. Finally, the resulting reversible circuit is mapped to a quantum network with the same algorithm used in the standard flow. The number of NCV gates of the resulting circuit is 9 (compared to 21) and the T-depth is 3 (compared to 12).

5   Experimental Evaluation

In order to confirm the benefits of incorporating the Boolean decomposition technique into the mapping flow of reversible circuits to quantum circuits described in Section 4, we have implemented the proposed idea in the open source toolkit *RevKit* [19]. The starting point is reversible circuits obtained from applying the BDD-based version of the Young subgroup synthesis [7], which creates reversible circuits composed of single-target gates[1]. We used the BDS-PGA tool [20] to decompose each control fucntion of a single-target gate to smaller ones. We restricted the decomposition of each single-target gate to at most 3 smaller single-target gates to limit the use of additional lines to at most 3. To map the resulting smaller gates into cascades of Toffoli gates we used the XOR minimization algorithm implemented in EXORCISM [21]. Finally, we applied the quantum

---

[1] Benchmarks were taken from http://webhome.cs.uvic.ca/~dmaslov/ and http://www.revlib.org

mapping algorithm explained in[4]. The experimental evaluation has been carried out on an Intel Core i5 processor with 4 GB of main memory.

Table 1 summarizes the obtained results. All benchmark names and original lines are listed in the first and second column, respectively. Then, the number of lines (L), the number of gates G, the NCV quantum costs (NCV), the *T-depth* (TD), the *H-count* (HC), and the required run-times (TIME) are provided for the synthesized circuits based on standard mapping and the synthesized circuits based on Boolean decomposition as explained in Section 4.

We provide absolute and relative improvement in the last two columns for quantum costs in terms of the NCV and the Clifford+T gate libraries. The NCV quantum cost reductions and its relative improvement of the circuits obtained by the proposed technique with respect to the realized circuits without taking into account the Boolean decomposition are given in the columns denoted by ΔNCV and IMP.NCV, respectively. The procedure presented above yields circuits with lower NCV quantum cost comparing to circuits obtained by standard mapping. The table shows a percentage improvement in terms of NCV quantum cost by approx. 16%. In the best case improvements of up to 67% are observed (*cycle10_2_61*).

The *T-depth* cost reductions and its relative improvement are provided in the columns denoted by ΔTD and IMP.TD, respectively. Also for this gate library realizations with fewer *T-depth* are obtained when our technique is applied. On average, the size of the resulting quantum gate cascades was decreased by 20%. In the best cases, reductions of up to 47916 in the *T-depth* for the benchmark *bw_116* are obtained.

Remarks and Observations. When applying the BDS-PGA tool to find a decomposition for a Boolean function that controls a single-target gate, it first searches for an algebraic decomposition and only looks for a Boolean decomposition if the first attempt is not successful. This process is done recursively for each resulting sub-function until Boolean functions with at most 2 inputs are reached. We adapted the tool such that recursion stops after maximum three decompositions in order to keep a reasonable number of additional lines.

We refer to the *common set* as the intersection of bound set and free set in Ashenhurst-Curtis decompositions and as the intersection of supports in bi-decompositions. We have observed that for large common sets the results of the standard mapping approach outperforms our approach. To ensure good results, we only decomposed functions with a small common set.

We further noticed that bi-decompositions based on XOR and XNOR are less effective compared to the standard mapping since EXORCISM finds efficient ESOP representations. Consequently, we adapted the BDS-PGA tool such that it does not try to find bi-decompositions based on XOR or XNOR.

Finally, factorization with respect to a single variable can usually not improve the overall result since the incorporation of the variable on the helper line does not minimize the functional support. We have therefore turned off that option in the BDS-PGA tool.

Table 1. Experimental evaluation

Benchmark		Classical mapping						Boolean decomposition based mapping						Improvements			
ID	L	L	G	NCV	TD	HC	TIME	L	G	NCV	TD	HC	TIME	ΔNCV	IMP.NCV	ΔTD	IMP.TD
decod24	4	5	12	74	42	36	0.05	6	30	49	33	20	0.10	-25	33.78%	-9	21.43%
4-49	4	5	14	117	81	44	0.04	7	57	105	63	52	0.15	-12	10.26%	-18	22.22%
aj-e11	4	4	10	128	90	50	0.05	7	62	112	69	66	0.14	-16	12.50%	-21	23.33%
mod5mils	5	5	3	11	6	4	0.01	7	8	11	3	2	0.04	-16	0.00%	-3	50.00%
mod5d1	5	5	4	20	12	8	0.01	7	9	13	3	2	0.03	-7	35.00%	-9	75.00%
4gt11	5	6	13	248	147	102	0.06	7	40	171	108	76	0.13	-77	31.05%	-39	26.53%
4mod5	5	5	22	315	186	126	0.05	8	58	213	123	80	0.16	-102	32.38%	-63	33.87%
4gt12	5	6	16	304	183	124	0.05	7	46	125	114	52	0.14	-179	58.88%	-69	37.70%
hwb5	5	6	31	494	339	194	0.06	8	89	422	264	162	0.21	-72	14.57%	-75	22.12%
4mod7	5	6	33	591	381	238	0.07	8	91	510	303	196	0.21	-81	13.71%	-78	20.47%
mini-alu	5	6	23	368	279	150	0.06	8	83	317	195	140	0.19	-51	13.86%	-84	30.11%
alu	5	5	21	310	261	122	0.05	8	81	233	168	88	0.17	-77	24.84%	-93	35.63%
4gt5	5	5	24	524	312	212	0.06	9	85	357	216	146	0.18	-167	31.87%	-96	30.77%
cm82a	6	6	55	1479	939	590	0.10	9	98	1468	894	580	0.30	-11	0.74%	-45	4.79%
C17	6	7	52	1394	942	560	0.12	9	88	1329	831	530	0.31	-65	4.66%	-111	11.78%
ex3	6	7	46	1593	963	644	0.12	9	96	1275	825	518	0.32	-318	19.96%	-138	14.33%
decod24-en	6	7	28	1076	642	440	0.09	9	87	727	480	306	0.26	-349	32.43%	-162	25.23%
f2	7	8	77	4617	2763	1866	0.16	10	95	4509	2700	1826	0.36	-108	2.34%	-63	2.28%
ham7	7	7	44	429	300	164	0.10	11	273	303	186	120	0.28	-126	29.37%	-114	38.00%
z4ml	8	9	266	18204	11568	7276	0.54	11	521	18041	11349	7212	0.92	-163	0.90%	-219	1.89%
rd73	9	10	503	45567	28125	65625	2.3	11	313	45567	28038	18240	2.88	0	0.00%	-87	0.31%
squar5	9	10	440	31815	19098	12984	1.39	11	309	31342	18930	12566	1.80	-473	1.49%	-168	0.88%
wim	9	10	276	30145	18432	12082	1.60	11	309	29291	17955	11742	1.90	-854	2.83%	-477	2.59%
sym9	10	11	1175	137421	84426	196994	3.27	12	1186	137367	84393	54942	3.67	-54	0.04%	-33	0.04%
dc1	11	11	228	36363	22140	14576	1.21	12	252	35719	21750	14328	1.57	-644	1.77%	-390	1.76%
rd84	11	12	2063	303672	184290	121468	50.58	13	2076	303672	184245	121488	53.27	0	0.00%	-45	0.02%
cycle10	12	12	27	3182	1908	1272	0.14	15	113	1025	1032	448	0.23	-2157	67.79%	-876	45.91%
pm1	12	14	1580	427692	259134	171112	132.81	16	1624	425828	257880	170372	137.18	-1864	0.44%	-1254	0.48%
0410184	13	14	189	18108	10956	7238	0.13	17	199	14948	9057	5980	0.23	-3160	17.45%	-1899	17.33%
ham15	14	15	734	40510	25566	16156	13.68	18	734	34967	21963	13948	15.06	-5543	13.68%	-3603	14.09%
bw	15	18	2585	2690620	1614336	1076344	4678.56	18	3176	2598544	1566420	1039576	5367.99	-92076	3.42%	-47916	2.97%
Average														**-3401**	**16.63%**	**-1821**	**20.75%**

To summarize, we looked for function decompositions with a small common-set and allowed bi-decompositions only for the OR, AND, and MUX operator.

6   Conclusions

In this work, we proposed a mapping approach that starts with single-target gates and therefore significantly differs from the standard mapping approach that has been state-of-the-art for the last two decades. We observed that incorporating Boolean decomposition in the mapping process of single-target gates often leads to better quantum realizations. Motivated by this, we introduced an improved mapping scheme which uses a constant number of ancillary lines and exploits the Boolean decomposition when generating the quantum gate cascades for a given single-target gate. Including our approach results in quantum circuits with a smaller NCV quantum cost as well as a lower T-depth cost comparing to standard mapping results.

References

1. Devitt, S.J.: Classical control of large-scale quantum computers. In: Yamashita, S., Minato, S. (eds.) RC 2014. LNCS, vol. 8507, pp. 26–39. Springer, Heidelberg (2014)
2. Nielsen, M., Chuang, I.: Quantum Computation and Quantum Information. Cambridge Univ. Press (2000)
3. Fowler, A.G., Stephens, A.M., Groszkowski, P.: High-threshold universal quantum computation on the surface code. Physical Review A **80**, 052312 (2009)
4. Barenco, A., Bennett, C.H., Cleve, R., DiVinchenzo, D., Margolus, N., Shor, P., Sleator, T., Smolin, J., Weinfurter, H.: Elementary gates for quantum computation. Physical Review A **52**, 3457–3467 (1995)
5. Maslov, D., Dueck, G.W., Miller, D.M.: Toffoli network synthesis with templates. IEEE Trans. on CAD of Integrated Circuits and Systems **24**(6), 807–817 (2005)
6. De Vos, A., Van Rentergem, Y.: Young subgroups for reversible computers. Advances in Mathematics of Communications **2**(2), 183–200 (2008)
7. Soeken, M., Tague, L., Dueck, G.W., Drechsler, R.: Ancilla-free synthesis of large reversible functions using binary decision diagrams (2014). CoRR abs/1408.3955
8. Sasao, T.: AND-EXOR expressions and their optimization. In: Sasao, T., (ed.) Logic Synthesis and Optimization. Kluwer Academic Publisher, pp. 287–312 (1993)
9. Ashenhurst, R.L.: The decomposition of switching functions. In: Int'l Symp. on the Theory of Switching, pp. 74–116 (1957)
10. Curtis, H.A.: A new approach to the design of switching circuits. van Nostrand Princeton, NJ (1962)
11. Brayton, R.K.: Factoring logic functions. IBM Journal of Research and Development **31**(2), 187–198 (1987)
12. Sasao, T., Matsuura, M.: DECOMPOS: an integrated system for functional decomposition. In: Int'l Workshop on Logic Synthesis, pp. 471–477 (1998)
13. Mishchenko, A., Brayton, R.K., Chatterjee, S.: Boolean factoring and decomposition of logic networks. In: Int'l Conf. on Computer-Aided Design, pp. 38–44 (2008)

14. Mishchenko, A., Steinbach, B., Perkowski, M.A.: An algorithm for bi-decomposition of logic functions. In: Design Automation Conference, pp. 103–108 (2001)
15. Bertacco, V., Damiani, M.: The disjunctive decomposition of logic functions. In: Int'l Conf. on Computer-Aided Design, pp. 78–82 (1997)
16. Yang, C., Ciesielski, M.J.: BDS: a BDD-based logic optimization system. IEEE Trans. on CAD of Integrated Circuits and Systems **21**(7), 866–876 (2002)
17. Abdessaied, N., Soeken, M., Thomsen, M.K., Drechsler, R.: Upper bounds for reversible circuits based on Young subgroups. Information Processing Letters **114**(6), 282–286 (2014)
18. Van Rentergem, Y., De Vos, A., Storme, L.: Implementing an arbitrary reversible logic gate. Journal of Physics A: Mathematical and General **38**(16), 3555–3577 (2005)
19. Soeken, M., Frehse, S., Wille, R., Drechsler, R.: RevKit: A toolkit for reversible circuit design. Journal of Multiple-Valued Logic & Soft Computing **18**(1) (2012). RevKit is available at http://www.revkit.org
20. Vemuri, N., Kalla, P., Tessier, R.: BDD-based logic synthesis for LUT-based FPGAs. ACM Trans. Design Autom. Electr. Syst. **7**(4), 501–525 (2002)
21. Mishchenko, A., Perkowski, M.: Fast heuristic minimization of exclusive-sums-of-products. In: Int'l Workshop on Applications of the Reed-Muller Expansion in Circuit Design, pp. 242–250 (2001)

Towards Line-Aware Realizations of Expressions for HDL-Based Synthesis of Reversible Circuits

Zaid Al-Wardi[1], Robert Wille[1,2(✉)], and Rolf Drechsler[1,2]

[1] Institute of Computer Science, University of Bremen, Bremen, Germany
[2] Cyber-Physical Systems, DFKI GmbH, 28359 Bremen, Germany
rwille@informatik.uni-bremen.de

Abstract. *Hardware Description Languages* (HDLs) allow for the efficient synthesis of large and complex circuits. Consequently, researchers also investigated their potential in the domain of reversible logic. Here, existing HDL-based synthesis approaches suffer from the significant drawback of employing additional circuit lines in order to buffer intermediate results. In this work, we investigate the possibility of reducing this overhead. For this purpose, an alternative synthesis scheme is proposed and evaluated which aims at a more efficient realization of expressions. The general idea is to re-compute (i.e to undo) sub-expressions as soon as the respective intermediate results are not needed anymore. The observations and discussions result in initial guidelines on how to realize expressions more efficiently as well as a better understanding of the potential of HDL-based synthesis.

Keywords: Reversible circuits · Synthesis · Hardware description languages · Optimization

1   Introduction

Motivated by applications e.g. in quantum computation [1], low-power design [2], or encoder and decoder design [3], research in the design of *reversible circuits* received significant interest. In the past decade, some substantial progress has been achieved in the development of corresponding (automated) design methods. This led to a variety of design solutions for a wide range of design tasks such as synthesis (see e.g. [4–8]), optimization (see e.g. [9,10]), verification (see e.g. [11, 12]), debugging (see e.g. [13]), and even automatic test pattern generation (see e.g. [14,15]).

Each design scenario results in a different circuit with equivalent functionality but with different cost parameters. In general, reversible circuit designers tend to synthesize circuits with a minimum number of lines. This is mainly motivated by the possible applications of reversible circuits in the domain of quantum computing, where circuit lines (realized by so-called qubits) are a very limited resource [1]. However, circuits with a minimal number of lines can, thus far, only been guaranteed by approaches that rely on Boolean/truth-table like synthesis

© Springer International Publishing Switzerland 2015
J. Krivine and J.-B. Stefani (Eds.): RC 2015, LNCS 9138, pp. 233–247, 2015.
DOI: 10.1007/978-3-319-20860-2_15

approaches (e.g. [4–6]). These methods expand exponentially depending on the number of circuit inputs, which lead to the fact that these methods are practically applicable for simple design problems with a limited number of input signals only.

Investigating design flows that scale better and have the ability to handle complex systems with hundreds of input signals led to the hierarchical design approaches based on *Hardware Description Languages* (HDLs). *SyReC* is a reversible HDL, which has been introduced to facilitate the description of reversible circuits by means of simple high level codes [16]. A corresponding synthesis scheme showed the ability to describe and synthesize complex functionality such as a reversible CPU[17].

However, a major drawback of this approach is that it requires a significant number of additional circuit lines. These additional lines are used to buffer intermediate results needed in order to realize entire HDL-statements. Although first approaches aiming at the reduction of additional lines in HDL-based circuits have been introduced [18], they mainly focused on the realization of entire statements. However, further potential exists when also the realization of expressions (used in statements) are considered. This is motivated in more detail later in Section 3.

In this work, we investigate the possibility of improving the realization of expressions within the HDL-based synthesis of reversible circuits. The general idea is to re-compute (i.e. to undo) intermediate results of expressions as soon as they are not needed anymore. While this basically continues the idea of the "reversible undo" to the circuit realization of expressions, it also leads to new questions on how to realize the respective expressions in detail. Hence, we discuss some of the respective cases and provide suggestions on how to handle them best. Experimental case studies confirm the findings. This eventually provides new insights as well as ideas on how to improve HDL-based synthesis in general and leads to a better understanding of the remaining potential.

The remainder of this paper is structured as follows. The next section briefly reviews the background on reversible circuits, the HDL considered here, as well as the corresponding HDL-based synthesis scheme. Section 3 provides a motivation of this work and illustrates the general idea which, eventually, leads to an improved HDL-based synthesis scheme proposed in Section 4. Observations and discussions on the applicability of the proposed approach are given in Section 5. This is finally confirmed by an experimental case study summarized in Section 6 before the paper is concluded in Section 7.

2   Background

This section briefly reviews the basics on reversible circuits, a reversible HDL, as well as the corresponding HDL-based synthesis. It provides the necessary background to keep the paper self-contained.

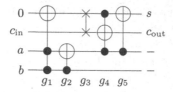

Fig. 1. Reversible circuit realizing a full adder

2.1   Reversible Circuits

Reversible circuits realize functions $f : \mathbb{B}^n \to \mathbb{B}^n$ with a unique input/output mapping, i.e. bijections. A reversible circuit $G = g_1 \ldots g_d$ is composed as a cascade of reversible gates g_i [1]. The inverse of G (representing the function f^{-1} and denoted by G^{-1}) can be obtained by cascading $g_d^{-1} g_{d-1}^{-1} \cdots g_1^{-1}$, where g_i^{-1} is the inverse gate of g_i. Since the self-inverse Toffoli and Fredkin gates are considered in this paper (see below), $g_i = g_i^{-1}$ holds and, thus, G^{-1} can simply be obtained by reversing the order of the gates of G.

For a set of Boolean signals $X = \{x_1, \ldots, x_n\}$, a *reversible gate* has the form $g(C, T)$, where $C = \{x_{i_1}, \ldots, x_{i_k}\} \subset X$ is the set of *control lines* and $T = \{x_{j_1}, \ldots, x_{j_l}\} \subseteq X$ with $C \cap T = \emptyset$ is the non-empty set of *target lines*. The gate operation is applied to the target lines if, and only if, all control lines meet the required control conditions. Control lines and unconnected lines always pass through the gate unaltered.

In the literature, several types of reversible gates have been introduced. Usually, circuits realized by *Toffoli gates* and *Fredkin gates* are considered. A Toffoli gate has a single target line x_j and uniquely maps the input $(x_1, x_2, \ldots, x_j, \ldots, x_n)$ to the output $(x_1, x_2, \ldots, x_{i_1} x_{i_2} \cdots x_{i_k} \oplus x_j, \ldots, x_n)$. That is, a Toffoli gate inverts the target line if, and only if, all control lines are assigned the logic value 1. A Fredkin gate has two target lines x_{j_1} and x_{j_2} and interchanges their values if, and only if, the conjunction of all control lines evaluates to 1.

By definition, reversible circuits can only realize reversible functions. In order to realize non-reversible functions, *additional circuit lines* with constant inputs and garbage outputs (i.e. don't care outputs) are applied (see e.g. [19,20]). Furthermore, additional circuit lines are also used frequently in hierarchical synthesis approaches (e.g. [7,16]).

Example 1. Fig. 1 shows a reversible circuit realization of a 1-bit adder. Black circles represent control lines while $\oplus$ and $\times$ represent the target lines of a Toffoli and Fredkin gate, respectively. Since the adder is a non-reversible function, one additional circuit line is used to realize this function as a reversible circuit. The gates g_1, g_2, g_4, and g_5 are Toffoli gates, while the gate g_3 is a Fredkin gate.

2.2   Reversible HDL

A major motivation of research in the domain of reversible circuit synthesis is the strive for a better scalability in order to enable the efficient design of complex

```
1  module example(in a(16), in b(16), in c(16), out f(16))
2    wire x(16)
3    x ^= (a & b)
4    x += (((a * b) + (a / b)) - ((a + c) / b))
5    f ^= (((x + b) ^ c) * ( a - b ))
```

Fig. 2. Simple SyReC program example

functionality. Consequently, HDLs became a focus of ongoing research. A first version of an HDL for reversible circuits named *SyReC* has been introduced in [16]. SyReC is based on the reversible software language *Janus* [21], which has been enriched by further concepts (e.g. declaring circuit signals of different bit-widths), new operations (e.g. bit-access and shifts), and some restrictions (e.g. the prohibition of dynamic loops). In the following, we briefly review the main concepts of this HDL by means of Fig. 2 which depicts a simple SyReC specification[1].

This simple example shows that an HDL-circuit is described as a module. A module declaration starts by naming the module and, then, declaring the port signals for this module as in Line 1. This signal list associates each signal name with a type (i.e. in/out) and a bit-width (16 in the example above). Internal wire signals are defined within the scope of the module (Line 2) and are intermediately used to simplify the internal description of a module. These signals are transparent outside of the module. All signals represent non-negative integers or, in case of bit-width of 1, a Boolean.

A variety of statements and expressions are available to specify the functionality of the circuit without losing reversibility. Because of this, direct signal assignments of the form $(x = a)$ are not allowed (as this would lead to a loss of the original value of x and, hence, will make the computation non-reversible). Consequently, signal assignments are restricted to so-called *reversible assignment operations*, i.e. the operations increase (+=), decrease (-=), and bit-wise XOR (^=). These operations preserve the reversibility (i.e. it is possible to compute these operations in both directions) and they are generally denoted by $\oplus =$.

In contrast to the reversible operations, *binary operations* (denoted by $\odot$) which are not necessarily reversible (e.g. arithmetic, bit-wise, logical, or relational operations) and to be used only in right-hand expressions which preserve the values of the respective inputs. In doing so, all computations remain reversible since the input values can be applied to reverse any operation. For example, to specify the AND-operation in Line 3, a new free signal x in combination with a reversible assignment operation is applied. That results in the statement $x ^\wedge = (a\&b)$. All binary operations are written in the form: $(Operand_{left} \odot Operand_{right})$. An *Operand* can be a simple *signal*, an *integer*, or even another *expression* that has

---

[1] For a more detailed treatment, we refer to [16] as well as to the detailed documentation provided at the RevLib benchmark webpage [22].

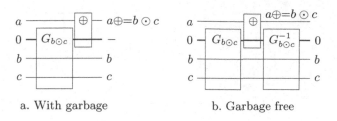

a. With garbage   b. Garbage free

Fig. 3. Synthesis scheme

the same form. Nesting binary operations in such hierarchy, gives SyReC the ability to generate complex functions out of this basic set of binary-operators.

2.3   HDL-Based Synthesis

In order to automatically synthesize the resulting designs, a hierarchical synthesis method is applied [16]. That is, existing realizations of the individual operations (i.e. building blocks) are combined so that the desired circuit is built. Fig. 3a illustrates the resulting scheme for the (generic) statement a $\oplus=$ (b $\odot$ c). The $\oplus$-block ($\odot$-block) denotes thereby a building block for a reversible assignment operation (expression). Solid lines that cross the box represent the signals on the right-hand side of the statement, i.e. the signals whose values are preserved.

More precisely, the following two steps are performed:

1. Compose a sub-circuit $G_\odot$ realizing all the right-hand side expressions in the statement. For this purpose, use the respective building blocks. The result of the expression is buffered by means of additional circuit lines with constant input values.
2. Compose a sub-circuit $G_\oplus$ realizing the overall statement using the existing building blocks of the statement itself together with the buffered results of the expressions.

Obviously, this procedure leads to a significant number of additional circuit lines (and corresponding garbage outputs), since new circuit lines with constant values have to be introduced for each statement. Hence, an alternative has been evaluated in [18] where partial results (buffered in additional circuit lines) are inversely re-computed as soon as they are not needed anymore. This process (also called *reversible undo*) yields the original (constant) values on the already existing circuit lines which can be re-used e.g. in order to realize the following statements. More precisely, the synthesis scheme reviewed above is extended by a third step (see also Fig. 3b):

3) Add the inverse circuit from Step 1, i.e. $G_\odot^{-1}$ to the circuit in order to set the circuit lines buffering the result of the right-hand side expressions back to the constant 0.

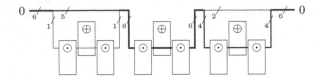

Fig. 4. Effect of the expression size

In other words, the first sub-circuit $G_{b\odot c}$ ensures that the right-hand side expression is realized, sub-circuit $G_{a\oplus=b\odot c}$ ensures that the entire statement is realized, and sub-circuit $G_{b\odot c}^{-1}$ sets the circuit lines buffering the result of $b \odot c$ back to the constant 0.

3   Motivation and General Idea

Following the synthesis scheme reviewed in Section 2.3, the number of additionally required lines for the entire circuit depends on the statement with the "largest" expression. This is illustrated by means of the following example.

Example 2. Consider a sequence of three statements to be synthesized. Additionally, assume that 1, 6, and 4 circuit lines are needed to realize the respective expressions. Then, in total $\max\{1, 6, 4\} = 6$ additional circuit lines are needed to realize the respective circuit. Fig. 4 illustrates how these circuit lines are applied.

However, in many cases, even large expressions can be realized with a significantly smaller number of lines. To this end, consider the realization of arbitrary expressions. Expressions can be formulated as a variety of combinations of binary operations $\odot$ over circuit signals and (nested) sub-expressions. Each expression can thereby be represented as a binary-tree, where each node represents a binary operator which receives two inputs (operands) and buffers an output. The root node represents the entire expression, while the leafs represent the circuit signals. Obviously, it is impractical to provide a building block for each and every of such combinations. Hence, only building blocks (denoted by G_O) for each binary operation O are provided. Then, an expression E is realized by cascading the respective building blocks for each binary operation $\odot$ of E. For this purpose, additional circuit lines are required in order to buffer the respective intermediate results. The eventually resulting circuit is denoted by G_{E_i}, whereby i denotes the index of the root node of the expression E. This circuit requires a total of $(k \times w)$ additional circuits lines in order to buffer the intermediate results of the binary operations, whereby w denotes the bit-width of the circuit signals and k is the number of binary-operations (nodes) in the expression.

Example 3. Consider the expression E=(((a * b) + (a / b)) - ((a + c) / b)) which has been taken from Line 4 of the SyReC code shown in Fig. 2 and is composed of six binary expressions over 16-bit signals. The binary tree for this expression is shown in Fig. 5. Each node represents a binary operation (enumerated

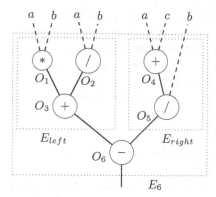

Fig. 5. The binary tree for the expression in Fig. 2 Line 5

from O_1 to O_6) to be realized using the respective building blocks (i.e. $G_{O_1}, \ldots,$ G_{O_6}). This leads to a reversible circuit $G_{E_6} = G_{O_1} \, G_{O_2} \, G_{O_3} \, G_{O_4} \, G_{O_5} \, G_{O_6}$ which requires a total of $6 \times 16 = 96$ additional circuits lines in order buffer the respective intermediate results.

When realizing such an expression, it is obvious that, eventually, only the result of the root operation is of interest. Circuit lines storing intermediate results can be re-computed back to their initial (constant) value as soon as they are not required anymore. Then, those lines would, in principle, be available to store other intermediate results needed in order to compute the overall expression. As a consequence, even large expressions could be realized with a significantly smaller number of additional circuit lines compared to the currently applied synthesis scheme. Again, this is illustrated by means of an example.

Example 4. Consider again the expression $\mathtt{E} = (((\mathtt{a} * \mathtt{b}) + (\mathtt{a}/\mathtt{b})) - ((\mathtt{a} + \mathtt{c})/\mathtt{b}))$ from Example 3, which contains 6 operations. The actually desired result of the root operation (the subtraction O_6) is obtained using the intermediate results from the sub-expressions $E_{left} = ((\mathtt{a} * \mathtt{b}) + (\mathtt{a}/\mathtt{b}))$ and $E_{right} = ((\mathtt{a} + \mathtt{c})/\mathtt{b})$. The left sub-expression is realized as $G_{E_{left}} = G_{O_1} \, G_{O_2} \, G_{O_3}$ which requires a total of $3 \times 16 = 48$ additional circuit lines. However, once this sub-expression is realized and its result is buffered, the intermediate results of operations O_1 and O_2 are not needed anymore and can be recomputed back to their initial (constant) value – resulting in a circuit $G'_{E_{left}} = G_{O_1} \, G_{O_2} \, G_{O_3} G_{O_2}^{-1} \, G_{O_1}^{-1}$. By this, 32 circuit lines with constant values become available and can be used in order to realize the right sub-expression. The entire expression E is then realized as

$$G_{E_6} = G'_{E_{left}} \, G_{E_{right}} \, G_{O_6} = G_{O_1} \, G_{O_2} \, G_{O_3} \, G_{O_2}^{-1} \, G_{O_1}^{-1} \, G_{O_4} \, G_{O_5} \, G_{O_6}$$

and requires a total of 64 additional circuit lines (a significant reduction compared to the 96 additional circuit lines needed in Example 3).

Note that, in the following, we denote (sub-)circuits which immediately re-compute all not needed intermediate results back to the initial (constant) value by G'.

In this work, we are aiming for investigating this potential in more detail. For this purpose, we propose a revised synthesis scheme for hardware description languages which re-computes circuit lines buffering intermediate results back to their initial (constant) value as soon as the respective intermediate value is not needed anymore. Afterwards, the effect as well as the possibilities of these changes in HDL-based synthesis are discussed in Section 5 and experimentally evaluated in Section 6.

4   Line-Aware Synthesis of Expressions

Left and right operands in a binary expression E are independently considered as shown in Fig. 5. Therefore, they can be synthesized as two different building blocks $G_{E_{left}}$ and $G_{E_{right}}$, respectively. Afterwards, the corresponding results are fed to the building block G_{O_k} realizing the root-operation O_k. Now, realizing the left sub-expression not according to the original synthesis scheme (i.e. as $G_{E_{left}}$), but according to the ideas sketched in the previous section (i.e. as $G'_{E_{left}}$), circuit lines applied in order to store intermediate results from E_{left} can be re-used for the realization of E_{right}. Then, the overall expression E can be realized as follows:

$$G_{E_k} \;=\; G'_{E_{left}} \; G_{E_{right}} \; G_{O_k}$$

This scheme can recursively be applied for all sub-expressions eventually leading to the following (proposed) synthesis procedure:

Given An expression E to be realized,
       An indication whether a circuit G or a circuit G' shall be realized
  1. **IF** (E is a circuit signal only), **THEN** terminate the execution of this algorithm (base case of the recursion).
     ELSE, consider $E = E_{left} \odot E_{right}$ with $\odot$ being the root-operation O_k realized by G_{O_k}.
  2. Recursively invoke this algorithm for expression E_{left} in order to generate a sub-circuit $G'_{E_{left}}$ realizing the left-operand.
  3. Recursively invoke this algorithm in order to to generate a sub-circuit $G_{E_{right}}$ realizing the right-operand.
  4. Combine the resulting sub-circuits to the following cascade:
     $G := G'_{E_{left}} \; G_{E_{right}} \; G_{O_k}$
  5. **IF** a circuit G' shall be realized **THEN**, re-compute intermediate results by adding the respective building blocks in a reverse fashion, i.e. extend the circuit to the following cascade:
     $G' := G \; G_{E_{right}}^{-1} \; G_{E_{left}}'^{-1}$

5   Observations and Discussion

Having the scheme proposed in the previous section, a detailed analysis and discussion on the potential of re-computing intermediate results as soon as possible can be conducted. This section is devoted to that. More precisely, several cases are discussed showcasing when the application of the proposed algorithm is beneficial and when it may turn out to be disadvantageous. This can be used to get inspirations for best practices as well as an understanding of the characteristics that apply when synthesizing HDL descriptions as reversible circuits.

5.1 Reducing the Number of Lines Is Not Always Rewarding

The ideas in the proposed synthesis scheme are based on the desire of reducing the number of lines in the resulting circuit. The total number of additionally required circuit lines is still bounded by the number of lines required for synthesizing the largest statement. Hence, improving the number of lines for a "smaller" statement does not really help in reducing the total number of lines in the circuit. Moreover, reducing the number of lines for this smaller statement leads to additional circuit costs, since re-computing intermediate results is conducted by adding further building blocks in a reverse fashion.

Example 5. Consider again the program from Fig. 2 as well as the sketch of its realization in Fig. 4. As can be seen, the statement in Line 4 has the largest expression and would require 6 additional circuit lines when synthesized using the original synthesis approach[2]. The statement in Line 5 has the second-largest expression and would require 4 additional circuit lines.

Now, if the synthesis approach proposed in Section 4 is applied in order to realize the largest expression, a reduction from 6 additional circuit lines to 4 circuit lines can be achieved. This is worthwhile as it indeed reduces the total number of circuit lines required for the entire circuit. However, applying the same scheme in order to improve the the second-largest expression does not lead to further global reductions. Although the expression itself could be realized with 3 rather than 4 additional circuit lines, the number of lines for the entire circuit would not change. Moreover, this reduction would increase the number of building blocks required for re-computing. Hence, this expression should be realized using the original synthesis scheme.

5.2 The Shape of the Expression Tree Has an Impact

In contrast to the original synthesis scheme (reviewed in Section 2.3), the proposed synthesis scheme from Section 4 depends on the operation precedence within the expression. In the worst case, the proposed procedure results in the same result as when the original scheme would have been applied. This worst case occurs whenever all operations in the expression have a primary value (i.e. a signal or a number) as an operand. Then, the circuit lines can not be re-used until the root operation is calculated. In this case, a circuit with a linear number of lines results, i.e. with k additional circuit lines and k building blocks (k

---

[2] Note that the number of circuit lines has to be multiplied by the bit-width w of the circuit signals, however, is assumed to be constant and, hence, omitted for sake of clarity.

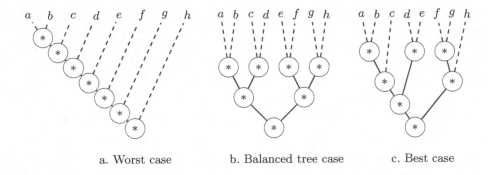

a. Worst case   b. Balanced tree case   c. Best case

Fig. 6. Expressions with seven multiplication in different orders of precedence

being the number of operations). An example of such case is shown in Fig. 6a. This case occurs when the precedence of operations is ordered either from left to right, or vice versa.

On the other hand, an expression which can be represented by a completely balanced tree can be realized with a logarithmic number of lines. Then, both operands always require the same number of lines which can frequently been re-computed and, hence, re-used. However, as already mentioned above, this comes with the price of larger gate costs as additional building blocks are required[3]. More precisely, this case would result in a circuit with $2 \cdot (\lceil log_2(k+1) \rceil) - 1$ additional circuit lines and $3^{(\lceil log_2(k+1) \rceil - 1)}$ building blocks. An example of such a case is shown in Fig. 6b.

The best case, which shows the biggest potential for the proposed procedure with respect to the number of lines, is observed when, for all the stages of the expression, the right operand requires exactly one circuit line less than the left operand. Then, the right operand can always reuse the buffers lines from the left operand and does not need to allocate an own one. An example of such a case is shown in Fig. 6c. The number of resulting circuit lines for this best can be approximated by the function $f(n) = f(n-1) + f(n-2) + 1$, whereby $f(0) = 0$ and $f(1) = 1$ (this sequence is related to the *Fibonacci sequence*), for example, if there are $n = 6$ lines, then $f(6) = 20$, i.e. an expression arranged in the best case with up to 20 operations, can be calculated by using 6 lines. With increasing k, the reduction ratio in the number of lines becomes even better – although, it is, practically, unlikely for such a single expression to occur in typical HDL statements.

Example 6. The following three expressions are actually equivalent to each other, each has 7 multiplication operations and the result is simply the product:

1. $((((((((a * b) * c) * d) * e) * f) * g) * h)$
   This case represent the worst case. It requires 7 additional circuit signals and requires 7 cascaded blocks to be realized.

---

[3] In this sense, the proposed synthesis scheme goes in line with previous observations on the trade-off between circuit lines and gate costs as e.g. conducted in [23].

2. $(((a*b)*(c*d))*((e*f)*(g*h)))$

   This case is the completely balanced case, which requires 5 additional circuit signals, but 9 cascaded blocks.
3. $((((a*b)*c)*(d*e))*((f*g)*h))$

   This case is the best case where only 4 additional circuit signals are sufficient to realize the circuit by cascading 12 basic blocks.

For a designer writing HDL programs to be synthesized as a reversible circuit, it is important to be aware of the synthesizer features when writing the expression in order to write expressions, whenever possible, in the way that result in better circuits.

5.3   Exchanging the Sub-expressions Has an Impact

As long as the left and right sub-expressions of an expression E are calculated independently, it is possible to exchange the order by which the respective sub-circuits are synthesized. This can be exploited when the right sub-expression requires a larger number of additional circuit lines for buffering intermediate results. Then, the expression E should be realized as $G := G'_{E_{right}} G_{E_{left}} G_{O_k}$. This has a slight benefit (precisely one signal is saved) compared to the original order: If the larger sub-expression is realized first, more signals can be re-computed. One of them can be used to buffer the result of the larger sub-expression. This signal is not needed to realize the other sub-expression since, as assumed before, this sub-expression is smaller. Because of the recurrent nature of the procedure, this one line reduction can be accumulated and result in a tangible reduction in the number of lines.

If the two expressions require the same number of signals, then no improvement with respect to the number of signals can be gained. Nevertheless, even then it might be beneficial to switch the sub-expressions. In fact, the sub-expression realized first is subject to an early re-computation. This gets more expensive for more "costly" operations. Hence, in case both sub-expressions require the same number of signals, the sub-expression with the "cheaper" building blocks should be realized first. This is illustrated by the following example.

Example 7. Consider E_{left} =((a*b)*(c*d)) and E_{right} =((a^b)^(c^d)). If E_{left} is synthesized first, a circuit $G'_{E_{left}} := G_{O_1} G_{O_2} G_{O_3} G_{O_2}^{-1} G_{O_1}^{-1}$ has to be generated, i.e. five building blocks for multiplication are required. The right sub-expression is then realized by $G_{E_{right}} := G_{O_1} G_{O_2} G_{O_3}$, i.e. three building blocks for the XOR operation are required. Exchanging the order would reverse that, i.e. result in five building blocks for the XOR operation and three building blocks for the multiplication. Since the realization of the multiplication requires a more expensive building block compared to the realization of the XOR operation, this would result in a much cheaper circuit.

Note that if the realization of the sub-expression is switched, this exchange must also be reflected in the respective re-computing cascade. That is, a corresponding circuit would have to be defined as $G' := G G_{E_{left}}^{-1} G_{E_{right}}'^{-1}$, i.e. again with the right and left sub-circuit interchanged.

6   Experimental Case Studies

In order to experimentally evaluate the proposed concepts as well as the considered cases, the proposed synthesis approach has been implemented in C++. The resulting algorithm can be applied to various expressions and determines the number of lines as well as the number of required building blocks of the respectively resulting realization.

A main problem for the evaluation is that, thus far, not a very huge variety of HDL descriptions which are useful for benchmarking are available.

Hence, we manually created an initial benchmark set composed of two types of expressions which cover different cases, namely a *polynomial factored form* and a *majority function*.

These cases offer properties allowing to evaluate the behavior of representations e.g. in terms of a balanced tree or in the best possible case as discussed in Section 5.

In the following, the respective cases will explicitly be discussed. In addition to that, Table 1 provides a numerical summary. The first columns denote thereby the name of the respective case (*Case*), its order (*Order*, i.e. the size of the respective instantiation, and the number of operations in the resulting expression (*Op.*). Afterwards, the number of additionally required lines (*Lines*[4]) as well as the number of Blocks (*Blocks*) are provided for (1) the original synthesis approach as reviewed in Section 2.3 (*Orig. synth.*), (2) the proposed synthesis approach assuming the expression is/can be represented in terms of a balanced tree (*Balanced tree*), and (3) the proposed synthesis approach assuming the expression is/can be represented in the best case (*Best case*). In addition to the absolute values, also the percentual difference to the original synthesis approach is provided in columns labeled by %.

Already the numerical evaluation shows the potential of the proposed synthesis approach. In fact, significant reductions in the number of lines can be achieved. As discussed above, this comes at the price of an increased number of building blocks. In this sense, the proposed synthesis scheme goes in line with previous observations on the trade-off between circuit lines and gate costs as e.g. conducted in [23]. More detailed discussions follow with respect to the considered cases.

6.1   Polynomial Factored Form

The first case considers polynomials in the factored form, i.e. expressions of the form

$$(x + a_1)(x + a_2)\dots(x + a_m),$$

where m is the order of the polynomial. This form contains $(2 \times m - 1)$ operations and has been chosen to demonstrate a fully balanced-tree expression. In fact, this

---

[4] Note that, again, the number of circuit lines has to be multiplied by the bit-width w of the circuit signals which, however, is assumed to be constant and, hence, omitted for sake of clarity.

Table 1. Experimental case studies

Case	Order	Op. (k)	Orig. synth.		Balanced tree			Best case		
			Lines	Blocks	Lines	%	Blocks	Lines	%	Blocks
Factored Polynommial	4	7	7	7	5	29%	9	5	29%	15
	8	15	15	15	7	53%	27	6	60%	41
	16	31	31	31	9	71%	81	8	74%	205
Majority function	3	5	5	5	4	20%	7	4	20%	7
	5	29	29	29	8	72%	102	8	72%	170

expression can be structured in a fashion so that sub-expressions of equal length result. This allows to represent the entire expression in terms of a balanced-tree. We can see from that the tendency to make both operands of the same size can dramatically decrease the number of additionally required lines. Furthermore, it can be noticed from Table 1 that the best case is not that much better in terms of the number of lines. In contrast, this may lead to significantly higher cost with respect to the needed building blocks.

6.2   Majority Function

The second case is considered in order to evaluate the algorithm on a logical expression that lacks the possibility to get represented either in form of a balanced tree or a best case tree. This case is carried out with the majority function, i.e. a Boolean function defined to determine if the majority of inputs are set to 1 or not. Two sub-cases are considered: the first is the majority of three inputs which is defined in the sum-of-products form as $(a\&b)|(a\&c)|(b\&c)$ and an according version for five inputs. For the first sub-case, this function shows only a slight change in the number of additionally required circuit lines, while the second sub-case unveils drastic reductions.

7   Conclusion

In this work, an alternative procedure for HDL-based synthesis has been proposed which focused on a line-aware realization of expressions. The general idea was to re-compute intermediate results as soon as they are not needed anymore. By this, a significant amount of circuit lines can be saved. Nevertheless, the applicability of the proposed scheme significantly depends on the respectively applied expressions. Hence, we discussed possible cases and, by this, provided a better insight into the possible potential. Experimental case studies confirmed the findings. Future work will focus on the development of strategies for code optimization, e.g. term rewriting techniques that best exploit the potential of the proposed synthesis method. Besides that, how to reduce the number of required building blocks and, hence, the resulting gate costs of the obtained circuit remains an open issue to be addressed.

References

1. Nielsen, M., Chuang, I.: Quantum Computation and Quantum Information. Cambridge Univ. Press (2000)
2. Berut, A., Arakelyan, A., Petrosyan, A., Ciliberto, S., Dillenschneider, R., Lutz, E.: Experimental verification of Landauer's principle linking information and thermodynamics. Nature **483**, 187–189 (2012)
3. Wille, R., Drechsler, R., Oswald, C., Garcia-Ortiz, A.: Automatic design of low-power encoders using reversible circuit synthesis. In: Design, Automation and Test in Europe, pp. 1036–1041 (2012)
4. Miller, D.M., Maslov, D., Dueck, G.W.: A transformation based algorithm for reversible logic synthesis. In: Design Automation Conf., pp. 318–323 (2003)
5. Shende, V.V., Prasad, A.K., Markov, I.L., Hayes, J.P.: Synthesis of reversible logic circuits. IEEE Trans. on CAD **22**(6), 710–722 (2003)
6. Wille, R., Le, H.M., Dueck, G.W., Große, D.: Quantified synthesis of reversible logic. In: Design, Automation and Test in Europe, pp. 1015–1020 (2008)
7. Wille, R., Drechsler, R.: BDD-based synthesis of reversible logic for large functions. In: Design Automation Conf., pp. 270–275 (2009)
8. Soeken, M., Wille, R., Hilken, C., Przigoda, N., Drechsler, R.: Synthesis of reversible circuits with minimal lines for large functions. In: ASP Design Automation Conf., pp. 85–92 (2012)
9. Feinstein, D.Y., Thornton, M.A., Miller, D.M.: Partially redundant logic detection using symbolic equivalence checking in reversible and irreversible logic circuits. In: Design, Automation and Test in Europe, pp. 1378–1381 (2008)
10. Soeken, M., Wille, R., Dueck, G.W., Drechsler, R.: Window optimization of reversible and quantum circuits. In: IEEE Symposium on Design and Diagnostics of Electronic Circuits and Systems (2010)
11. Viamontes, G.F., Markov, I.L., Hayes, J.P.: Checking equivalence of quantum circuits and states. In: Int'l Conf. on CAD, pp. 69–74 (2007)
12. Wang, S.A., Lu, C.Y., Tsai, I.M., Kuo, S.Y.: An XQDD-based verification method for quantum circuits. IEICE Transactions **91−A**(2), 584–594 (2008)
13. Wille, R., Große, D., Frehse, S., Dueck, G.W., Drechsler, R.: Debugging of toffoli networks. In: Design, Automation and Test in Europe, pp. 1284–1289 (2009)
14. Polian, I., Fiehn, T., Becker, B., Hayes, J.P.: A family of logical fault models for reversible circuits. In: Asian Test Symp., pp. 422–427 (2005)
15. Wille, R., Zhang, H., Drechsler, R.: ATPG for reversible circuits using simulation, boolean satisfiability, and pseudo boolean optimization. In: IEEE Annual Symposium on VLSI, pp. 120–125 (2011)
16. Wille, R., Offermann, S., Drechsler, R.: SyReC: A programming language forsynthesis of reversible circuits. In: Forum on Specification and Design Languages. pp. 184–189. Springer, Heidelberg (2010)
17. Wille, R., Soeken, M., Große, D., Schönborn, E., Drechsler, R.: Designing a RISC CPU in reversible logic. In: Int'l Symp. on Multi-Valued Logic, pp. 170–175 (2011)
18. Wille, R., Soeken, M., Schönborn, E., Drechsler, R.: Circuit line minimization in the HDL-based synthesis of reversible logic. In: IEEE Annual Symposium on VLSI, pp. 213–218 (2012)
19. Maslov, D., Dueck, G.W.: Reversible cascades with minimal garbage. IEEE Trans. on CAD **23**(11), 1497–1509 (2004)
20. Wille, R., Keszöcze, O., Drechsler, R.: Determining the minimal number of lines for large reversible circuits. In: Design, Automation and Test in Europe, pp. 1204–1207 (2011)

21. Yokoyama, T., Glück, R.: A reversible programming language and its invertible self-interpreter. In: Symp. on Partial Evaluation and Semantics-Based Program Manipulation, pp. 144–153 (2007)
22. Wille, R., Große, D., Teuber, L., Dueck, G.W., Drechsler, R.: RevLib: an online resource for reversible functions and reversible circuits. In: Int'l Symp. on Multi-Valued Logic, pp. 220–225 (2008). RevLib is available at http://www.revlib.org
23. Wille, R., Soeken, M., Miller, D.M., Drechsler, R.: Trading off circuit lines and gate costs in the synthesis of reversible logic. INTEGRATION, the VLSI Jour. **47**(2), 284–294 (2014)

Synthesis of Quantum Circuits for Dedicated Physical Machine Descriptions

Philipp Niemann[1], Saikat Basu[2], Amlan Chakrabarti[2], Niraj K. Jha[3], and Robert Wille[1,4](✉)

[1] Institute of Computer Science, University of Bremen, D-28359 Bremen, Germany
pniemann@informatik.uni-bremen.de
[2] A.K. Choudhury School of I.T, University of Calcutta, Calcutta, India
acakcs@caluniv.ac.in
[3] Department of Electrical Engineering,
Princeton University, Princeton, NJ 08544, USA
jha@princeton.edu
[4] Cyber-Physical Systems, DFKI GmbH, D-28359 Bremen, Germany
rwille@informatik.uni-bremen.de

Abstract. Quantum computing has been attracting increasing attention in recent years because of the rapid advancements that have been made in quantum algorithms and quantum system design. Quantum algorithms are implemented with the help of quantum circuits. These circuits are inherently reversible in nature and often contain a sizeable Boolean part that needs to be synthesized. Consequently, a large body of research has focused on the synthesis of corresponding reversible circuits and their mapping to the quantum operations supported by the quantum system. However, reversible circuit synthesis has usually not been performed with any particular target technology in mind, but with respect to an abstract cost metric. When targeting actual physical implementations of the circuits, the adequateness of such an approach is unclear. In this paper, we explicitly target synthesis of quantum circuits at selected quantum technologies described through their *Physical Machine Descriptions* (PMDs). We extend the state-of-the-art synthesis flow in order to realize quantum circuits based on just the primitive quantum operations supported by the respective PMDs. Using this extended flow, we evaluate whether the established reversible circuit synthesis methods and metrics are still applicable and adequate for PMD-specific implementations.

1 Introduction

Supporting the design of quantum circuits is one of the main applications of reversible logic. Quantum circuits [1] promise to significantly speed up solutions for computing problems of practical interest. This is enabled by quantum mechanical properties, such as superposition and entanglement. Quantum circuits execute a sequence of quantum operations. These quantum operations are inherently reversible. Often, significant parts of a quantum computation (e.g., database search [2] and modular exponentiation [3]) are Boolean in nature.

© Springer International Publishing Switzerland 2015
J. Krivine and J.-B. Stefani (Eds.): RC 2015, LNCS 9138, pp. 248–264, 2015.
DOI: 10.1007/978-3-319-20860-2_16

Thus, leveraging existing reversible logic synthesis methods for implementing those parts is an obvious first step.

Over the past few years, a popular synthesis flow has been to

- realize the desired functionality as a reversible circuit and
- map the resulting reversible circuit to an equivalent cascade of quantum gates/operations.

A large body of research has been targeted at both these steps (e.g., reversible circuit synthesis [4–9] and mapping to quantum circuits [10–13]). Most of these methods target NOT, controlled-NOT, and controlled-**V** as the set of primitive quantum operations. This set is popularly referred to as *NCV* and its use was originally motivated by one of the first works on reversible-to-quantum circuit mapping by Barenco et al. [10]. However, several new quantum systems have emerged in recent years. The ARDA quantum computing roadmap [14] lists some of them. These systems are described using *Physical Machine Descriptions* (PMDs) [15]. They describe different technologies for the realization of quantum circuits based on the respective quantum mechanical properties. Moreover, each PMD supports a specific set of primitive quantum operations. Thus, mapping a quantum circuit to a PMD is not yet compatible with the established synthesis flow that targets NCV-based circuit implementations only.

In this work, we investigate and evaluate the applicability of the state-of-the-art NCV-based synthesis flow, which has emerged over the last 10-20 years, for mapping quantum circuits to a particular PMD [15]. We first review today's established NCV-based synthesis steps. Then, we propose extensions to this flow, e.g., mapping schemes from reversible circuits or NCV-based quantum circuits to PMD-specific quantum circuits, and analyze the circuit cost. Finally, we perform an experimental evaluation to a) compare synthesis flows with different extensions and b) investigate whether the established synthesis methods and metrics are still applicable and adequate for the PMD-specific circuit realization. This can throw light on the drawbacks and provide potential for improvements in quantum circuit synthesis.

The remainder of this paper is organized as follows. The next section briefly reviews the basics of quantum and reversible circuits. Then, a review of the PMDs targeted in this work is provided in Section 3. Section 4 describes the synthesis flows. First, the state-of-the-art synthesis flow is discussed, followed by its extension to a PMD-specific synthesis flow. Then, the cost metrics used in the evaluation are described in Section 5. The evaluation and discussion follow in Section 6 and the paper is concluded in Section 7.

2   Background

This section reviews the basics of quantum and reversible circuits.

2.1   Quantum Circuits

First, we discuss the preliminaries of quantum logic. Quantum operations manipulate qubits rather than classical bits. A qubit can represent 0 or 1 as well as superpositions of the two. More formally:

Definition 1. *A qubit is a two-level quantum system, described by a two-dimensional complex Hilbert space. Two orthogonal quantum states $|0\rangle \equiv \binom{1}{0}$ and $|1\rangle \equiv \binom{0}{1}$ are used to represent Boolean values 0 and 1. The state of a qubit may be written as $|x\rangle = \alpha|0\rangle + \beta|1\rangle$, where α and β are complex numbers and $|\alpha|^2 + |\beta|^2 = 1$.*

The quantum state of a single qubit is denoted by the vector $\binom{\alpha}{\beta}$. The state of a quantum system with $n > 1$ qubits is given by the tensor product of the respective state spaces and can be represented as a normalized vector of length 2^n, called the state vector.

According to the postulates of quantum mechanics, the evolution of a quantum system can be described by a series of transformation operations satisfying the following:

Definition 2. *A quantum operation over n qubits can be represented by a unitary matrix, i.e., a $2^n \times 2^n$ matrix $\mathbf{U} = [u_{i,j}]_{2^n \times 2^n}$ with*

- *each entry $u_{i,j}$ assuming a complex value and*
- *the inverse $\mathbf{U}^{-1}$ of $\mathbf{U}$ being the conjugate transpose matrix (adjoint matrix) $\mathbf{U}^\dagger$ of $\mathbf{U}$ (i.e., $\mathbf{U}^{-1} = \mathbf{U}^\dagger$).*

Every quantum operation is reversible since the matrix that defines any quantum operation is invertible. At the end of the computation, a qubit can be measured, causing it to collapse to a basis state. Then, depending on the current state of the qubit, either a 0 (with probability $|\alpha|^2$) or a 1 (with probability $|\beta|^2$) results. The state of the qubit is destroyed by the act of measuring it.

Example 1. Consider the quantum operation H defined by the unitary matrix $\mathbf{H} = \frac{1}{\sqrt{2}}\left(\begin{smallmatrix} 1 & 1 \\ 1 & -1 \end{smallmatrix}\right)$, which is the well-known Hadamard operation [1]. Applying H to the input state $|x\rangle = \binom{1}{0}$, i.e., computing $\mathbf{H} \times |x\rangle$, yields a new quantum state $|x'\rangle = \frac{1}{\sqrt{2}}\binom{1}{1}$. In $|x'\rangle$, $\alpha = \beta = \frac{1}{\sqrt{2}}$. Measuring this qubit would either lead to a Boolean 0 or Boolean 1, each with probability $|\frac{1}{\sqrt{2}}|^2 = 0.5$. This computation represents one of the simplest quantum computers – a single-qubit random number generator.

Complex quantum operations are usually realized by a *quantum circuit*, which executes a series of elementary quantum operations using quantum *gates*. Such a composition of gates can be expressed by a direct matrix multiplication of the corresponding gate matrices. Alternatively, this process can be viewed as the implementation of a quantum algorithm in which a series of low-level quantum operations or quantum computational instructions is represented by a sequence of individual transformation (i.e., gate) matrices.

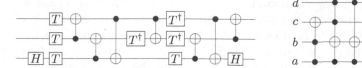

Fig. 1. A quantum circuit   **Fig. 2.** A reversible circuit

Example 2. Consider the 3-qubit quantum circuit shown in Fig. 1. It realizes a 2-controlled NOT operation known as the *Toffoli gate*. More precisely, the basis states of the third qubit are swapped if and only if the first and second qubits are in the $|1\rangle$-state. Conventionally, horizontal lines represent qubits. Operations $\boxed{H}$ (as in Example 1), $\boxed{T}$ with $\mathbf{T} = \left(\begin{smallmatrix} 1 & 0 \\ 0 & e^{i\pi/4} \end{smallmatrix}\right)$, $\bullet\!\!\oplus$ ($CNOT$), etc. are applied successively from left to right.

Several libraries of quantum operations have been presented in the literature. From a theoretical point of view, the set of arbitrary one-qubit gates (unitary 2×2 matrices) and a single 2-qubit gate, namely the controlled-NOT ($CNOT$) gate, is sufficient to approximate any quantum operation to an arbitrary precision [1]. However, the technologies that are actually used for the physical realization of quantum circuits support a small subset of quantum operations only. This is discussed in more detail in Section 3. Moreover, these technologies are much more fault-prone than classical technologies since the phenomenon of quantum decoherence forces the qubit states to decay – resulting in a loss of quantum information. To address this issue, specific *fault-tolerant* (FT) quantum gate libraries have been presented for the synthesis of quantum circuits.

2.2 Reversible Circuits

A special case of unitary matrices are permutation matrices. These matrices only contain entries 0 and 1 (there is a single 1 in every row/column) and represent classical reversible functions, i.e., Boolean functions $f : \mathbb{B}^n \to \mathbb{B}^n$ that map each input pattern to a unique output pattern. In other words, reversible functions are bijections that perform a permutation of the set of input patterns. A large body of research has focused on synthesizing initial representations of reversible functions, e.g., in terms of truth tables, two-level representations, binary decision diagrams, and permutation matrices, to *reversible circuits* [4–9]. These circuits commonly consist of a set of lines (corresponding to qubits) and reversible gates. The most established type of reversible gates is the *multiple-controlled Toffoli* (MCT) gate. MCT gates consist of a possibly empty set of control lines and a single target line that is inverted if and only if all control lines carry the value 1. Note that the MCT gate library also includes the special cases of NOT (empty set of controls) and controlled-NOT ($CNOT$) gates (singleton set of controls). For historical reasons and for brevity, we will simply use Toffoli gate to refer to the 2-controlled Toffoli gate.

Example 3. Consider the reversible circuit shown in Fig. 2 that realizes a modulo 10 counter. More precisely, if the input – taken as a binary number $dcba_2$ – is less than or equal to (the decimal number) 10, then the output is incremented and taken modulo 10, i.e., the output is $((dcba + 1)\%10)_2$. For binary numbers larger than 10, the circuit does not behave according to this formula. However, it is clear that – due to reversibility – the output also has to be larger than 10.

It is a common phenomenon that, as in the previous example, reversible circuits have a meaningful output only for a subset of the input patterns. This is because many reversible functions are obtained by *embedding* an irreversible function into a reversible one [16], by adding extra input/output lines in order to ensure a bijective mapping.

3   Physical Machine Descriptions

The physical realization of quantum circuits is a difficult task – especially for circuits with a large number of qubits [1]. It needs well-formed qubit states and their transformation through the time-dependent Hamiltonian of the physical system [1]. In general, a quantum circuit implements the unitary operator corresponding to the Hamiltonian evolution of the qubit states. A quantum technology describes a physical system for qubit realization and a set of primitive quantum operations for realizing the Hamiltonian. A broad survey of quantum systems has been conducted in the ARDA quantum computing roadmap [14]. This motivates the consideration of *Physical Machine Descriptions* (PMDs) [15]. Each PMD is different in terms of its quantum mechanical properties. This leads to different Hamiltonians and, hence, a different set of supported (primitive) operations.

In this work, we target PMDs of six quantum systems, namely *Quantum Dots* (QD), *Superconducting Qubits* (SC), *Ion Traps* (IT), *Neutral Atoms* (NA), *Linear Photonics* (LP), and *Non-linear Photonics* (NP). In this section, we provide a brief review of these quantum systems[1]. Then, we summarize the primitive quantum operations supported by the respective PMDs. This provides the basis for a detailed consideration of synthesis issues in the remainder of this paper. The targeted PMDs are described next.

– *Quantum Dots (QD)*
  In this system, a qubit is defined by the spin state of a single-electron quantum dot, which is confined by electrostatic potential. The desired quantum operations are implemented by gating of the tunneling barrier between neighboring dots [17].
– *Superconducting Qubits (SC)*
  In a superconducting system, a qubit is simply represented by the two rotation directions of the persistent super-current of Cooper pairs in a superconducting ring containing Josephson tunnel junctions [18]. The state of a qubit is defined by a distribution of voltages or currents, each characterized by an amplitude and phase, which are functions of time.

---

[1] We keep the respective descriptions brief, but provide references for further reading.

- *Ion Traps (IT)*
  Ion-trap quantum computation can be implemented by confining a string of ions in a single trap, exploiting their electronic states as qubit logic levels, and using mutual Coulomb interaction for transferring quantum information between ions [19].
- *Neutral Atoms (NA)*
  A system of trapped neutral atoms is a good candidate for implementing scalable quantum computing [20] [21]. That the atoms are neutral means that they are feebly coupled to the environment. Hence, decoherence is minimized. Trapped atoms can be cooled to the motional ground state of the quantized potential wells, and the initialization of the internal atomic states can be performed using standard techniques of laser spectroscopy. The different qubit levels can be described by various motional and internal states of the neutral atoms.
- *Linear Photonics (LP)*
  In linear photonics, the qubits are represented by the quantum state of single photons. Quantum logic gates can be constructed using only linear optical elements, such as mirrors and beamsplitters, additional resource photons, and triggering signals from a single-photon detector [22].
- *Non-Linear Photonics (NP)*
  In nonlinear photonics, quantum logic gates are implemented using interactions of photons with nonlinear photonic crystals. The photonic crystals include layers of a Kerr medium [23] and, thus, perform a nonlinear shift of the photonic wave function.

Each of the PMDs described above relies on a different quantum mechanical property and, hence, a different set of supported (primitive) quantum operations. Table 1 provides a list of supported one-qubit and two-qubit operations [15]. More precisely:

- R_x, R_y, and R_z realize rotations around the x, y, and z axis of the Hamiltonian, respectively. They are parametrized by a rotation angle θ. The corresponding matrices are

$$R_x(\theta) = \begin{pmatrix} \cos(\frac{\theta}{2}) & -i\sin(\frac{\theta}{2}) \\ -i\sin(\frac{\theta}{2}) & \cos(\frac{\theta}{2}) \end{pmatrix}, R_y(\theta) = \begin{pmatrix} \cos(\frac{\theta}{2}) & -\sin(\frac{\theta}{2}) \\ \sin(\frac{\theta}{2}) & \cos(\frac{\theta}{2}) \end{pmatrix}, \text{ and } R_z(\theta) = \begin{pmatrix} e^{-i\frac{\theta}{2}} & 0 \\ 0 & e^{i\frac{\theta}{2}} \end{pmatrix}.$$

  For FT implementations, the angle θ must be a multiple of $\frac{\pi}{4}$ [24].
- The Pauli operations σ_x (=NOT), σ_y, and σ_z (sometimes also denoted by X, Y, and Z) are special cases of these rotations for $\theta = \pi$ (up to global phase, i.e., a physically indistinguishable multiplicative factor).
- $S = \begin{pmatrix} 1 & 0 \\ 0 & i \end{pmatrix}$ and $T = \begin{pmatrix} 1 & 0 \\ 0 & e^{i\pi/4} \end{pmatrix}$ are special cases of the R_z gate with rotation angle $\theta_S = \frac{\pi}{2}$ and $\theta_T = \frac{\pi}{4}$, respectively (also up to global phase).
- R_{xy} and A_{squ} are multi-rotation gates with two parameters. For our purpose, it is sufficient to know that R_x and R_y are special cases of R_{xy} and that R_z rotations can be implemented by two R_{xy} rotations.
- In the case of two-qubit operations, it is sufficient to know about operations CZ and G, which perform phase shifts. CZ denotes the controlled-Z

Table 1. Primitive quantum operations supported by different PMDs

PMD	ONE-QUBIT OPERATIONS	TWO-QUBIT OPERATIONS
QD	$R_x, R_z, \sigma_x, \sigma_z, S, T$	CZ
SC	R_x, R_y, R_z	$iSWAP, CZ$
IT	R_{xy}, R_z	G
NA	R_{xy}	CZ
LP	$R_x, R_y, R_z, \sigma_x, \sigma_y, \sigma_z, S, T, H$	$CNOT, CZ, SWAP, ZENO$
NP	$A_{squ}, R_x, R_y, R_z, H$	$CNOT$

operation (defined analogously to the controlled-NOT operation). It is represented by the 4×4 diagonal matrix $CZ = \mathrm{diag}(1, 1, 1, -1)$, whereas the parametrized G operation is represented by $G(\theta) = \mathrm{diag}(1, e^{i\theta}, e^{i\theta}, 1)$.

These different PMD-specific sets of supported operations pose a significant challenge for synthesis: mapping of the circuit has to be performed to each PMD separately. Most existing synthesis methods do not target the gate libraries given in Table 1. Hence, in the remainder of this paper, we address the question of how we can utilize existing synthesis flows for the synthesis of PMD-specific quantum circuits.

4 Synthesis Flow

Since synthesis of quantum circuits is a complex task, many (automatic) methods employ a synthesis flow that *does not directly* realize the given quantum functionality, but employs a *multiple-step* approach. For this purpose, two main characteristics are exploited, namely

- many important quantum algorithms, like Grover's database search algorithm [2] and Shor's factorization algorithm [3], contain a considerable reversible (Boolean) component that needs to be synthesized, and
- all quantum operations are inherently reversible.

Consequently, the quantum functionality of Boolean components is first realized as a reversible circuit, rather than a quantum circuit. This significantly reduces synthesis complexity. Besides, a huge variety of synthesis approaches is already available (e.g., [4–9]). Then, the resulting reversible circuit is mapped to an equivalent quantum circuit representation.

In this section, we first review this established synthesis flow and its current assumptions. Then, we discuss how this flow can be extended to obtain PMD-specific realizations that can be executed in the respective technologies. A comparison of these different extensions at a theoretical level (with respect to the resulting cost metrics) as well as through an experimental evaluation will follow in Sections 5 and 6, respectively.

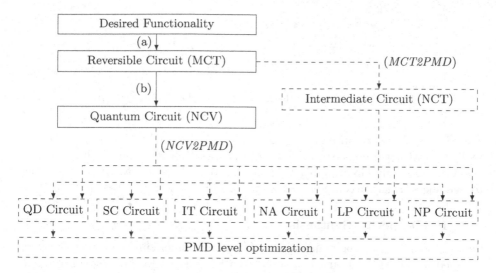

Fig. 3. Synthesis flow for reversible circuits

4.1 State-of-the-Art Synthesis

The established synthesis flow for quantum circuits is sketched by solid lines and boxes in Fig. 3. Starting with the desired functionality (e.g., provided in the form of truth tables, two-level representations, binary decision diagrams, or permutation matrices), the first step is to generate a reversible circuit realizing the corresponding function (Step (a) in Fig. 3). A large body of research has focused on this step [4–9].

In the following step, the resulting reversible circuit is mapped to an equivalent quantum circuit representation (Step (b) in Fig. 3). The key to this task can be found in the seminal work by Barenco et al. [10] for realizing the Toffoli gate at the quantum level. This is done using the *NCV* library that is composed of

- NOT gates,
- controlled-NOT (*CNOT*) gates, as defined in Section 2,
- controlled-**V** gates that are defined analogously, but, when activated, perform the operation $\mathbf{V} = \frac{1+i}{2}\left(\begin{smallmatrix} 1 & -i \\ -i & 1 \end{smallmatrix}\right)$, and
- controlled-$\mathbf{V}^\dagger$ gates[2] that realize the inverse operation $\mathbf{V}^\dagger = \frac{1-i}{2}\left(\begin{smallmatrix} 1 & i \\ i & 1 \end{smallmatrix}\right)$.

Fig. 4 shows the mapping of the Toffoli gate (with two control lines) to the NCV library. This mapping can be extended to MCT gates. A naive way to do this would be to decompose the MCT gate into a cascade of Toffoli gates that can, in turn, be mapped to the NCV library (Fig. 4). However, researchers have come up with highly optimized, direct mapping of MCT gates to the NCV library (e.g., [10–13]). These mapping methods have had a significant impact on how

---

[2] Since two **V** gates or two $\mathbf{V}^\dagger$ gates in a sequence realize a *CNOT* operation, their corresponding operation is usually called "the square root of NOT".

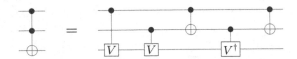

Fig. 4. Quantum level decomposition of the Toffoli gate [10]

reversible circuits are optimized. In fact, the number of NCV gates required to realize an MCT gate has become a major optimization criterion for the synthesis of reversible circuits in Step (a). This has led to *NCV library based quantum cost* to become a widely accepted cost metric for evaluating reversible circuits.

4.2 PMD-Specific Synthesis

Quantum circuits can be mapped to PMDs in a manner similar to how they are mapped to the NCV library, i.e., actual synthesis is conducted at the reversible circuit level whereas the desired PMD-specific circuit is obtained through a mapping scheme. Since PMD-specific mappings tend to create the potential for further circuit minimization at the PMD level, another optimization step is usually carried out at this level [15,24,25].

The above considerations lead to the synthesis flow for PMD-specific quantum circuits sketched by dashed lines and boxes in Fig. 3. More precisely, the mapping to PMD-specific circuits can be accomplished in two ways, namely by

- a mapping from a reversible circuit based on MCT gates (*MCT2PMD*) or
- a mapping from the NCV library based quantum circuit (*NCV2PMD*).

As neither the MCT nor the NCV library is directly supported by any of the PMDs (see Table 1), both approaches eventually require a mapping scheme of the respective gates from these libraries to the PMD level. However, since it is already a challenging task to find corresponding mappings for gates operating on a small number of qubits, we do not aim to obtain direct mappings for large MCT gates with more than two control lines. Instead, we propose to employ the decomposition of large MCT gates into cascades of Toffoli gates [10]. In this way, an arbitrary MCT gate can be implemented using the reduced *NCT* library composed of only *N*OT, *C*ontrolled-NOT, and *T*offoli gates. With this intermediate representation, a mapping to the PMD level is finally required for only three gates (NCT). Moreover, these mappings can be reused to also generate PMD-specific circuits from NCV representations – only one additional mapping, namely for controlled-**V** gates, is required for this purpose[3].

Mappings for the controlled-NOT, controlled-**V**, and Toffoli gates are shown in Fig. 5, Fig. 6, and Fig. 7, respectively[4]. Note that the presented mappings

---

[3] Note that mappings for the controlled-**V**† gate are not needed explicitly as they can be derived by applying the corresponding mapping of the controlled-**V** gate in reverse order and with inverted gates.

[4] Mappings for the *CNOT* gate were presented earlier in [15], however, are shown here for the sake of completeness.

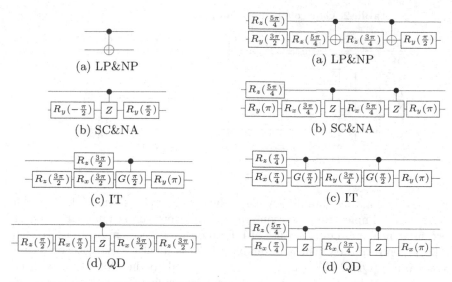

Fig. 5. Mapping a $CNOT$ to PMDs   **Fig. 6.** Mapping of controlled-**V** gate to PMDs

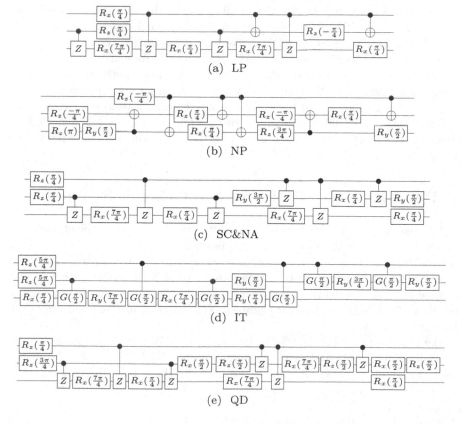

Fig. 7. Mapping of Toffoli gate to PMDs

Table 2. Gate counts of the mappings from Figs. 5-7

PMD	NOT	CONTROLLED-NOT	CONTROLLED-**V**	TOFFOLI
QD	1	5	6	18
SC	1	3	7	15
IT	1	5	6	15
NA	1	3	8	17
LP	1	1	7	13
NP	1	1	7	16
NCV	1	1	1	5

employ an FT quantum gate library [24]. Cheaper mappings are available when dropping the FT implementation requirement [15]. However, as faults are a major concern in quantum circuits, the use of FT quantum gates is important. To this end, the FT gate library which we employ here is ideal to use with quantum error-correcting (QEC) codes as it is closely related to the Clifford+T library (as also discussed in [24]). In fact, some post-processing is necessary to use a specific QEC code, but this is beyond the scope of this paper.

The above mappings enable the application of the two proposed schemes, *MCT2PMD* and *NCV2PMD*, for the synthesis of quantum circuits for direct execution on the corresponding PMD. We have summarized the respective costs of single NCT/NCV gates for each PMD in Table 2[5]. As can be seen, the costs are significantly different across PMDs. Even more importantly, the actual costs of implementing a $CNOT$, controlled-**V**, and Toffoli gate are up to a factor of 8 higher than in the case of the NCV library based quantum cost. The consequences of these cost differences will be further analyzed in the following section. Then, the efficiency of both schemes will be compared through an experimental evaluation in Section 6.

5   Resulting Cost Metrics for MCT Circuit Synthesis

In the previous section, we proposed two different extensions to the state-of-the-art synthesis flow to obtain quantum circuits that can be executed on particular PMDs. More precisely, in the *MCT2PMD* scheme, MCT circuits are, first, transformed to an intermediate representation in terms of NCT gates which are, then, mapped step-by-step to their respective PMD implementations. In contrast, in the *NCV2PMD* scheme, highly optimized NCV circuits are mapped directly to the particular PMD.

We observed that the PMD-specific costs of NCV and NCT gates are substantially higher compared with the usually applied NCV library based quantum costs. As a consequence, MCT gates – which are the actual input of both synthesis schemes – are significantly more expensive when realized on PMDs and

---

[5] Recall that an R_z rotation is implemented by two R_{xy} rotations in NA. Consequently, an R_z operation has a gate count of 2.

Table 3. PMD-specific cost metrics for MCT gates

#CONTR.	MCT2PMD									NCV2PMD								
	N	C	T	QD	SC	IT	NA	LP	NP	N	C	V	QD	SC	IT	NA	LP	NP
0	1			1	1	1	1	1	1	1			1	1	1	1	1	1
1		1		5	3	5	3	1	1	1			5	3	5	3	1	1
2			1	18	15	15	17	13	16		2	3	28	27	28	30	23	23
3			4	72	60	60	68	52	64		4	10	80	82	80	92	74	74
4			8	144	120	120	136	104	128		4	16	116	124	116	140	116	116
5			12	216	180	180	204	156	192		8	24	184	192	184	216	176	176
6			26	468	390	390	442	338	416		8	36	256	276	256	312	260	260
7			32	576	480	480	544	416	512		12	44	324	344	324	388	320	320
8			40	720	600	600	680	520	640		14	62	442	476	442	538	448	448
9			48	864	720	720	816	624	768		18	70	510	544	510	614	508	508
10			56	1008	840	840	952	728	896		20	88	628	676	628	764	636	636

the PMD-specific costs differ significantly for the various technologies. Hence, the NCV library based cost metric is no longer valid for PMD-specific synthesis. This poses a problem since NCV library based costs are commonly used in almost all synthesis approaches aimed at generating MCT circuits. Consequently, it could have a significant impact on the synthesis process if PMD-specific cost metrics were used when synthesizing MCT circuits.

In fact, the two mapping schemes give rise to their *own dedicated cost metrics*, as shown in Table 3. Here, the first column denotes the number of control lines of the MCT gate. In the following columns, the costs for the *MCT2PMD* scheme are given. In the first three columns, the required numbers of NOT, $CNOT$, and Toffoli gates for realizing the corresponding MCT gate in the NCT library are provided (based on the decomposition in [10]). Based on these numbers, PMD-specific costs are computed using Table 2 and presented in the following six columns. In the remainder of the table, this procedure is likewise performed for the *NCV2PMD* scheme: first, the numbers of NOT, $CNOT$, and controlled-**V** gates are obtained (based on the state-of-the-art mapping [12]) and, then, the PMD-specific costs are computed and shown in the remaining columns.

Overall, the numbers indicate a significant difference between the two mapping schemes with a clear advantage for *NCV2PMD*. However, the actual difference between the two approaches and comparison with NCV library based quantum costs need to be evaluated in practice, especially with respect to optimization performed at the PMD level after technology mapping. This experimental evaluation is conducted in the following section.

6 Experimental Evaluation

In this section, we summarize the experimental evaluations conducted using the newly proposed synthesis flows: *MCT2PMD* and *NCV2PMD*. More precisely, we investigate which of the two flows actually performs better. In addition, we also evaluate the difference between the commonly used NCV library based cost metric and the PMD-specific cost metrics presented in the previous section.

We synthesized various MCT circuits from the RevLib benchmark suite [26] as PMD-specific quantum circuits using both flows. More precisely, we synthesized medium-sized circuits with an NCV library based quantum cost in the 100 to 15,000 range, such that, on the one hand, the circuits are large enough to enable a meaningful evaluation and, on the other hand, are still amenable to the application of highly elaborate NCV optimization.

We used the state-of-the-art NCV library based mapping scheme presented in [12] to generate the NCV circuits for the *NCV2PMD* scheme. This scheme uses optimized mappings for MCT gates and then performs several heuristic optimizations on the resulting NCV circuit. In both approaches, we used the FTQLS tool [24] – enriched by the FT mappings presented in Section 4.2 – to generate the FT PMD-specific implementations from the NCV and NCT circuits. After this mapping, additional optimization steps, as described in [24], are performed.

6.1   Comparison of the Synthesis Flows

In the first evaluation, we compared the efficacy of the two proposed synthesis flows with respect to circuit cost. The results are summarized in Fig. 8. In each graph, the y axis represents the quantum cost when using the *MCT2PMD* mapping, whereas the x axis represents the quantum cost when using the *NCV2PMD* mapping. The diagonal line represents the cost equilibrium, i.e., circuits that have the same cost for both mapping schemes appear on this line. Circuits that can be realized cheaper with the *MCT2PMD* scheme than with the *NCV2PMD* scheme appear below this line, whereas circuits that can be realized cheaper with the *NCV2PMD* scheme than with the *MCT2PMD* scheme (modulo better future mappings of MCT gates in the latter scheme) appear above this line.

In summary, a small advantage of the *NCV2PMD* scheme can be observed for all PMDs as indicated by the cost metric presented in Section 5.

6.2   Comparison of PMD and NCV Costs

In the second evaluation, we were interested in the difference between the NCV library based quantum costs and the two PMD-specific quantum costs (as proposed in Section 5). This is of particular interest because, thus far, reversible circuits are still being optimized with respect to an NCV library based cost metric. Hence, it is important to understand whether and, if so, what differences exist between these cost metrics.

For this purpose, we compared the obtained NCV library based quantum costs of the initial MCT benchmark circuits to their PMD-specific costs. The relationship between these costs is summarized in Fig. 9 for both mapping schemes. The x axis depicts benchmarks circuits, whereas the y axis provides the ratio of the PMD costs to the NCV costs. Average values and standard deviations for all PMDs are shown in Table 4.

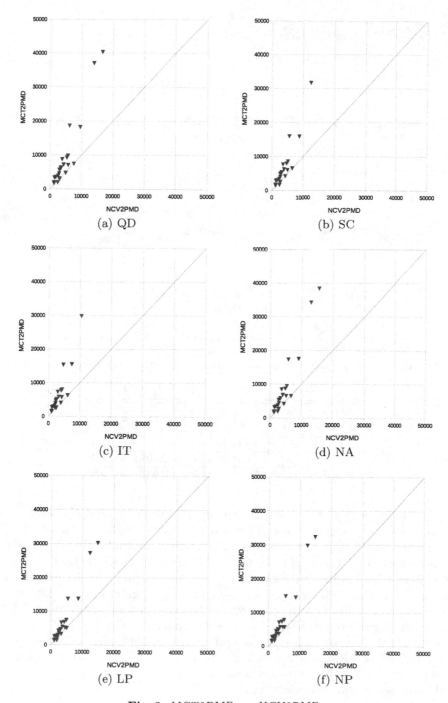

Fig. 8. *MCT2PMD* vs. *NCV2PMD*

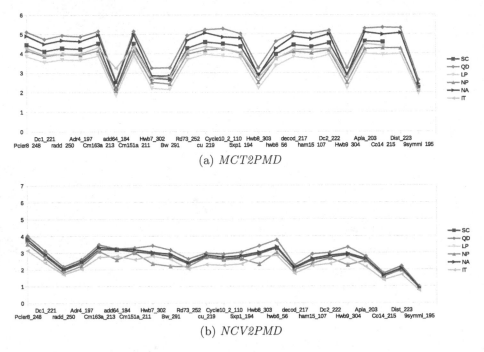

(a) *MCT2PMD*

(b) *NCV2PMD*

Fig. 9. NCV library based quantum cost vs. PMD-specific cost

Table 4. Statistics for the ratio between PMD-specific and NCV library based cost

MCT2PMD	QD	SC	IT	NA	LP	NP
Average value	4.54	3.90	3.78	4.27	3.35	3.63
Standard deviation	0.95	0.85	0.70	0.97	0.78	0.79
NCV2PMD	QD	SC	IT	NA	LP	NP
Average value	2.89	2.61	2.28	2.70	2.40	2.40
Standard deviation	0.68	0.61	0.55	0.63	0.56	0.56

First of all, we observe that for many circuits the cost ratio is close to the average value, i.e., the real cost of the circuit differs from the estimated NCV library based cost only by a constant, PMD-specific, multiplicative factor. This holds for both the *MCT2PMD* and *NCV2PMD* mapping schemes. In these cases, NCV library based quantum cost can be used as a useful proxy for actual cost estimation. However, there are several circuits that significantly deviate from the average, both towards the top and the bottom. In these cases, using NCV library based quantum cost is not an adequate proxy.

Overall, the use of PMD-specific cost metrics as optimization criterion is likely to lead to MCT circuits that are better suited for a later mapping to PMDs. Nevertheless, the currently popular NCV library based cost metric may still serve as a useful approximation.

7   Conclusions

In this paper, we considered the design of PMD-specific quantum circuits. PMDs correspond to quantum systems whose quantum mechanical properties are used to implement quantum circuits. As part of its specification, each PMD supports only a restricted set of primitive quantum operations. Consequently, when synthesizing quantum circuits for these PMDs, the specific gate library has to be taken into account. The commonly used synthesis flow for quantum circuits employs a multiple-step scheme in which a reversible circuit (based on MCT gates) is realized first and then mapped to an equivalent cascade of quantum gates. However, this mapping leads to NCV library based quantum circuits that are not directly supported by any of the PMDs. To overcome this problem, we proposed extensions to the existing synthesis flow aimed at synthesis of PMD-specific quantum circuits. To this end, we proposed FT mappings to the PMD level for various quantum gates (from the NCV and the NCT library). An analysis showed that these mappings lead to much higher costs for the realization of MCT gates compared to the commonly used NCV library based quantum costs. An experimental evaluation indeed indicated that there is no simple relation between PMD-specific and NCV library based cost. This motivates the need for a more detailed consideration of PMD-specific synthesis at the reversible circuit level based on the metrics proposed in this work.

References

1. Nielsen, M., Chuang, I.: Quantum Computation and Quantum Information. Cambridge Univ. Press (2000)
2. Grover, L.K.: A fast quantum mechanical algorithm for database search. In: Theory of Computing, pp. 212–219 (1996)
3. Shor, P.W.: Algorithms for quantum computation: discrete logarithms and factoring. In: Foundations of Computer Science, pp. 124–134 (1994)
4. Shende, V., Prasad, A., Markov, I., Hayes, J.: Synthesis of reversible logic circuits. IEEE Trans. on CAD **22**(6), 710–722 (2003)
5. Gupta, P., Agrawal, A., Jha, N.K.: An algorithm for synthesis of reversible logic circuits. IEEE Trans. on CAD **25**(11), 2317–2330 (2006)
6. Fazel, K., Thornton, M., Rice, J.: ESOP-based Toffoli gate cascade generation. In: IEEE Pacific Rim Conference on Communications, Computers and Signal Processing, pp. 206–209, August 2007
7. Wille, R., Drechsler, R.: BDD-based synthesis of reversible logic for large functions. In: ACM Design Automation Conference, pp. 270–275, July 2009
8. Soeken, M., Wille, R., Hilken, C., Przigoda, N., Drechsler, R.: Synthesis of reversible circuits with minimal lines for large functions. In: ASP Design Automation Conference, January 2012
9. Lin, C.-C., Jha, N.K.: RMDDS: Reed-Muller decision diagram synthesis of reversible logic circuits. ACM J. Emerg. Technol. Comput. Syst. **10**(2) (2014)
10. Barenco, A., Bennett, C.H., Cleve, R., DiVincenzo, D., Margolus, N., Shor, P., Sleator, T., Smolin, J., Weinfurter, H.: Elementary gates for quantum computation. The American Physical Society **52**, 3457–3467 (1995)

11. Maslov, D., Young, C., Dueck, G.W., Miller, D.M.: Quantum circuit simplification using templates. In: Design, Automation and Test in Europe Conference, pp. 1208–1213 (2005)
12. Miller, D.M., Wille, R., Sasanian, Z.: Elementary quantum gate realizations for multiple-control Toffoli gates. In: Int. Symposium on Multiple-Valued Logic, pp. 288–293 (2011)
13. Wille, R., Soeken, M., Otterstedt, C., Drechsler, R.: Improving the mapping of reversible circuits to quantum circuits using multiple target lines. In: ASP Design Automation Conference, pp. 145–150, January 2013
14. ARDA: Quantum computation roadmap. http://qist.lanl.gov/qcomp_map.shtml
15. Lin, C.-C., Chakrabarti, A., Jha, N.K.: Optimized quantum gate library for various physical machine descriptions. IEEE Trans. on Very Large Scale Integration (VLSI) Systems 21(11), 2055–2068 (2013)
16. Wille, R., Keszöcze, O., Drechsler, R.: Determining the minimal number of lines for large reversible circuits. In: Design, Automation and Test in Europe Conference, pp. 1204–1207 (2011)
17. Taylor, J.M., Petta, J.R., Johnson, A.C., Yacoby, A., Marcus, C.M., Lukin, M.D.: Relaxation, dephasing, and quantum control of electron spins in double quantum dots. Phys. Rev. B 76 (2007)
18. Strauchand, F.W., Johnson, P.R., Dragt, A.J., Lobb, C.J., Anderson, J.R., Wellstood, F.C.: Quantum logic gates for coupled superconducting phase qubits. Phys. Rev. Lett. 91 (2003)
19. Cirac, J.I., Zoller, P.: Quantum computations with cold trapped ions. Phys. Rev. Lett. 74(20), 4091–4094 (1995)
20. Deutsch, I., Brennen, G., Jessen, P.: Quantum computing with neutral atoms in an optical lattice. Fortschritte der Physik [Progress of Physics] 48, 925–943 (2000)
21. Briegel, H.J., Calarco, T., Jaksch, D., Cirac, J.I., Zoller, P.: Quantum computing with neutral atoms. Journal of Modern Optics 47, 415–451 (2000)
22. Knil, E., LaFlamme, R., Milburn, G.J.: A scheme for efficient quantum computation with linear optics. Nature 409, 46–52 (2001)
23. Inoue, S.I., Aoyagi, Y.: Design and fabrication of two-dimensional photonic crystals with predetermined nonlinear optical properties. Phys. Rev. Lett. 94 (2005)
24. Lin, C.-C., Chakrabarti, A., Jha, N.K.: FTQLS: Fault-tolerant quantum logic synthesis. IEEE Transactions on Very Large Scale Integration (VLSI) Systems 22(6), 1350–1363 (2014)
25. Lin, C.-C., Chakrabarti, A., Jha, N.K.: QLib: Quantum module library. ACM J. Emerg. Technol. Comput. Syst. 11(1) (2014)
26. Wille, R., Große, D., Teuber, L., Dueck, G.W., Drechsler, R.: RevLib: An online resource for reversible functions and reversible circuits. In: Int. Symposium on Multiple-Valued Logic, pp. 220–225 (2008). http://www.revlib.org

Short Papers

Power-Clock Generator Impact on the Performance of NEM-Based Quasi-Adiabatic Logic Circuits

Samer Houri[1(✉)], Gerard Billiot[2], Marc Belleville[2], Alexandre Valentian[2], and Herve Fanet[2]

[1] Molecular Electronics Devices, Department of Quantum Nanoscience, Faculty of Applied Science, Kavli Institute of Nanoscience, Delft University of Technology, Lorentzweg 1, 2628 CJ Delft, The Netherlands
S.Houri@tudelft.nl
[2] DACLE, CEA-LETI, Minatec Campus, 17 rue des Martyrs, Grenoble, France
{Gerard.Billot,Marc.Belleville,Alexandre.Valentian,
Herve.Fanet}@cea.fr

Abstract. The influence of the power-clock generator on the global energy-performance relationship of nanoelectromechanical (NEM) switch-based quasi-adiabatic logic circuits is investigated in this paper. This investigation is undertaken the capacitor bank type generator, it is found that the leakage current of the MOSFET switching devices used within the generator constitutes an important source of performance degradation. Capacitor type generators are found to be most efficient for low operating frequencies (less than a MHz).

Keywords: Power-clock generator · Adiabatic charging · Adiabatic logic · Quasi-adiabatic logic · Nanoelectromechanical relays

1 Introduction

Although reversible and adiabatic computing, that can be traced back to [1], is an interesting approach to low power energy efficient computing, solutions based on this approach have yet to gain wide adoption. This is in part due to the introduced complexity overhead in the case of reversible and adiabatic logic [2,3], but also due to the fact that MOSFET devices are simply not well suited to fully apply such circuits.

This fact stems from limitations that are inherent to MOSFET devices, mainly their leakage and low gradient subthreshold slope. If these two issues are circumvented, then reversible and quasi-adiabatic logic become more energy efficient when compared to other available alternatives such as subthreshold logic. And while advanced semiconductor-based solutions are able to promise improvements on current MOSFET performance, such as in the case of finFETs [4] and tunnel FETs [5], these solutions remain limited by the semiconductor physics itself. Therefore, metal-insulator type combinations are being pursued instead of semiconducting ones, this approach explains the recent revival in interest in mechanical relay type switches, albeit at the nanoscale [6-10], thus nanoelectromechanical (NEM) switches are a promising and viable candidate to replace MOSFET

© Springer International Publishing Switzerland 2015
J. Krivine and J.-B. Stefani (Eds.): RC 2015, LNCS 9138, pp. 267–272, 2015.
DOI: 10.1007/978-3-319-20860-2_17

devices, at least in certain niche applications, particularly promising is their implementation to adiabatic and quasi-adiabatic logic [11-12].

While previous work explored NEM-based quasi-adiabatic logic and reported encouraging results, little attention was given to the question of the necessary ramped-voltage generator, i.e. power-clock, necessary for quasi-adiabatic logic circuits to function. Indeed, in one case when a power-clock generator-NEM quasi-adiabatic logic combination was explored [13], it was found that the generator constitutes a limiting factor to the energy saving potential that accompanies the use of NEM switches.

2   NEM-Based Quasi-Adiabatic Logic

A typical electrostatically actuated NEM relay is a suspended nanomechanical structure, usually a beam or a cantilever, that bends under the effect of an applied electrostatic force in order to establish direct mechanical contact between two electrodes, here denoted source (S) and drain (D), the electrostatic relay may therefore be regarded as a variable capacitor. NEM switches of various dimensions, designs, and materials have been fabricated, see for example [6], but all electrostatic NEM switches may be reduced mathematically, as a first order approximation, to a single degree of freedom lumped elements mass-spring system like the one shown in Fig. 1(a).

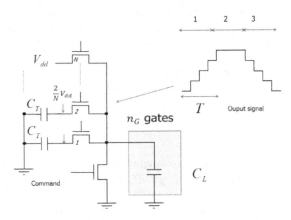

Fig. 1. Schematic representation of a capacitive bank generator, each transistor opens sequentially to increase the voltage by V_{dd}/N thus generating the shown stepwise voltage ramp

In fig. 1(a), k represents the equivalent spring constant, i.e. structural stiffness, of the nanomechanical structure, g is the electrostatic actuation gap, and d is the contact gap. While these parameters and others affects the behavior of the system, in the current analysis only the device open capacitance C_{OPEN}, and the device closed capacitance C_{CLOSED}, dictated by g and d respectively, are of interest.

The nano-relay commutes under the effect of a slowly ramped voltage waveform, like the one shown in Fig. 1(b), during a complete ON/OFF cycle the device and line capacitances are charged and discharged adiabatically, therefore it is assumed *a priori* that the ramp-up and ramp-down times T are significantly larger than the circuit's electrical time constant given roughly by $R_S C_L$, (where R_S is the circuit equivalent series resistance and C_L is the interconnect capacitance), thus $T \gg R_S C_L$.

It is now possible to calculate the dissipation that accompanies such charge-discharge cycle. It is important to note that the dissipation that accompanies such a cycle varies widely depending on the ratio of mechanical time constant, i.e. mechanical commutation time τ_{Mech}, to that of the ramp-up and ramp-down periods T. While in previous work the case where $\tau_{Mech} \gg T$ was explored [11, 12], here circuits operating under the condition $\tau_{Mech} \approx T$ are investigated as this does not require modifying the voltage waveforms as proposed in [12] or excessively slow circuit operation [11, 12].

Thus, by considering the simplified circuit model shown in Fig. 1(b), it is possible to express dissipation during the charging cycle by integrating the power dissipated in the series resistance, it is assumed that the discharge cycle dissipates a similar amount. Thus the total dissipated energy is given by:

$$E_{Electrical} = 2 \int_0^T R_S i^2 dt = 2 \int_0^T R_S (i_1 + i_2)^2 dt = 2 \int_0^T R_S \left(i_1^2 + i_2^2 + 2 i_1 i_2 \right) dt. \quad (1)$$

where i is the current going through the series resistance R_S, the current splits into two components, i_1 goes through the interconnect capacitance and i_2 through the NEM relay.

By using the following equalities:

$$V(t) = V_{dd} f(t), \quad (2.a)$$

$$\text{and } C(t) = C_0 g(t). \quad (2.b)$$

where $V(t)$ is time varying waveform, $f(t)$ is the time dependence of the waveform, $C(t)$ is the NEM relay time dependent capacitance, C_0 is the device's open capacitance, i.e. C_{OPEN}, and $g(t)$ is the time dependence expression of the NEM capacitance.

The energy injected into the NEM switch is obtained from the following integration:

$$E_{Injected} \approx \int_0^T i_2 V_{dd} dt = C_0 V_{dd}^2 \int_0^T \left(g(t) \frac{df(t)}{dt} + f(t) \frac{dg(t)}{dt} \right) dt \quad (3)$$

Thus, the energy dissipated by the NEM switch is given by:

$$E_{NEM} \approx C_0 V_{dd}^2 \left[\int_0^T \left(g(t) \frac{df(t)}{dt} + f(t) \frac{dg(t)}{dt} \right) dt - \frac{g(T)}{2} \right] \quad (4)$$

3   Capacitor Bank Generator

The capacitive bank generator approximates the ideal trapezoidal power-clock with a series of stepwise signals [14]. Therefore the charging of the outputs is not abrupt but

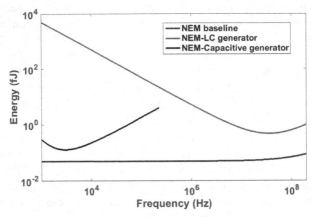

Fig. 2. Comparison of different combinations of generators with NEM-based quasi-adiabatic logic, NEM baseline (blue plot). The LC resonant generator (red) and the capacitive (black).

divided into N steps as shown in Fig. 2. The voltages of the tank capacitors are respectively $\frac{V_{dd}}{N}$, $\frac{2V_{dd}}{N}$ ... V_{dd}, and it is possible to demonstrate that the system converges towards this equilibrium when the supply voltage is applied [14].

To energize the gates, switch 1 is closed and the output is charged to V_{dd}/N, then switch 1 is opened and switch 2 is closed, the output is then charged to $2V_{dd}/N$. The process continues up to switch N at which point the gates are charged to V_{dd}.

Assuming CMOS technology is used for implementing the staircase generator, it is necessary to calculate the adiabatic dissipation in the switching transistors and in the charging of their gates, along with the dissipation due to leakage, where the leakage dissipation is calculated for the three phases shown in Fig. 2. The optimal switching condition established in [14] for the *kth* transistor is applied, where R_k is the passing resistance of the transistor, thus:

$$2.2R_k n_G (C_L + C_0) = \frac{T}{N} \tag{5}$$

And by defining the leakage dissipation during phases 1 and 3 as:

$$E1_{lk} = \sum_{i=0}^{k-1} 2.2 n_G (C_L + C_0) \frac{1}{N} v_t^2 exp\left(\frac{-V_T}{nv_t}\right) e^{1.8} exp\left(-\frac{i}{N}\frac{V_{dd}}{nv_t}\right)\frac{k-i}{1-\frac{i}{N}} \tag{6}$$

$$E3_{lk} = \sum_{i=k+1}^{N} 2.2 n_G (C_L + C_0) \frac{1}{N} v_t^2 exp\left(\frac{-V_T}{nv_t}\right) e^{1.8} exp\left(-\frac{i}{N}\frac{V_{dd}}{nv_t}\right)\frac{i-k}{1-\frac{i}{N}} \tag{7}$$

It is now possible to write the overall dissipated energy as:

$$E \approx 2NC_iV_{dd}^2 + 2\sum_{k=1}^{k=N}(E1_{lk} + E3_{lk})$$
$$+ 2.2\, n_G(C_L + C_0)e^{1.8}v_t^2 exp\left(\frac{-V_T}{nv_t}\right)\frac{N}{1-\frac{1}{N}}$$
$$+ n_G(C_L + C_0)\frac{V_{dd}^2}{N} + n_G(C_L + C_0)\frac{V_{dd}^2}{N} + n_G\eta C_0 V_{dd}^2$$
(8)

The first term in (8) is the switching dissipation of the N command transistors, the second term is the leakage energy of the N transistors during phase 1 and 3, the third term is the leakage dissipation during the phase 2, the fourth term is the active switching energy dissipated in the transistors and the last two terms are the adiabatic dissipation and non-adiabatic residue dissipation in the gates. The fourth and fifth terms are equal since the load capacitance is supposed to be the sum of the capacitive loads of the gates. The first term is considered negligible.

By optimizing energy dissipation it is possible to calculate N_{opt} numerically. For simplicity the dissipated energy is re-expressed as:

$$E = n_G(C_L + C_0)V_{dd}^2 f(N) + n_G\eta C_0 V_{dd}^2$$
(9)

where $f(N)$ represents the function to be minimized.

By using nominal circuit parameter values of $n_G = 10^6$, $C_L = 10^{-15}F$, $C_0 = 10^{-15}F$, $\eta = 0.05$, $n = 1.5$, $V_{dd} = 1\,V$, $R_k \approx 1k\Omega$ it is possible to obtain $N_{opt} = 50$ ($V_T = 150$ mV) and $N_{opt} = 75$ ($V_T = 200$ mV), and $T_{opt} = 2.10^{-4}s$, and $3.10^{-4}s$. The corresponding optimum operating frequency and optimal energy dissipation are calculated and summarized in Table 1. Thus the stepwise charging generator is an interesting solution if low operating frequencies are allowed (< 1 MHz).

Table 1. Comparison of optimal operating frequency and minimal dissipated energy per gate for the two generator types

Generator	Optimal frequency	Minimal energy
LC [13]	35 MHz	$4.8\ 10^{-16}$ J
Capacitive	5 KHz	$1.3\ 10^{-16}$ J

4   Discussion and Conclusions

By combining the dissipation expressions obtained for the NEM relays with those of the generators it is possible to estimate the optimum operating frequencies and minimum dissipated These optimal values are summarized in Table 1 along with those obtained in [13] for the LC generator. Furthermore, the performance of the different NEM-generator combinations are plotted in Fig. 3 along with NEM-only baseline plot for comparison.

From Fig. 3, it is visible that while the NEM-quasi-adiabatic logic combination on its own show a very promising energy saving, particularly a somewhat frequency flat response for low operating frequencies, its combination with the power-clock generators changes the performance of the circuit. Each of the two generators shows a different operating minimum, where the LC generator tend to be in the 10s of MHz range, while that of the capacitive generator tend to be less than a MHz range.

In summary this paper presented an analysis of the energy-performance relation of NEMS-based quasi-adiabatic logic circuit, the papers mainly aims to explore the performance limitations imposed by the power-clock generators.

Acknowledgments. The project was funded by the French program 'CARNOT'. Partial funding comes from FP7 grant No. 318287, project LANDAUER.

References

1. Landauer, R.: Irreversibility and heat generation in the computing process. IBM Journal of Research and Development **5**, 183–191 (1961)
2. De Vos, A.: Reversible Computing: Fundamentals, Quantum Computing, and Applications. Wiley (2010)
3. Morrison, M., Ranganathan, N.: Synthesis of Dual-Rail Adiabatic Logic for Low Power Security Applications. IEEE Transactions on Computer-Aided Design of Integrated Circuits and Systems **33**(7), 975–988 (2014)
4. Hisamoto, D., Lee, W.C., Kedzierski, J., Takeuchi, H., Asano, K., Kuo, C., Anderson, E., King, T.J., Bokor, J., Hu, C.M.: FinFET-A Self-Aligned Double-Gate MOSFET Scalable to 20 nm. IEEE Transactions on Electron Devices **47**, 2320–2325 (2000)
5. Zhang, Q., Zhao, W., Seabaugh, A.: Low-Subthreshold-Swing Tunnel Transistors. IEEE transactions on electron devices **27**(4), 297–300 (2006)
6. Loh, O., Espinosa, H.D.: Nanoelectromechanical contact switches. Nature Nanotechnology **7**(5), 283–295 (2012)
7. Lee, J.O., Song, Y.-H., Kim, M.-W., Kang, M.-H., Oh, J.-S., Yang, H.-H., Yoon, J.-B.: A Sub-1-Volt Nanoelectromechanical Switching Device. Nature Nanotechnology **8**, 36–40 (2013)
8. Pawashe, C., Lin, K., Kuhn, K.J.: Scaling limits of electrostatic nanorelays. IEEE Transactions Electron Devices **60**, 2936–2942 (2013)
9. Kam, H., King Liu, T.-J., Stojanovic, V., Markovic, D., Alon, E.: Design, Optimization, and Scaling of MEM Relays for Ultra-Low Power Digital Logic. IEEE Transactions on Electron Devices **58**, 236–250 (2011)
10. Kam, H., Chen, Y., King Liu, T.-J.: Reliable micro-electro-mechanical (MEM) switch design for ultra-low-power logic. In: 2013 IEEE Reliability Physics Symposium (IRPS), Anaheim CA (2013)
11. Houri, S., Valentian, A., Fanet, H.: Comparing CMOS-based and NEMS-based adiabatic logic circuits. In: Dueck, G.W., Miller, D. (eds.) RC 2013. LNCS, vol. 7948, pp. 36–45. Springer, Heidelberg (2013)
12. Houri, S., Poulain, C., Valentian, A., Fanet, H.: Performance Limits of NEMS-Based Adiabatic Logic Circuits. Journal of Low Power Electronics and Applications **3**, 368–384 (2013)
13. Houri, S., Billot, G., Belleville, M., Valentian, A., Fanet, H.: Limits of CMOS Technology and Interest of NEMS Relays for Adiabatic Logic Applications. Unpublished (2015)
14. Svensson, L.J., Koller, J.G.: Adiabatic charging without inductors. In: International workshop on Low-Power Design, pp. 159–164 (1994)

Towards a Cost Metric for Nearest Neighbor Constraints in Reversible Circuits

Abhoy Kole[1], Kamalika Datta[2], Indranil Sengupta[1], and Robert Wille[3,4]($\boxtimes$)

[1] Department of Computer Science and Engineering, Indian Institute of Technology, Kharagpur, India
abhoy.kole@yahoo.com
[2] Department of Computer Science and Engineering, National Institute of Technology Meghalaya, Shillong, India
kdatta@nitm.ac.in
[3] Institute of Computer Science, University of Bremen, 28359 Bremen, Germany
isg@iitkgp.ac.in
[4] Cyber-Physical Systems, DFKI GmbH, 28359 Bremen, Germany
rwille@informatik.uni-bremen.de

Abstract. This work in progress report proposes a new metric for estimating nearest neighbor cost at the reversible circuit level. This is in contrast to existing literature where nearest neighbor constraints are usually considered at the quantum circuit level. In order to define the metric, investigations on a state-of-the-art reversible to quantum mapping scheme have been conducted. From the retrieved information, a proper estimation to be used as a cost metric has been obtained. Using the metric, it becomes possible for the first time to optimize a *reversible* circuit with respect to nearest neighbor constraints.

Keywords: Quantum cost · Nearest neighbor cost · Quantum circuit · Reversible circuit

1 Introduction

Motivated by the promises of quantum computation [6] researchers started to investigate how to efficiently synthesize quantum circuits. This eventually established a design flow for quantum circuits representing Boolean components which (1) realizes the desired functionality as a reversible circuit (using methods e.g. proposed in [4,7,11–13]) and (2) maps the resulting circuit in its respective technological quantum circuit description (using mapping schemes as e.g. proposed in [1,3,5,14]).

However, while this design flow leads to proper results, it does not consider certain technological constraints. In particular, so-called *nearest neighbor constraints* are not considered by this flow, although many important quantum computing technologies heavily rely on them. In order to satisfy these constraints, it has to be ensured that computations are only performed between adjacent (i.e. nearest neighbor) signals.

© Springer International Publishing Switzerland 2015
J. Krivine and J.-B. Stefani (Eds.): RC 2015, LNCS 9138, pp. 273–278, 2015.
DOI: 10.1007/978-3-319-20860-2_18

A major problem is thereby that methods considering nearest neighbor constraints are usually applicable at the quantum circuit level only (see e.g. [9,10,16]). This is mainly caused by the absence of proper cost metrics which could be applied at the reversible logic level. In the established design flow sketched above, the handling of nearest neighbor constraints is indeed considered as another separate (third) design step which is applied not until the technology mapping of the second step has been completed.

In this work in progress, we aim for overcoming this drawback and for allowing nearest neighbor optimization at the reversible logic level – the abstraction level in which the actual synthesis is performed. For this purpose, we propose a cost metric which, for the first time, can be used to evaluate nearest neighbor constraints for reversible circuits rather than quantum circuits. In order to define the metric, investigations on a state-of-the-art reversible to quantum mapping scheme have been conducted. From the retrieved information, a proper estimation to be used as a cost metric has been obtained.

2   A Nearest Neighbor Cost Metric for the Reversible Logic Level

In general, the *Nearest Neighbor Costs* (NNC) for a quantum gate circuit are defined as the number of SWAP gates needed to make it nearest neighbor compliant. Thus far, the various works that have been reported to make a circuit nearest neighbor compliant target quantum circuits only and are unable to provide any cost estimate e.g. for synthesis at the reversible logic level[1]. In this work, we propose a cost metric which serves this purpose. To this end, we investigate a state-of-the-art reversible to quantum mapping scheme and derive systematic information to be utilized in order to formulate an NNC metric for the reversible logic level. In this section, the underlying reversible to quantum mapping scheme is reviewed first. Afterwards, we summarize our analyzes and, eventually, present the resulting metric.

2.1   Mapping of Reversible to Quantum Circuits

Our investigations are based on the mapping scheme as introduced by Miller et al. in [5]. The general idea is to partition a Toffoli gate $g(C;t)$ with a set of control lines C into a cascade of smaller gates including subsets C_1, C_2 with $C = C_1 \cup C_2$ and $C_1 \cap C_2 = \emptyset$. For this purpose, a so-called *ancilla line* (denoted by a) with $a \notin C$ and $a \neq t$ is additionally applied. More precisely,

$$T(C;t) = V(a;t)T(C_1;a)V^\dagger(a;t)T(C_2;a)$$
$$V(a;t)T(C_1;a)V^\dagger(a;t)T(C_2;a) \tag{1}$$

---

[1] Note that the authors of [2] proposed a solution to achieve adjacency of Toffoli gates. But as discussed in the previous section, this is not sufficient to also ensure nearest neighbor compliance at the quantum logic level. In [15], nearest neighbor compliance at the reversible circuit level was investigated. But here a special model (based on multi-level quantum systems) has been assumed.

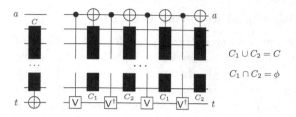

$$C_1 \cup C_2 = C$$
$$C_1 \cap C_2 = \phi$$

Fig. 1. Reversible to quantum mapping scheme

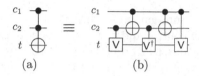

Fig. 2. Toffoli gate and its equivalent NCV cascade

is applied where $T(C; t)$ denotes an MCT gate, $V(a; t)$ denotes a V-gate, and $V^\dagger(a; t)$ denotes a $V^\dagger$-gate with the respective control and target lines. Fig. 1 illustrates the resulting structure.

This partitioning is repeated until only Toffoli gates with two control lines result. While decomposing C_1 in the respective iterations, some of the control lines in C_2 can be used as ancilla. However, further ancilla lines may be required to decompose C_2. Those can be chosen as follows:

a) *First choice:* Use the target line t (this is possible only one time).
b) *Second choice:* Use any other free line a' with $a' \notin C_1 \cup C_2 \cup \{t\}$.
c) *Third choice:* Use any of the control lines in C_1 (this results in higher quantum cost compared to options (a) and (b)).

After all iterations have been completed, a circuit results which is composed of either V- and $V^\dagger$-gates (which are already quantum gates) or Toffoli gates with at most two control lines. These Toffoli gates are eventually mapped to quantum gate cascades as shown in Fig. 2. Overall, the functionality of the original Toffoli gate has been realized as a quantum circuit.

In [5], further simplifications are conducted which allow for reducing the number of quantum gates in the resulting cascade by a so-called line labeling procedure. However, considering those simplifications would make the derivation an NNC cost metric significantly harder. Hence, they have been omitted in our investigations. Initial evaluations show that this has an acceptable effect on the precision of the proposed metric.

2.2   Investigations and Resulting Cost Metric

The mapping scheme reviewed above provides the basis of our investigations towards an NNC metric for the reversible logic level. According to Eqn. 1, each MCT gate $T(C;t)$ is mapped into four quantum gates $V(a;t)$ with the same control and target lines[2], two identical MCT gates $T(C_1;a)$, and another two identical MCT gates $T(C_2;a)$. Hence, the NNC resulting from the mapping from the gate $T(C;t)$ has to be the sum of the NNCs resulting from each of these gates. This leads to:

$$NNC(T(C;t)) = 4 * NNC(V(a;t)) + 2 * NNC(T(C_1;a))$$
$$+ 2 * NNC(T(C_2;a)), \tag{2}$$

The NNC of the quantum gates can directly be determined by considering the distance between the control and the target line. It is usually assumed that two SWAP gates are required in order to decrease this distance by one [8] – (one SWAP gate for moving the control and the target line together; another to restore the original order). Hence, assuming a numerical encoding of the control and target lines from the topmost line to the undermost line, the NNC of the quantum gates is $NNC(V(a;t)) = 2(|a - t| - 1)$.

The NNC of the respective $T(C_i;a)$ gates can be computed by recursively applying Eqn. 2 together with the following base conditions:

a) $|C_i| = 1$:

$$NNC(T(\{c\};t)) = 2(|c - t| - 1)$$

That is, similar to the quantum gates, the NNC is determined by considering the distance between the control and target lines.

b) $|C_i| = 2$:

$$NNC(T(\{c_1, c_2\};t)) = 4(|c_1 - c_2| - 1)$$
$$+ \min\{4(|c_1 - t| - 1), 4(|c_2 - t| - 1)\}$$
$$+ \max\{2(|c_1 - t| - 1), 2(|c_2 - t| - 1)\}$$

Here, the mapping of a Toffoli gate $T(\{c_1, c_2\};t)$ into a a cascade of five quantum gates (shown in Fig. 2) is considered. The NNC value of the two controlled-NOT gates can be estimated as $4(|c_1 - c_2| - 1)$ – this is reflected in the first term. Similarly, the second term indicates the NNC value for the two controlled-V and controlled-$V^\dagger$ gates. Finally, the third term contributes to the NNC due to the controlled-V or controlled-$V^\dagger$ from the cascade. For the latter two terms, the respective configuration of the Toffoli gate $T(\{c_1, c_2\};t)$ with respect to its control and target lines has to be taken into account. Fig. 3 shows the two possibilities. This motivates the respective application of the min/max-values.

All these observations eventually result in the following cost metric for nearest neighbor costs to be applied at the reversible logic level:

---

[2] For simplicity, V and $V^\dagger$-gates are used interchangeably in the following.

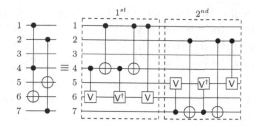

Fig. 3. Toffoli gates and their respective decomposed netlist

Algorithm NNC (C, t, a)

Inputs: MCT gate with a numerical encoding of the set of
control lines C, the target line t, and the ancilla line a
Outputs: NNC of that gate

begin
    if ($|C| = 1$)
        then $NNC = 2(|c - t| - 1)$;
    else if ($|C| = 2$)
        then $NNC = 4(|c - t| - 1)$
            $+ \min \{4(|c_1 - t| - 1), 4(|c_2 - t| - 1)\}$
            $+ \max \{2(|c_1 - t| - 1), 2(|c_2 - t| - 1)\}$;
    else
        begin
            Split C into C_1 and C_2 such that $C_1 \cup C_2 = C$
              and $C_1 \cap C_2 = \phi$;
          $NNC = 4 * NNC(a, t, \phi) + 2 * NNC(C_1, a, a_1)$
             $+2 * NNC(C_2, a, a_2)$;
          // a_1, a_2 are selected ancilla lines for the mapping
        end
    return NNC;
end

Fig. 4. Algorithm determining the NNC of a reversible gate

Definition 1. *Given a reversible circuit $G = g_1 g_2 \ldots g_{|G|}$ composed of multiple control Toffoli gates. The* Nearest Neighbor Costs (NNC) *of G is defined as the sum of the NNCs of its gates, i.e. $NNC(G) = NNC(g_1) + NNC(g_2) + \cdots + NNC(g_{|G|})$. The NNC of a gate g_i is defined as the result of the linear-time algorithm given in Fig. 4.*

3   Conclusions and Future Work

In this work in progress report, we proposed a cost metric that, for the first time, allows for the consideration of nearest neighbor constraints at the reversible circuit level. Thus far, corresponding optimizations could usually be applied after technology mapping only, i.e. rather late in the design process. By investigating a state-of-the-art reversible to quantum mapping scheme, we were able to derive a proper approximation which, eventually, allows those considerations e.g. directly during the synthesis of the reversible circuit. Evaluations on the accuracy as well on the applicability of the proposed metric are left for future work.

Acknowledgments. This work has been supported by the Department of Science and Technology (DST) and the German Academic Exchange Service (DAAD).

References

1. Barenco, A., Bennett, C.H., Cleve, R., DiVinchenzo, D.P., Margolus, N., Shor, P., Sleator, T., Smolin, J., Weinfurter, H.: Elementary gates for quantum computation. Physical Review A (Atomic, Molecular, and Optical Physics) **52**(5), 3457–3467 (1995)
2. Chakrabarti, A., Sur-Kolay, S., Chaudhury, A.: Linear nearest neighbor synthesis of reversible circuits by graph partitioning. CoRR (2011)
3. Maslov, D., Young, C., Miller, D.M., Dueck, G.W.: Quantum circuit simplification using templates. In: Design, Automation and Test in Europe, pp. 1208–1213 (2005)
4. Miller, D.M., Maslov, D., Dueck, G.W.: A transformation based algorithm for reversible logic synthesis. In: Design Automation Conference, pp. 318–323 (2003)
5. Miller, D.M., Wille, R., Sasanian, Z.: Elementary quantum gate realizations for multiple-control Toffolli gates. In: Intl. Symposium on Multi-valued Logic (ISMVL), pp. 288–293, May 2011
6. Nielsen, M., Chuang, I.: Quantum Computation and Quantum Information. Cambridge Univ. Press (2000)
7. Saeedi, M., Sedighi, M., Zamani, M.S.: A novel synthesis algorithm for reversible circuits. In: Intl. Conference on CAD, pp. 65–68. IEEE (2007)
8. Saeedi, M., Wille, R., Drechsler, R.: Synthesis of quantum circuits for linear nearest neighbor architectures. Quant. Info. Proc. **10**(3), 355–377 (2011)
9. Shafaei, A., Saeedi, M., Pedram, M.: Optimization of quantum circuits for interaction distance in linear nearest neighbor architectures. In: Design Automation Conf., pp. 41–46 (2013)
10. Shafaei, A., Saeedi, M., Pedram, M.: Qubit placement to minimize communication overhead in 2D quantum architectures. In: ASP Design Automation Conf., pp. 495–500 (2014)
11. Shende, V.V., Prasad, A.K., Markov, I.L., Hayes, J.P.: Synthesis of reversible logic circuits. IEEE Trans. on CAD of Integrated Circuits and Systems **22**(6), 710–722 (2003)
12. Soeken, M., Wille, R., Hilken, C., Przigoda, N., Drechsler, R.: Synthesis of reversible circuits with minimal lines for large functions. In: Asia and South Pacific Design Automation Conference, pp. 85–92 (2012)
13. Wille, R., Drechsler, R.: BDD-based synthesis of reversible logic for large functions. In: Design Automation Conference, pp. 270–275 (2009)
14. Wille, R., Soeken, M., Otterstedt, C., Drechsler, R.: Improving the mapping of reversible circuits to quantum circuits using multiple target lines. In: ASP Design Automation Conf., pp. 145–150 (2013)
15. Wille, R., Lye, A., Drechsler, R.: Considering nearest neighbor constraints of quantum circuits at the reversible circuit level. Quantum Information Processing **13**(2), 185–199 (2014)
16. Wille, R., Lye, A., Drechsler, R.: Exact reordering of circuit lines for nearest neighbor quantum architectures. IEEE Trans. on CAD **33**(12), 1818–1831 (2014)

Towards Modelling of Local Reversibility

Stefan Kuhn$^{(\boxtimes)}$ and Irek Ulidowski

Department of Computer Science, University of Leicester, Leicester LE1 7RH, UK
{shk12,iu3}@le.ac.uk

Abstract. We describe a new operator for reversible process calculi that allows us to model locally controlled reversibility. In our setting, actions can be undone spontaneously or as a part of pairs of so-called concerted actions, where performing forwards a weak action forces undoing of another action, without the need of a global control or a memory. We model an example from chemistry, the simple interaction of two water molecules, and give an informal explanation of the role of the new operator.

Keywords: Reversible process calculi · Out-of-causal order reversibility · Local reversibility · Modelling of chemical reactions

1   Introduction

There are many different computation tasks which involve undoing of previously performed steps or actions. Consider a computation where the action a causes the action b, written $a < b$, and where the action c occurs independently of a and b. There are three executions of this computation that preserve *causality*, namely abc, acb and cab. We note that a always comes before b. There are several conceptually different ways of undoing these actions [15]. *Backtracking* is undoing in precisely the reverse order in which they happened. So, undo b undo c undo a is a backtrack of the execution acb. *Reversing* is a more general form of undoing: here actions can be undone in any order provided causality is preserved (meaning that causes cannot be undone before effects). For example, undo c undo b undo a is a reversal of acb for the events a, b and c as defined above.

In biochemistry, however, there are networks of reactions where actions are undone seemingly *out of causal order*. The creation and breaking of molecular bonds between the proteins involved in the ERK signalling pathway is a good example of this phenomenon [13]. Other examples are given in [6], [11] and [12]. Let us assume for simplicity that the creation of molecular bonds is represented by actions a, b, c where, as above, $a < b$ and c is independent of a and b. In the ERK pathway, the molecular bonds are broken in the following order: undo a undo b undo c, which seems to undo the cause a before the effect b. The aim of this short paper is to explore the usefulness of a new operator for representing some forms of *out-of-causal order reversible* computation. We do this

© Springer International Publishing Switzerland 2015
J. Krivine and J.-B. Stefani (Eds.): RC 2015, LNCS 9138, pp. 279–284, 2015.
DOI: 10.1007/978-3-319-20860-2_19

by modelling a simple example of reversible chemical reactions. The first process calculus for the out-of-causal order reversible computation was proposed in [13]. It is the calculus CCSK [9,10] which is extended with an execution control mechanism for managing the pattern and the direction of computation. The control mechanism is external to the processes it controls, and it can have a global scope. In contrast our new operator is purely local in character and internal to (the syntax of) the process itself. This is carefully described in Section 2 which introduces our process calculus informally, including the new general prefixing operator $(s; b).P$, while presenting an intuitive model of the autoprotolysis of water. A more abstract denotational model of causal and out-of-causal order reversible computation is given in terms of event structures in [11].

The new prefixing construct $(s; b).P$, where s is a sequence of actions or executed actions and b is a *weak* action, provides a mechanism for local reversibility. Informally, actions in s can take place in any order, and b can happen if all actions in s have already taken place. Once b takes place, one of the executed actions in s must be undone immediately. We shall model this with a pair of *concerted* actions: do b and, at the same time, undo one of the action in s. In our view, this is a simple but realistic representation of a very common mechanism of covalent bonding.

We demonstrate the usefulness of our calculus by modelling autoprotolysis of water, where two water molecule interact by exchanging a proton. The two water molecules are modelled as appropriate compositions of oxygen and hydrogen atoms. Then, the molecules are composed into a process, and the computation of the process is represented by a pair of concerted actions.

Starting with Regev et al. [14] process calculi, specifically the π-calculus, were used to model biochemical systems. For this the biological units in question (often macro molecules like proteins) are represented as processes, binding sites are modelled as channel ports and binding and unbinding is represented as establishing and breaking a communication, respectively, on a channel. Process calculi developed in order to model in a better way different aspects of such systems are causal π-calculus [2] or the κ-calculus [4] amongst others. Apart from CCSK, other reversible process calculi are RCCS [3] and the variants of the π-calculus addressed in [7,8] and in [1].

2   Autoprotolysis of Water

In this section we introduce our calculus informally, concentrating on the new general prefixing operator $(s; b).P$ which produces pairs of *concerted* actions, while presenting an intuitive model of the autoprotolysis of water.

We consider a reaction that transfers a proton between two water molecules. Since the reaction takes place in water it is also known as autoprotolysis of water. The reaction is shown in Figure 1. It is reversible and it takes place at a relatively low rate, making pure water slightly conductive.

In order to model this reaction we need to understand what it is that makes it happen. The main factor is that the oxygen in the water is *nucleophilic*. Oxygen has a high electro-negativity, meaning it attracts electrons. Furthermore, oxygen

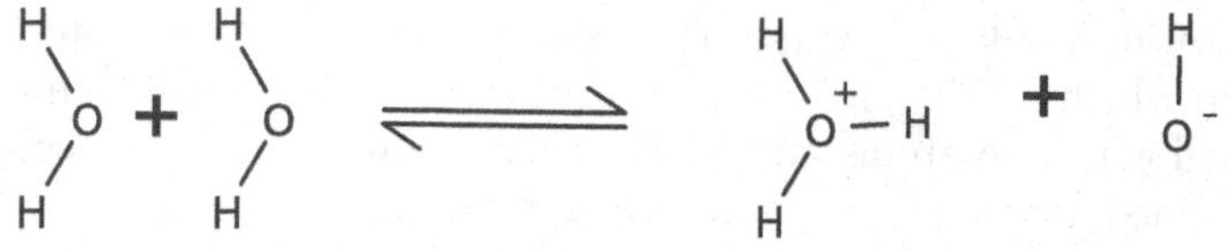

Fig. 1. Autoprotolysis of water

has electrons in its outer shell which are not involved in initial bonding (two lone electron pairs, or four electrons in total). All this makes oxygen nucleophilic: it tends to connect to another atomic nuclei. Since the oxygen attracts electrons, the hydrogens in water have a positive partial charge and the oxygen a negative partial charge. The reaction starts with the oxygen (in a water molecule) being attracted by a hydrogen in another water molecule due to their charges (this attraction is called a hydrogen bond). Due to the nucleophilicity of the oxygen, a covalent bond can form to the hydrogen. This bond is formed out of the electrons of one of the lone pairs of the oxygen. Since a hydrogen cannot have more than one bond the creation of a new bond is compensated by breaking of the existing hydrogen-oxygen bond. These reactions are *concerted*, namely they happen together without a stable intermediate configuration. As a result we have reached the state where one oxygen has three covalent bonds to hydrogens and is positively charged. And the other oxygen bonds to only one hydrogen and is negatively charged, having an electron in surplus.

We notice the reaction is reversible: the oxygen, which has lost a hydrogen, can pull back one of the hydrogens from the other water. This is the case since the negatively charged oxygen is a strong nucleophile and the hydrogens in the H_3O molecule are all positively charged. Therefore, any of the hydrogens can be abstracted, making both oxygens formally uncharged, and restoring the two water molecules.

We shall model the hydrogen and oxygen atoms as processes H and O as follows, where h, o are actions representing the bonding capabilities of the atoms and n, p representing negative and positive charges respectively. And, H', O' are process constants.

$$H \stackrel{def}{=} (h; p).H'$$
$$O \stackrel{def}{=} (o, o, n).O'$$

We use a general prefixing construct $(s; b).P$ where s is a sequence of actions or executed actions, and b is a *weak* action. Sometime the weak action is omitted (as in the definition of O). Informally, actions in s can take place in any order and b can happen if all actions in s have already taken place. Once b takes place, it must be accompanied by undoing immediately one of the actions in s.

We use a synchronisation function γ which tells us which actions can combine to produce bonds between atoms. We define γ in the style of ACP [5], where actions ho, np, nh, no represent the created bonds:

$$\gamma(h, o) = ho \quad \gamma(n, p) = np$$
$$\gamma(n, h) = nh \quad \gamma(n, o) = no$$

Each water molecule is a structure consisting of two hydrogen atoms and one oxygen atom which are bonded appropriately. We shall use subscripts to name the individual copies of atoms and actions; for example H_1 is a specific copy of hydrogen defined by $(h_1; p).H_1'$, similarly for O_1 defined as $(o_1, o_2, n).O_1'$. The atoms are composed with the parallel composition operator "$|$" using the *communication keys* (which are natural numbers) to combine actions into bonds. So a water molecule is modelled by the following process, where the key 1 shows that h_1 of H_1 has bonded with o_1 of O_1 (correspondingly for key 2) and $\setminus\{h_1, h_2, o_1, o_2\}$ is the restriction operator keeping the bonds together.

$$(h_1[1]; p).H_1' \mid (h_2[2]; p).H_2' \mid (o_1[1], o_2[2], n).O_1') \setminus \{h_1, h_2, o_1, o_2\}$$

The system of two water molecules in Figure 1 is represented by the following process where the restriction $\setminus\{n, p\}$ represses actions n, p from taking place separately by forcing them to combine into bonds (according to γ).

$$(((h_1[1]; p).H_1' \mid (h_2[2]; p).H_2' \mid (o_1[1], o_2[2], n).O_1') \setminus \{h_1, h_2, o_1, o_2\} \mid$$
$$((h_3[3]; p).H_3' \mid (h_4[4]; p).H_4' \mid (o_3[3], o_4[4], n).O_2') \setminus \{h_3, h_4, o_3, o_4\}) \setminus \{n, p\}$$

Due to the structural congruence laws for restriction, the process can be represented equivalently by grouping all the restricted actions as follows:

$$((h_1[1]; p).H_1' \mid (h_2[2]; p).H_2' \mid (o_1[1], o_2[2], n).O_1' \mid$$
$$\mid (h_3[3]; p).H_3' \mid (h_4[4]; p).H_4' \mid (o_3[3], o_4[4], n).O_2') \setminus \{h_3, h_4, o_3, o_4, h_1, h_2, o_1, o_2, n, p\}$$

Now actions n, p can combine, representing a transfer of a proton from one atom of oxygen to another oxygen. We show the transfer from O_2 to O_1, where $\rightarrow$ is a transition relation denoting a reaction taking place, here a creation of a bond:

$$\rightarrow ((h_1[1]; p).H_1' \mid (h_2[2]; p).H_2' \mid (o_1[1], o_2[2], n[5]).O_1' \mid (h_3[3]; p[5]).H_3'$$
$$\mid (h_4[4]; p).H_4' \mid (o_3[3], o_4[4], n).O_2') \setminus \{h_3, h_4, o_3, o_4, h_1, h_2, o_1, o_2, n, p\}$$

The creation of the bond with key 5 forces us to break the bond with key 3 (between H_3 and O_2) due to the property of the operator $(s; b).P$ discussed earlier, where $\rightsquigarrow$ is a transition relation that denates breaking a bond:

$$\rightsquigarrow ((h_1[1]; p).H_1' \mid (h_2[2]; p).H_2' \mid (o_1[1], o_2[2], n[5]).O_1' \mid (h_3; p[5]).H_3'$$
$$\mid (h_4[4]; p).H_4' \mid (o_3, o_4[4], n).O_2') \setminus \{h_3, h_4, o_3, o_4, h_1, h_2, o_1, o_2, n, p\}$$

These two reactions happen almost simultaneously so we model them as a pair of *concerted actions* where h_3o_2 represents that the bond h_3o_2 is broken:

$$((h_1[1]; p).H_1' \mid (h_2[2]; p).H_2' \mid (o_1[1], o_2[2], n[5]).O_1' \mid (h_3[3]; p[5]).H_3'$$
$$\mid (h_4[4]; p).H_4' \mid (o_3[3], o_4[4], n).O_2') \setminus \{h_3, h_4, o_3, o_4, h_1, h_2, o_1, o_2, n, p\}$$
$$\xrightarrow{\{np[5], \underline{h_3o_2}[3]\}}$$
$$((h_1[1]; p).H_1' \mid (h_2[2]; p).H_2' \mid (o_1[1], o_2[2], n[5]).O_1' \mid (h_3; p[5]).H_3'$$
$$\mid (h_4[4]; p).H_4' \mid (o_3, o_4[4], n).O_2') \setminus \{h_3, h_4, o_3, o_4, h_1, h_2, o_1, o_2, n, p\}$$

We have now arrived at the state on the right hand side in Figure 1. There are weak bonds between n and p and *strong* bonds between h_i and o_j for all appropriate i, j. Since H_3 is weakly bonded to O_1 and its strong capability h_3 has become available, the bond 5 gets promoted to a stronger bond, releasing the capability p of H_3. We represent this structural change as a rewrite (and not as a transition) using a symbol, $\triangleright$:

$$\triangleright ((h_1[1]; p).H_1' \mid (h_2[2]; p).H_2' \mid (o_1[1], o_2[2], n[5]).O_1' \mid (h_3[5]; p).H_3'$$
$$\mid (h_4[4]; p).H_4' \mid (o_3, o_4[4], n).O_2' \setminus \{h_3, h_4, o_3, o_4, h_1, h_2, o_1, o_2, n, p\}$$

After returning restrictions to the original positions we get this process:

$$(((h_1[1]; p).H_1' \mid (h_2[2]; p).H_2' \mid (o_1[1], o_2[2], n[5]).O_1') \mid (h_3[5]; p).H_3')$$
$$\setminus \{h_1, h_2, h_3, o_1, o_2\}$$
$$\mid (h_4[4]; p).H_4' \mid (o_3, o_4[4], n).O_2') \setminus \{h_4, o_3, o_4\}) \setminus \{n, p\}$$

Oxygen O_1 is still blocked, which represents it being fully bonded (and positively charged). Oxygen O_2 has a free n capability and can abstract any of the hydrogens from O_1. As a result the process can reverse to its original state or to equivalent states where different hydrogen atoms are bonded to O_1 and O_2.

Note that in water the n of O_1 can combine with the p of one of its hydrogen atoms, say H_1. Due to the property of the operator $(h_1[1]; p).H_1'$, this must be followed immediately by breaking the bond 1 on h_1 with O_1, giving

$$((h_1; p[5]).H_1' \mid (h_2[2]; p).H_2' \mid (o_1, o_2[2], n[5]).O_1')) \setminus \{h_1, h_2, h_3, o_1, o_2\}.$$

Now the system is converted to a system which is equivalent to the original formulation of water by promoting the bond 5 to a strong bond:

$$((h_1[5]; p).H_1' \mid (h_2[2]; p).H_2' \mid (o_1[5], o_2[2], n).O_1')) \setminus \{h_1, h_2, h_3, o_1, o_2\}$$

3 Conclusion

We have introduced a new operator to a reversible process calculus that allows us to model locally controlled reversibility by performing pairs of concerted actions, where the first element of the pair is a creation of a (weak) bond and the second element is breaking one of the existing bonds. This mechanism has purely a local character; there is no need for an extensive memory or global control. We have modelled a simple example of a chemical reaction using our calculus, and we have seen that this can be modelled realistically.

In the future, we shall give the calculus operational semantics and explore reachable states with a view to show that some reachable states are not reachable by computing forwards alone. One of the main motivations for our calculus is to model faithfully chemical reactions, so we shall consider a wider range of examples to explore fully the usefulness of our new reversibility mechanism. In this, we shall aim to address undoing of steps of reactions in both the causal as well as out-of-causal order.

References

1. Cristescu, I., Krivine, J., Varacca, D.: A compositional semantics for the reversible p-calculus. In: LICS 2013, pp. 388–397. IEEE Computer Society (2013)
2. Curti, M., Degano, P., Baldari, C.T.: Causal pi-calculus for biochemical modelling. In: Priami, C. (ed.) CMSB 2003. LNCS, vol. 2602, pp. 21–33. Springer, Heidelberg (2003)
3. Danos, V., Krivine, J.: Reversible communicating systems. In: Gardner, P., Yoshida, N. (eds.) CONCUR 2004. LNCS, vol. 3170, pp. 292–307. Springer, Heidelberg (2004)
4. Danos, V., Laneve, C.: Formal molecular biology. Theoretical Computer Science 325(1), 69–110 (2004)
5. Fokkink, W.: Introduction to Process Algebra (Texts in Theoretical Computer Science. An EATCS Series). Springer (2000)
6. Lanese, I., Lienhardt, M., Mezzina, C.A., Schmitt, A., Stefani, J.-B.: Concurrent flexible reversibility. In: Felleisen, M., Gardner, P. (eds.) ESOP 2013. LNCS, vol. 7792, pp. 370–390. Springer, Heidelberg (2013)
7. Lanese, I., Mezzina, C.A., Schmitt, A., Stefani, J.-B.: Controlling reversibility in higher-order pi. In: Katoen, J.-P., König, B. (eds.) CONCUR 2011. LNCS, vol. 6901, pp. 297–311. Springer, Heidelberg (2011)
8. Lanese, I., Mezzina, C.A., Stefani, J.-B.: Reversing higher-order pi. In: Gastin, P., Laroussinie, F. (eds.) CONCUR 2010. LNCS, vol. 6269, pp. 478–493. Springer, Heidelberg (2010)
9. Phillips, I., Ulidowski, I.: Reversing algebraic process calculi. In: Aceto, L., Ingólfsdóttir, A. (eds.) FOSSACS 2006. LNCS, vol. 3921, pp. 246–260. Springer, Heidelberg (2006)
10. Phillips, I., Ulidowski, I.: Reversing algebraic process calculi. The Journal of Logic and Algebraic Programming 73(1–2), 70–96 (2007)
11. Phillips, I., Ulidowski, I.: Reversibility and asymmetric conflict in event structures. In: D'Argenio, P.R., Melgratti, H. (eds.) CONCUR 2013 – Concurrency Theory. LNCS, vol. 8052, pp. 303–318. Springer, Heidelberg (2013)
12. Phillips, I., Ulidowski, I., Yuen, S.: Modelling of bonding with processes and events. In: Dueck, G.W., Miller, D.M. (eds.) RC 2013. LNCS, vol. 7948, pp. 141–154. Springer, Heidelberg (2013)
13. Phillips, I., Ulidowski, I., Yuen, S.: A reversible process calculus and the modelling of the ERK signalling pathway. In: Glück, R., Yokoyama, T. (eds.) RC 2012. LNCS, vol. 7581, pp. 218–232. Springer, Heidelberg (2013)
14. Silverman, W., Regev, A., Shapiro, E.: Representation and simulation of biochemical processes using the pi-calculus process algebra. In: Proceedings of Pacific Symposium on Biocomputing 2001, pp. 459–470. World Scientific Press (2001)
15. Ulidowski, I., Phillips, I., Yuen, S.: Concurrency and reversibility. In: Yamashita, S., Minato, S. (eds.) RC 2014. LNCS, vol. 8507, pp. 1–14. Springer, Heidelberg (2014)

Application of Functional Decomposition in Synthesis of Reversible Circuits

Mariusz Rawski[✉]

Institute of Telecommunications, Warsaw University of Technology, Warsaw, Poland
rawski@tele.pw.edu.pl

Abstract. The design of reversible circuits differs significantly from the design of conventional circuits. Although many methods to synthesize reversible functions have been developed, most of them are not scalable. In this paper an application of the *divide and conquer* paradigm is proposed that adopts for reversible logic synthesis the concept of functional decomposition developed for conventional logic synthesis. The initial function is decomposed into a network of smaller sub-functions that are easier to analyze and synthesize into reversible blocks. The final circuit is then composed of these blocks. The results of experiments reported here demonstrate the potential of the proposed approach.

Keywords: Reversible circuits · Logic synthesis · Functional decomposition

1 Introduction

Recently, reversible circuits have attracted much attention as they can be used in photonic, nano-computing technologies and quantum algorithms. Reversible logic circuits are also one of the promising alternatives to traditional digital circuits, as conventional microelectronic technology is going to reach its limits in the near future.

One of the very important areas of research are methods for reversible circuit implementation. Designing efficient methods for reversible synthesis is of particular importance to the development of quantum circuit construction (in particular, oracles) and may well result in much more powerful computers and computations [10].

Although there is a variety of synthesis techniques for reversible logic reported in literature, the scalability of all these approaches is limited, i.e. the methods are only applicable for relatively small functions – exact approaches reach their limits with functions having more than 6 variables [2]. Therefore a number of heuristic approaches have been proposed, e.g. [1,3–5,8]; however, most of them are also only applicable for functions with up to about 30 variables.

In [11] and [13] a hierarchical synthesis approach has been proposed that can cope with significantly larger functions. The basic idea is to represent the function to be synthesized as BDD, then substitute each node of this BDD

© Springer International Publishing Switzerland 2015
J. Krivine and J.-B. Stefani (Eds.): RC 2015, LNCS 9138, pp. 285–290, 2015.
DOI: 10.1007/978-3-319-20860-2_20

with a cascade of reversible gates. Since BDDs may include shared nodes causing fan-outs (which are not allowed in reversible logic), this approach leads to
implementations requiring significant number of additional circuit lines.

In this paper a novel approach is proposed. It is based on the application of the
divide and conquer paradigm. A functional decomposition algorithm developed
for conventional logic synthesis is used to decompose initial Boolean function into
a network of smaller sub-functions, which are easier to analyze and synthesize into
reversible blocks – then the final circuit is composed of these blocks.

2   Functional Decomposition

Functional decomposition relies on breaking down a complex system into a network of smaller and relatively independent co-operating subsystems, in such a
way that the original system's behavior is preserved. A system is decomposed
into a set of smaller subsystems, such that each of them is easier to analyze and
synthesize.

For a Boolean function F, the set X of the function's input variables is
partitioned into two subsets: *free variables* U and *bound variables* V, such that
$U \cup V = X$. Assume that the input variables x_1, ..., x_n have been relabeled
in such a way that $U = \{x_1, \ldots, x_r\}$ and $V = \{x_{n-s+1}, \ldots, x_n\}$. Let G be a
function with s inputs and p outputs, and let H be a function with $r + p$ inputs
and m outputs. The pair (G, H) represents a serial functional decomposition of
F with respect to (U, V), if $F(X) = H(U, G(V))$. G and H are called blocks of
the decomposition (Fig. 1).

Fig. 1. Schematic representation of the serial functional decomposition

Functional decomposition is widely recognized as one of the best logic synthesis methods targeting FPGAs (*Field Programmable Gate Arrays*) [9]. However
it is not limited to logic synthesis of digital circuits. The strong motivation for
developing decomposition techniques comes from such modern research areas
as pattern recognition, knowledge discovery and machine learning in artificial
intelligence [6].

3   Proposed Synthesis Approach

Reversible circuits are digital circuits with the same number of input signals and
output signals that map each input vector to a unique output vector (i.e. they realize bijections). To implement an irreversible specification using reversible gates,
constant inputs and *garbage outputs* should be added to the original specification.

There exist a variety of approaches to reversible logic synthesis that construct reversible circuits satisfying a reversible specification. Since most circuits of practical interest are too large for optimal synthesis, heuristic algorithms have been proposed.

Another approach is to apply the *divide and conquer* paradigm to decompose the initial circuit into a network of smaller units that are then synthesized into reversible blocks. Application of the concept of functional decomposition developed for conventional logic synthesis allows decomposing Boolean function into a network of smaller sub-functions that are easier to analyze and synthesize. Since the size of blocks of the decomposition network generated in this process can be controlled, it is possible to decompose a function into so small sub-functions that each of them can be synthesized with exact reversible synthesis methods.

This approach is schematically presented in Fig. 2. The description of a Boolean function to be implemented is given in the *espresso* format (*pla* file). The whole process consists of several main elements.

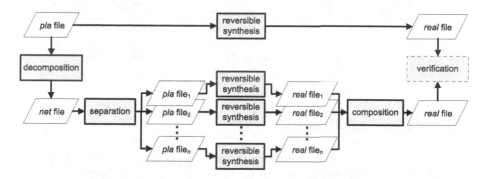

Fig. 2. Synthesis flow – functional decomposition application approach

1. *decomposition* – the initial function is decomposed into a network of blocks. The synthesis can be controlled by setting the maximal size of blocks that can be obtained in subsequent decomposition steps. The algorithm iteratively applies decomposition from Fig. 1 to blocks obtained in earlier iterations until all blocks have the required size. This process results in a network of blocks (Fig. 3a) each of them described in the *espresso* format (*net* file).
2. *separation* – each block of the decomposition network is extracted from the *net* file and placed in a separate *pla* file. Since, in general, blocks obtained in the decomposition process are irreversible, at this stage functions represented by each *pla* file may be subject to *irreversible function embedding* if needed for the subsequent steps. At this stage the information about decomposition network structure can also be saved, and used at the *composition* stage if necessary.
3. *reversible synthesis* – each function from the set of *pla* files is synthesized using a reversible synthesis method of choice and the results are stored as

real files. Since at the *decomposition* stage the maximal size of the resulting blocks can be controlled, at this stage exact synthesis methods can be used if the blocks are small enough.

4. *composition* – here the final reversible circuit is formed by composing single *real* files from the previous stage into one *real* file (Fig. 3b).
5. *verification* – this nonobligatory stage may be used to verify the functional correctness of the obtained implementation. However, it requires a reference *real* file generated using any reversible synthesis method directly from the description of the initial Boolean function.

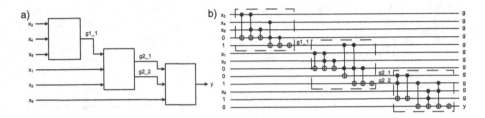

Fig. 3. a) Decomposition network. b) Reversible circuit implementing the decomposition network

4   Experimental Results

For the experiment, several single-output functions have been selected, as well as single-output functions have been constructed by extracting separate outputs of several multi-output functions. No argument reduction have been performed.

For the decomposition, a synthesis tool developed for synthesis of combinational circuits targeting programmable logic devices FPGA has been used. Each function has been decomposed into a network of blocks with no more than three inputs. Reversible synthesis has been performed using *RevKit v1.3* [11].

The synthesis of blocks of the decomposition network has been performed with an exact algorithm [2], which guarantees to find a network with the minimal number of gates.

Since exact synthesis cannot be applied to functions with more than six input variables due to its high computational effort, non-decomposed functions have been synthesized with heuristic algorithms based on BDDs [13], KFDDs [12], ESOPs [1] and Reed-Muller spectra [7]. For each of the synthesis methods the number of gates (G), the number of lines (L) and the quantum cost (Q) have been reported.

Table 1 presents a comparison of the results obtained with the approach presented in this paper and the results of the synthesis obtained with the algorithms implemented in *RevKit*. It can be noticed that the new approach allows obtaining better results with respect to the gate count and the number of lines for almost all functions used in the experiment. Although the exact synthesis used to synthesize blocks of the decomposition network focuses on optimizing the gate count, the quantum costs for many of these functions are also lower.

Table 1. Synthesis results comparison

benchmark	DEC G	L	Q	BDD G	L	Q	KFDD G	L	Q	ESOP G	L	Q	RM Spectra G	L	Q
5xp1f3	25	9	117	20	12	64	30	8	483	23	13	67	142	7	2076
5xp1f4	14	7	66	17	11	53	22	8	259	15	11	39	10	7	79
5xp1f5	5	5	25	7	9	19	13	8	86	6	10	18	4	7	24
5xp1f9	8	10	52	13	12	41	3	8	78	9	13	33	7	8	517
add6f1	4	4	8	5	13	9	13	13	111	5	15	9	5	12	9
add6f2	13	7	33	15	16	43	33	13	481	15	17	35	10	12	50
add6f3	19	10	63	21	17	61	71	13	1451	24	19	64	21	12	249
add6f4	24	12	76	32	20	100	145	13	3869	32	21	92	45	12	913
add6f5	29	14	89	39	22	127	291	13	11391	40	23	120	97	12	2873
add6f6	32	14	100	41	23	141	63	13	3223	41	23	141	63	13	3223
life	40	16	188	66	27	210	468	10	143268	67	26	195	184	10	7172
parity	24	19	32	31	17	31	120133	17	4294956357	31	31	31	15	16	15
rd84f0	7	8	7	15	9	15	461	9	65485	15	15	15	7	8	7
rd84f1	27	9	63	38	15	114	398	9	61358	36	15	116	28	9	140
rd84f2	31	12	123	50	21	158	482	9	82778	51	21	159	70	9	1820
rd84f3	4	12	44	7	15	35	1	9	509	7	15	35	1	9	509
ryy6	47	26	291	39	26	119	128	17	5040	43	29	139	80	17	7569
sym10	49	17	229	77	32	253	2513	11	1713341	81	32	257	266	11	14785
sym6	23	9	99	29	14	93	150	7	6350	27	14	87	36	7	777
sym9	41	15	194	62	27	206	264	10	7137	66	27	222	210	10	4368
t481	59	23	247	52	30	152	1551	17	73352	42	26	118	41	17	481

5   Conclusions

To the author's best knowledge, the approach that applies the *divide and conquer* paradigm to reversible logic synthesis proposed in this paper has not been previously investigated in the literature.

The results presented in this paper show that the presented approach may have great potential for reversible logic synthesis. It is important to notice that in the experiments reported here a decomposition tool has been used which was initially developed for synthesis of combinational circuits targeting FPGA devices. Designing dedicated decomposition algorithms that take into account specifics of reversible synthesis would certainly improve the quality of results obtained using the proposed approach. The author believes that this approach may be a viable initial stage of designing such decomposition methods.

References

1. Fazel, K., Thornton, M., Rice, J.: ESOP-based toffoli gate cascade generation. In: IEEE Pacific Rim Conference on Communications, Computers and Signal Processing, pp. 206–209. Citeseer (2007)
2. Große, D., Wille, R., Dueck, G.W., Drechsler, R.: Exact multiple-control toffoli network synthesis with SAT techniques. IEEE Transactions on Computer-Aided Design of Integrated Circuits and Systems 28(5), 703–715 (2009)
3. Gupta, P., Agrawal, A., Jha, N.K.: An algorithm for synthesis of reversible logic circuits. IEEE Transactions on Computer-Aided Design of Integrated Circuits and Systems 25(11), 2317–2330 (2006)
4. Kerntopf, P.: A new heuristic algorithm for reversible logic synthesis. In: Proceedings of the 41st Annual Design Automation Conference, pp. 834–837. ACM (2004)
5. Khan, M.H., Perkowski, M.: Multi-output ESOP synthesis with cascades of new reversible gate family. In: Proceedings of the 6th International Symposium on Representations and Methodology of Future Computing Technology, pp. 144–153 (2003)
6. Lewandowski, J., Rawski, M., Rybinski, H.: Application of parallel decomposition for creation of reduced feed-forward neural networks. In: Kryszkiewicz, M., Peters, J.F., Rybiński, H., Skowron, A. (eds.) RSEISP 2007. LNCS (LNAI), vol. 4585, pp. 564–573. Springer, Heidelberg (2007)
7. Maslov, D., Dueck, G.W., Miller, D.M.: Techniques for the synthesis of reversible toffoli networks. ACM Transactions on Design Automation of Electronic Systems (TODAES) 12(4), 42 (2007)
8. Miller, D.M., Maslov, D., Dueck, G.W.: A transformation based algorithm for reversible logic synthesis. In: Proceedings of the Design Automation Conference, pp. 318–323. IEEE (2003)
9. Rawski, M., Selvaraj, H., Falkowski, B.J., Łuba, T.: Significance of logic synthesis in FPGA-based design of image and signal processing systems. In: Pattern Recognition Technologies and Applications: Recent Advances, pp. 265–283. IGI Global (2008)
10. Shende, V.V., Prasad, A.K., Markov, I.L., Hayes, J.P.: Synthesis of reversible logic circuits. IEEE Transactions on Computer-Aided Design of Integrated Circuits and Systems 1(03), 710–722 (2003)
11. Soeken, M., Frehse, S., Wille, R., Drechsler, R.: RevKit: an open source toolkit for the design of reversible circuits. In: De Vos, A., Wille, R. (eds.) RC 2011. LNCS, vol. 7165, pp. 64–76. Springer, Heidelberg (2012)
12. Soeken, M., Wille, R., Drechsler, R.: Hierarchical synthesis of reversible circuits using positive and negative davio decomposition. In: 2010 5th International Design and Test Workshop (IDT), pp. 143–148. IEEE (2010)
13. Wille, R., Drechsler, R.: BDD-based synthesis of reversible logic for large functions. In: Proceedings of the 46th Annual Design Automation Conference, pp. 270–275. ACM (2009)

Author Index

Printed in the United States
By Bookmasters